Francesca Alfano M

Extreme B ies

The Use and Abuse of the Body in Art

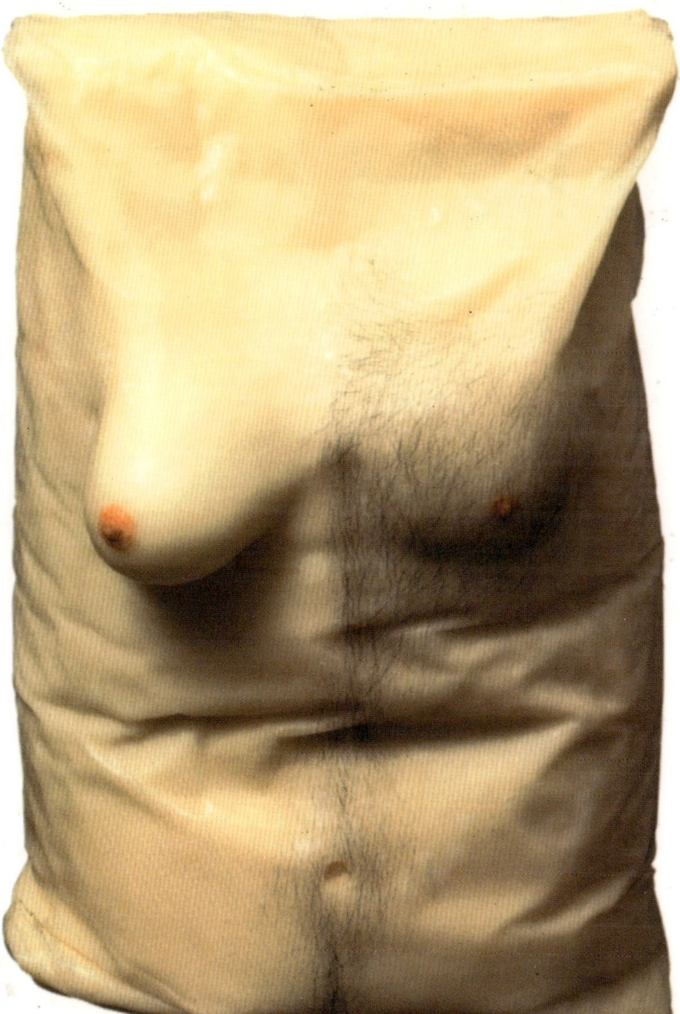

EXTREME BODIES

Francesca Alfano Miglietti (FAM)

EXTREME BODIES

The Use and Abuse of the Body in Art

SKIRA

Graphic design and layout
Studio Cesare Fullone, Milan

Translation from Italian
Antony Shugaar

Special thanks to
Silvia Evangelisti
Silvia Palombi
Stefano Piantini
Archivio Conz, Verona; Edizioni Charta, Milan; Barbara Gladstone Gallery, New York; Cristinerose Gallery, New York; Fondazione Prada, Milan; Galerija Kapelica, Ljubljana; Luciano Inga-Pin, Milan; Fiorella La Lumia, Lattuada Studio, Milan; Galleria Lia Rumma, Milan; Satany Gallery, Tokyo; Archivio Scala; The Andy Warhol Foundation for the Visual Arts, New York

A very special acknowledgement to the archives of the magazine *Virus Mutations* for their fundamental contribution to the iconography of this volume

First published in Italy in 2003
by Skira Editore S.p.A.
Palazzo Casati Stampa
via Torino 61
20123 Milano
Italy
www.skira.net

Printed and bound in Italy. First edition

ISBN 88-8491-379-9

Distributed in North America and Latin America by Rizzoli International Publications, Inc. through St. Martin's Press, 175 Fifth Avenue, New York, NY 10010.
Distributed elsewhere in the world by Thames and Hudson Ltd., 181a High Holborn, London WC1V 7QX, United Kingdom.

CONTENTS

Classification is not the beginning of the study of a problem — it is the end. For me all the small acts I perform are research, experimental probes. That is why I feel free to make them appear as outrageous as possible. Unless research is rendered extreme, it is not effective. Research, in order to be effective, must have incisiveness, power and pressure. Naturally, it appears very dogmatic. That does not mean we are tied to it. We can throw it away.

Marshall McLuhan

This book has no bibliography because there are an infinite number of books, films, videos, artworks, cities, meetings and days that all flowed into its "implementation". The most immediate references are scattered through the body — my own body and the body of the book — but I would still like to take this opportunity to acknowledge some of those who contributed to its completion.
This book could not have been created without Cesare Fullone, with whom I continue to dream, weep and laugh, and Giuditta, with whom I play, stumble and lose myself.
It is also dedicated to all those who think, affectionately, that I am not well, or more simply, disturbed.
I would like to thank all the artists and authors who contributed to creating the multiple structure of this book, and especially Lea Vergine, who practically demanded it.

INTRODUCTION

In the churches of the south where combat raged
I looked upon those paintings,
Those great bloody stains.
Canvases begin to lose their power…
We should have others, yes.
Well: this is what it means to praise artworks.
No, not the works: the art.
That which is purest in us,
Cannot always be reached through the same works of art,
But they are in any case artworks…
Death is not such a serious thing, after all:
But pain is.
Art is a paltry thing in the face of pain
and, unfortunately,
no painting can withstand comparison with
a patch of blood.
André Malraux

The embryonic forms of some of the essays and certain of the encounters in this book have been part and parcel of my life and my theoretic choices over the past decade, a series of cultural feelings and emotions have characterised my progress, and the purpose of this book is precisely that of identifying and indicating some of the works that have become intense cultural feelings of art, those that have untangled in the collective imagination and taken form in some of the most important transformations of our social reality.

This book, the research for which has evolved into a theoretical reflection on the use of the body in art, has adopted a methodology that tends to emphasise comparison, and has thus become a work with a staggered, altered, modified time frame, a time frame that is neither linear nor chronological.

And so there have developed a series of zones of coexistence and interpenetration, mingling cultures and times that have resulted in startling links and connections, hybrids, visions, identifying the path of "impure" subjects, the trail of deviation, of a hidden melancholy. Subjects and works that share the determination to "say", to "show", point out, indicate.

The body of this book is a theoretical subject in which art is central, but which implies its links to various institutions and society at large. The book analyses the body, which has always been manipulated, by its relationship with cultural, religious and political institutions, right up to the threshold of a self-mutation. A special body. Exploration of a body as the construction of forms of discourse, obligations and the instruments of control.

A temporal dimension that chooses its tensions, becoming a cartography of the most significant iconographies of the special body that has always inhabited art. It is specific to our contemporary era that a body is chosen, subject and object of a multitude of events that suggest continuous references to classical iconography, emphasising the varied analogies and affinities amongst the experiences and experiments of contemporary artists and the more traditional iconography of Western tradition.

In late Latin antiquity, the term "classical" was used to describe something that excelled in its class, and in Romanticism it was defined as a perceptible form that has been transfigured in order to attain the dimension of a self-aware spirit, the classical as context in which the infinite idea found an ideal form in which to express itself: the human figure. And the human figure is the true protagonist of this book, a body directly taken from the Western iconographic tradition, a body that has persisted through centuries and centuries of art, the body investigated in art, revealed, shown, the wounded, martyred, anatomised, cut open, tortured, executed and crucified body; the body that is depicted and presented as an extreme tension. Selected bodies, special bodies, classical bodies. "A classic, I told myself, can be a challenge or a confederate. It is a challenge when it is presented as a system, a linguistic and fantastic universe that is consistent and compact, inviolable. A supreme classic, which acts however only with a challenge, precisely because of its remarkable precision and aptitude; but it does not allow itself to be employed, it is intimately ironic, fascinating and repellent.... Or else there is the accomplice: the classical that offers an alluring image, murky and dicey, offering words, images, colours, situations and rhythms, like someone humming a few bars of a tune so that a listener can carry on with the melody." (Giorgio Manganelli)

Not a "capricious" and excessive tendency, not the perverse predilection of an extreme dimension, but rather a planetary sensibility that changes and intervenes directly on the body of art. A sophisticated and fierce vision, a very specific sense of the spirit of the time, the presentation of macrocosms that include modes, trends, rebellions, mutations, images of humanity in transformation. Wounds, crosses, torture, blood, transfigurations, extensions, as well as saints, heroes, princes and kings, as reference symbols for existence, as squandering, as a break with the authoritarian schemes that can be glimpsed in the hypocritical lie that presents art as the site of a reassuring vision, sweet and pacific.

"An organism, either social or physical, is a system of judgement, if for no reason other than that the organic body, made in the image of God, has always been the metaphorical reference for the organisation of the cosmos or the city; in exchange, all social, metaphysical and religious movements have the right to exert control and judgement over the body of every man and the use that is made of it." (Camille Dumoulié)

And art bursts into reality and becomes visible through "scandal", almost always a scandal that has to do with morality, sexuality, norms, prohibitions, a form of visibility that often succeeds in transcending the artwork itself. It is always the same categories that provoke indignation, it is always the display of the body that creates irritation, discomfort, reaction. Not all bodies, but in every case, and as long as art has existed, the body that art chooses. The social danger of bodily desires was already guessed at by Plato, who established a process of sublimation of the body, taken as the site of sensory gratification, decisive to the purpose of a well-balanced social organisation. Plato sensed, therefore, a sort of incompatibility between the tensions of the body and the organisation of personal relationships. The concept of morality and the ensuing norms change from season to season, something that just a short while before was intolerable and forbidden to the eyes of the pure rapidly becomes a perceptual habit; but art continues to create scandal. And it is scandal for Caravaggio, the scandal created by the choice of Christ made man, depicted with the physicality of the human body, a dirty, whipped, executed body, with its shadows and dark colours, by that "Caravaggesque light" that seems to try to restore Christ to his rejected destiny of youth, aging and death. A Christ without resurrection. And it is scandal for Renée Cox, the scandal created by the choice of a Christ who states that men were created in the image and resemblance of God, depicted therefore with the body of the artist herself, who takes this image and resemblance quite literally, setting herself at the centre of a Last Supper, herself, a woman. Black. Nude. And it is scandal.

FAM

Chosen Body

FOREWORD

There are no more connections necessary between culture and politics; now it is possible to be culturally at the vanguard but politically reactionary. Life style has abandoned its foundations in the realm of personal ethics, becoming an empty fluctuating object/sign — a piece of cynical merchandise — in the media landscape.
A. Kroker

Body and power, both religious and political, the body and the politics of power. The body has long since become one of the sites in which forms of knowledge converge, creating their own systems of awareness and understanding, a luminous field of uncertainty upon which to establish an intensely violent politics, though apparently liberating, a culture with a winking, conspiratorial tone that from time to time threatens death on the bonfire, employs tortures or promises youth and beauty. Everything that has to do with the body, that manifests itself as transparent or seductive or threatening, becomes an irreversible sign of a power that changes but still persists in its multiple incarnations. With Michel Foucault we seem to have a clearer view of the totalitarian practices of powers that, from case to case, establish themselves in the context of human bodies and the degree to which those powers, however coercive and apparently all-powerful they may be, always encounter opposition of one sort or another that reduce them almost to a condition of powerlessness. It is precisely in the bodies, from whose disciplinary organisation the powers take their very legitimacy, that this conflict takes place.

Sex, disease, desires, oppressions, pain, neurosis, constrictions: power acts on bodies, leaving its signs — brands, tortures, constrictions, disciplines, cures, diets, rules, taboos and transgressions, structuring them into what Foucault himself called the "charnel house of signs".

The body is, for power, the privileged site through which it is possible to channel needs and desires, physiological processes and metabolisms, attitudes to be controlled and repressed. And art chose the body, a body that had been used, usurped, abused, displayed, a body that had been cut, wounded, dramatised, the body as loss of self, the body of Antonin Artaud and the acts of cruelty, the body without organs of Gilles Deleuze and Félix Guattari, bio-power as the cultural disciplining of the bodies of Foucault, the body that struggles, rebels, that indicates the escape from the coercions of power, indicating the relations that are exercised by powers and knowledges over the bodies.

Gina Pane, *Action psyché*, 1974. Photo by Françoise Masson

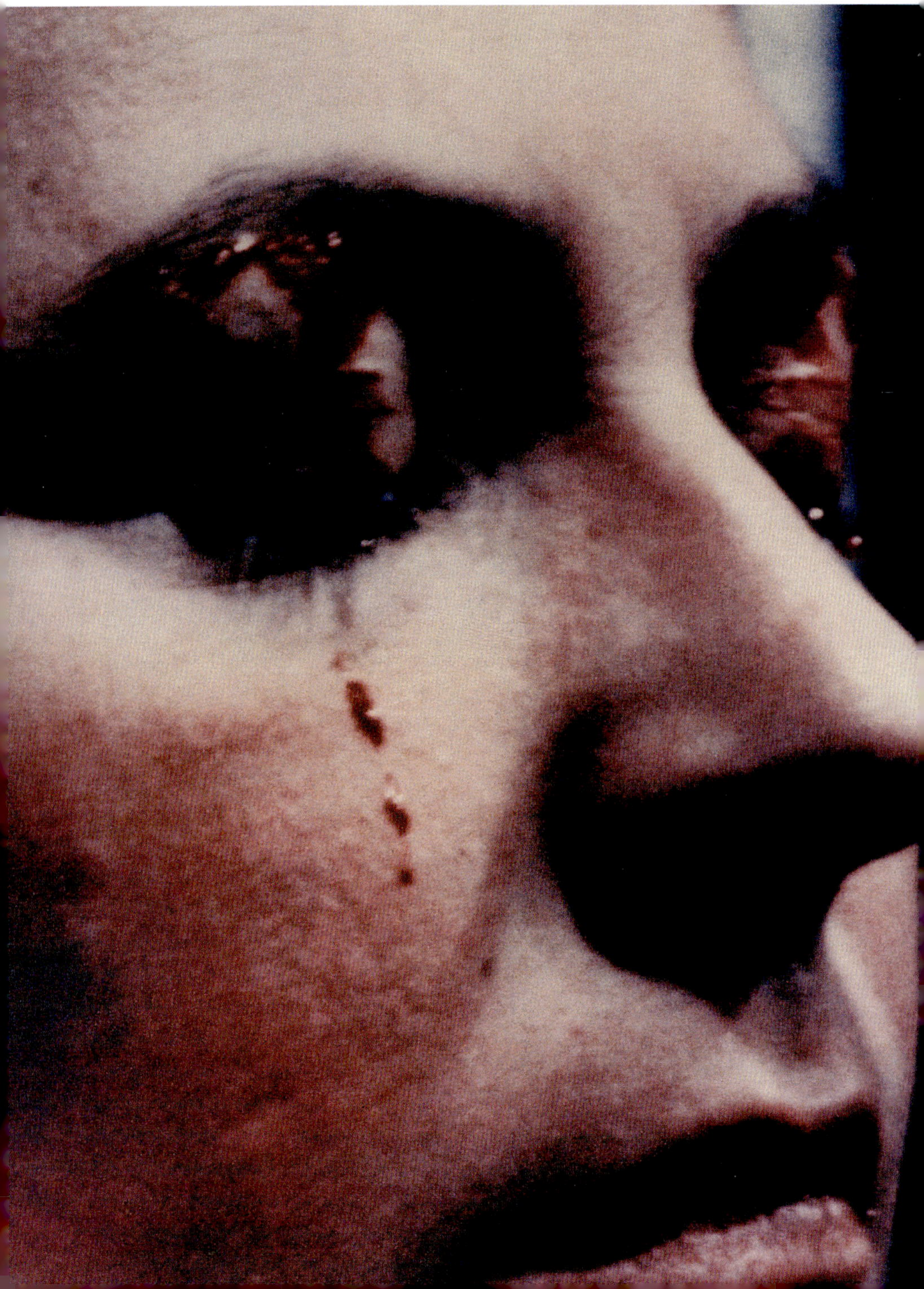

The history of the body, historians have begun to work on it for some time now.... But the body is also directly immersed in a political field: the relationships of power operate an immediate grasp upon it, they attack it, they mark it, they train it, they torture it, they force it to perform certain tasks, they oblige it to participate in ceremonies, and they demand certain signs from it.
Michel Foucault

ABOUT WOUNDS

Being able to inhabit the world. Moving beyond reality to gain access to the universe of possibilities, to be in the world, to provide oneself with a body. A physiological body, anatomical, organic, a body that changes with events, with actions, with behaviours, to the point of unhinging the dogmatic and repetitive commonplaces of belief. "There is... a common ground for the arts, a shared problem. In art, in painting just as in music, it is not so much a matter of copying or inventing certain forms, as much as receiving certain forces. And that is why no art is actually figurative.... The task of painting is defined as the attempt to render visible forces that are invisible. This is evident. The force is closely related to sensation: it is enough that a force be exerted on a body, that is, on a specific point of the wave, for there to be sensation" (Gilles Deleuze): a question of forces, sensations, stimuli that act directly on the spectator's nervous system. Precarious, wounded, mortal body. And the iconography of pain, of the mortal offence, of savagery inflicted on the body, can be found everywhere in the artworks of Western culture over the past eighteen centuries and more. It is art itself, in its history, that gives itself a body, a mythical, spiritual, glorious body.

"For the sole reason that they suffered, in themselves, the shared slaughter, their bodies, unlike ours, were able to give themselves up to the luminous colour of health; but he himself, Fra Angelico, could be said to have been born with his body already luminous" (Elsa Morante). Roberto Longhi dates the *Christ with Crown of Thorns* by Fra Angelico (Guido di Pietro), now in the church of Santa Maria del Soccorso in Leghorn, to 1430–35; shortly after the painter began working as an artist, he took holy vows and entered the monastery of San Domenico in Fiesole. The *Christ with Crown of Thorns* is a portrait of physical pain that emerges from the red that is so much a feature of this work: the mouth is red, as are the eyes, red are the drops of blood dropping from the thorns in the crown pressed onto Christ's head, and some sections of Christ's halo and clothing are also red. The evocation of martyrdom appears in the context of a sort of inadequate melancholy, within the discipline of spatial rules that seem to ward off the announced immortality; the entire image is an attack on equilibrium, a repressed weeping, a moment's interval that becomes the power of a vision. Light is the

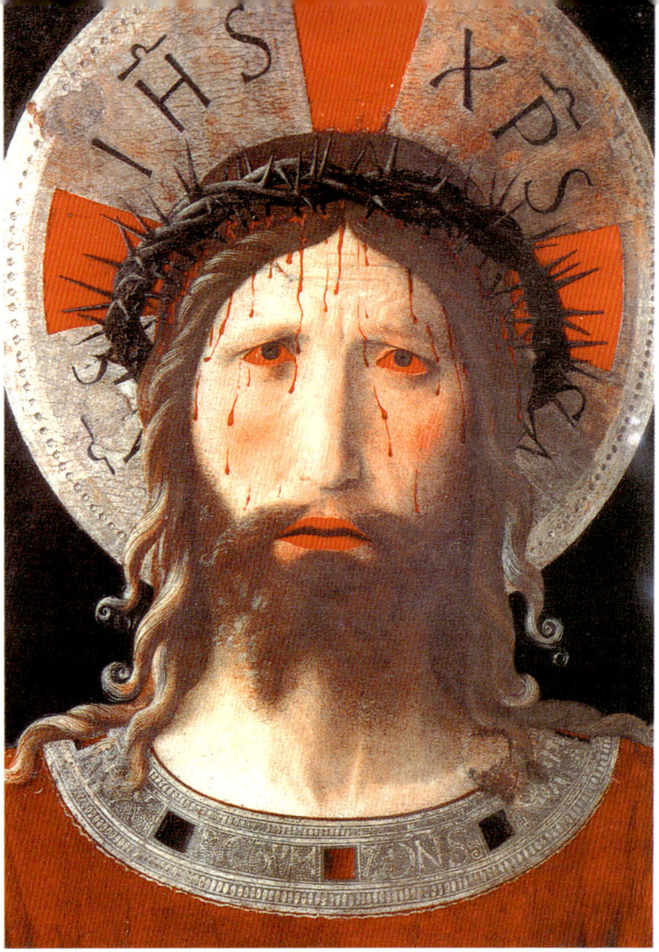

Fra Angelico,
Christ with Crown of Thorns, 1450

characteristic feature of the works by Fra Angelico, a concept of light that for him is not merely a component of vision and colour but rather the central subject of the art and the image, an ascetic light: he painted absolutely diaphanous figures that become the bodies of everyday perceptible light. The vision of Fra Angelico is an alchemy of contrasts, an alchemy that ranges from the darkness of "evil", lit only by the fires of the Inferno, all the way up to a radiant vision that allows us into the halls of light. And gold is one of the lighting strategies of Fra Angelico: clothing, hair, furniture, floors and thrones all create a sort of temporal indeterminacy that enters the realm of light and baffles the vision. The very idea of depiction is involved in this shift: the *Frescoes of San Marco*, the *Crucifix and Saints* and the *Last Judgment*, the *Altarpiece of San Marco*, the vision of Fra Angelico offers the viewer a sense of security based on the conviction that light can constitute the possibility of seeing, and structures a vision that becomes a process creating an order in the infinite flow of perception, while light becomes a metaphor for religious truth. Fra Angelico intuits and introduces a concept of vision as a subjective action, and the gazes begin to proliferate in a visual narrative that becomes a history of fragments, splinters of discourse, notes of meetings between the light of depiction and the light from within. "No rhetorical conceits, no pious unction corrupts his enamoured gestures. The ambiguity of false religions, or 'lovely eras', has tried to bring him down to the level of its own instrumental uses, transforming his great art into household saints or a kind of furnishing. But in reality his gifts of the Epiphany, finished with his own hands, are delivered to the home of light, where vulgar or prepared eyes cannot reach", continues Elsa Morante on the subject of Fra Angelico, where "vulgar or prepared eyes" cannot see in his works the body of the wound, the cruelty inflicted, the derision. Fra Angelico's body of Christ is a wounded body; at the foot of the crucifixion in the main panel of the altarpiece of San Marco, as in other crucifixions he painted, there is a skull drenched with blood, a place of alienation, the paradox of the symbol of life, i.e. blood, which abandons the corporeal solidity in a transgression of obedience to the fate announced. A deviation from the relation with the divine, the possibility of a radical otherness: in the despairing and incredulous face of the Christ crowned with thorns, the recognition of an alienation.

It is the body that reemerges under layers of symbolism and sublimations, to be exhibited, pulsating nervously, participating in a series of uncomfortable references, hidden, secret, which declare the plane of existence, the escape from the totalitarian and anonymous system of the mask, the functional gap of the bureaucracies of socially accepted behaviours. And the certainties of normality crumble under the blows of a succession of emotional implosions that create a radical and desperate attempt to reappropriate one's self.

It is evident that the future belongs to the possibility of metamorphoses of identities, the exhibition of intensities in the escape from the level of "hijacking" of the image, of all images, and it breaks out onto the level of violence and pain that characterises the margins of existence.

The end of the 1960s was a time of open and wide-ranging debate over some of the fundamental rules that guide society. A number of the more hypocritical social conventions were the target of a series of rebellious actions that involved nearly every walk of life: the talk was of liberty, and the body constituted one of the sites in which the revolt chose to take place.

And so people began to question the conventional structures, be they public or private, individual or collective; they began experimenting with pain and cruelty as methods that power has always used to hold sway, to leave its own traces on human beings. They began to discuss the precarious nature of existence in relation to the rules of society, to reveal the effects of coercion, to denounce the methods of indirect tyranny. In these same years, some of the most significant artistic movements chose the body as the site of extensive experimentation. Almost always the body used is the artist's own; tensions are transferred onto the artist's own body to the point of rendering them visible, giving them a physical dimension. Anguish, repression, violence, and even madness, fear, disease, perversion and panic all became materials for investigation and artistic experimentation. Bruce Nauman, Arnulf Rainer, Vito Acconci, Gina Pane, Urs Lüthi, Chris Burden all investigate and bear witness to the discomfort, they opt for the power of putting on display their innermost drives, they choose to show off, to reject the fear of diversity. Each of them, in their own actions, works to demolish the conventions that regulate social relations, thus beginning to shatter the taboos that insist that public and private should be different and separate. Both the artists and the leading figures of the protest movements choose to communicate through the testimony of their own experience, their own existence, their own nightmares. They put on display the fragments of their own private lives, and they exhibit their personal effects and begin to think of the traces and remnants of their own lives as material to display, to open to discussion, to use as a document of testimonial.

The true protagonists of these actions were repression, censorship and lack of liberty, and Viennese Actionism became the most significant challenge of the 1960s. "In a word, we are convinced that there are living forces in so-called poetry, and that the image of a murder presented in appropriate theatrical conditions is infinitely more terrible for the spirit than the actual implementation of that same murder", wrote Artaud, and Actionism staged the death of the self, the destruction of the being, the invisible violence suffered on a daily basis, the repression that operates through taboos, in a sort of performance that demands and obtains an audience that will be obliged to take note of its own psychological and existential condition.

The theoretical and aesthetic transition that selected the body, one's own body as an artistic material, was almost obligatory, as was the decision to make flesh, skin, one's own senses the tools of communication, the substitution of the body itself for written pages and lectures. "I said 'cruelty' just as I would have said 'life' or 'necessity', especially to emphasise that in my view, theatre is a perpetual act and emanation", wrote, once again, Artaud. Bodies as places of existence, the body that decides wittingly to give life to existence, and therefore willing to think and rethink itself, bind, multiply itself, belong to itself, bend, excite, stretch itself and take possession of itself. Thus existence becomes a form of expression, and it is this same expression that is inscribed in the body, through the cruel and necessary signs that transform it into a manifesto in which the obligatory and catatonic docility to which the body has been abandoned is opposed by the evidence of a body exhibited to society, witting and scandalous, against a body that is captive and resigned to muteness. Tension is the wild heart of the performances of Actionists, who create ceremonies in which they emphasise the perversity of a useless and harmful normality in which one is obligated to recognise oneself. Thus wounds, stabbings, attacks are staged, blood is spattered, blades are used, death is theatricalised. The social rules that have chosen to conceal or obscure suffering or irregular bodies, systematically repressing the instincts and slowly but incessantly domesticating the mind, are opposed by the Actionists with exposed bodies, bodies that reveal themselves to be irregular and diseased, emphasising and staging some of the mechanisms of the social machinery. The spectator is provoked, during the course of the performances, through a sense of disorientation, disquiet and aggression, which tends to weaken the power of the systems of oppression by concentrating attention on the suffering, on exploitation, and the annihilation of the individual which becomes a norm, a habit of perception, an everyday experience. "But while the murderer exhausts in the commission of his crime the potential of his action, the actor preserves intact an emotional potential..." In these words, Artaud reaffirms the superiority of the "virtual revolt" over the social revolution, inasmuch as it operates on the spiritual level and provokes disturbances that "empty themselves, with the power of an epidemic, into the sensibility of the audience", as Camille Dumoulié puts it. And the marginal takes centre stage.

Shame is the feeling of an original fall, not because of the fact that I may have committed this or that particular fault but simply that I have "fallen" into the world in the midst of things and that I need the mediation of the Other in order to be what I am.... This is why the Biblical symbol of the fall after the original sin is the fact that Adam and Eve "know that they are naked".
(Jean-Paul Sartre)

Nudity and coverings, dressing and undressing become pretexts for being born, dying, laughing, trembling and unveiling; they become a method, at once intimate and political, of order or disorder in interpersonal relationships, as well as in the social context in which the bodies were exhibited or covered. And the choice falls on the wound as a symbol of disorder, of the rupture of an equilibrium.

Art no longer wants just spectators, but now chooses to have witnesses... accomplices... The body as blood, skin, limbs, senses, but also body as fear, panic, anguish, depression, tension... The Viennese Actionists incarnate the maximum limits of bodily experiences, accomplishing actions with a sharp tension towards cruelty, a cruelty physically employed upon themselves and psychologically upon their audience. Still with the backcloth of Austrian Expressionism, the powerful neurotic metaphor of art under the decadent Austro-Hungarian monarchy, at the beginning of the 1960s in Vienna the artistic extremisation of Egon Schiele, the philosophical tensions of Ludwig Wittgenstein and the psychoanalytical revolutions of Sigmund Freud were developed. All of these currents would converge in the formation of Viennese Actionism, which included Rudolf Schwarzkogler, Hermann Nitsch, Günter Brus, Otto Muehl and Arnulf Rainer. The Wiener Aktionismus was not a full-fledged group, there was never a proper manifesto, nor even a unity of poetics: it was a meeting of solitary artists who represented in their works the anguished complexity of a life that had by now been definitively compromised by the various forms of "existential diseases".

"Just like Artaud they want to try all the possibilities available to know themselves by means of the body and its exploration. The denuding of the body becomes the final effort to win the right to put themselves in the world again. Those who feel pain need to be right", writes Lea Vergine concerning the protagonists of the Body Art movement, and it is precisely the profound meaning of Artaud's cruelty that provides one of the ways into an understanding of Viennese Actionism, whose protagonist is a human being entirely held captive by his or her own body, a body dehumanised by external violence. This led to a series of scandalous and irritating actions that staged, or exhibited in the streets of a respectable Vienna, the most hidden and secret taboos, involving the public in an absolutely intolerable visual, mental, and corporeal dimension: the body of the Viennese Actionists was a body obliged to undergo mortification, humiliation, laceration, self-mutilation, before it could finally and once and for all strip off the skin of the respectable middle class.

Rudolf Schwarzkogler was born in Vienna in 1940, and died there, a suicide, in 1969, in the wake of a serious depressive crisis triggered by a drastic crash diet. Concerning his life and death, over the years, various versions have successively been put forth, many claiming that he killed himself during the course of a self-castrating action, while others speak of his death as a consequence of a performance in which he "removed" his skin piece by piece in public. Schwarzkogler is one of the most complex and widely quoted artists of Viennese Actionism; he

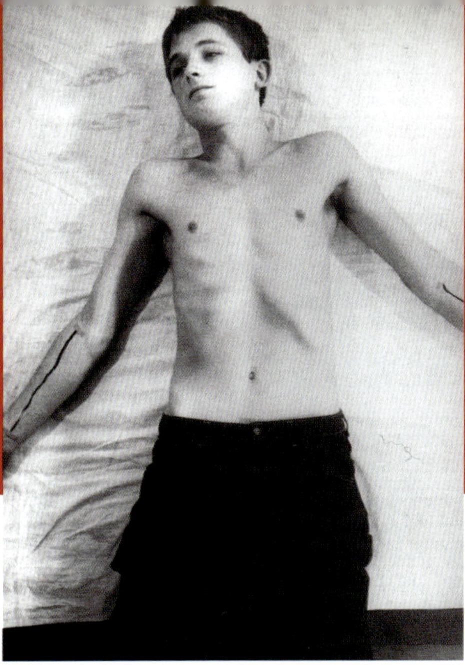

Rudolf Schwarzkogler,
4 Aktion, 1965,
actor Heinz Cibulka.
Photo by F. Cibulka

achieved an indissoluble relationship between art and life, a life and an art in which pain, anguish and a sense of impotence constituted the dramatic and suffocating dimension of his creations. Art was for Schwarzkogler a "purgatory of senses and a detox cure", and he upheld the justification of art in a "regeneration of the interior capacity". His actions, which became increasingly cruel and extreme as he tested and pushed the envelope of the threshold of tolerability, were executed in private and then exhibited and documented photographically only amongst the smallest circles of his friends, in accordance with his own programmatic intentions. Schwarzkogler created a sort of laboratory of the body, featuring choices and privations; the works that he himself called "table actions" established relations amongst various materials, arranged on a table, with the human body and the surrounding space.

Let the beard and hair grow
Fast and take steam baths
Hold your breath
Eat nothing salty
Don't look into fountains
Don't look out windows
Stay awake
Sleep in a green house on the bare earth
As long as it's raining.
(Rudolf Schwarzkogler, Art as Purgatory of Senses*, 1968)*

In his actions he inflicted wounds and mutilations upon himself and, often photographed covered with gauze bandages, he achieved a powerfully symbolic atmosphere aimed at a society that was deaf and dumb with respect to the individual. Emblematic, in this sense, was *2 Aktion*, which called for the presence of

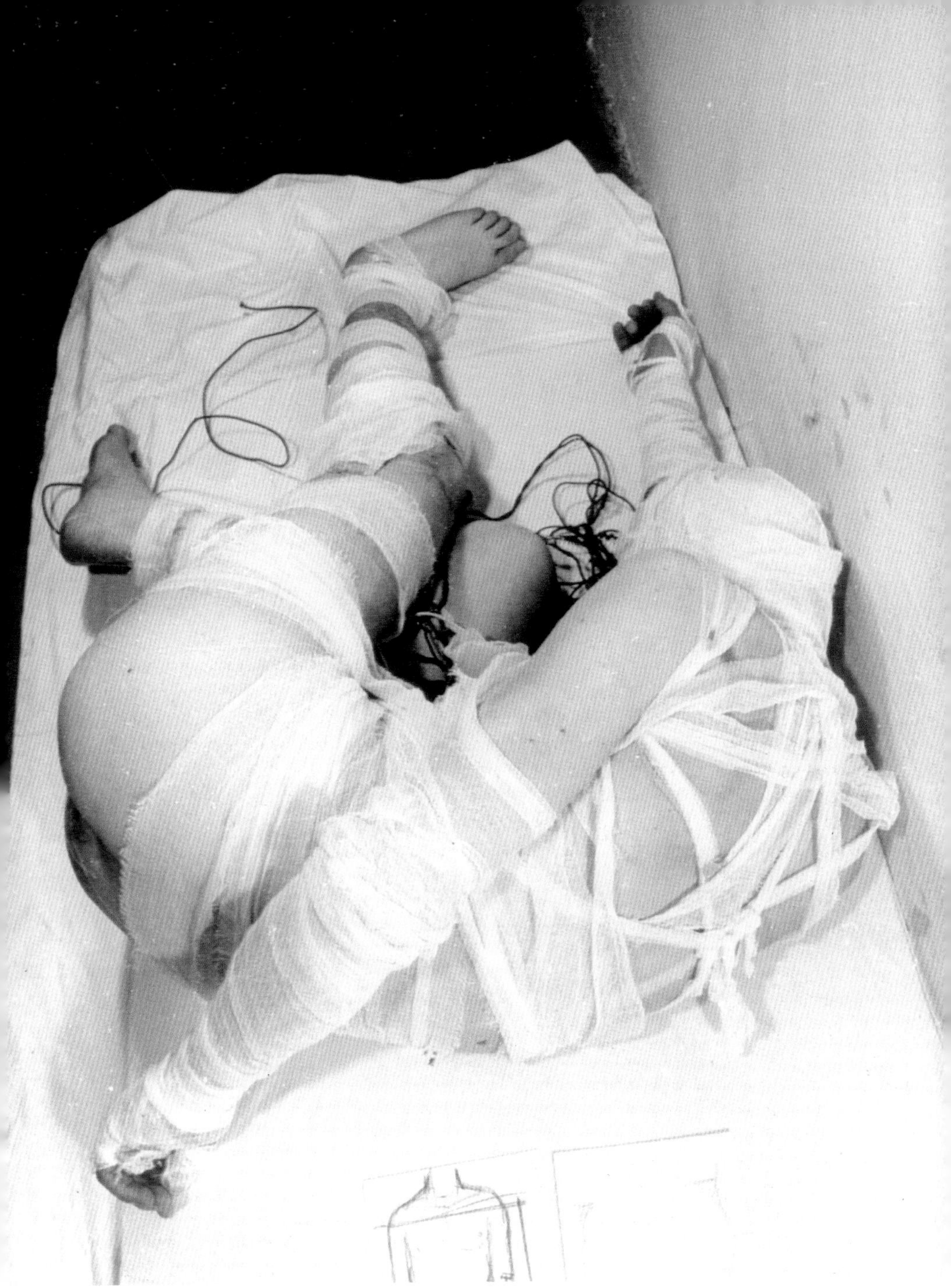

Rudolf Schwarzkogler, *3 Aktion*, Vienna, 1965

a gutted fish, the bandaging of his penis and the application of the fish's head to his penis: wound and castration. The image was disturbing and extremely powerful: with the elimination of the penis Schwarzkogler seemed to want to lose the masculine self-consciousness of power and suppress himself as a masculine being. And again, in his work, bandaged fish on his body, tampons in his throat, bleeding wounds, bandaged heads and rocks, stains and tubing and razor blades. The photographs show him (him or else Heinz Cibulka, an invaluable colleague and often the protagonist of his artworks, who in 1965 took most of Schwarzkogler's photo actions) sideways, in a sort of suffocation produced by the bandages, laid out on what would seem to be an anatomic table, in the blocked, unkempt position of violent death, of someone that has suffered violence, in anonymous and deserted rooms. He simulated processes of castration, sadomasochistic aggressions, macabre disguises, he repeatedly made use of white spaces, a white ball, white bandages, a square of black glass, fish, electric wires and surgical materials: materials that reproduce the chill and emptiness of panic, fear and anguish; which reproduce threats, death, aggression. His indifference to pain was a provocative weapon towards those who assign a negative meaning to pain, and who consider the discussion of the concept of identity a waste of time, and its inevitable transformation a loss. Between 1960 and 1964, aside from reading the French Romantics and Symbolists, Rudolf Schwarzkogler explored Artaud, Duchamp, Schwitters, Malevich, Klein, Eastern philosophies, and the Bible. In the same years, he began to devote himself to actions, and on 6 February 1965, after his first performances with Nitsch, he executed *Wedding*, the first of his actions, in which he introduced and presented his very unusual relationship between body and objects.

Schwarzkogler's actions were private actions, without audience and carried out in an enclosed space, of which we have static photographic sequences where the artist, through his urge for perfection, exerts an exasperated control over the slightest details, and where he becomes at the same time actor and spectator. For him, the action is a representation of self-control, a self-control exercised in any situation: he simulates castration processes, he disguises himself, he ties himself up, he cuts himself, in a room whose lighting suggests the clinical and sterile atmosphere of an operating chamber, in which we see a generic body, entirely covered with bandages. A suffering man is transformed into a bandaged body devoid of social identity; the face of the individual has vanished and what remains is a generic body, bandaged and hobbled in its movements in a reality of punishment in which the suffering body becomes the symbol of a revolt aimed at neutralising the tools of violence and control.

Schwarzkogler clearly shows all the loneliness and the alienation of the individual within society, a self-segregation, a cruel disguise that forces the spectators to experience symptoms of repulsion and discomfort in the face of an outsider, a reject of society, a lonely man, desperate, sick, who displays mental and corporeal pain. Schwarzkogler's work is powerfully political stuff, but at the same time it is strongly lyrical and poetic: "[In Schwarzkogler] it is possible to distinguish that febrile erotic sweetness that can be traced back to the Viennese tradition, where the extreme determination of expression rises to the level of erotic cruelty, but is always aesthetically overcome", Nitsch would later write, describing the work of his friend as "Apollonian".

The body in Schwarzkogler's work is a living body, made of flesh and blood, a body of shame, taboos, fear and violence. Aside from a series of poetic statements, the artist executed a part of his artworks as static photo-sequences. It is not that the action is so important, for Schwarzkogler, as much as the photographs in which all of the processes of activation of the mechanism of violent revolt are simulated: castration, transvestitism, death. Clinical and sterile backgrounds are the setting for the "fixed" shots of a body that is tortured, abused and damaged, the bandages that wrap it bring us back immediately to the canonical portraits of suffering, accidents, hospitals, psychic and physical discomfort, the anonymous desperation of an agonising existence. A rigid series of sequences records the maniacal and repeated selection of familiar objects and elements, which are transformed into estranging materials and objects: we see the private iconography of a man who is persecuted, accused, tortured, from whom submission is being demanded. A being segregated first and foremost in its own corporeality, which is configured as an organic prison, living, dehumanised by the violence to which it is subjected. Instinct, psychosis and neurosis all appear on stage, escaping individual annihilation through a self-inflicted violence that displaces the brutal external impositions. Beyond the limit, outside of the boundary, within the moral, sexual, identity-linked and social outrage, Schwarzkogler, with his violated and bandaged body, displays self-mutilation, alteration and sadomasochism, and indelibly marks the distance between himself and his spectators.

"The enemy is the organism. The BwO is opposed not to the organs but to the organisation of the organs called the organism... The BwO is not opposed to the organs; rather, the BwO and its 'true organs', which must be composed and positioned, are opposed to the organism, the organic organisation of the organs. The judgement of God, the system of the judgement of God, the theological system, is precisely the operation of one who makes an organism, an organisation of organs that is called organism, because it is not possible to tolerate the BwO, because He persecutes it, disembowels it to go on ahead and to send the organism on ahead. The organism is already this, the judgement of God, which the doctors take advantage of and from which they draw their power. The organism is absolutely not the body, the BwO, but rather a layer over the BwO..." write Deleuze and Guattari, and it is a body that has been cut, mortified, rendered docile, which the Actionists show, a body that is bound, torn, squeezed, and which expresses and appropriates the signals of a condition, the condition of revolt and rebellion. In their actions, it is as if the organs had been modified, rethought, removed and repositioned. Ways to undo the body, observe it, remake it. This expresses an attempt to be an "organism" subject to itself, to emerge from an idea of the organism that often becomes the body itself. The BwO of Deleuze and Guattari is a material undergoing transformation, a production of intensity that is opposed to the dualisms of Western culture, a body that no longer wants to forget any aspect of itself, that no longer wishes to renounce its multiplicity. "The exceptional individual has many possible positions", and the work of the Actionists becomes a form of creative aggression, obscenity: it commands its own flagellation, thus determining a plan of revolt in which all the actions become metaphors for the imbalance of power.

And the body becomes a substrate, and will succeed in becoming a signifier, a sign capable of action, it becomes the extra-artistic medium most typical of the

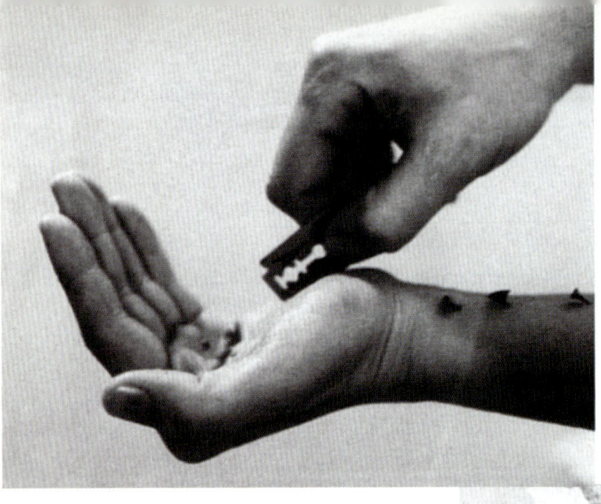

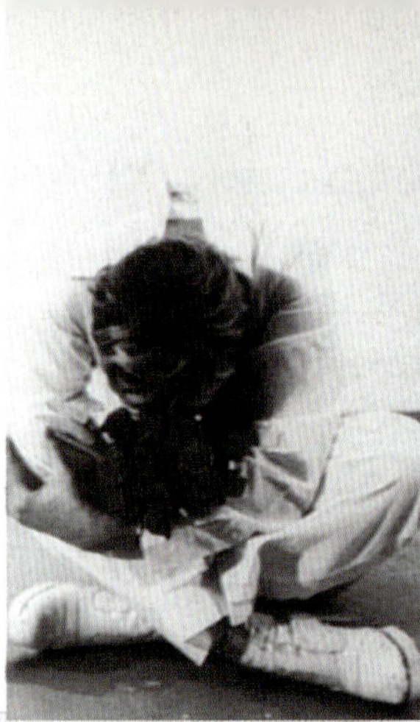

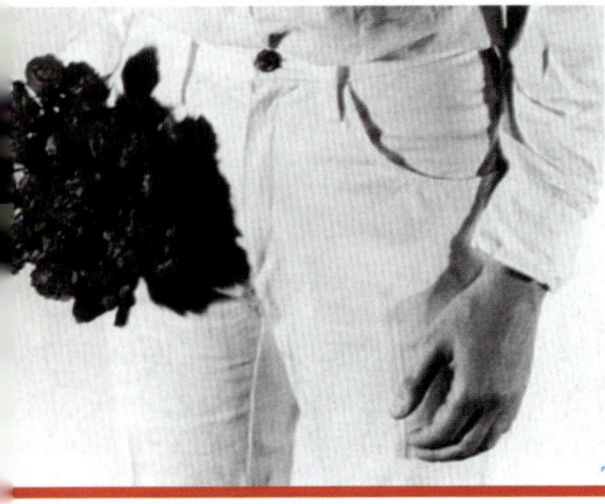

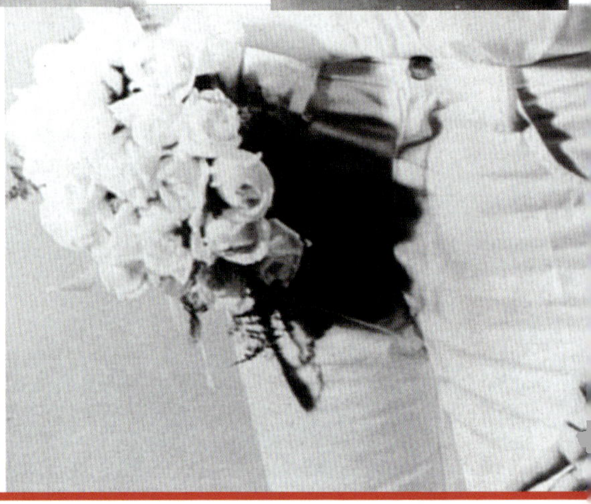

art of the 1970s. An attempt is made to recover bodily freedom buried beneath the hypocrisies of conventions and the rules of a power based upon control, there is a rejection of the emergency exits of the media that ensnare and hypnotise on the existence of others, provided that there is no focus on their own existence. Reports of war, student riots, police brutality, sexual taboos, everything passes on the body which tends toward a state of suspension in which the breakdown and the crumbling of the subject opens the path toward the overcoming of the self in the will to power. "And where then do we want to arrive? Beyond the sea? Where does this powerful greed of ours drag us, so much more powerful than any other desire? And why precisely in that direction, down there where all the suns of humanity have set until today? One day will it be said of us that, turning our bow toward the west, we too hoped to reach an India, but that it was our destiny instead to shipwreck in infinity? Or else, my brothers? Or else?"; thus Nietzsche intuits the nomadism that would in time explore new dimensions of being, a search that disposes us toward contact, encounters, which accepts the risks of displaying one's own interior. A foreign self in one's own body, a body that is revolted, displayed, wounded, which expands until it coexists with the things

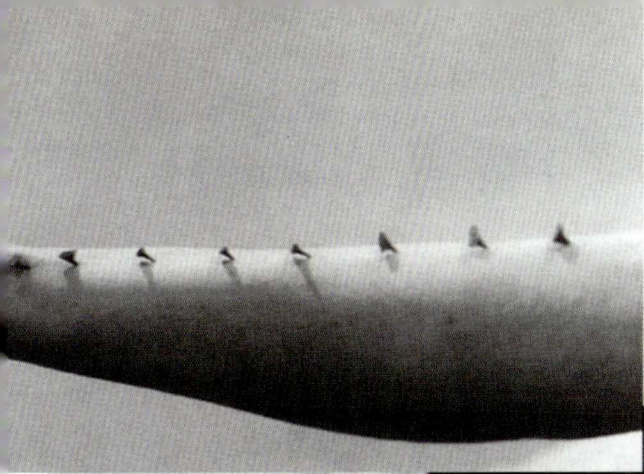
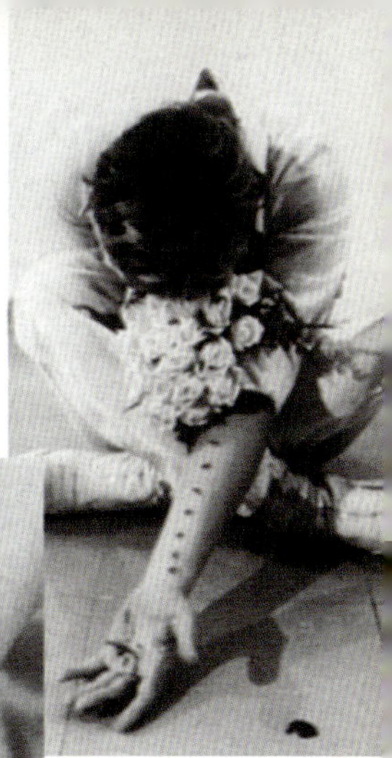
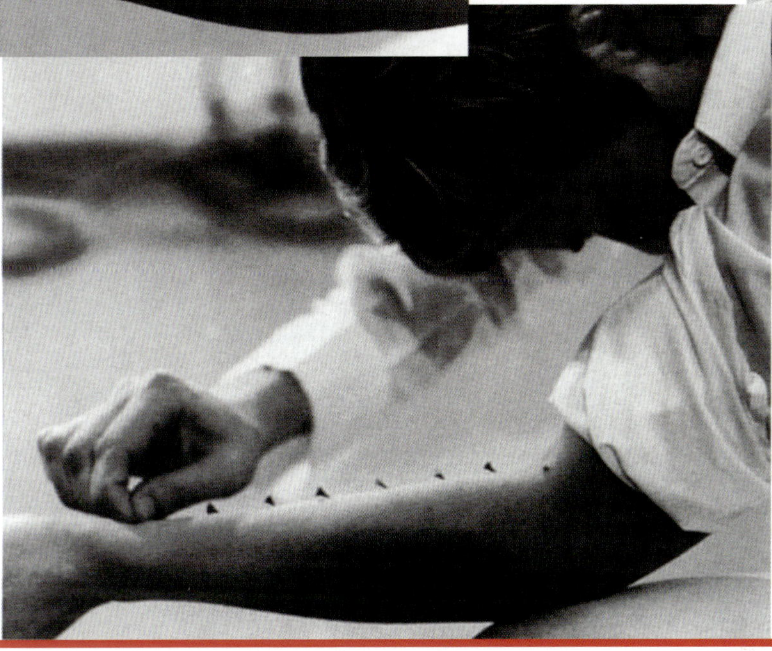

Gina Pane, *Azione sentimentale (Action)*, Galleria Diagramma, Milan, 1973. Photo by Françoise Masson

of the world, a body that is transformed into the flesh of the world. “And conscience makes cowards of us all…” as Shakespeare has his Hamlet say, and it is recklessness that, when fear restrains us, triggers the liberating accident, makes things happen. And wounds are created and shown, and the world is inscribed in the body displaying its own collapse. The body exposed, wounded, manipulated is an escape from the obstacle that prevents us from living and that renders visible the interplay of dovetailing of the submission to the everyday, a real motive for yielding, the habituation to the rigidity provoked by a control that prevents existence from becoming destiny. Thus we create a new code of signs that provoke a crisis amongst the instances that determine the fear of the future; there is a disruption of the maps of the territory of control, and there is an attempt to provoke the incident in which things dramatically begin once again to communicate.

The exhibition of the self, of one’s own body, of the intimacy of one’s own fears and one’s own individual desires becomes at the same time a shock and an instant of wonder, surprise, and the event itself; it chooses to explore the areas of collapse.

Gina Pane began to work with the medium of the body in 1968, and her artwork has been preserved in the form of film and photography taken by the photographer Françoise Masson. The first action in which Gina Pane wounded herself was *Escalade*, in 1971: "...My works were based on a certain kind of danger. I often tested some pretty extreme limits, but always in front of an audience. I was exhibiting the danger, my limits, but I never offered answers. The result was not genuine danger, but only a structure that I had created. And this structure gave the viewer a certain type of shock. The viewer no longer felt safe. He or she would be caught off balance, and this would give them a certain internal emptiness. And they were obliged to remain in that void. I would give them nothing.... In my work, pain was almost the message itself. I would cut myself, whip myself, and my body would just be overwhelmed.... Physical suffering is not merely a personal problem but also a problem of language.... The body becomes the idea itself, whereas before it was nothing more than a transmitter of ideas. There is quite a broad territory worthy of investigation. From there, it is possible to enter other spaces, such as from art to life, where the body is no longer a representation but rather a transformation". Always and unfailingly dressed in white, she would cut her lips with a razor blade, she would cut her face, she would display her body covered with worms, she would stab her arm with thorns from bunches of roses, she would roll on a floor covered with broken glass... she would display the signs of power on the body as a gesture of rebellion and she would take the language upon herself... she would climb barefoot up a ladder with nails sticking out of each rung, she would put out fires with her feet, she would eat rotten meat until she vomited... Her extraordinary physical and psychological stamina and energy are evidence that Gina Pane had an inner experience that emerged in her body directly from the deepest recesses of her subconscious to become a conscious thought that was displayed as a truth that could produce lesions and wounds. What is most striking about her actions is the incredible calm and self-control that contrasts so sharply with her blood-spattered clothing, pain as a strategy for losing one's identity, as a form of corporeal revolt, as an insult to the somnolent quiet in which others try to relegate human life. Gina Pane displayed herself in a ritual that laid out a special archaeology of existence, of her own life, her memories, experiences and feelings, which she ritualised in a series of gestures that would open a gash or a wound, both physical and mental. With Gina Pane, the private became public in a dimension that was poetic even more than political, she established a personal autonomy in which the wound allowed a language, a communication, a dialogue, that would break into the absent relations amongst beings whose existences were separated by conventions, choices and references. All of Gina Pane's work seems directed toward the creation of a suspension of time, a crystallisation of language: all of her energy was concentrated into a redefinition of the world beginning from the communication amongst living beings. It is an exhibition of diversity, of illness, of rejection, and the wound becomes the passage from depiction to reality, an attempt to destroy a separate attitude, an escape from the functional calculus of utilitarian relationships and the revolutionary decision to opt for an immediate communication amongst individuals. She dipped her hands into boiling chocolate, she would put out fires with her bare feet and hands, she would cut herself and mix the blood with milk... Gina Pane took upon her own body the signs of a society that programmes indifferent individuals, and created the shock of participation; she transformed her own body into a site of rebellion, she sought to name that which in reality has no name, she proposed actions that had a powerfully political connotation: the passion of recognition of the other, moral requirements, the energy of participation. And she opened a wound: "...unless you feel love in the most universal sense of the word, you cannot do something like this. It is impossible", she said in an interview about her cutting of her skin. With Gina Pane the metaphorical power of art was reactivated, revealing the links with Western religious iconography, and with the revolt that was exciting young minds in those years, with the general subject of transfiguration: she presented her body as the original site of emotions and excitement. In a society based on the principle of reality, Gina Pane's work broke in like a conscious and possible laceration that illuminated the possibility of a symbolic exchange: "The symbolic is neither a concept, an instance nor a category, nor is it a structure, but is an act of exchange and a social relation which puts an end to the real, which resolves the real and at the same time the opposition between the real and the imaginary... The symbolic is that which puts an end to this code of disjunction and the disjoint terms. It is the utopia that puts an end to the topics of the soul and the body, man and nature, the real and the unreal, and birth and death", writes Jean Baudrillard in connection with the replacement of exchange value, in contemporary society, with the "accounting order of value". The work of Gina Pane, her "donating", "opening" and "exhibiting" of herself, her transformation of the body into research on being is an extreme attempt at exchange value, in which that which is donated, opened or shown is precisely the uniqueness of the emotions and the authenticity of the passion, of the contact between individuals, who are able to intuit the meaning of the complexity in which the action takes place and in which our daily struggle occurs.

And these are real drops of blood on the arms in which rose thorns are driven for a "sentimental action", just as the abrasions on the bodies are real, from the repeated rubbing and caressing, the grimaces are real, and the whispers and the litanies... Art does not declare a body, but it creates the event of a presence: a dark blue breast, a rivulet of blood, an ampoule of breath... The idea develops of a body that becomes a new territory for discussion, a new indication of the escape route from the blind alleys of a reality that has transformed us into users, consumers, voters, patients, clients, debtors and rivals... A bite, a cut, a bruise, hickeys from kisses on the skin, an expanded consciousness, out of the body, in the explosion of identity and all its cages of recognition. "Your secret can always be seen on your face and in your gaze. Lose your face. There should only be flows, which at times dry up, freeze, or overflow, and at other times join or divide." (Gilles Deleuze)

Losing one's identity, allowing it to drop away, scattering it to the winds... And the body returns to being a protagonist on the contemporary artistic scene, in a geography of mutations that repropose it as a possibility of self-production: the truth of a body that emerges more and more in its acceptation as a cultural construct subject to a perennial and rapid transformation; if for the Body Art of the 1970s the body constituted a place to be explored in its most recondite recesses, it now becomes a decision to be faced. With all of the questions, the perplexities and the problems that are thus entailed. A body that takes into account the changes that emerge from the social and cultural fabric and which becomes a social body that enters and mutates the individual body. This is the most radical evidence of the contemporary, the challenge against the theories of a virtual and dematerialised body, the truth of flesh, blood, sperm, sweat... the truth that emerges, in this view on the future, with the taboos of all time... "The history of the body, historians began writing it long ago... They have examined it as a seat of needs and appetites, as a place of physiological processes and metabolisms, as the target of microbial or viral attacks... But the body is also directly immersed in a political field: the relationships of power operate upon the body an immediate manipulation, they invest it, they mark it, they train it, they torture it, they oblige it to perform certain jobs, they oblige it to take part in ceremonies, they demand signs from it", again Foucault, again the close and direct relationship between body and power, between body and politics, between bodies and the politics of power. The body is the place in which a series of relationships of power converge and tend to transform it into a territory of experimentation. A body that is educated, trained, marked, detained and regulated. A body "disciplined" by a progressive and hyper-specialised refinement of the techniques of control, privation and detainment. A control that includes the body in its biological whole, but especially its instincts, its desires, its obsessions, its liberties or its deliriums. And which operates directly upon the individual actions and attitudes.

"You will be organised, you will be an organism, you will articulate your body — otherwise you will be nothing but a depraved individual. You will be signifier and significance, interpreter and interpretation — otherwise you will be nothing but a deviant. You will be a subject, and fixed as such, the subject of an enunciation folded over a subject of enunciate — otherwise you will be nothing but a vagabond." This dense network of rules and fixed points is expressed on a daily basis in those sites through which power can act effectively, but especially "in concealment": total institutions.

Foucault defines these sites as heterotopical, sites where "the set of vital, organic and psychic manifestations of an individual seem to implode in a fully codified existential space".

"One does not punish", in an exclusive manner, "the *korper* [physical body], but rather the *leib*, which is to say, the relations of the body in society.... Not the marks of torture, but rather the signs of internment, or perhaps we should say the signs of social representation." A coercive system encloses the bodies in pre-codified spaces, structures and constructs sites in which the perception of oneself and the external context is modified, in which the relationship with other bodies is interdicted and modified, and modifies sexual attitudes, anaesthetises the senses.

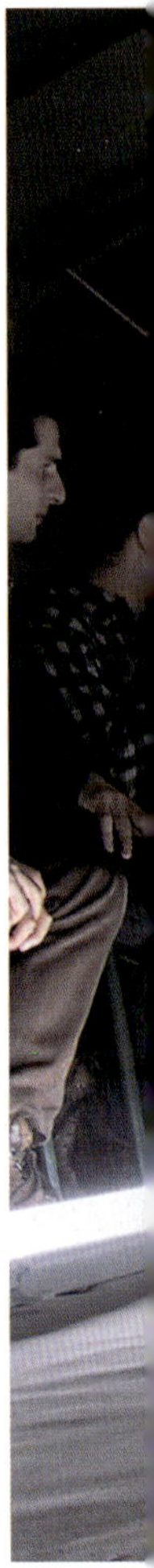

Franko B moves in a context where one of the most intense relationships between body and power becomes evident, the power that covers the surface of the body, marking it, carving it, subjectifying it according to certain previously established categories. The actions of Franko B are obsessive, they take place emotionally in the exchange with the audience (the reactions are manifold: fear, annoyance, attraction, flight): an audience that is silent and disturbed because it is witnessing performances and actions that indicate the invasiveness of places of detention, enclosure of the body, the paralysis of social relationships, the threat of pain. And blood is the element that Franko B chooses for his performances, his own blood, an act of inverting the internal/external relationship of the body, the expulsion of one's own liquids onto the "external façade", the external aspect of things; he chooses to put the more intimate and personal and hidden dimension of a being on show: one's own interior.

Franko B, *I Miss You*, performance at the ArtLive Festival, Turin, 2000. Photo by Manuel Vason

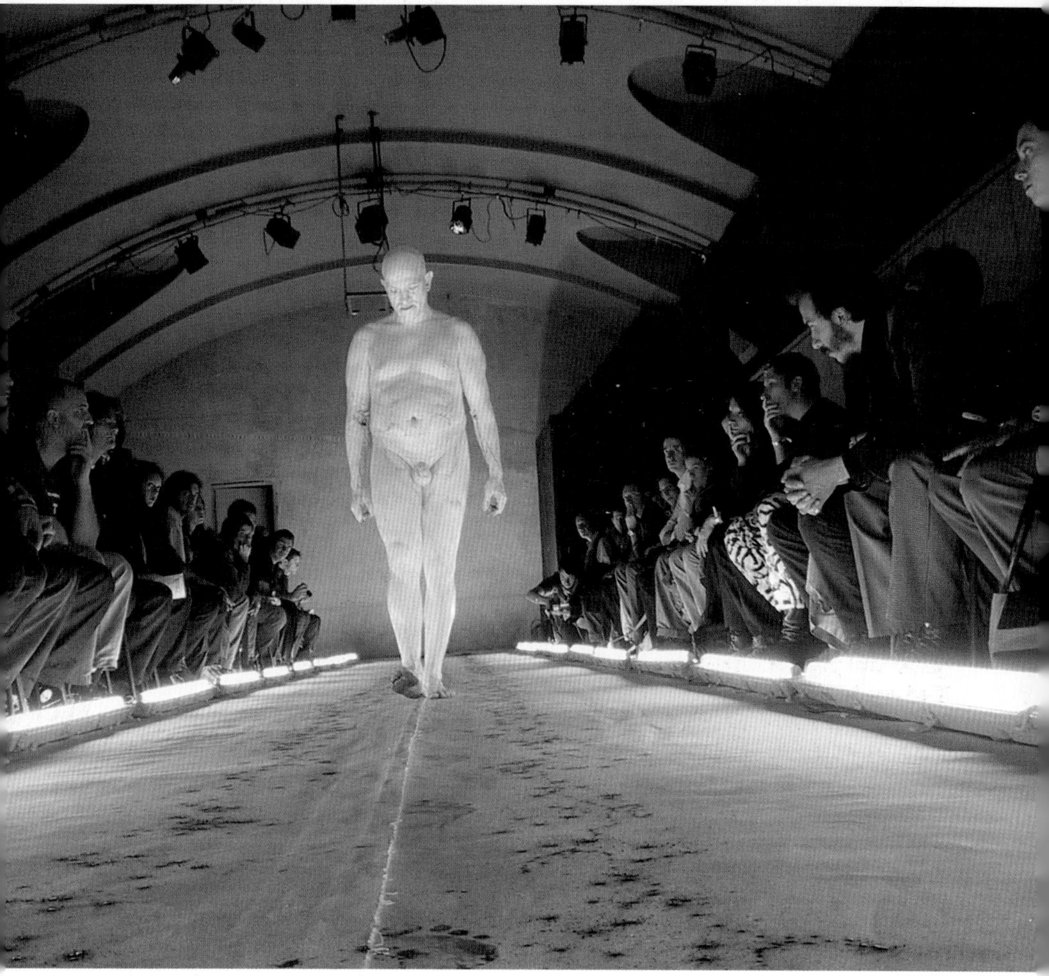

Foucault points out that in the decision to make use of physical pain, in the exposure of a tortured body, a body that has been amputated, branded, displayed alive or dead in a public "spectacle", there was a commemoration and demonstration of the triumph of the law, but at the same time, it became possible to suspect perverse relationships between crime and power. For many acts of torture, the public dimension was chosen in order to make clear to all the certainty of the penalty in case of infraction, and the populace was summoned to witness the punishment so that it might "learn" not to transgress; but the condemned man, once he had become aware of his imminent end, would lose all hope of salvation, and would scream against power and its means of coercion, inquisition, and violence, reversing his own position as a condemned man into the evident con-

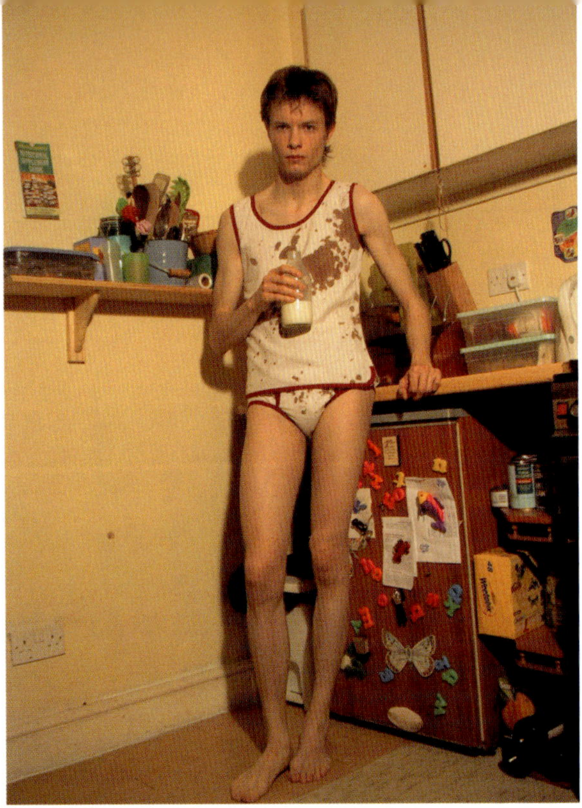

Franko B,
Milk and Blood,
2000

demnation of an absolute power, in an extreme attempt to transform his own body and the torture it had suffered into a site open to the discussion of power itself and its methods. And so public executions were abolished. Franko B carried out his first actions in an attempt to recreate images of the discovery of his own body as a pretext for provoking questions about very specific subjects: belonging, individuality, identity. In 1990 he did a series of cuts of skin, in 1995 with *Mama I Can't Sing!* he had himself slapped, in *I'm Not Your Babe* (1996) he showed his body abused, cut and bloody.

For Gilles Deleuze, as for Antonin Artaud, the world of the organic becomes the extreme metaphor of an organisation, the social organisation, in which what rules is the principle of the division and assignment of roles, hierarchies: "the BwO screams: they turned me into an organism! They bent me without having any right to do so! They have stolen by body!...", and Franko B opposes to the rigid schemes of the powers/knowledges an experimentation in which he sets himself forth as the object of an existence that becomes body, he performs an act of reappropriation and reconstruction of the self. Franko B is an unrequited artist, an artist that has the features of the specific cultural history of those who spend an entire lifetime passing through different places, both mental and geographical. An idealist and realist at the same time, with a cunning assortment of formalism and formal anarchy, concreteness and abstraction, he belongs to the tradition of visionaries, of the constructors of new visions, capable of structuring an artwork in the simultaneous presence of heterogeneous tensions, capable of

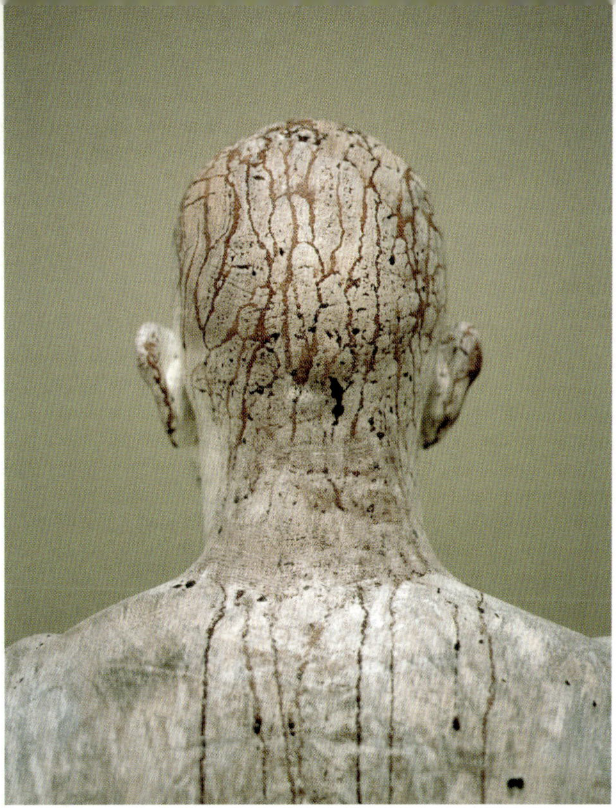

Franko B,
Oh Lover Boy,
performance
in Malmö, Sweden,
September 2000.
Photo by Manuel Vason

being shocked and generating a crisis in every criterion of reality, capable of enacting an attempt to render the beauty of actions at the farthest limit. Franko B is essentially a classical artist, capable of capturing the element of disquiet and contradiction and therefore worthy of the most provocative avant-garde. Franko B affirms the reasons of rebellion, a rebellion that is timeless, as is art. Everything is opened to discussion: relationships, equilibriums, planes, colours. Who are the protagonists and who are the extras in the performances by Franko B? There is no representation, no seduction from reality, no concession to the "rule": the final vision is an excessive movement between a formal progression that is apparently respected in an arbitrary, irrational space. These are visions that conceal fields of force activated from time to time by almost haphazard elements, interplays of force, brusque movements, unusual expressions, irregular progressions that like an alarm siren place us face to face with a horizon that seeks out life, with all the emotions that it can provoke, from laughter to anguish, from panic to happiness. Franko B creates the subterranean "subconscious" of a vision that has no desire to be conciliating, he seeks the path of personal liberty with a discussion through the luminous and the irreducible, through the courage that develops out of fear, pain, discomfort and shame. He invites us to seek our own way out, an "intellect of love" capable of inventing beauty. Imprints of original gestures, these are the artworks of Franko B, an "irregular" full of tension, a universe that draws upon the multiplicity of the human condition transmuted into a poetic and luminous presence. Beauty to the limit of the visual, auditory, and mental collapse. In the endless interplay of transformations that are made possible by metaphor, Franko B produces a new vision of art by showing an unprecedented vision of the world, and chaos is transformed into a rigorous performative presence, contributing to the destruction of facile images of an excessively optimistic world of aesthetic order. The metaphor is for Franko B the place of beauty: "The irregular, that is the unexpected, surprise, astonishment, all represent an element that is as important as it is beautiful" (Charles Baudelaire).

Franko B creates with the spectator an intimate relationship of tacit implications in a series of excessive images; it is the apparition of a representation of the world as a world of images: art always focuses on exceptional cases.

"The force of great personalities lies in precisely this fact, that they do not choose, but in full and by their nature they are what they will and achieve... it is the pride and boast of great personalities that they are guilty." (Hegel)

For Franko B the image (both in his performances and in his objects) is never the pretext for a transgression, rather it is the quest for a world that is present before the eyes of one and all, a world that has momentarily been dissimulated but is still perceptible to those who know how to summon up its presence. Everything begins with a sort of blinding, a blinding that places itself as a sort of filter between the world of the artwork and the world of things. For Franko B a glorious discourse is not sufficient: it is necessary to add gestures, expressions, atmospheres and sensations. It is an interplay of gazes, gazes that express tension, attention, astonishment, indifference, desperation, obsession, a series of controversial and contrasting emotions. It is a condition that comes to be condemned from the depths, inasmuch as every desire is destined to plunge into the failure of the gaze, a gaze that replaces the theatrical gesture: for Franko B, far from any temptation, whether theatrical or ritual, the gesture, the behaviour, the presence become the act par excellence. What seems to be activated is the unpredictable gaze of the dreamer, in a structure of the artwork (whether it is performance-driven or takes the form of an object) which, once distances have been abolished, traces the imprints of a potent and direct symbolism: the heart, the red cross, the syringe... imprints of red crosses and hearts on strollers, shoes, furniture, trays, car doors, file cabinets, trousers... *I Love Mr. Woodcock*, 1998: hearts and crosses, objects carved the way he has done so many times before on his own body, an "accumulation" of artifacts that become so many votive objects in a disposable society, a society of discards, survivors, human beings bent like so much sheet metal. The actions and the objects of Franko B are done with the images of the discoveries upon his own body. "Many of my obsessions have created marvellous images, which are marvellous for me, otherwise they would be intolerable and they would also be dangerous. What I am doing is to render tolerable the intolerable... I make an icon of the things that are over-hastily branded as intolerable. I see my own neuroses, my own fears, my 'trips', my negative experiences with a creative approach, I try not to contaminate them, I try to express them in a direction that is pure, as it is in my mind. It is a process of liberty, my quest is a research project on individual liberty... My blood is my body. When I feel it, it gives me a sense of freedom, especially the fact that it is my blood..." It is towards a total complicity that Franko B leads us, towards an impassioned participation in the perceptible experience of a world that deploys itself through the artwork, an artwork that rejects neither the vertigo of distance nor that of proximity: on the threshold of the desire of a two-fold excess in which the gaze is each time on the very verge of losing all its power. And in that way the artwork disappears and the world that constructed it instead appears. And it is at this point that one learns to regulate the exercise of one's gaze, in the face of an artwork that questions us: to keep one's eyes open in order to capture the gaze that seeks us. There is no doubt about it, you must look if you wish to be looked at.

A filter of decadence, an interval between melancholy and discomfort, the choice of displaying a pain that refuses to be caught up in the celebration of healing but rather seeks out the depth of the world, the "bottom without abysses" of Nietzsche, the "necessary for survival". And the gesture becomes the resistance of the body to the order of reason: events selected and incessantly inserted into reality, predetermined images which act on the social brain grafting in a sort of epidemic that manifests itself in the cycle of panic-depression-anguish.

Everyday life has been colonised by an economic system that in order to exist must necessarily produce standardised images according to the very principle of economics, and depression springs out of the incapacity to perceive and act upon one's own singularity, a singularity understood as difference and opposition: "Depression is the emotional experience of a state of impotence and impoverishment of the ego: it originates from the tension between powerfully based narcissistic aspirations and an awareness on the part of the ego of its own impotence and incapability of living adequately with respect to these models" (Jacobsen). A singularity, the instinct that rejects depression as a way of life and as a by-product of imagination.

"Physical pain can cancel out psychological pain because it annuls all of the psychological contents, whether they be painful, pleasurable or neutral. Our acceptance of its capacity to put an end to madness is one of the ways in which we, consciously or unconsciously, recognise its power of putting an end to all aspects of the self and the world." (Elaine Scarry) The representation of pain, of wounds, of the irreversible signs of disease upon the human body almost always provokes reactions of rejection, disgust and fear, which often lead to the need to establish a certain distance from the subject of the artwork. This sort of "impurity" of the body terrorises and frightens, almost appears as a threat, as a demonstration of the precariousness of our own body. A wound obliges us to an almost primitive confrontation and relationship in an era in which we often claim that the image has lost all power.

"My relationship with chocolate in an autobiographical sense comes from when I worked in a candy store. Careful you don't melt, candyman! they would say to me when I would go to take a shower after football practice. Later, at university, when I began to formulate my artistic language, I started using food as the temporal element of my pieces. Immediately after university, I completed my first installation, developed with chocolate in a slaughterhouse. In general, my artwork consists of different works that use chocolate as a fundamental ingredient. Looking at and smelling the *Morgue Chocolates*, a spectator tries to distance pleasure from himself or herself. For me giving the spectator a complete vision of the artwork means making him or her work with all five senses." Stephen J. Shanabrook is an American artist who lives half the year in Russia and half in Holland. Some of his early pieces were done with sugar and sweets, but it was with *Unknown Resurrections*, using chocolate, that Shanabrook's work became

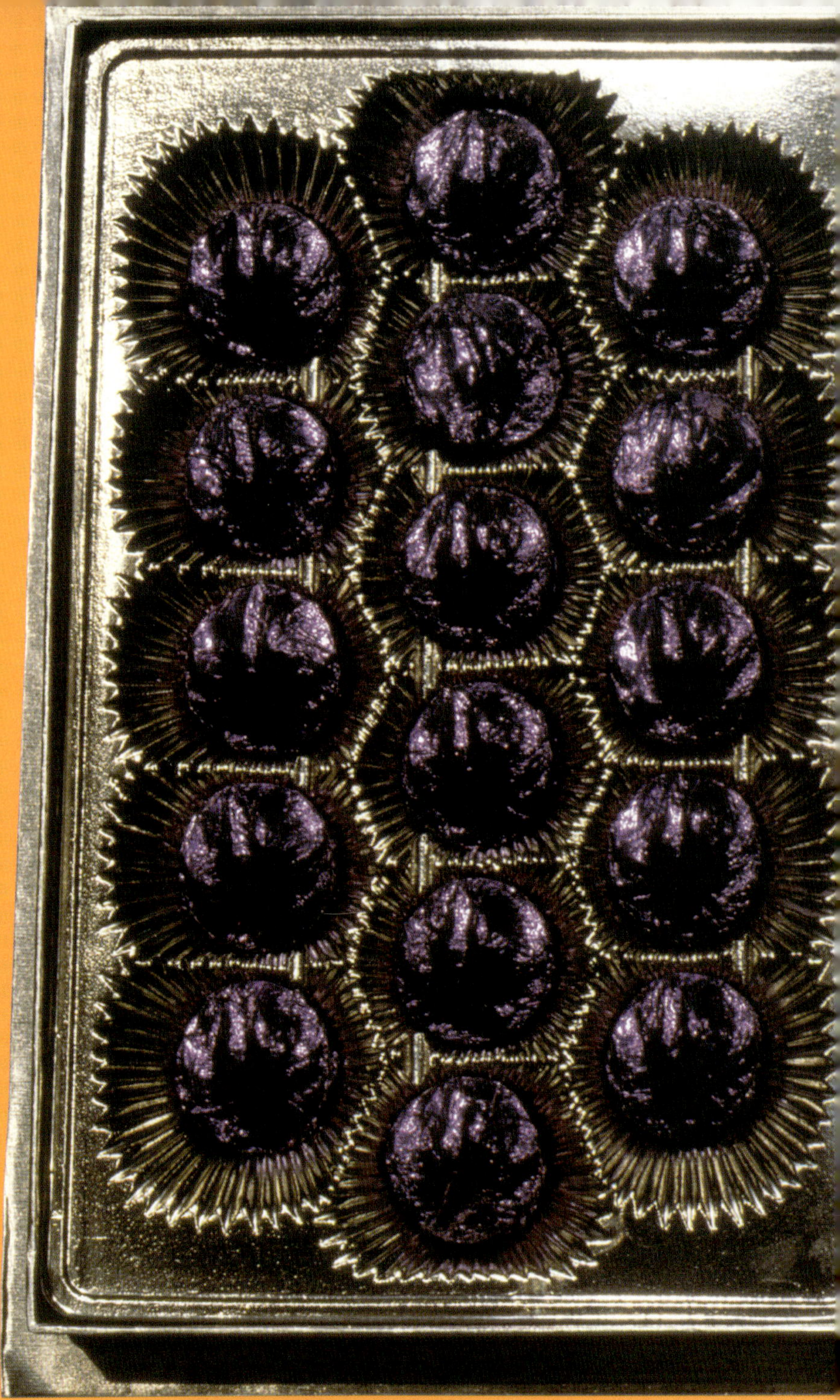

Stephen J. Shanabrook, *Halcyon Nest (Open Eyes)*, Moscow. Photo by Igor Andelic

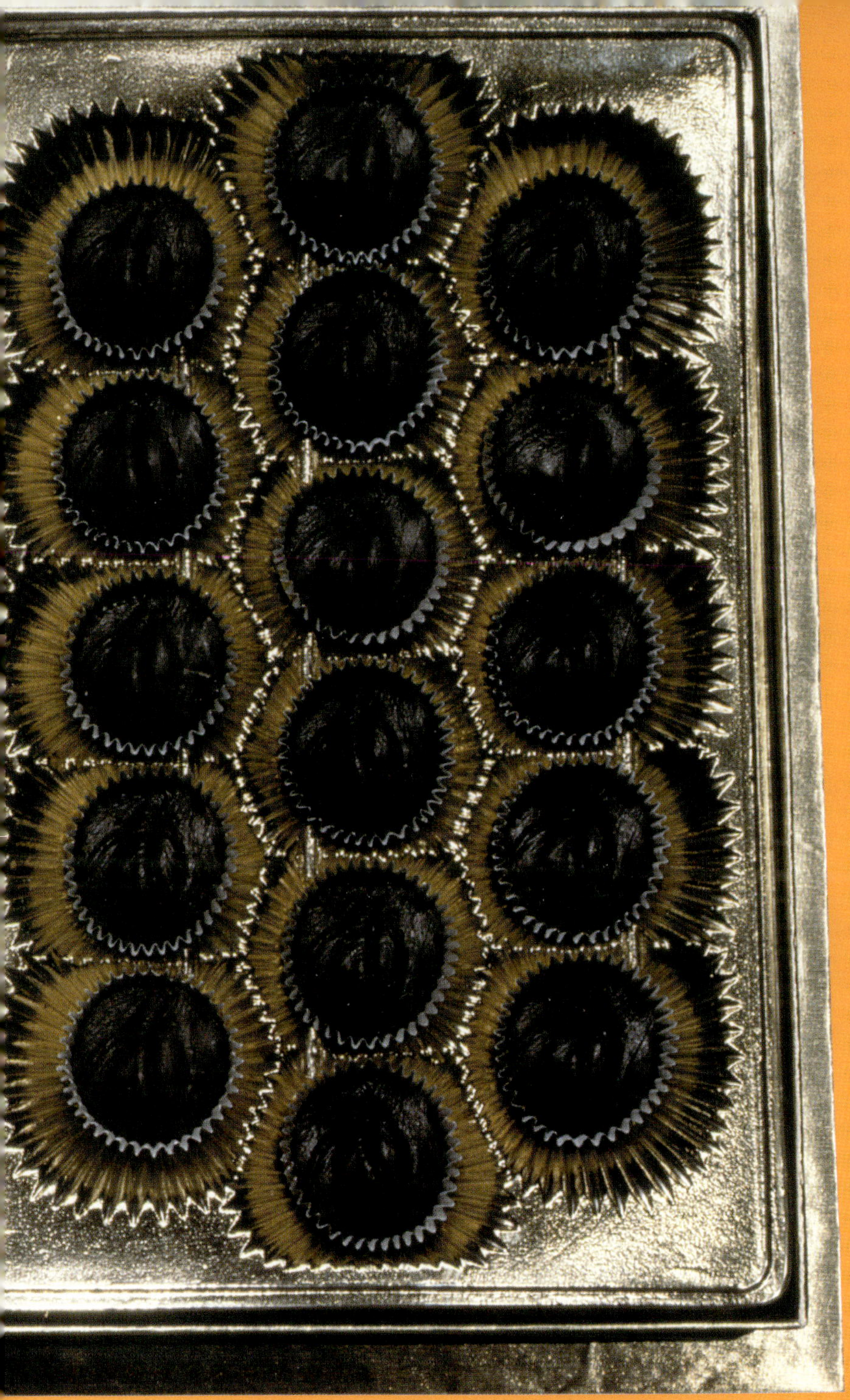

Stephen J. Shanabrook, *Evisceration of Waited Moments*. *Morgue Chocolates*, Toledo, Ohio. Photo by Igor Andelic

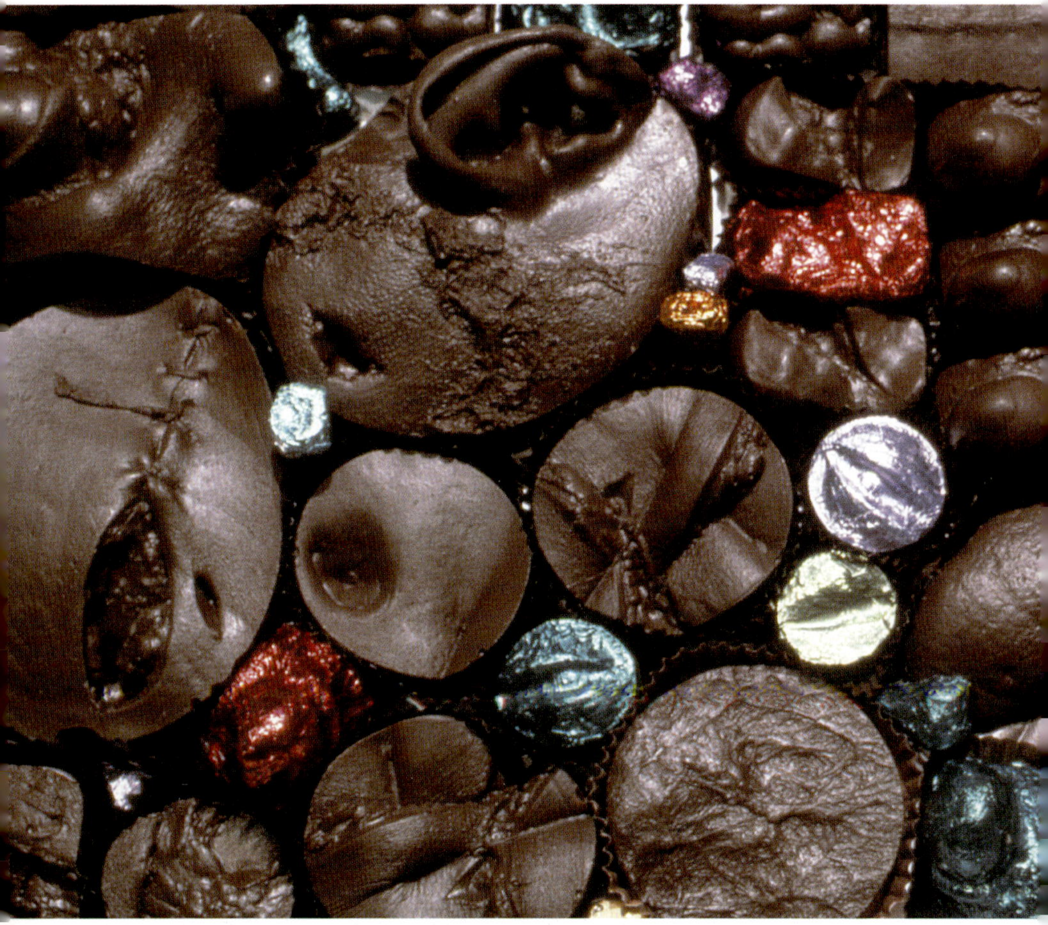

radical, aggressive, powerful. He intertwines and merges two metaphorical shadows that have nothing in common: chocolate and wounds. Two metaphorical shadows, of the metaphor of chocolate, joy without sin, and of the metaphor of death, sin without joy. The symbolic meaning of chocolate, linked to the imperative of pleasure, and the symbolic meaning of the wound, linked to the dimension of pain, creates a sort of disorientation in Shanabrook's work, an effect of nausea, waste, sabotage and excitement.

Sickeningly sweet remains that are in no way symbolic, like the recognition of something which we are incapable of understanding, like the very substance that sublimates fear and beauty, in which we find renewed emphasis of the paradigm that art is stronger than death. Chocolate casts that in aesthetic terms lose track and reference to the proportions of "good taste", and which in ethical terms pre-

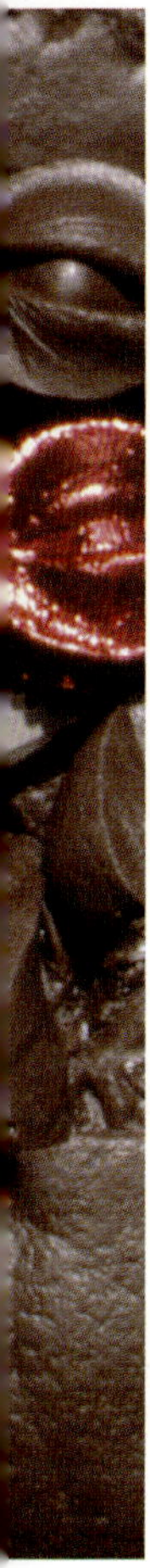

sent themselves as an imperative of the ego that demands that we hold out to the very end, whatever the cost. For the American and Russian series, *Unknown Resurrections*, Shanabrook chose the bodies of the "different ones", those whom society tries to repress or insult because they make us feel uneasy. These lives and the traumatic experiences they have undergone are the motifs of Shanabrook's casts. A detailed description of body parts, living evidence of the end, impersonal parts of injured bodies, that have been shot, crushed, or stitched carelessly back together, which can only be classified in accordance with the findings of forensic medicine. These casts, made in Moscow, look like so many chocolate bonbons laid out in a sampler box, a vision of violent death rendered peaceful and consumable by the decision to make the casts in chocolate. The bonbons of the *Morgue Chocolates* series are a symptomatic product of the artist's vision of life and death in America: the remains of people who have been brutally murdered, bodies that could not be reassembled, constitute a "silent lament". Gunshot wounds, protruding eyeballs, knife wounds stitched up with ordinary string, in his works become so many fragments of a horrible and everyday reality that hits us in the solar plexus through the precise little casts made of chocolate. This vision and this presence of violent death in "chocolate" frightens us and irritates us, much more than the death that we witness daily in the pages of the morning newspaper and the evening television news: 32 casts of an eye in the box of *Halcyon Nest* seem to be covered, through the chocolate, by an inevitable death, a series of eyes open and sleepless that seem to want to affirm the refusal to die, an inability to resist and, at the same time, the suggestion that in the face of violent death we cannot close our eyes.

And once again art chooses the rejected, the unwatchable, the close-up.

It is precisely the banality of chocolate that renders the image so powerful, because the spectator is caught by surprise. The familiarity, the odour and the sensory stimulation of the pleasure that the chocolate provokes are the influential aspects of the *Morgue* series. A cloying and banal package of chocolate bonbons, which reproduce a case of gangrene, a gunshot wound, a suture of lacerated tissues, is seductive and stimulating, and until the horror takes over it is desirable. Even if we don't admit it rationally, the desire is there and so, for the spectator, the conflict begins: the odour of the chocolate is so powerful that he cannot manage to face what he sees, even before he begins to ask himself exactly what he is seeing. As Gilles Deleuze has written: "...every man who suffers is flesh. Flesh is the common territory shared by man and beast, an indistinguishable territory, flesh is this 'fact', in which we identify with the objects of horror and compassion". The sensation and the impact are powerful, clashing, disquieting and seductive. We feel guilty, we feel the disagreeable sensation of wanting to eat the proof and the outline of someone else's pain. Shanabrook makes chocolate shapes that are apparently similar, in their manufacturing and in their visual impact, to those ordinarily available on the market, and he uses as containers the "classic" gift packs: but the decorations on the chocolates themselves, customarily signs of a roguish and popular romanticism — little hearts, flowers and cameos — instead reproduce the signs of physical pain, desperation and fear, a sort of necessity of recognising the presence of the abject. We recognise the need to maintain the fear of the abject within the superficial pleasure of the taste buds in order to provoke a complex imbalance: remembering life through the contact with the death of another. "Consumption has become the way in which life sustains itself. In this moment the process of life does not close its circle. It goes in a single direction, the physical and psychological movement becomes reactionary and artificial", states Shanabrook, who sees in chocolate a close relationship with the idea of blood, both fluids that have passed through history as offerings for the gods or as a simple remedy for inner melancholy. After his first performances and exhibitions, in which he utilised only his own body, the artist began to work on other identities and other anatomies, including dead bodies, always using food as a metaphor for the human condition; nonetheless, it was with the *Morgue Chocolates*, the artworks made of chocolate that contain signs of wounds, death, and those of the internal workings of the human body after death that Shanabrook begins to approach the limit, the place that is forbidden: the place of the artists. These pieces of chocolate represent the dichotomy that is always present between life and death: utilising both the sensory stimulations of taste and the "information" of disgust in the rational sphere, the spectator finds himself or herself trapped in that dimension in which things, sensations and attractions have no name and are nothing more than a sum total of opposites. "While I was working in the Moscow morgue, the idea of identity was not particularly important to me, because it was a morgue for unidentified people. In fact the title of those works was *Unidentified*, and this word or a derived word was usually written in green on a leg. Moreover, in Moscow, when I first exhibited these artworks, I presented them intentionally in an old information kiosk not far from Red Square. In this way, the identity of the corpses was replaced by the identity of the living people through their oral or visual participation." One year after the presentation of *Unidentified,* Shanabrook exhibited *Evisceration of Waited Moments*, in which all of the images of death are "taken" from an American morgue. "The situation there was quite different. I was extremely aware that I did not want to be involved in the past of these corpses. What I was doing was intended merely as a way of representing death in general, not in particular, not in any connection with a specific personal history. Concentrating on the narrative part would have been an unacceptable invasion of privacy and would have added only a component of useless shock. When I work with these subjects I am keenly aware that the component of shock has no value or purpose and undermines the work, taking it down to the level of a scandal rag. The pieces of chocolate are generic representations of death, and for me they need to remain anonymous in order to preserve their universality and their cutting edge."

A later series involved the production of masks of young Russian poets done in chocolate, creating a powerful emotional impact in their manufacturing, simulating the form and the fixity of death masks. Once again the main theme of the artwork is the link between life and death; in place of chocolate surrounded by violence we find that it is poetry that now surrounds the chocolate. *Restitution After the Meeting of Thirteen* is an artwork executed with the co-operation of twelve Conceptual artists from Moscow: Shanabrook exactly reproduces the faces of each of the twelve artists, and then all of them are given an exact copy of their face in chocolate and their index finger in graphite. Each artist is given 24 hours to interact with the face as he thinks best, recording what happened on a piece of paper specially supplied, using his graphite finger as the main writing implement. "My role as antagonist (the thirteenth one) consisted of presenting the artist as a conflictual being, rendering his image desirable and digestible even if this meant in some cases inflicting a form of self-destruction, or taking revenge on one's own ego. Given the quality of the chocolate I did not expect that I would have many remains to display, but to my great surprise that is not at all what happened: at least half of the artists chose not to take part in this act of virtual cannibalism..." The chocolate masks are conceptually very similar to the *Morgue Chocolates*: the invitation to take into consideration the meaning of what it is to look at one's own death mask triggered various interventions, even though all the artists who took part in the project left on the masks clear signs of an inner conflict, a sort of restitution to their own funeral effigy of the most vital part of their own being. In Shanabrook's vision, the use of chocolate takes on the value of a very powerful weapon, since because of its ordinary and desirable appearance nobody is afraid of chocolate, "...indeed, the first thing that comes to the mind of most people is to eat it, while in a second phase they discover the message that I meant to hide in it. And there they are, like fish on a hook".

Disorderly bodies, falling bodies, fighting bodies, bodies that gather, bodies that show the impact of the assault on life, often bodies of anguish, a weight that breaks up the movements and alters the care for appearances, isolated bodies that have fallen into a lack of references, bodies of anguish, the anguish of history, the anguish that the body pays as the price for its semantic autonomy, anguish as physical impossibility, anguish as a critical moment, anguish as a total overwhelming individual revolt. Bodies that emerge from the representation, that "materialise" through the themes of power and violence that relegate men to a delirium of disturbing contortions, an anguish-making violence, subtle, that penetrates our everyday existence through the news, the mass media, the models of success. And the figures multiply in contortions or in classical poses of depositions, a rhythmic structure, movement and immobility, confused and muddled together, a voluntary procedure. There is an insistence on the anguish of the vanishing of meaning, there is a discussion of the legitimacy of all power, isolated contorted bodies are shown, torn in half, frightened, a precipitous sentimentality, and the anguish surfaces, in the images of works that declare their own will, their determination not to condescend. An assault.

The organism, social or physical as it may be, is a system of judgement, even only for the fact that the organic body, made in the image of God, has always been the metaphoric point of reference of the organisation of the cosmos or city; in exchange, all social, metaphysical and religious requirements have the right to exert control and judgement over the body of every man and upon the use that is made of that body.
Camille Dumoulié

STIGMATA

A body, the body of contemporary art, which in its less predictable iconography takes upon itself the tensions of a tradition of images that have decided to show the signs of a laceration, a detachment, a fracture. It is a scandalous idea which is engendered directly from the determination to proceed through the "unspeakable" which becomes name and image. The body of art is scarred, wounded, raped. Art leaves to the advertising image the glistening and ironic provocation, and keeps for itself the possibility of subverting the established order which re-establishes itself on a daily basis and, joking at time's expense, indicates as a danger signal the vulnerability of Western culture to manipulation. Art keeps for itself the corporeal, the organic which for Antonin Artaud becomes the cry that names the flesh, the theatre, cruelty, existence and the body. Artaud indicated the path to the destruction of the dualist metaphysics of soul and body which is the beginning of the separation between word and existence, the duality between text and body. He indicated the modes of de-construction of the body, beginning from the concept of a "body without organs".

- What do you mean, Monsieur Artaud?
- I mean to say that I have found the method for dispensing once and for all with this ape, and that if no one believes in God anymore, everyone increasingly believes in man. And therefore it is man that we must make up our minds to avoid.
- And how can we do that?
- By laying him down once more, but for the last time, on the autopsy table to readjust his anatomy. I say, to readjust his anatomy. Man is sick because he is badly made. We must make up our minds to strip him naked and scrape away that animalcule that itches him so, mortally, God, and with God, his organs. And tie me up if you want, but there is nothing more useless than an organ. When you have made for man a body without organs, you will have then freed him from all his automatic instincts and endowed him with an authentic liberty. Then you will teach him once again to dance backwards as in the delirium of the dancehalls, and backwards will be his authentic place.

In the insane asylum of Rodez, Artaud's inferno takes form, an inferno that passes through fifty electroshocks: "Electroshock, Mister Latremolière, plunges me into despair, it erases my memory, it dulls my brain and my heart, it makes me an absent individual, aware that he is absent, watching himself chase after his being for weeks, like a dead man next to a living man who is no longer himself, demanding that he come, into which he can no longer enter".

It was in this traumatic experience that Artaud sought to reappropriate that body that had become an absent body, a divided, alienated, disincarnated body, a phantasmagorical body that becomes a goal to attain, a place of reconjunction. *Histoire vécue d'Artaud-Momo*, *Tête à tête par Antonin Artaud* and the radio broadcast *Pour en finir avec le jugement de dieu* are just some of the texts of Artaud in which we see the structure of a new terminology that defines its own vocabulary: the body, the flesh, the organisation of the organism, theatre and cruelty. Artaud violently attacks that absolutely arbitrary "construction" that is the body, and that "unequal" division, imposed at God's behest, whereby he keeps for himself spirit and light and immortality, leaving to man the sexual existence, the putrefaction of the flesh, and an organic and therefore mortal life. And flesh, for Artaud, becomes the cause of organic death, it no longer coincides with the body; flesh is the very death of the body, the reason for which all of the organism must be placed in discussion once again. "Apparatus for the insertion and expulsion of flows, the organ in its modalities of mouth, ear, eye, nose, anus, and sex is the aperture, the cut through which vital substance is expelled.... These humours which abandon us, this spreading pool of shit, sperm, urine, saliva, coughing, wax, snot, are all indications of the impure body.... The body is the body, it stands alone and has no need of organs, the body is never an organism, the organisms are the enemies of the body, the things that are done happen on their own without the assistance of any organ, every organ is a parasite, it serves only a parasitic function destined to support the life of a being that should not exist." Artaud defines the individual as a being devoid of any real self-knowledge, a being in prey to a "word", a partial understanding, a being whose origins and whose final destination plunge into scientific or religious hypotheses, and establishes the definition of "impouvoir", the non-power of/over oneself. All of his theoretical work is focused upon the possibility of presenting the danger on the stage, the possibility of breaking the schemes of a reassuring theatre, a reassuring art: "The truly diabolical and authentically cursed thing about our era is its clinging to outmoded artistic forms, instead of finding oneself condemned to the pyre while making signs through the flames". And Artaud chose to emphasise the progressive paralysis of thought, of the word, and of one's own being/body he chose to emphasise the desert-like, the gelid, the coagulant, the glacial aspects that in the theatre, for instance, take the word away from the actor, imposing upon him instead the word of the written text. Artaud determines and creates a form of theatre that demands the totality of the existence of the creative gesture and which rejects the manners of recitation and performance; for Artaud it is necessary, in the theatre, to be emancipated from the text, from a text that does not take into account the physicality of the actor, and which seems to need only mechanical and rigid gestures. He defines theatre as a total act, "...In the final instance we are referring to the impossibility of separating the spiritual side from the physical side". And he creates a "word" that overflows, that is lost, that escapes, and which becomes the subtraction from one's own being and one's own existence, a subtraction from one's own body and from the flesh. All of Artaud's literary production is an act of accusation against a theatre that expresses psychological conflicts, a theatre that gives pride of place to the word as extrapolated from a written text: "The word can only withhold thought, it delimits, but it exhausts it; it is quite simply a point of arrival". Artaud conceives a language that is independent from the word, a language destined directly to the senses, a theatre of the gesture, of the physical, of the spatial, the creation of alphabets independent of the limitations of verbal language, "...the gestures... represent ideas, attitudes of the spirit, aspects of nature, and that in so effective and concrete a manner, not unlike that Oriental alphabet that represents night as a tree on which a little bird has closed one eye and is beginning to close the other.... Such a language gives a good idea of what could be done with a theatre that was a poetry of space independent of articulated language".

Artaud chooses the gesture to define the creation of the cruelty on the scene.

"I employ the word 'cruelty' in the sense of an appetite for life, a cosmic rigour, an implacable necessity, in the gnostic sense of a living whirlwind that devours the darkness, in the sense of that pain apart from whose ineluctable necessity life could not continue; good is desired, it is the consequence of an act; evil is permanent.... Above all, cruelty is lucid, it is a kind of rigid direction, submission to necessity. And theatre understood as continual creation, as a total magical action, complies with this necessity. A drama in which this determination did not exist, visible in every gesture and in every act, and in the transcendent aspect of the action, this blind appetite for life, capable of overcoming every obstacle and hindrance, would be a useless and inadequate drama. What is more, this act of extreme sincerity is fused into a living organism, into its impulses, into its breathing, a rhythm of thought and the circulation of the blood....[A]nd I will devote / myself from now on / exclusively / to the theatre / as I conceive it, / a theatre of blood, / a theatre which at each performance will stir / something / in the body / of the performer as well as the spectator of the play, / but actually, / the actor does not perform, / he creates. / Theatre is in reality the genesis of creation."

Artaud attacks the organisation of the body, the organs: the body can no longer be an organism, corporeality can no longer be organised, and therefore the sole hope of mankind is to reconstruct itself, regenerate itself as a new body, and the theatre for Artaud is the sole place in which it is possible to take this step: "The theatre has always appeared to me as the exercise of a dangerous and terrible act, in which for that matter both the idea of theatre and spectacle is eliminated and the idea of all science, all religion and all art. The act of which I am speaking tends toward the organic and physical transformation of the human body. Why? Because the theatre is not the prepared set in which a myth is developed, virtually and symbolically, but rather the crucible of fire and real flesh in which anatomically, by compression of bones, limbs and syllables, the bodies are rebuilt, and the mythical act of creating a body is presented, physically and naturally". And he defines the "glorious body", a body liberated from the heavy weight of the organs, just like the language which, in parallel with the body, must be rethought, reformulated, freed of the "organs" that limit its potential.

And it is poetic language that determines the symbolic exchange, that structures an economics of expression, an economics of relationships, an economics of passion. The opening of a debate over extermination in the name of God. Thus are created the actions *qua* manifesto, the excesses of a discipline are pointed out, paradox is shown and the excesses and the violence in the contortions of a language that claims to be "spiritual" are identified.

> *In brief, you should consider that we are made of nothing but dust. It's not much to go on, I admit that, and we should never forget that it's true. But even considering this, this sort of lousy beginning, we're not really doing all that badly. And so, for my part, I am convinced that, despite the lousy current situation, we can survive. Have I been perfectly clear?*
> *(Philip K. Dick)*

Born and raised in the Mojave Desert, not far from Los Angeles, where he spent his youth in a family that was deeply religious and attended the Pentecostal church, active in the Charismatic Movement, Ron Athey was educated in a religious tension filled with fanaticism, apocalyptic prophecies, and ecstatic rituals. At first he transferred his background into a punk experience and later into a series of performance and theatre works, earning him a reputation as one of the most important artists of the Bodily Mutations movement. Performer, writer and critic, Ron Athey believes that nothing is too extreme in the pursuit of truth: "My work is difficult to describe, I am an extreme performance artist… I work on pain, suffering". The body is the absolute protagonist for Ron Athey, a body-object that is expropriated, tortured, offended, the site of disease and death, and yet at the same time the instrument of reappropriation of an identity chosen and no longer suffered. He is openly homosexual and sero-positive, and with his group he stages apocalyptic and truly shocking performances, in which self-mutilation, cutting, incisions and blood-spilling all trace the outlines of a dynamic otherness of the body and physicality. Reality, for Ron Athey, is not perceived: it is created. And he creates a universe of creatures that are courteous, courageous, lonely, cruel, people who are filled with love. Reality, for Ron Athey, is what man recreates continually by means of passions and determination, accidents and happenings. Reality is that which one is able to construct with senseless fragments and incoherent shrapnel, days and events that surround us and that at times appear to us as forgotten bits, discarded pieces of a reality that does not belong to us, of a completely different world that may have once made sense, but which now appears solely in its exquisite illogic.

"In my work I feel the need to continue to act out this religious comedy through my characters, I play the part of a frightened preacher, and with technology I have succeeded in recreating a sort of surgical stigmata using twenty-five needles in a crown and in the same way I have re-staged the scene of the martyrdom of Saint Sebastian.... I don't believe that it is necessary for my audience to explore in depth the meaning of what I do. Everything is structured more or less as if for a television programme, or for a musical: things have a beginning and an end, and not everything that comes between them is entirely understandable. This is because our background is given for the most part by a series of spectacular events that are offered by and large by television: talk shows and liturgical ceremonies coexist daily on American television screens, perfectly integrated one with the other. It is the set of multiple cultures, it is the American dream going down in flames. I contrast shit with glitter, atheism with mysticism, it all forms part of a plane upon which it is possible to act and become someone or something else. The roles meet phase transitions, linked to the elements of the earth, flesh, blood, repentance and mystification."

Art for Ron Athey is an event, the construction of an artist who chooses the action, a story of tenderness and fury, a flashback, a declaration that condenses necessity and the desire of life in a landscape by this point characterised by anxiety. Ron Athey stages what mediaeval *Pietà* were alluding to, he transfers onto his body something absolutely original and invisible to our eyes: piety as a living reality, the piety of the modern world, ugly, ordinary and ubiquitous. "If a *Pietà* of a thousand years ago could hand us... an image of our future world, what would be the modern-day equivalent of such a precognitive artifact? What do we have, nowadays, in the twentieth century, that is as habitual and familiar as one of those *Pietà* could have been for a Christian in the fourteenth century and which can serve as a representative microcosm of a distant future?... Not Christ lying dead in the arms of his eternal Mater Dolorosa, but rather a pile of Budweiser beer cans standing a hundred feet tall... Thousands of beer cans, toppling noisily, clanking and shifting, showering and crackling, and a giant homeostatic factory, automatic, run by a computer..." wrote Philip K. Dick, identifying paranoia as the lack of surprise, which has become a recurring feature of the contemporary world. Ron Athey "incarnates" intolerable situations and actions, a complex of mystery, nonsense, contradictions, hostility, passions and religion, and chooses to emphasise the inexplicable and generous totality of a human being in relation to another human being, the complicated, subtle, disconcerting, learned, warm behaviour with which we become visible to the eyes of another.

In the field of psychopathology, the structure of the schizoid personality is well established: its chief characteristic is a constant lack of feeling. Carl Gustav Jung has long maintained that most of reality should be approached with one's emotions. And the feeling becomes the rebellious emergence from mechanical thought, reflex, from the incapacity of making exceptions, the escape from stable, predictable, controllable thought. Ron Athey uses as "working" material for his performances pain, rage, fear, love, and all sorts of intense sensations. And that is what creates unease and prejudice against his work: the use of powerful emotions as shocks in order to emerge from the catatonic and schizoid situation in which the contemporary world has relegated us. It is typical of the lower forms of existence to continually provide an identical response.

This is no longer simple opposition, but rather a different trajectory, it is the manifestation of a system that operates through prohibitions and concessions, a system based on intentional misunderstandings, a foreshortened view of a precipice that has made the obsession with the failure of the individual a control machine. It is the emergence from the intimidations that rely upon regimes of dogmatic knowledge, it is a flight from the functional taboo, it is the choice of being lost in the face of the regressions of refuges of manner, the shabby transgressions, it is the possibility of withstanding the pressures of "fashionable artworks", revealing the proliferating triumph of media-oriented kitsch. And it is suddenly scandal.

Body I am, in all ways, and nothing more; and soul is nothing other than a word to describe a part of the body.
(Friedrich W. Nietzsche)

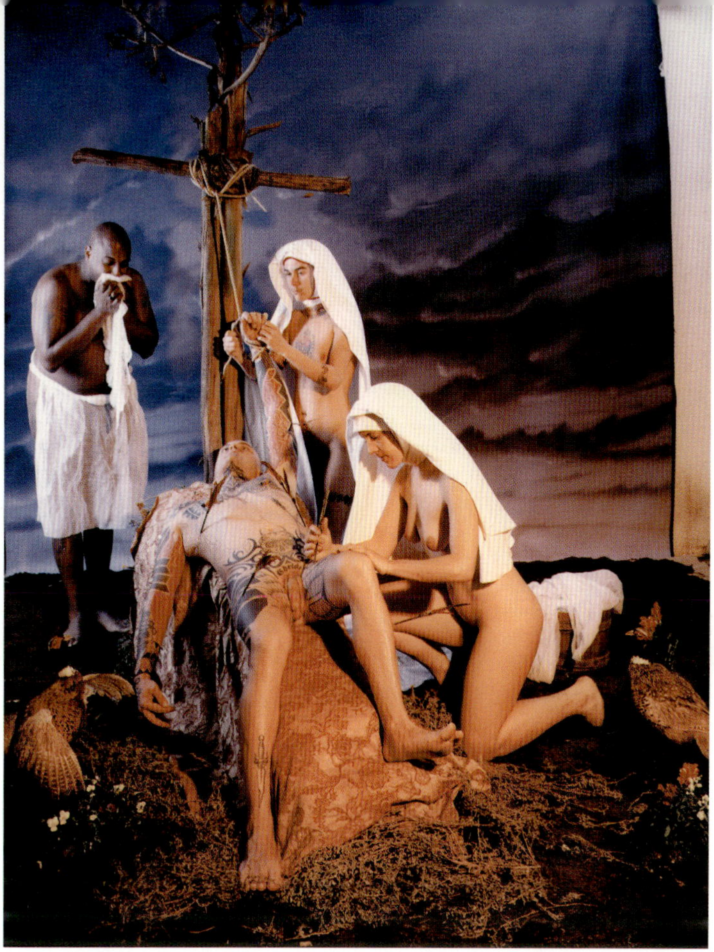

Ron Athey, *Saint Sebastian Removed from the Stake*, 1997. Photo by Catherine Opie

The condition of Rosso Fiorentino is not that of a man who lives "in nature", nor does he live in harmony: it is an interplay of equilibriums in which the rules do not seem to have been changed, and yet the final result is entirely modified. Imagination is used by Rosso Fiorentino as a force that serves to foment dissatisfaction, obliging the mind to live far from itself; imagination "is dangerous" and opens the eyes to a world that is no longer the world of things but rather the world of the various sites of desire and thought.

And the world becomes intolerable: Rosso Fiorentino chooses "perverse" visions, different trends that pull away from the normal direction of representation. His images are unsettling, absorbed in who-can-say-what meditations, sometimes visionary, lunatic, or excessively desperate: surreal colours, exploded spaces, and a construction of the artwork that is a testimonial to a classicism in complete revolt. Rosso Fiorentino captures all the elements of disquiet and contradiction, mysterious and sinister lights, counterpoints of colours, perspectival breakthroughs, interplay of volumes and planes, dissolutions and dematerialisations: an anti-classical repertory, at times strangely "cinematographic". Completely invented planes of sequencing, main characters and actors, "sudden un-

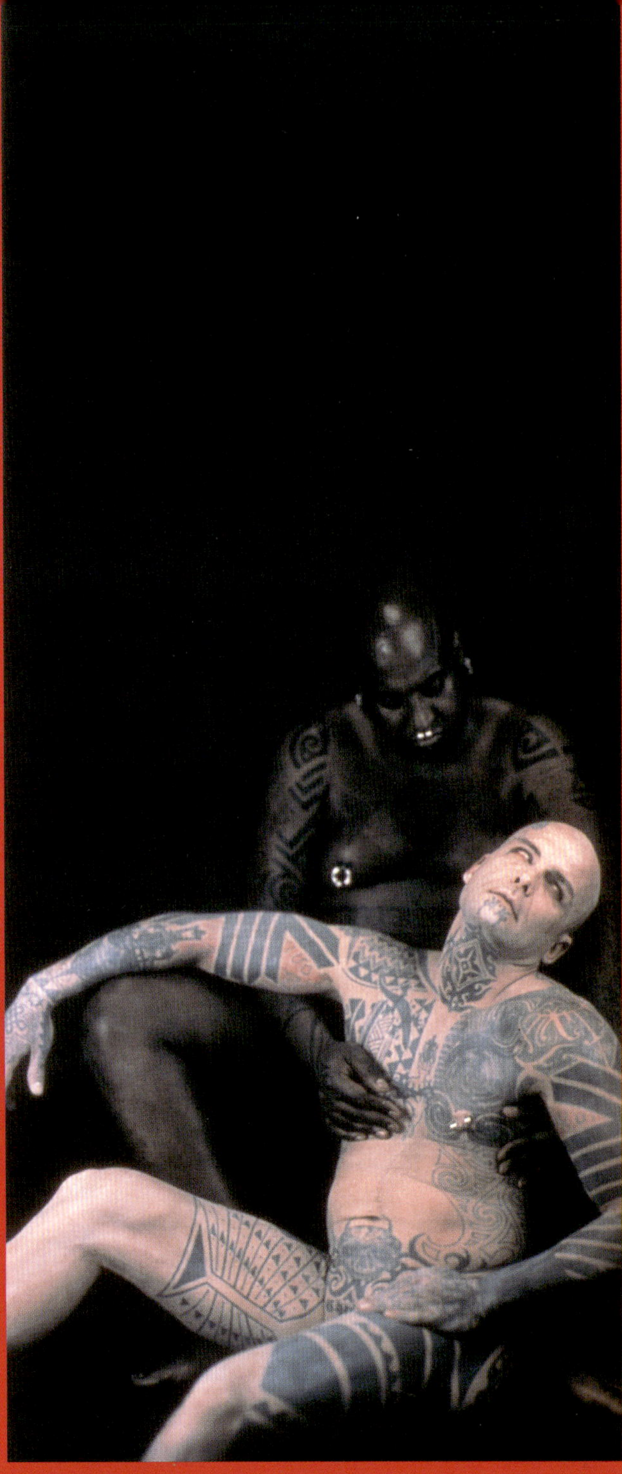

Ron Athey, 2000.
Photo by
Catherine Opie

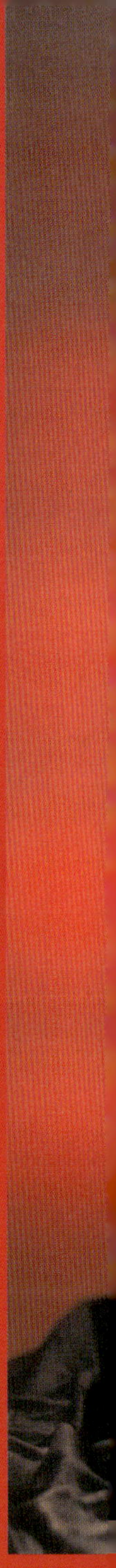

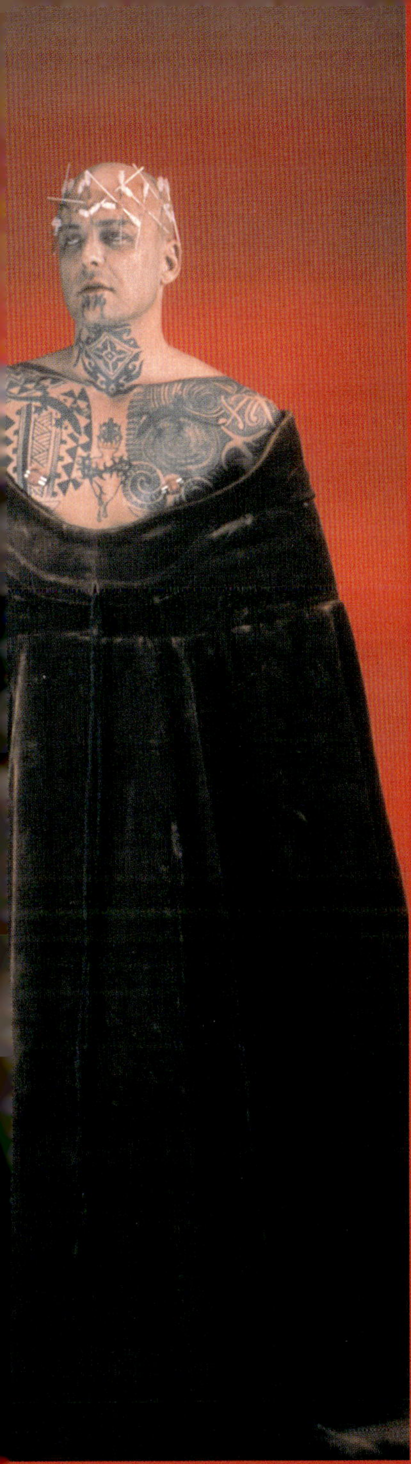
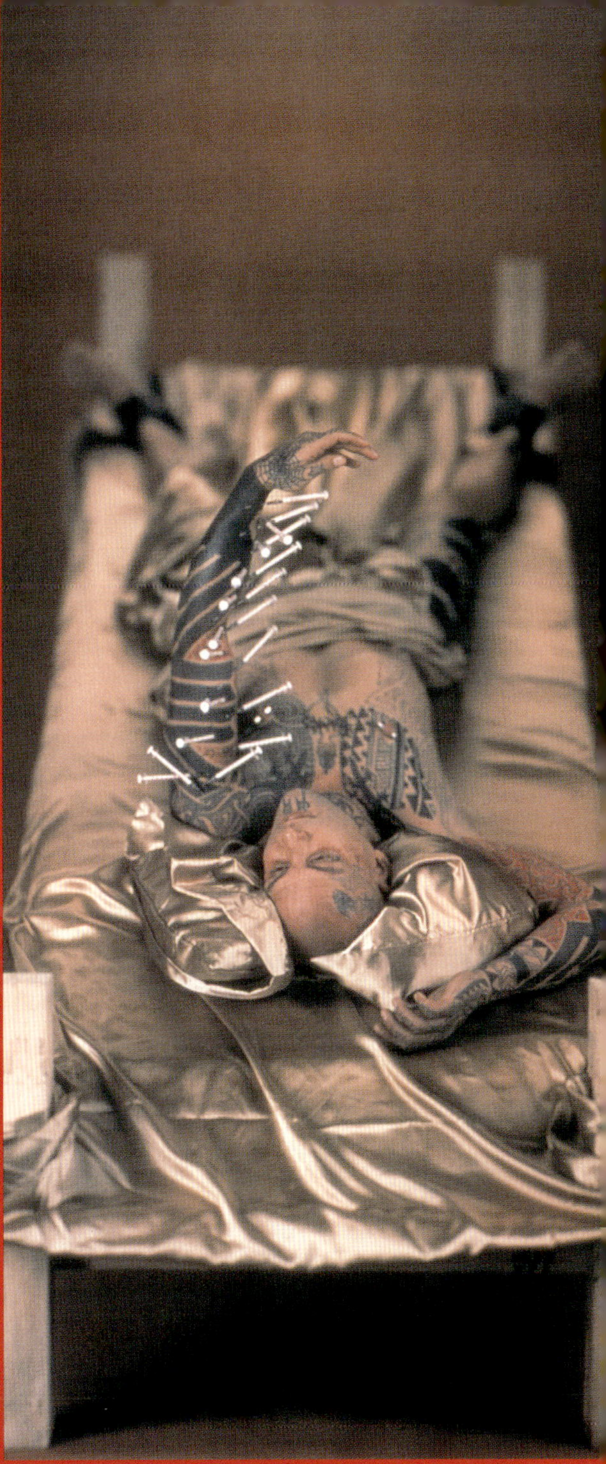

expected turns of events", irregular time frames, and above all a language that seeks out no pacification, no witnesses, no evidence, the language of an enigma that does not ask us to be anonymous spectators, but rather obliges us to emotion and participation, the same demands made by noir.

In the *Deposition* of Volterra (1521), Rosso Fiorentino sharply defines the figures against the background, agitating them in an excessive fit of frenzy, everything is excessive, nothing exists in a state of calm. An eccentric dimension, an "assortment" of bizarre poses, an abstract and vivid colouring and an entirely distorted space. The background of the artwork is neutral, absolutely devoid of any naturalistic indications: nothing remains of fifteenth-century representation. For Rosso Fiorentino man is not the centre of the universe, instead it is imagination, his solitary and individual vision. All of the dramatic tone is reserved for the expression and the bodies agitated by a desperation without comfort. The artwork emphasises the mental aspect over representation itself, the "fact" is a pretext: the pretext for a construction that bases its symmetry on contradiction, a nervous composition, all jerks, angles, diagonals and sharp points. The figures move on ladders, as if in a foreshadowing of movement, work; nothing is motionless, neither history nor vision nor destiny, every character is involved in a deeply felt and painful part, every character is agitated in a dimension that rejects the "background", all of them are protagonists of a single, total, clamorous drama. The pacing that Rosso Fiorentino uses is an accelerated rhythm: everyone is doing something, the action prevails over the immobile desperation. There is a continuous climbing and descending of ladders, consoling, despairing, hiding, twisting, and shame. Not even the figure of Christ is motionless: moved by those who are taking him down, he appears to be in the motion seen in the flow that surrounds him, an energy that transcends death, the event, and even destiny. In many of the *Pietà* in the history of art, the face of Christ appears older than the face of his mother, an old man in the arms of a young man, the face of a man who did not survive events. For Rosso Fiorentino the face of the dead Christ is exhausted, all the same his expression is unusually peaceful, destiny has run its course, the earthly moments, with all of its drama, is over, now it is possible to raise his eyes a little higher, the achieved dimension of the unique and unrepeatable event. The figures of Rosso Fiorentino are elongated, their placement is uncomfortable; what is being shown here is tension, and in order to do so there is a need for a disequilibrium, altered proportions. Nothing is contained; it is the rhythm of life over death, it is mobility over the immobility of history, of representation, of the history of representation, it is the verticality of desire against the horizontality of history: a capricious and stimulating vision as only desire can be. A feverish intensity, a dream-like dimension, a delirious vision, a surprising spirituality, a deeply moved expressionism: in this painting by Rosso Fiorentino we can already see the distinctive signs of the most original languages of art, from Surrealism to the Cubist vision, from the Futurist movement to the chaotic lifestyle of the visionaries, to the tensions of the contemporary, from the abolition of space to the confluence of dissonant parallelisms. Three ladders, a massive cross, four groups of figures and a clashing coloration: these are the elements of the painting. And yet from the young man at the bottom right to the old man set up high, on the cross, from the figure covering its eyes at the bottom right to the gaze of the woman who is holding up the Virgin Mary at the bottom left, from the horizontal

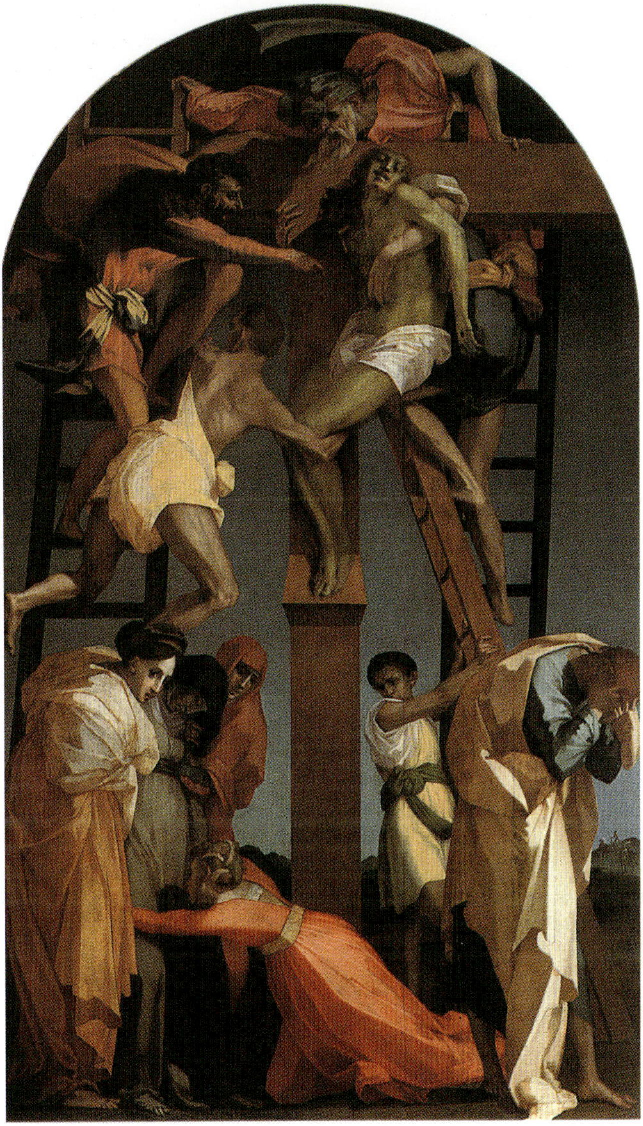

Rosso Fiorentino,
Deposition, 1521

structure of the upper part — where the characters face each other around the cross — to the woman throwing herself on the ground and embracing the knees of the Virgin Mary, all of the painting is constructed with an almost geometric rigour, with a cunning skill at staging worthy of the finest scheme of tension, and this also thanks to the use of sharp corners and points, straight lines and diagonals. The characters seem to be so many projectiles launched toward the event, obliged to take a position in the face of the event, involved in the destiny that has brought them all together in the face of the singular.

In 1963, in the "Ricotta" episode of the film *Rogopag*, Pasolini reconstructed the *tableau vivant* in colour (the rest of the episode was in black and white) of the *Deposition of Christ* by Rosso Fiorentino and the *Deposition* by Pontormo. He set the stage for the *Deposition* of Rosso Fiorentino by shooting it at first as a total vision, and successively breaking the picture down into a sequence with an increasingly frenetic rhythm and pace, compressing the depth of field (just as Rosso Fiorentino had done) and emphasising the painterly quality of the figures.

The *Deposition* by Rosso Fiorentino appears to us as a vision worthy of the finest tradition of hallucinogenic drugs, with brilliant and chilly colours, overstated, the figures all shrapnel of a single diamond captured by a light that is not so much revelation as action, revolution; everything that selects movement over stasis is revolution, everything that selects a gaze "elsewhere" is innovation. And Rosso Fiorentino is an innovator, an "irregular", one who chooses not the canon, but instead the daring vision, the reckless dimension. Everything in this artist's oeuvre tells us that he relies not on the real but rather sets out, from the very beginning, to abstract from reality, and he founds upon abstraction a form of realistic vision, a realism marked by a terrified vision, capable of capturing only the dramatic events, the disquieting implications, the exaggerated aspects.

Andante
The sun is dying on my young boy and on Saint Peter's Square,
The Red Bus bus goes by at the end of Via delle Guje,
Red as the morning stars, in the trousers of the dark young man the sun is red,
The dark young man is sitting beneath a column, and he lights a cigarette,
red as the sun,
With death and with life under the sky of the Prati.
(Pier Paolo Pasolini)

The life that Pasolini instils in the figures of Rosso Fiorentino is real life, a life that speaks to us of an unknown reality, of a reality that has never been narrated, of a possible reality, but possible only against the back-cloth of a dimension of total time, of a life in expansion, and it is here that the meeting takes place between Rosso Fiorentino and Pasolini, between the streets of rebellion, in the alleyways of transgression, in the plazas of those who do not accept the state of things, in the outlying areas of an imagination that does not resign itself to organised life.

In the *Deposition* by Rosso Fiorentino, the cross and the ladders, asymmetrical with respect to one another, establish an anguished instability, emerging against the back-cloth of a sky clean and sheer as a slab of steel; the scene testifies to the disappearance of nature, the lack of substantiality of any element outside of the chosen event, a dimension without information, without traces, entirely focused on that which sweeps through and moves the bodies: no other element need disturb the disorder of agitated life.

Rosso Fiorentino is a rebel of representation, and the delirious imagination that renders the bodies strident and sharp leaves the entire scene without air; it is a remarkable effect of abstraction that he presents us with, a dimension left speechless and shaken by the very specificity that engendered it.

Rosso Fiorentino chooses neither an aseptic nor a repetitive representation, rather he fills his painting in every one of its parts, and in all of its parts he modifies the customary and the "recognised": from the dimensions of the artwork, "excessively" vertical, to its very structure. The existence of the figures is completely devoid of naturalness: it is entrusted to the imagination; and the pictorial language that results is mental, visionary, excessive. It is the shipwreck of classicism: no pacification, no equilibrium. The reference is to the mind and to dreams, and in the encounter between a mind that is opposed to the world and a dream that recognises no place, if not in another atmosphere, one of the masterpieces of art is born.

And, the contradiction
a thousand times, a thousand times alluded to
of my irreducible Christ,
who winds up being defended by some demented Herodianus
gruesomely devoid of a sense of the ridiculous.
(Pier Paolo Pasolini)

Removing the veil, entering directly into the heart of the iconography, exploring, penetrating, investigating the image from "within", from within the artwork itself, by crossing the boundary and cutting into the space and time that separate the artist from the artwork, identifying with the support. A chameleon-like way of putting oneself into play, of becoming an artwork. "Mine was a criticism of all of the methods of the past and all of the taboos of the present, photography remained the best instrument for achieving this process of self-revelation... every human being in these images was my own self. I wanted to photograph those parts of myself that were unknown, the fear of my own being, in all of the potential of its anonymous perdition, hoping to face it and thus become free of it... the images described the battle field and the assassination of my own spirit", declares Joel-Peter Witkin, the artist who proposes a classical encounter between life and death, a form of celebration of the difference and the marvellous in the contemporary. Witkin photographs life, love, death, terror, fear, anguish, estrangement, the different, forgiveness, images that many feel should never be photographed, but which, when painted, belong to the most classic of Western iconography; the need to "capture" and "capture for oneself" wonder, and not only the subjects of exposure. Theatralisation and exasperation of the classical and the mythological, juxtaposition of artworks, periods, fears, taboos, beauty and expectation... the works of Witkin create a sophisticated equilibrium of wonder, beauty and incredulity. Once again art makes fun of language, and nature becomes physically a *natura morta*, a "dead nature", as the Italian describes a still life. Images of freaks and hermaphrodites, dwarfs and dismembered bodies that treat the relationship between love and death, pain and sex, the passage from light to dark. The attraction to the different is a distinguishing feature of the artworks of Witkin, the marvellous, the bizarre, the whimsical, an attraction that art has been producing and reproducing for centuries, an out-of-control temporal mechanism in which the dates no longer count, but the essential is focused upon a series of "natures", whether dead or alive, in which we see humanities altered, modified, alien, which are often born in nature and not in the altered and scandalous imagination of art. The paths of the sacred, of mythology, of revelation... Joel-Peter Witkin seems to want to take into account a culture that bases its very existence on an alchemy of powerful and clashing elements, and chooses simultaneously and in the same image that which terrifies, that which astounds, that which attracts us, that which overthrows us, that which liberates us,

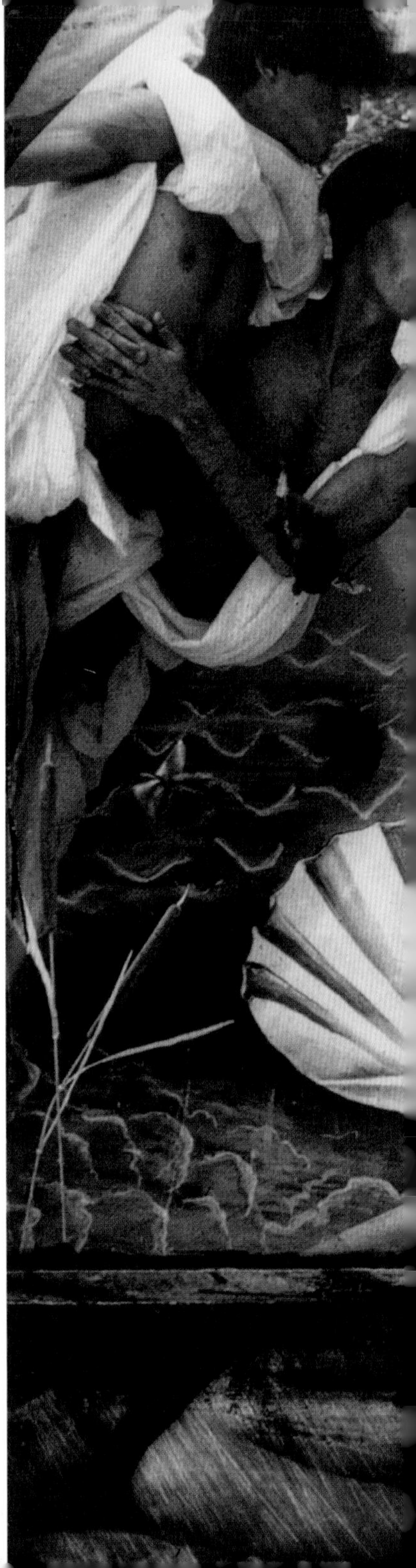

Joel-Peter Witkin,
Gods of the Earth and the Sky,
Los Angeles, 1988

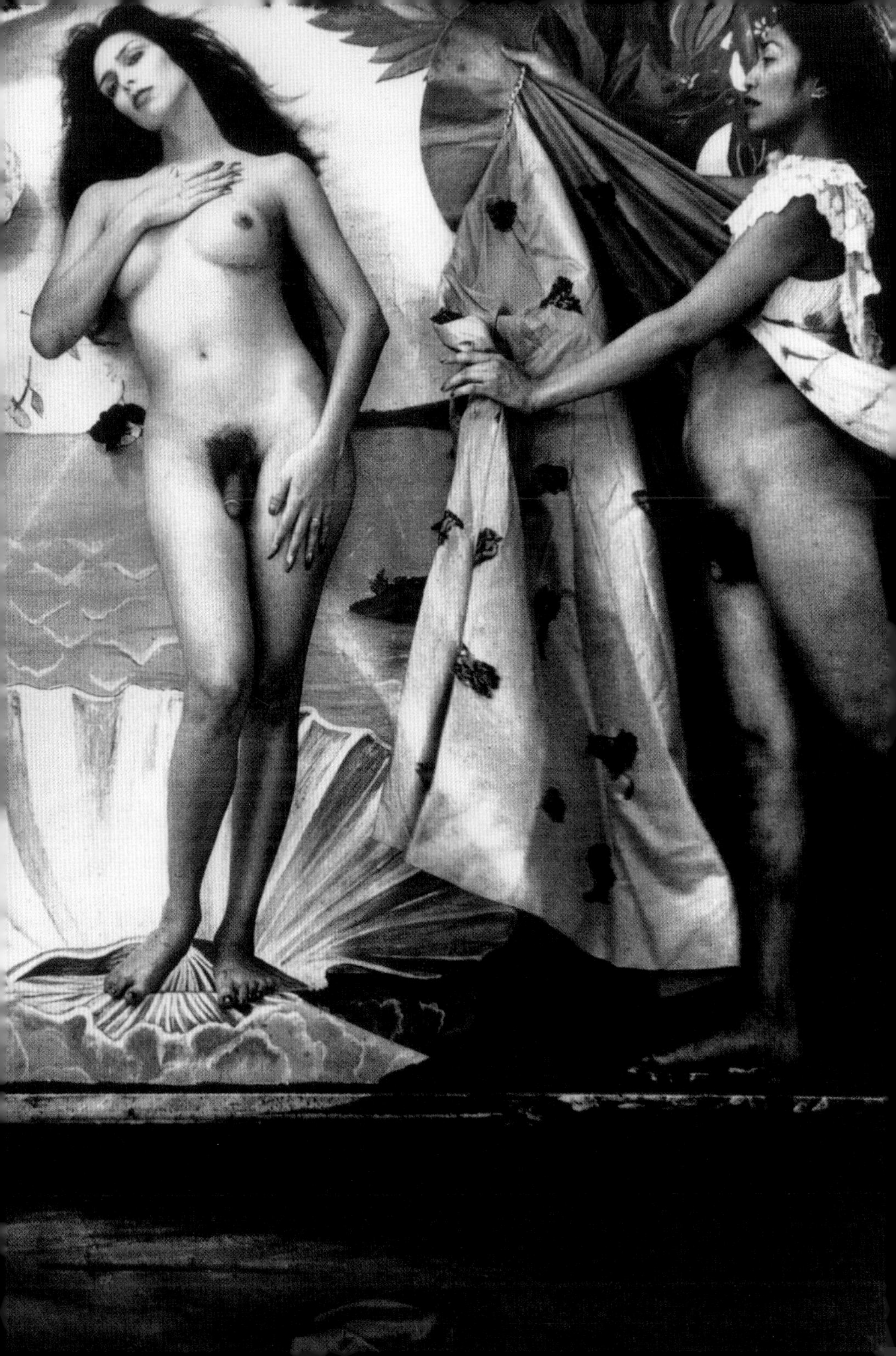

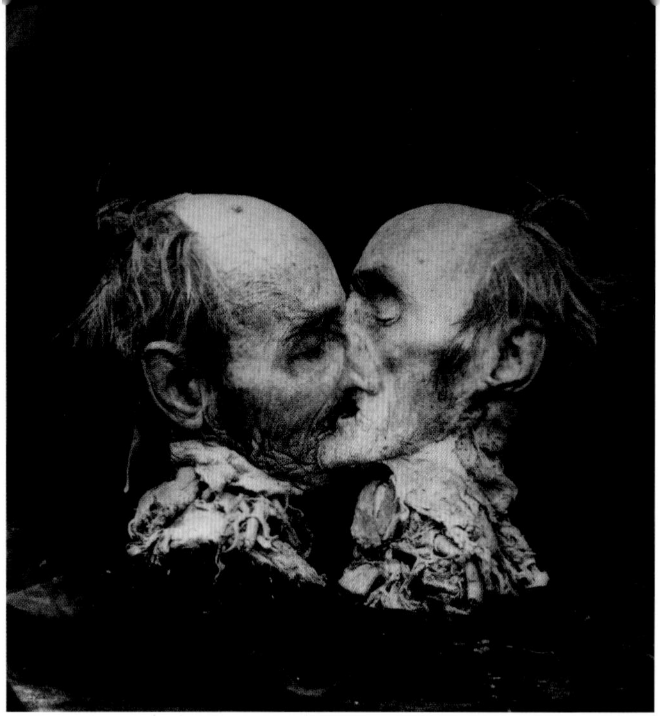

Joel-Peter Witkin,
The Kiss,
New Mexico,
1982

that which imprisons us, that which distinguishes us, and that from which we flee: diversity. Witkin places us face-to-face with the monster, with the chameleon-like, kaleidoscopic possibilities of an unexpected identity that escapes the rules of uniformity. And the spectators raise up barriers of psychological defence and rejection, as if the monstrous identity of the individual were to appear in the images shown, and the process of reading could be transformed into a process of identification, contagion and familiarity.

The visual trap acts as a supplementary operation: the images of Witkin allow no truce, they do no admit identity, equivalence, refractions of the identical, they simply act as the destruction of an identity, confounding and hybridising human, animal and vegetable species, merging together life and death, the animate and the inanimate, the visible and the invisible, destroying the grid-work of normality and unhinging the laws that gravitate upon the norms and rules of the commonly tolerable. And we speak of perversion, sadism, violence, blasphemous desecration, deviation, mental insanity... the discovery of the monster, its presence, the certainty of its existence, the evidence that "monsters really do exist": and the mechanisms of defence and exorcism are triggered, and we find irrational reasons that are adduced as would-be explanations. What seems to emerge is a religious component with an apocalyptic and intimidating tone, which seems intended to hint that at the roots of any monster is guilt, and so the monster becomes a symbol of a primordial danger, hovering between aggression and vendetta, a sort of infection, a kind of virus that diseases the social and political body by introducing itself from without and propagating with its very presence its own pathogenetic elements: a sort of intimidatory explanation based on a widespread sense of guilt.

And once again we clearly see the presence of a censorious and reactionary culture, which instrumentalises diversity and transforms it into monstrosity, while pointing out the monster as a general admonishment; and once again chooses to show its force of persuasion guided by the fear and amplification of taboos; and once again we are shown that fear and the monstrous are instruments of power, and power does not gladly tolerate diversity, and singles out monsters and the different as the fruit reaped due to the transgression of the rules that power established. "I believe that much of the world is ugly. In its place I want to create a space, take the best of what I have seen, and put it in that space." With these words Joel-Peter Witkin seems to want to show difference as the living imagination that crosses through all of the iconography of all eras of history: dwarfs, fat people, cripples, amputees, people missing limbs from birth; it is as if normality were meaningless to him, aesthetically unattractive, and as if he recognised in anomaly meaning and a richness of meaning. Without trying to give the different a "normal life", he amplifies their very difference in an exasperated, dramatic iconography, producing a secret and forbidden image of them: he recognises and shows and displays diversity, proposing it in the most classical of iconographies. The abolition of diversity is to Joel-Peter Witkin clear evidence of an imbalance, of an absence of determination to change that prohibition; hunted and denounced, the diverse through Witkin are "shown", they emerge from the apocalyptic folklore and from the judgement of the universal reason, and emerge from a human condition that has chosen to bury information, knowledge, emotions, beauty, imagination, outside of oneself and one's own body, in the apotheosis and in the necessity of economic relations that base their own power on the fragility that upholds the necessity of a "handsome presence", on the structuring of a society that has chosen the functionary, the manager, the entrepreneur, the computer programmer and the computer itself as icons. "Our real necropolises are no longer the cemeteries, the hospitals, the wars, the hecatombs, and death is not at all where people expect it to be — it is no longer biological, psychological, metaphysical, it is not even homicidal anymore — its necropolises are in the basements or the halls of the huge electronic data-processors, blank spaces, purged of all human sound — glass caskets in which all of the sterilised memory of the world is congealed.... Against our dream of losing everything, forgetting everything, we elevate a great inverse wall of relations, connections and information, a dense and inextricable artificial memory, and we are buried alive in this fossil hope of being rediscovered one day." (Jean Baudrillard) The beings of Joel-Peter Witkin do not belong to any functional category, their very presence is scandalous, obscene, abject, they live constantly under the gaze of those who want them under control, their very existence creates an interruption in a collective that has structured its own existence on the power of taboos, on the mechanism of censorship and removal from which anguish takes form. Corpses, fœtuses, human and animal skeletons, freaks, deformities, mutilations, love and necrophilia. Witkin works directly upon the materials of the Romantic "sublime", as he himself states: "The contemplation of destruction is not destructive, but rather takes part in the construction of the sacred and the modern", operating in a dimension of the myth and the representation that seems to come directly from the imagination of such great visionaries as Arcimboldo, Goya, Bosch, Moreau, Canova, Velázquez and Picasso. He cre-

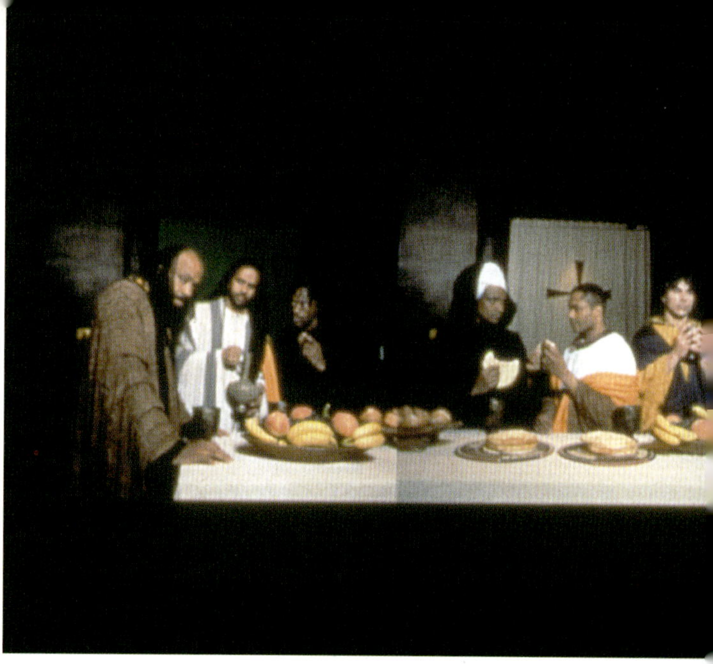

Renée Cox,
Yo Mama's Last Supper,
1996

ates an equilibrium of suggestions that become scandalous in the choice to use the photographic medium, an artifact of reality, testimonial and evidence of rejection, taboo and marginalisation. "My images are not necessarily beautiful because I was photographing that which commonly represents beauty. I was very excited to know that I could find beauty even in the most vile and ugly things... a way of rescuing the phantoms of the present from rejection, of justifying them through the traditions and the accounts of ancient communities." Joel-Peter Witkin seems to be seeking a redemption from an idea of life and death that both appear to be signified only by a passion for the artificial.

To tell the truth, there remains nothing upon which to base oneself. All we have left is theoretical violence. Speculation to death, whose only method is the radicalisation of all hypotheses.
(Jean Baudrillard)

All that awaits us is the extermination of awareness that vision has amongst its component parts; increasingly, the image is inscribed everywhere and becomes functional to an operative logic, a radical finality, a series of images that follow and torment us: in the houses, in the streets, in the transit points, in the monitors... The end of ambiguity, metaphor, cerebral death by blinding, by excessive vision. Everything becomes reversible and everything belongs at the same time to determination and to indetermination.

Everything is acceptable and everything seems to belong to the state of things, everything has a Universal Reason, everything is justified: discrimination, violence, racism. Racism is a modern phenomenon: cultures or races were ignored or annihilated in the past, but never in the name of a Universal Reason. Differences in the past were dealt with and fought over, at times to the death; but it is only with the new and modern concept of "undifferentiated", that the idea of

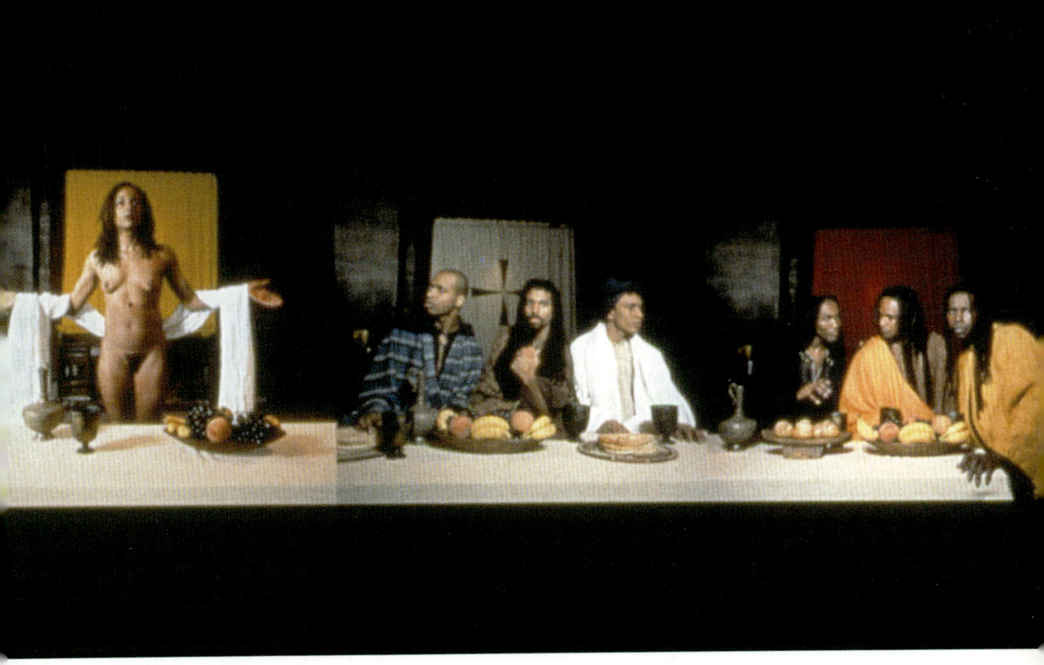

discrimination arises. "...Only afterward did we become racists, because we have made great progress. And not only in relation to Indians and cannibals — our culture, by deepening its rationality, has successively extradited into the inhuman all of inanimate nature, the animals, the lesser races. Then this cancer of the Human attacked the very society that it was attempting to circumscribe in its absolute superiority." (Jean Baudrillard)

Woman, black and naked is the figure of Christ at the Last Supper by Renée Cox, and equally black is the Christ on the Cross, depicted from various distances and "edited together" with all the various perspectival alterations. And the reversal of roles is evident and poetic, as is the opening of the discussion of identities, the ferocious critique of the narrative. Equally classical are the themes and the iconography, scandalous is the extraneous body at the centre of the artwork, a shift that activates a capacity of modification of things and perceptions, of sensibilities, a technique for the modification of reality implemented through a calculus of power that Renée Cox succeeds in opening once again to discussion and shifting. "The more human God appears to be, the greater we try to make the distance that separates him from man, that is, the more religious speculation and theology deny the identity of the divine being with the human being, the more the human being is degraded." (Ludwig Feuerbach) Renée Cox began her career as a fashion photographer, thus laying the foundations for her present activity. In much of her output, especially in projects such as the series *Yo Mama* or the series on pregnancy, the very body of the artist has become an integral part of the artwork. Renée Cox chooses to emphasise the shared sense that some women have of the body, especially in the Afro-American community, modest and conservative. In this series, the nude pregnant body was photographed and shown under a glorious light and, at the same time, as a body that is going through a phase that historically was always concealed, put in a corner and hidden from view, with the sole exception of the mystical conception, the sacred motherhood.

At the dawn of Western modernity all of the crazy people were "extradited", followed by the children, in the progressive detention in their idealised standing of infancy, into the "ghetto of the childish universe, into the abject state of innocence", followed by the old people, pushed to the outskirts of normality. *Yo Mama* by Renée Cox sets forth a powerful and dogmatic image of maternity, an image against the stereotypes of passive mothers, hopeless victims. Artworks that are powerful and dense with humour. *Yo Mama* is a series of self-portraits that loom over the spectator: the artist portrays herself naked, wearing nothing but a pair of black high-heeled shoes, while she carries her two-year-old son in her arms. An image that is regal and at the same time erotic, which underscores the change in the representations of mothers throughout history, a new approach to a mentality that no longer wants to submit to the concept of "category", the segregation in common places that marked the static nature of the culture — species, genders, sub-genders, cataloguing: the crazy, the black, the children, the elderly, the poor, the sick, and so on and so forth until we come to the transexuals, women, the gay, mothers, all categories based on an increasingly racist definition of the "normal man". With the series *Renaissance*, Cox's discourse becomes more explicit, a sort of genealogy of discrimination. The series developed out of her experience as a student in Florence, where the artist visited the major museums and looked closely at the most famous masterpieces of the Renaissance; it leapt to her eyes that in the context of the great iconography of Western culture, there are no black people, with a few exceptions, where the black person is a servant or a maid. Renée Cox thus began a series of artworks in which the original concept of the Renaissance is adapted to suit the tensions and the conquests of the 1990s: she chose to use blacks to depict David, the Virgin Mary and the Christ Child, Adam and Eve. The desire for grandeur so typical of the Renaissance reappears in the imposing size of her works: indeed, she chose a format that would provoke an even more powerful impact upon the spectators, the same format as the huge artworks that are so widely studied in the museums and churches of Florence. According to Renée Cox: "For the works that were part of the exhibition *Black Male* at the Whitney Museum, we should mention Catholicism, since it was a black crucifixion. I began to wonder what the influence of Catholicism had been on slavery, and how the Church of the fifteenth century had managed to earn a fortune and why the Church wondered whether or not Africans were human beings. And coming up to the nineteenth century, with the Jim Crow laws on hanging African-Americans on Sundays and on Catholic slave owners. These were the themes that emerged during the work for those photographs".

Reflective surfaces... hair food breasts carafes mouths... portraits and self-portraits of a history of the image that has selected the partiality of the triumphant. An interval, a chorus, the placement in the foreground of a captured gaze: spiritual disquiet, psychological introversion, and a special intellectual acuity that have all characterised the conviction that it is impossible to engage in art without violating the limits imposed by "manner", by the style of "that golden age" of art, so recent in time but already surrounded almost by an atmosphere of legend. What is striking in the works of Renée Cox is that tension, so distant and

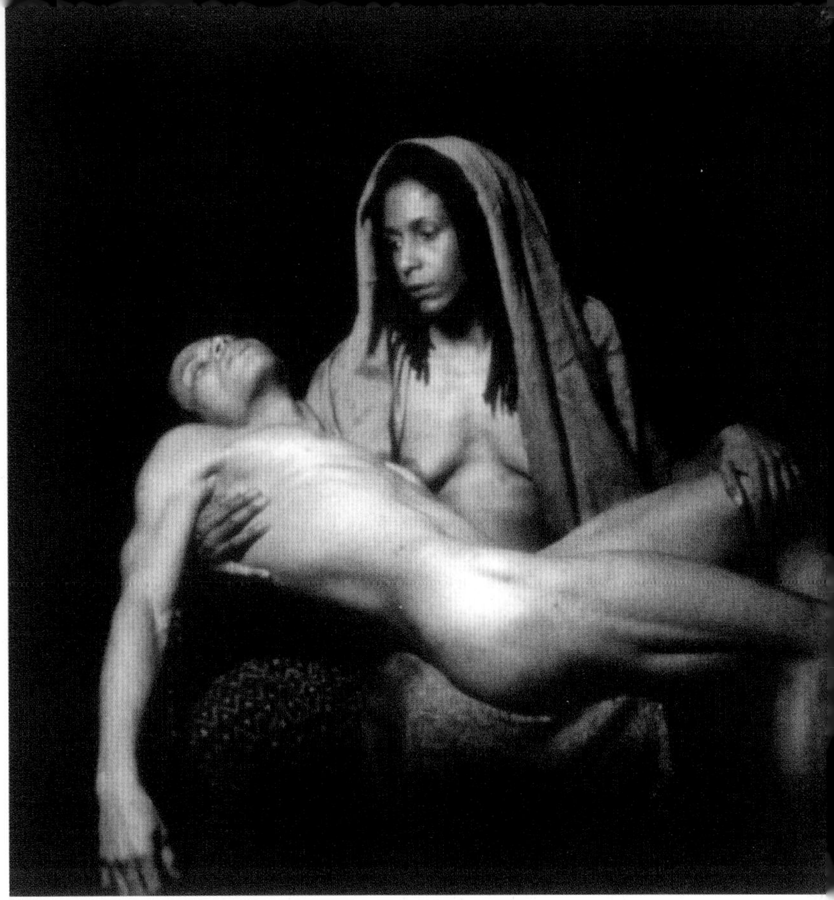

Renée Cox,
Yo Mama's Pietà, 1996

yet so present, that quiet and provocative sense of recovering myths, heroes, heroines and dreams, the rejection of proportion and balance, the placing in discussion of those canons that continue to live artificially in a sort of grammar of style. And it is an excessive, blinding, furious and lovely vision that Renée Cox sets forth, a magnificent tendency, capricious and extraordinary, that develops out of a sensibility that intertwines contorts displays and distracts the gaze; it tames it, hypnotises it, captures and seduces it. Once again the rule is broken and the vision is excessive, rational and scandalous.

A savage and almost fierce vision, a complacent exhibitionism, a romantic tendency toward the sensual, critical and sentimental, scandalously romantic. In the images of Cox we find a sense of mystical spiritualism and pantheistic naturalism, a cunning mixture of formalism and formal anarchy, concreteness and abstraction. With Renée Cox, the Virgin Mary, the most widely recognised icon on earth, has become a black woman who, choosing the action as her medium, changes the common significance of the equilibriums of submission: she launches a challenge in her determination to re-read both reality and history. And the spectators are thus obliged to review their cultural barriers, built on images and narratives that are negative with respect to other civilisations and other cultures.

In her more recent work, Renée Cox has shifted her references from the Renaissance to changes in the body, towards something new and more powerful about race, femininity and sexual stereotypes.

This is the figure of a super-heroine, influenced by the comics and constructed entirely through photography and digital manipulation. Raje is the "reincarnation" of Cox as a super-hero, a character championing the cause of African-Americans and all other minorities. Raje demands equality for all people who have been oppressed. Raje liberates Aunt Jemima and Uncle Ben from their chains and from a century of slavery, and transforms them into her allies and super-hero colleagues. She criticises Picasso for refusing to lend money and for refusing to give credit to the Cubists. She breaks the symbol of evil, that is, the swastika. She challenges the music industry for having denied so many young people their money.

Obviously, this work is a provocative indication and a clear accusation concerning the contribution that American blacks have offered and continue to provide in the United States. Moreover it communicates a sort of sense of power to girls and women, because this superhero can do what she wants and go where she wants without having to follow the laws of tradition and other limitations. Raje is opposed to any stereotype, and fights against all the forms of prejudice that exist in many countries around the world.

"Women's bodies have changed today, in physical terms as well, and I am an example of that change. Women's body image is undergoing a profound change, from the voluptuous body of the turn of the century to the strong and determined body of today. Today it is important to have a strong body, in part to demonstrate the increased power and the change in women's roles. Women are about to begin managing their bodies by themselves, without men having a prior say in the matter."

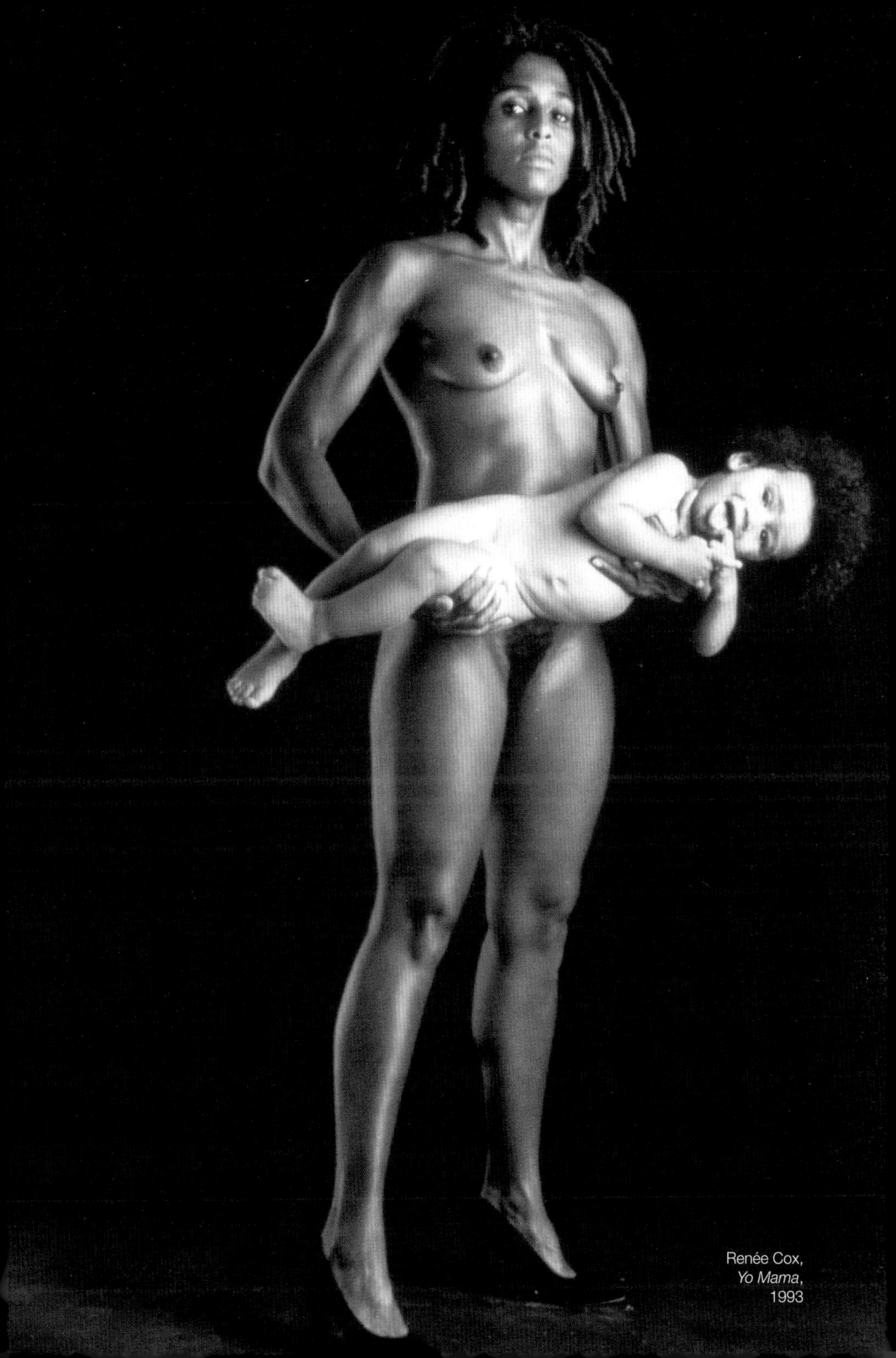

Renée Cox,
Yo Mama,
1993

Death, inasmuch as it is universal to the human condition, has only existed since there began to be a social discrimination among the dead. The institution of death, like that of survival and immortality, is a late conquest of the political rationalism of the priestly castes and the Church: it is upon the operation and management of this imaginary sphere of death that they found their power.
Jean Baudrillard

ABOUT DEATH

Art takes with it the fascination of suffering, the representation of the wounded, displayed, exalted body, and becomes an image of the Catholic world view that claims to include the possibility of salvation. And death appears on the horizon. Death enters art through the faces and the bodies of saints, heroes, warriors, princes and kings. The funereal games, macabre and obsessive, of the Middle Ages, the representation of the skeleton with the sickle, the Horsemen of the Apocalypse, Inferno and Paradise, and already in the sixteenth century we begin to see the first signs of that culture that wants life separate from death. And thus begins the long process of the "abolition" of death. "All of our culture is nothing other than an immense effort to dissociate life from death. ...Abolishing death is our ghost, which branches out in all directions: that of survival and eternity for religions, that of truth for science, that of productivity and accumulation for economics." (Jean Baudrillard) This separation is at the centre of Western culture: no other culture operates this "cut", this laceration, this tear, no other culture operates the two phases of existence as if they were autonomous.

And so death became epic, singular, exemplary death, it became the death of the "immortal" body, it became an event: a ritual that was repeated cyclically, the mythology of the end linked back to the myth of origin in the figure of Christ.

At the very beginning of the fifteenth century the groundwork was laid for an altered political, philosophical and cultural conception. The new Italian courts of the Medici, the Visconti, the Anjou, the Sforza, the Aragon, the Malatesta and the Este, decided with their policies of art patronage that art would have an enormous impact on social life. Throughout the early Renaissance there emerged, powerfully, a reconsideration of mythology, the central role of alchemy and the esoteric sciences, new mathematical and astronomical hypotheses that took their places alongside the religious spirit, with respect to which they were no longer considered antithetical. Dating back to 1480 is the *Dead Christ*, or *Foreshortened Christ*, by Andrea Mantegna, which contains several of the most astonishing cultural revolutions of the time. "Man is as a mortal. He calls himself mortal because he can die. To be able to die means: being capable of death inasmuch as death.... Alone man dies, and that is a constant, as long as he lives on this earth, as long as he dwells" (Martin Heidegger); the vision of

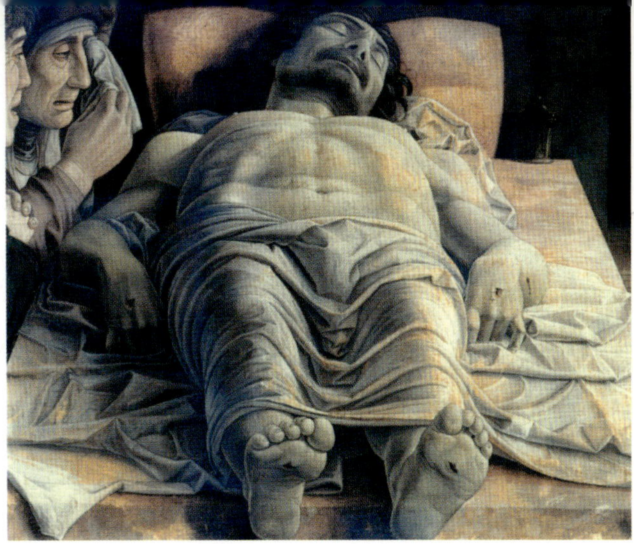

Andrea Mantegna, *Dead Christ in the Tomb and Three Mourners*, 1480

Mantegna opts for a perspectival delirium, an all-involving and dolorous closeness to the lifeless body, an almost inevitable contact with the idea of the end. The individual of the Renaissance is an "historical" individual, aware of being in the world, in a system of relationships, a being with a conscious baggage of emotion, a feeling that becomes a measure of the meaning of the time of life. The perspectival sense of existence is entirely revolutionised; the Renaissance chooses the vision from on high, chooses to look at the earth from the sky, from heaven, and to give a physical meaning to time: the physical condition of birth, life and death. The awareness of being on the earth, the sense of history, the walls, the stones, the possibility of desiring an iconography. Mantegna places us at the feet of the death of Christ, witnesses and accomplices of the most famous death sentence in Western history. A vision that appears constrained within the limits of the painting, which seems, like all desperation, unwilling to remain within the limits of self-control. The scene is excessively clean, as are tidy the wounds on the hands and the feet in which we see the holes left by the nails, clean is the cloth that covers the lower portion of the body, clean is the body and clean is the hair of Christ. Mantegna seems to be trying to suggest the scientific vision of an operating table, an anatomical awareness. The painting cannot contain the bodies of the women who weep at the side of the bare and essential representation. The overall view is heartbreaking, compressed and essential in the face of death, in the face of the pain of loss.

The entire strategy of the contemporary system tends to ward off the idea of death in a sort of interdiction, it cannot be named, death belongs now to the idea of disappearance, absence, distance. The civilisation of the image will not tolerate blood, disease, old age, and just as it conceals the sick and the old, in the same way it undertakes a systematic disappearance of death, which is named and viewed only in images linked to homicide, or in general the catastrophe from which it results. The only acceptable death is "accidental" death. Natural death no longer exists.

Death is no longer understood as a real moment of a subject, a body, but rather as the spectre of a dimension in which the social is lost, negated, given

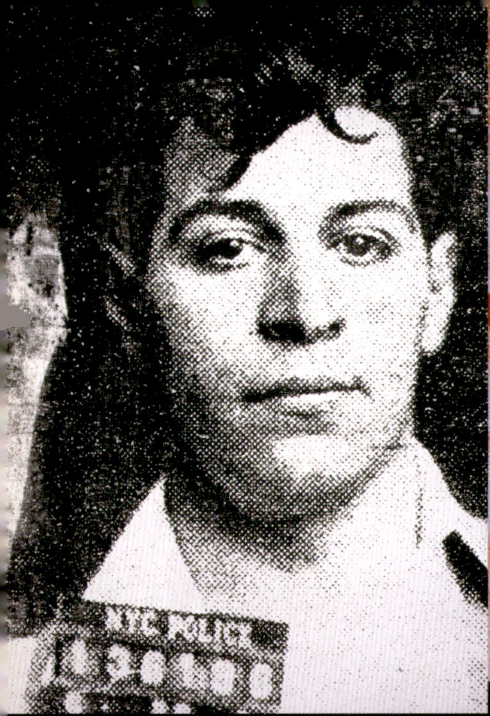

Andy Warhol, *Most Wanted Men n. 12 (Frank B.)*, 1964.
Photo by The Andy Warhol Foundation / Art Resource / Scala

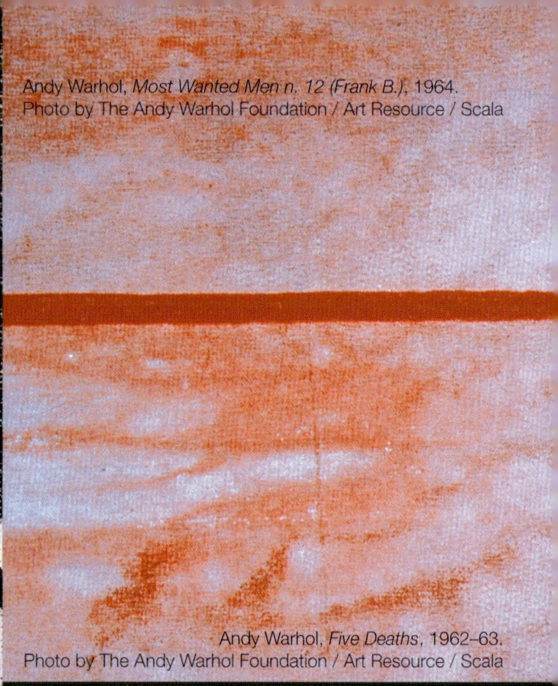

Andy Warhol, *Five Deaths*, 1962–63.
Photo by The Andy Warhol Foundation / Art Resource / Scala

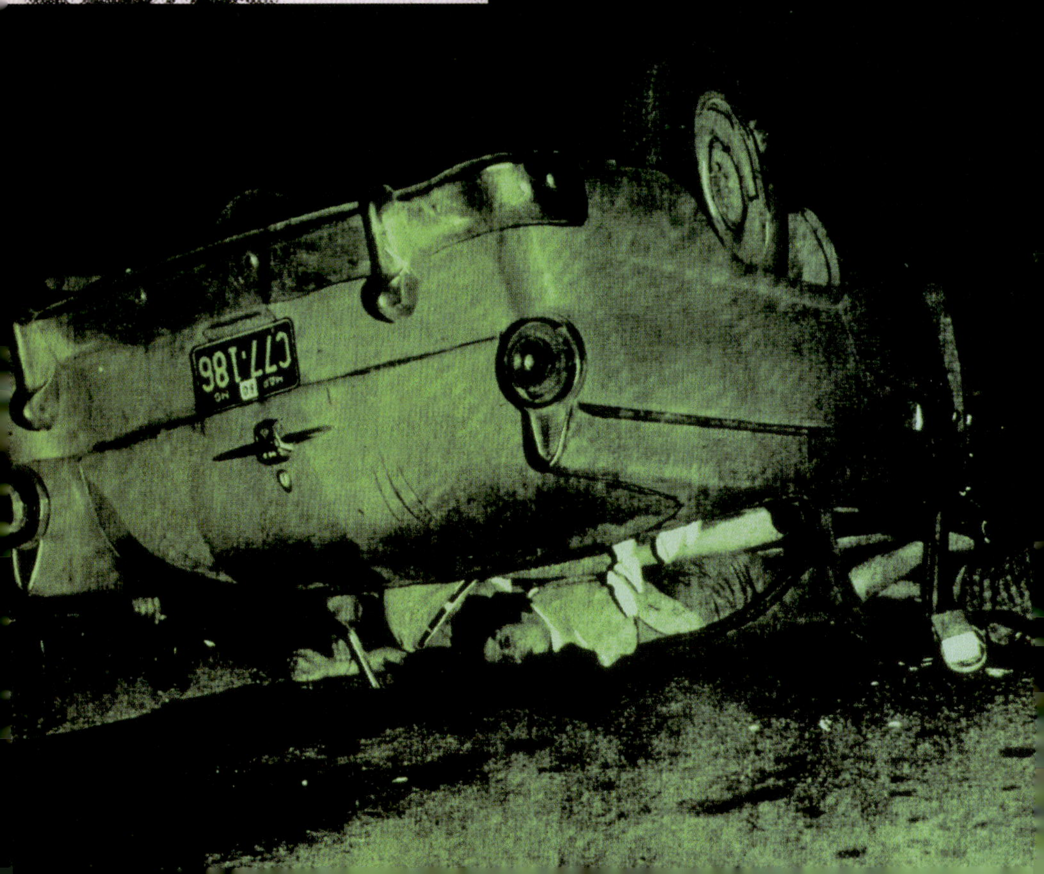

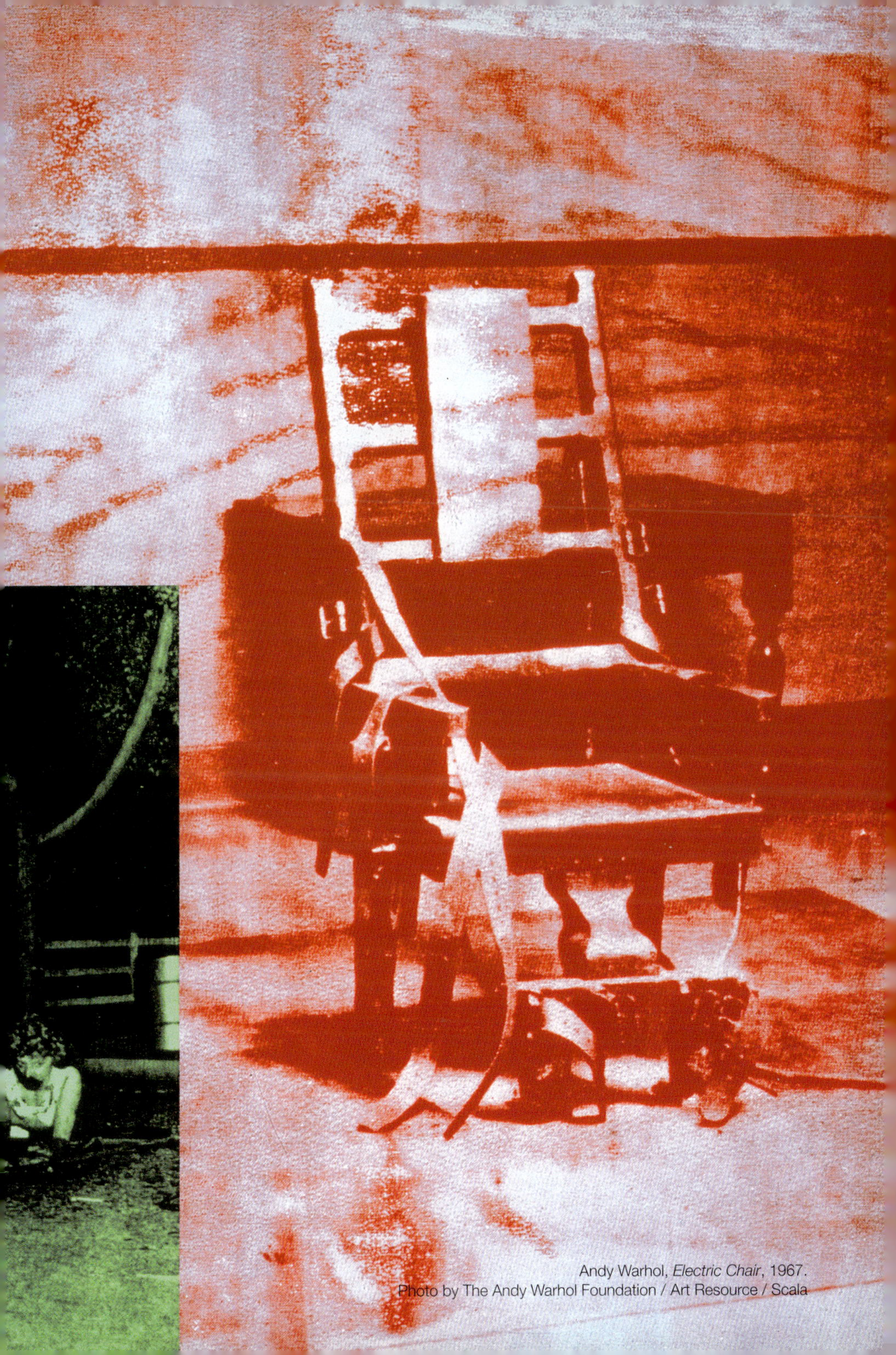

Andy Warhol, *Electric Chair*, 1967.
Photo by The Andy Warhol Foundation / Art Resource / Scala

over to flight. "These days men die and that's it", wrote Adorno, in his *Minima Moralia*. In hospitals or in hospices it is only possible to choose between a "clandestine" death or a "spectacularised death", assisted for pay, and just as in some primitive cultures, death is accompanied by collective wakes and public lamentations: nowadays there are institutions for profit that offer assistance on one's death bed. No other form of death is possible.

"The first image of death that I did, I think, was the photograph of the big plane crash, the front page of a newspaper: 129 Dead. I was also painting the *Marilyn* series. I realised that anything I was doing had to do with death.... Every time I turned the radio on, it would say things like: 'four million people are about to die'. That was the starting point. But then when you see a terrible photograph over and over again, it stops making much an impression at all.... I decided that my exhibition in Paris would be called *Death in America*. There would be reproductions of the electric chair and the dogs in Birmingham and car wrecks and other scenes of suicide.... I started the *Elizabeth Taylor* series many years ago, when she was very sick and everybody was saying that she was going to die soon", declared Andy Warhol, whose painting is increasingly associated with the idea of "superficiality".

With Andy Warhol, alongside the more media-driven behaviours of a Puritan consumer-oriented society, an underground became official, "his" underground, peopled with transvestites, homosexuals, drugs, and with him the art world emerged from its ghetto and became "fashionable".

The works of Warhol seem to be images extrapolated from an obsessive imagination that has chosen to create art through private nightmares and public nightmares from the collective American imagination: the assassination of John F. Kennedy, the suicide of Marilyn Monroe, the obsession with merchandise, the abnormal quantity of useless news, the endless series of evening news shows, the centrality of image... A genuine instigation to the psychotic imagination against a back-cloth of increasingly chilling images, increasingly shocking. Andy Warhol confronts us with a flat representation of death, with a screen that neutralises it and gobbles it up like all the other images of the society of the spectacle. Familiar images, and therefore innocuous images, indeed reassuring images, and thus themselves death; and it is with this awareness that Warhol creates his world. For him the human body seems to re-emerge everywhere in a mask of death, in the intrusiveness of duplication, globalisation, artifice, the representation of the world through the adaptation of the code of advertising. Warhol selects subjects that are already immersed in the dimension of the image: the advertising image, the mass media image, the image of social mythology, of the contemporary legend, the metropolitan consumption, a dimension in which the images originate already "flattened", already bodiless, in a sort of bizarre game in which the real has already disappeared behind its depictions, already in origin. A reality that already exists as a representation, a reality that is experienced as a "live report", as a sequence from the evening news, or a piece of fiction. In the face of the crisis of representation, the same crisis to which Duchamp had responded with an iconoclastic aesthetic, Warhol responds with a technique of saturation, an overdose of image, a multiplication of that which already originates as image.

"My series of paintings devoted to death was split into two parts: in the first part, the subject was famous dead people, in the second part, people that no one had ever heard of. I thought that people sooner or later should think about them: the girl that jumped off the Empire State Building, the women that ate spoiled tuna, and people that died in car crashes. I didn't feel any special compassion for them, but people go their way and they react, in the final analysis, in a very different way when a dead person is a stranger. So I said to myself that it would be nice for these unknown people if, just for once, people, who usually are indifferent, were to think of them just once." For Roland Barthes, only the images that belong to one's own history become a "wound"; the others, those that form part of the history of a stranger, or even those of someone who never existed, are taken as symbols of evidence. The electric chair, twisted lengths of sheet metal that once formed an automobile, the photographs of wanted men, images taken from the photographs of the newspapers that "illustrate" their articles about crime and scandal, from the rogues' galleries of the FBI, from the police photographs shot on the "scene of the accident". Warhol knows that everything is merely image, and even the quality of the photograph is not particularly important: screened, scratched images, missing sections, the only thing that is important is that the chosen image should already be an image, already have been used as an image, even an image of death. "From savage societies to modern societies, evolution is irreversible: bit by bit the dead cease to exist, they are pushed out of the symbolic circulation of the group. They are no longer full-fledged beings, partners worthy of exchange, they are pushed further and further away from the group of the living, from domestic intimacy to the cemetery, the first grouping still at the centre of the village or the city, then the first ghetto and foreshadowing of all future ghettos, pushed further and further away from the centre towards the outskirts, finally nowhere, as in the new cities or the contemporary metropolises, in which nothing is planned any longer for the dead, neither a physical nor a mental space. Even the mad, the criminals, the abnormal can find structures offering assistance in the new cities: that is, in the rationality of a modern society, only the function of death can no longer be located. What to do with the dead? Nowadays it is not normal to be dead. Being dead is an anomaly, a form of deviancy." (Jean Baudrillard)

An ordinary death

Today, with the exception of cemeteries, the last refuge of the dying imagination, the anthropomorphic representations of the afterlife, once so useful, are now out of date.
(Theodor Adorno)

An impressive body of work on the concept of identity is that done by Christian Boltanski, who reveals the fragility and the mechanisms of a political and institutional strategy that instead is meant to be a form of self-identification. A series of points of attachment, iconographic devices, alterations. "Certainly, everything must disappear. All of our efforts to struggle against death, against disappearance, are in vain. When someone dies, it is what I have called the little memory that truly disappears. Everything that they knew, their stories, their favourite books, their memories… Everything that forms us and constructs us disappears totally when we die. The great history is in books, but the little history is very fragile. At the beginning of my work, the first thing I tried to do was to preserve my life in so many cookie tins, to put everything into a sort of breadbox. Of course, I knew from the start that it was impossible and totally ridiculous. At the beginning

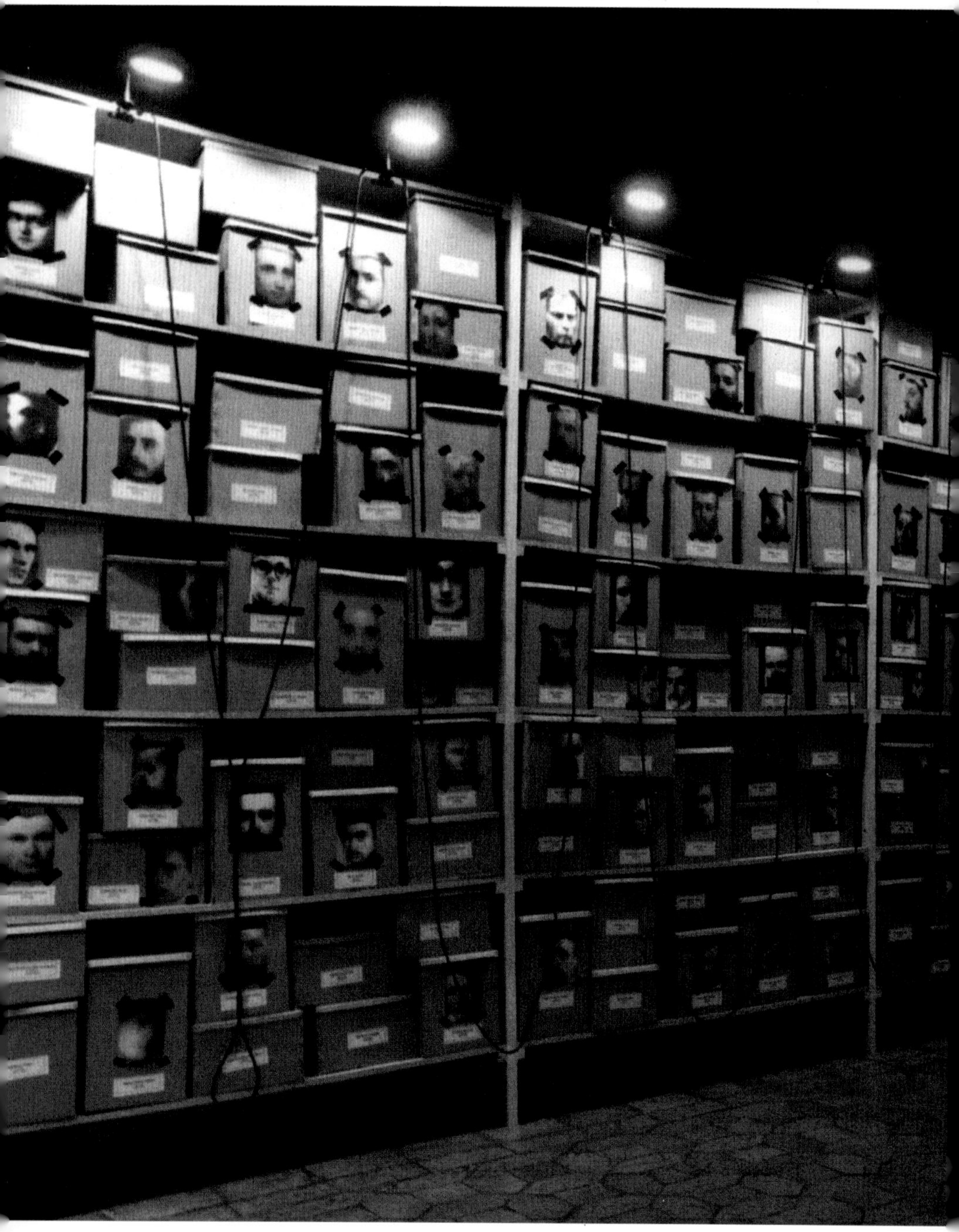

Christian Boltanski, *Les Pensionnaires de la Villa*, installation at Villa Medici, Rome, 1995. Photo by Claudio Abate

of my life, I spoke of my childhood, which is the common denominator for all of us. The more I work, the more I tend to disappear. What has truly disappeared is the boy that I was." (Christian Boltanski, 1997)

In his first artworks Boltanski tampers with and exchanges his identity, his origins, his relationships. He constructs a mutating identity in which his own childhood can be based upon stereotypes and clichés, or else he assumes a different childhood: he borrows a family picture album from a friend, and he appropriates it, reconstructing, through the photographs, an identity of his own, entirely built upon another person's life. For three years (from 1969 to 1971) all of Boltanski's artworks were a systematic construction of an impossible autobiography, created by making variations of facts, documents and things that had happened, to him but also to others. He utilised in fact his own information and that from the lives of others, he assembled pieces of different identities, he chose materials from his own past and from the past of others, selecting the shared information, the "memories of one and all", the memory of a past that "belongs to everyone". Accumulations of objects, photographs, clothing, furniture, memories, troves that Boltanski called *Réserves*; lists and images of dead people, such as *Les Suisses Morts*, 1991; walls of clothing, *Réserve*, 1990. Archives of memories, souvenirs, proofs of existences without history, without epic gestures, without heroic acts, objects that lay there like so many carcasses, like merchandise of no value, because their value was not intrinsic but rather was linked to the emotional makeup and the meanings of those who had once selected them and lovingly preserved them. Boltanski selected and put together, one by one, those elements that precisely because they could have belonged to anybody, succeed in suggesting a certain doubt about one's identity, a doubt that is insinuated in the identity of the spectator as well, likewise opened to discussion. A poetic investigation, cruel, about common sense, the constants and the variants of identity and its manipulations.

So, there are inventories of infancy, and identity becomes once again one of the places of manipulation in which Boltanski recomposes and breaks down biographies that intertwine true and false information, biographies that are quite simply possible. Photographs, testimonials, documents that trace the outlines, nebulous and rarefied, and yet still loaded with "evidence", of one's childhood, the possibility, intuitive and veiled, of being able to intervene on one's own autobiography, to make use of images that are so common, generic and stereotypical that they become ambiguous and false even when they truly do belong to our own childhood: the photograph on our parents' bed, the first day of nursery school, the birthdays, the school bench and desk. The ambiguity of images that are at once familiar and extraneous.

Boltanski is interested in everything that seems to contain life right up to and into the context of death. He chooses containers, which like the body have contained objects touched by life but which no longer contain it: what remains are letters, vitrines, the drawers of a dresser, books, various notes, clothing which appears to us like the phantom or ghost of the person that once wore it. And the objects, seen on their own, could have belonged to anyone, as if the "disappearance" of the subject had taken with it also the individual fragments that could narrate hundreds of different stories, stories of lives that have become stories of bodies, bodies of childhood, adolescence, maturity, diseased bodies, bodies dis-

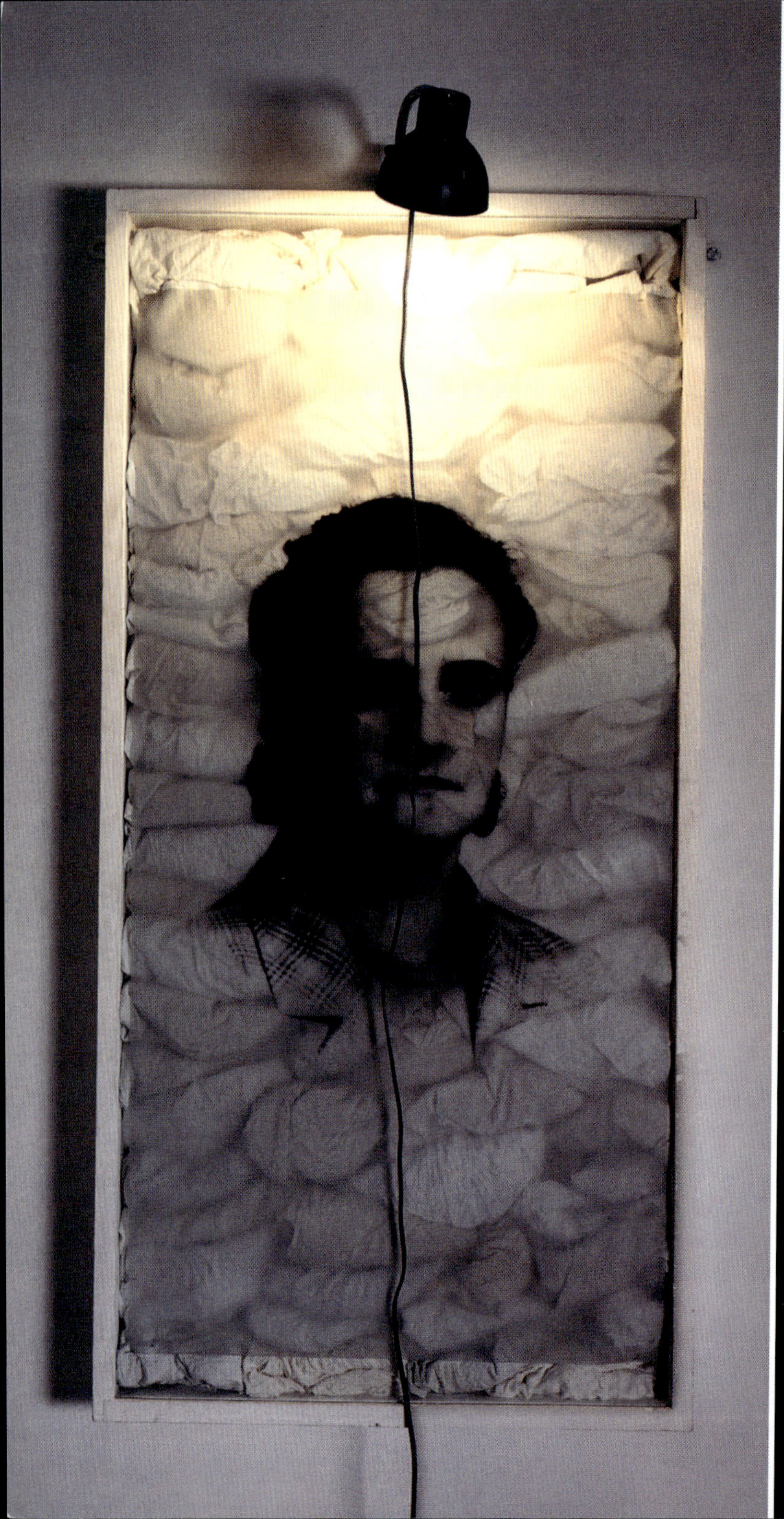

Christian Boltanski,
Padre Mariano,
1994

tanced, transformed, aged. “Oh Lord, give each of us our own Death. A dying that springs from a life in which each of us had love, meaning and pain.” (Rainer Maria Rilke, *The Book of Hours*) Dead bodies in place of which by now we find objects and fragments and clothing that survive them, objects that testify to their absence. Heartbreaking and dramatic are the places full of lifeless objects made by Boltanski, from the clothing of a child who perhaps has already become an adult or perhaps never grew up, to the clothing of adults: “Since 1988 I have worked extensively with clothing. Used clothing speaks of someone who was there but is no longer there. The odour and the folds have remained, but not the person.... That clothing, in some cases, possessed a certain connection with the idea of resurrection”. A collection of ordinary objects, anonymous, insignificant or charged with emotion: but all of them, paradoxically, instead of a testimonial to life seem to affirm the idea of a death. Especially emblematic is the case of photographs, almost always amateur pictures or identity pictures, such as the ones on passports: “Photographs are objects linked to a subject and its absence. For that reason, the photograph often evokes death, because we see an object that recalls an absent subject. I always make the comparison between a piece of used clothing, a dead body and a photograph of someone. In all three cases, we are dealing with an object that refers to a subject and its absence.... In my work, whether I make use of a piece of clothing or a photograph, one thing is not more important than the other. The most important thing is the effect of reality”.

Dead, 1993: a hallway, two shelves lit from above, a great many items of clothing, folded and placed on the light wooden counters: once again we see the remains of anonymous lives, the generic quality of dead people in no particular place or time, who have died for no special reason, piles of everyday clothing, a way of capturing the neutrality of grief, the absence of life and bodies, of which only meaningless and cumbersome details remain, such as the things that once belonged to the dead. And the imagination seems to come apart, as if all at once the fiction had fallen aside to give room to incredulity, silence, void. And so death, the death that belongs to ordinary individuals, seems to have vanished in the Western world, stripped of the metaphors and images that narrate it and represent it. A sort of new iconoclasm affects it, just as it is affected by a non-naming, a passing over in silence, and so dying becomes an obscene act, an event devoid of meaning. The clothing, the photographs, the notes, the names, the personal accessories, in their incredible quantity, in their orderly and systematic display, take on with Boltanski the aspect of improbable altars, systems of conservation, archives, containers of memories, whether they be cookie tins or love letters, clothing or photographs.

“The identity of the subject decays constantly, falling into the state of being forgotten by God. But there is nothing biological about this death”, wrote Jean Baudrillard. Images of death, images of the dead: death lives on in the images of art, with no desire for obscurity, no impulse toward darkness or oblivion.

An emotional fog, a residual mist of desperation, a fragment of memory. One’s own? Someone else’s? The suicide of identity. Boltanski undertakes a sort of reconstruction of an “individual mythology” through the collection, archiving and preservation of fragments of an individual existence and images of that existence. Photographs, clothing, hair, fingernails, as well as documents, relationships, childhood, family, loves and death. A series of documents and testimonials which the artist recovers and studies and analyses like a detective: a maniacal selection of the elements that have become the traces of an existence, the evidence of a life that was lived, the evidence of a memory of the individual that becomes the collective memory in the sphere of the relations and interactions of the chosen subject. Fragments, never complete nor exhaustive in a complex territory, passing through the identity of "another" at a distance. Another of whom, momentarily, Boltanski assumes the identity, which he sets forth in an invasive and awkward series of relics with an immaterial presence, the memory of a disappearance to which only the objects continue to bear witness. "The inventory of the objects that belonged to a woman from Bois-Colombes is the fifth project of this type that I have undertaken. Its execution complies with the same rules as the previous projects: to present, without any prior selection on my part, all of the objects that belonged to a person chosen at random in the city or the town where the exhibition takes place." (Christian Boltanski) An attitude typical of the forensic scientist and at the same time, typical of a chaplain in charge of votive offerings: monuments of objects that are transformed into an imposing form of existential architecture. Small stories narrated with that atmosphere of death that accompanies the iconography of the sacred. An obsessive and maniacal archive made up of accumulations, accumulations that seem to announce the melancholy and desperation that the emotion of the end brings with it. We find a silent and heartrending amplification, in Boltanski's work, of the fragility and brief duration in time of human beings, the traces of an anonymous existence with respect to the reasons and the invasiveness of the collective and of history. Evidence that for an anonymous subject the ending truly corresponds with death. Boltanski assembles and presents the remains of an absolutely individual everyday existence, of an individual that is not him and that, usually, is of no particular interest to anyone other than the protagonist of that existence: tables, chairs, photographs, letters, notebooks, writings, cookie tins, pieces of clothing… A sort of sacred assemblage, a set of votive offerings of an individual of no special interest, no renown, without any remarkable achievements, of no special heroic deeds.

Monuments, heartbreaking and melancholy, of ordinary deaths. An imposing and poetic collection of private histories, assembled by Christian Boltanski: "In my work I have always wanted for there to be lots of people: there are thousands of dead Swiss, thousands of persons, thousands of objects of inventory, extremely long lists… What I am attempting to show is at the same time the number and the unique nature of every individual. It is very important for me that they should all be apparently similar and yet all different, all unique, and therefore in this sense, saved. In 1994 I did *Menschilich*, an artwork that assembled 1600 images of human beings, a work on the loss of identity. In this mass of people, how could anyone recognise anyone?… All information about them has been lost, all that remains are these photographs that strangely mingle their presence and their absence. All of the difference has been eliminated, their little stories are lost… To name people seems very important to me, giving a name is tantamount to recognising the uniqueness of the person". All this emphasises the madness that selects the images that are to be preserved, the images of History, at the expense of the multitude of personal histories. "Everyone has had a death of their own. Those men who bore it within their armour, enclosed like a prisoner, those women who became exceedingly old and minute and then passed away on a huge bed, as if on a giant stage, before their entire family, the servants and the dogs, with discretion and control. Even the children, even the very smallest children, did not have just any infant death, they gathered themselves and they died in what they had already become and in which they would someday turn into. It was that which gave those women a melancholy beauty, when they were heavy with child and they stood there, their bodies huge, their small hands resting on those bodies, involuntarily concealing two fruits: a child and a death." (Rainer Maria Rilke, *Notebooks of Malte Laurids Brigge*)

The death of strangers. The morgue

The emergence of survival can therefore be analysed as the fundamental operation of the birth of power. Not only because this device will allow the requirement of sacrifice in this life and the redemption of a reward in the next life — all of the strategy of the priestly castes is summarised here — but even more for the establishment of a prohibition to die and at the same time the instance that supervises that prohibition: power.

(Jean Baudrillard)

"My artworks are clear. They speak of life, of death, of religion, of sex. They do it in a direct manner, but not brutally, because I always try to make them elegant", declares Andres Serrano, whose works reveal a body without mediation, without truce, without symbolism: it is still flesh, blood and skin, a crude and sensual anatomy in a series of artworks that photographically depict death, violence, sex, poverty, desperation and suicide. Dating from 1992 is the best-known series of artworks by Andres Serrano, *The Morgue*, a series of large-format Cibachromes (125.7 x 152.5 cm) depicting close-up details of corpses taken in a morgue, dead bodies, bodies with anonymous stories, unknown, repeated: suicides, homicides, disasters, overdoses, AIDS. Bodies reduced to a package, to surface, to flesh. "Has the living body become a gift-wrapping and has the dead body simply become a throw-away package?" (Paul Virilio) Serrano was authorised to take these pictures in an American morgue with permission to "work" on the corpses, but only following their autopsies. The images depict partial bodies: a hand, a silhouette, a torso, an eye, no reference to the surrounding environment: the morgue itself is never shown, the backgrounds are neutral, the details are well portrayed, the colours are pure, the corpses are real, so real that they appear to be false, pictorial, constructed, and so when death is finally discovered, it is yet more tremendous. During three months of work, Serrano photographed 95 percent of the corpses that passed through the morgue: abandoned bodies, segregated in the morgues, nomad bodies, exposed bodies. Serrano seems to approach us one by one to show us these photographs, photographs of corpses, anonymous, photographs of details of nameless beings whose only form of identification is the type of death, the cause of life's end: *Infectious Pneumonia*, *Rat Poison*, *Suicide II*, *Fatal Meningitis II*, *Gun Murder*, *Cardiac Arrest*, *Knifed to Death*... No social role, no name, no code, but a life and a fragment of personal history that emerges from the cause of death. Serrano chooses, in depicting these dead people, in depicting these deaths, a point of view that verges on the theatrical, certainly a part of a classical iconography: a black background, arrangement of the body or the fragment of the body as a composition, a uniform light and a symbolic approach to the

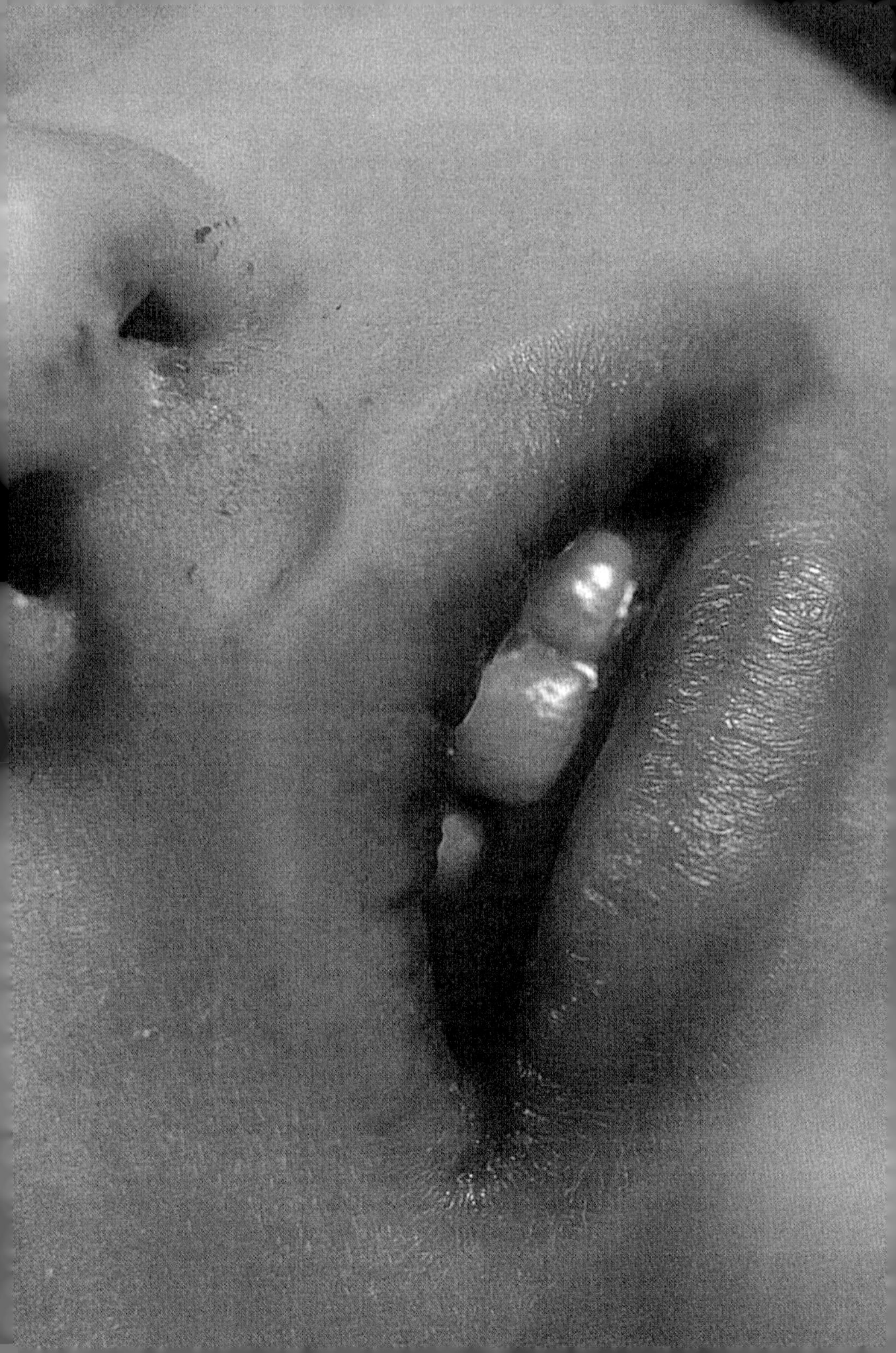

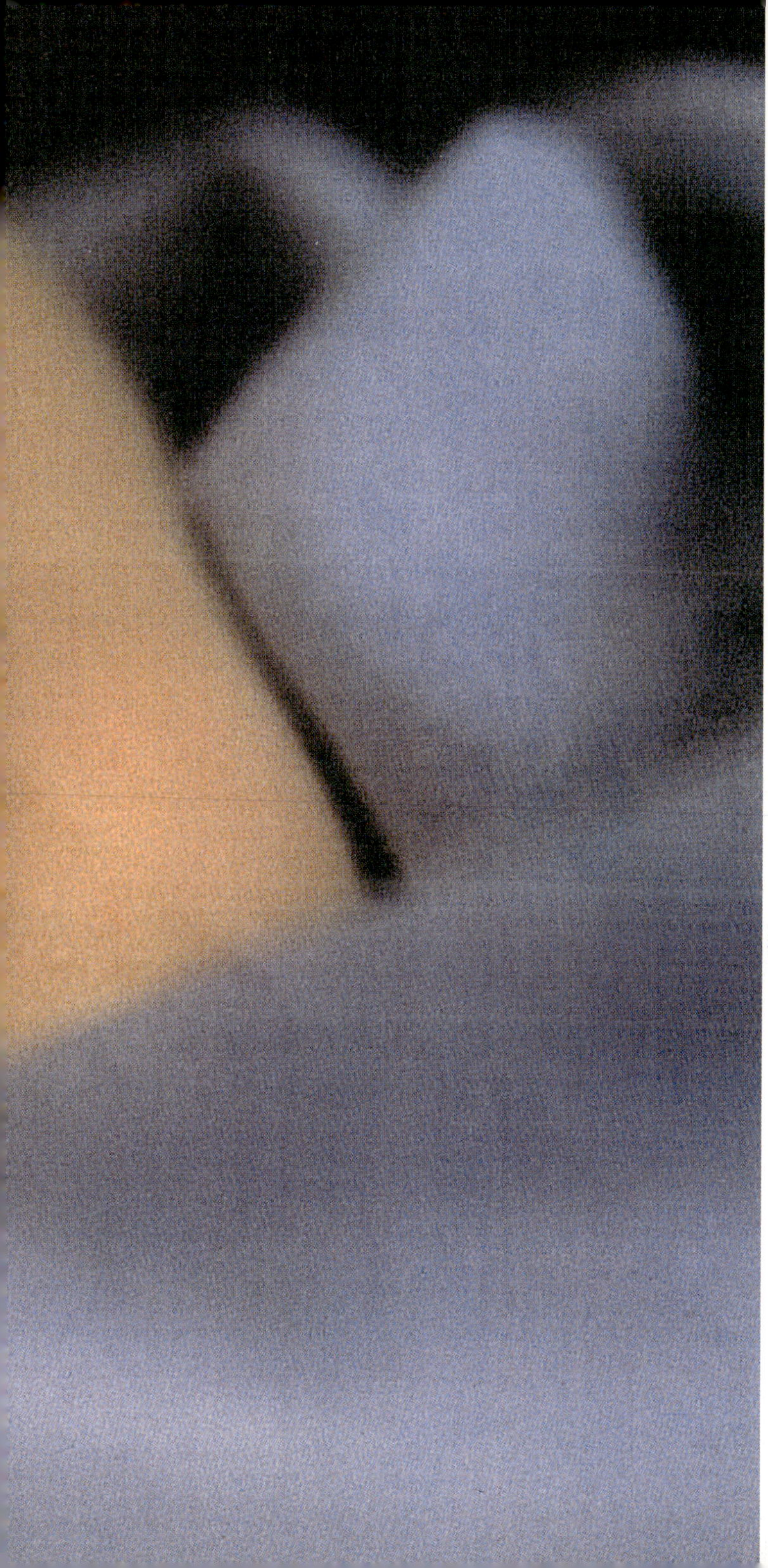

Andres Serrano,
The Morgue.
Pneumonia Due
to Drowning II,
1992

forbidden. What is shown is the corpse, a corpse that, stripped of the religious idea and outside of the scientific vision, becomes a sort of rough and irritating contact with the idea of death represented without filters and without escape, a death transformed into an immediate datum that plunges into the uselessness of necessity: death as a rebirth has been replaced by death as an annihilation. Faced with the artworks of the series *The Morgue* the spectator is obliged to confront the corpse, to come into close contact with the abject, and in the scandalous and excessive beauty of the composition the feeling that emerges, immediately after approach, is flight. There is no pious mourning in the images of *The Morgue*, no consolation in an account of the existence of the body on display; only an approach, a recognition, the recognition that never came for many of the bodies photographed. And so, deprived of the meaning of their existence, completely unaware of their lives and aware only of the manner of their death, these bodies are only so many corpses, the vision of which is intolerable to many. "Display does not mean, however, removing the intimacy from its portrayal and bringing it out, making it evident.... Displayed, then: but this is not the visibility of what in a first moments was concealed, closed. Here the exhibition is the being itself (it is called: being)", writes Jean-Luc Nancy. "I have the desire to monumentalise that which I photograph", dark atmospheres, black backgrounds, drapery, hands suspended in the void. The fixity and the immobility of death. Silence. The solitude of the empty body. Skin that changes colour over the course of a few days (white, greenish, dark blue, brown, purple). The serenity of the desperation of the moment of death impressed on the face. Hairs, tendons, muscles, humours, which can barely manage to hang on in the pores of the skin. And, again, skin: "goose bumps", skin upon which we begin to see the first signs of an inevitable decomposition; skin devastated by disease, skin ripped open in the autopsy and badly stitched back together. Foot, child's hand, bruised lips, legs, eyes closed forever: dead people put in a pose for the occasion. In this manner, by reducing death to so many neutral, impersonal details, Serrano strips the corpses of their identity, and what remains is only the flesh, the skin, the hair and the veins. "I asked myself: can I photograph someone that I did not know when they were alive?"

A body that expands, that becomes a terrible freedom of language, a body that becomes the body of taboos, becomes an ordinary form: disease, pain and death. Production times, which punctuate since the turn of the twentieth century, neither call for nor accept losses, they do not admit suspensions, they do not tolerate voids, and they transform the void and silence of death into a failure, into a rejection for the very idea of death which has become a brutal surprise; everything that has to do with death is rejected as if it were obscene, intolerable, unfair. Death is no longer symbolised, and it has become proof of the failure of science. Society therefore finds itself faced with a failure and no longer with a simple fatality, and we therefore see the structure of shame and concealment, a collective response in the inability to recognise death in the failure of the idea of life. "We no longer hope to survive our own death but only, through technology, to survive our own lives" (Jean Baudrillard); there develops an ideology of healing and simulation of age, and always healing, continually recovering, lengthening one's biological duration, comes to constitute a sort of eternalisation of survival. The photographs of *The Morgue* by Andres Serrano are set almost as a

Andres Serrano, *The Morgue. Rat Poison Suicide II*, 1992

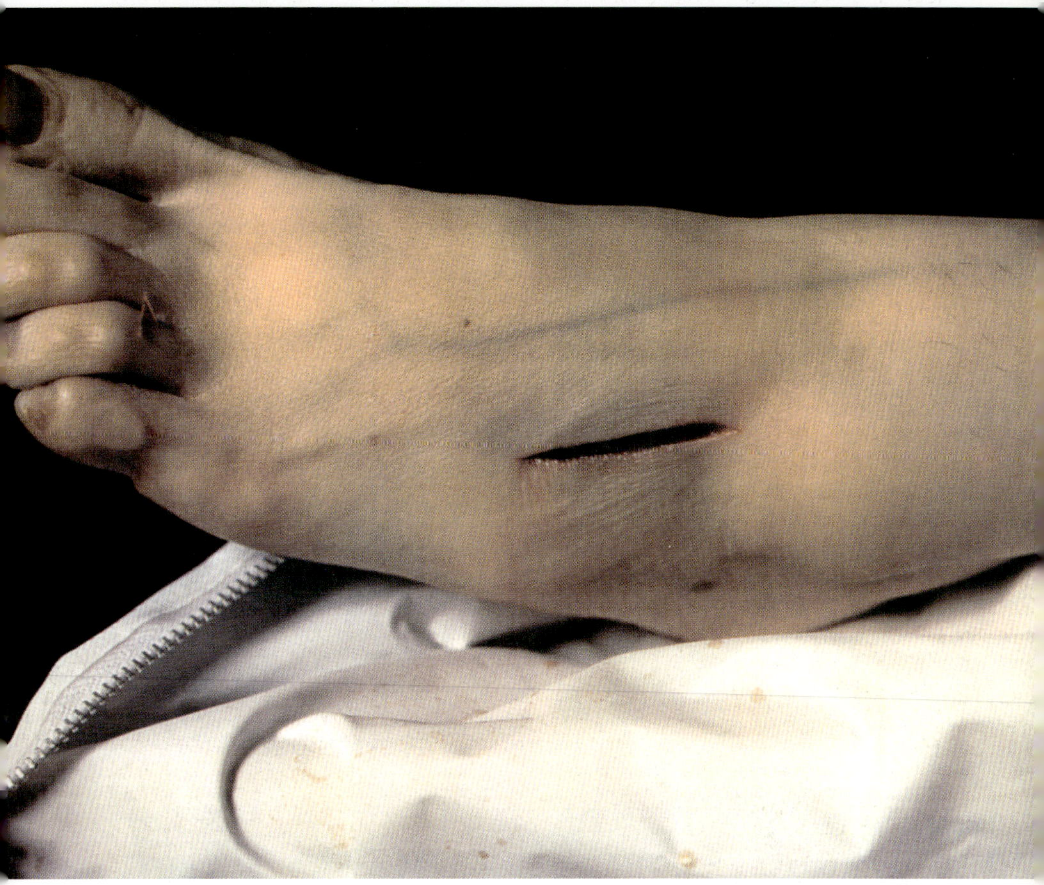

presence and an evidence that are uncomfortable, removed, abject, the image of cadavers is displayed, large-scale details of the thing we want to ignore, our inability to organise our own past, our own present, our own future, in exchange for a functionality that in the past promised an eternal life after death, and which now promises eternal duration within life.

It is a world
Of death —
Once people were born living and
Bit by bit
They died. Now people are born dead —
Some manage to come
Bit by bit
To life
(Bazlen)

Lucinda Devlin, *The Omega Suites. Gas Chamber*, Maryland State Penitentiary, Baltimore, Maryland, 1991

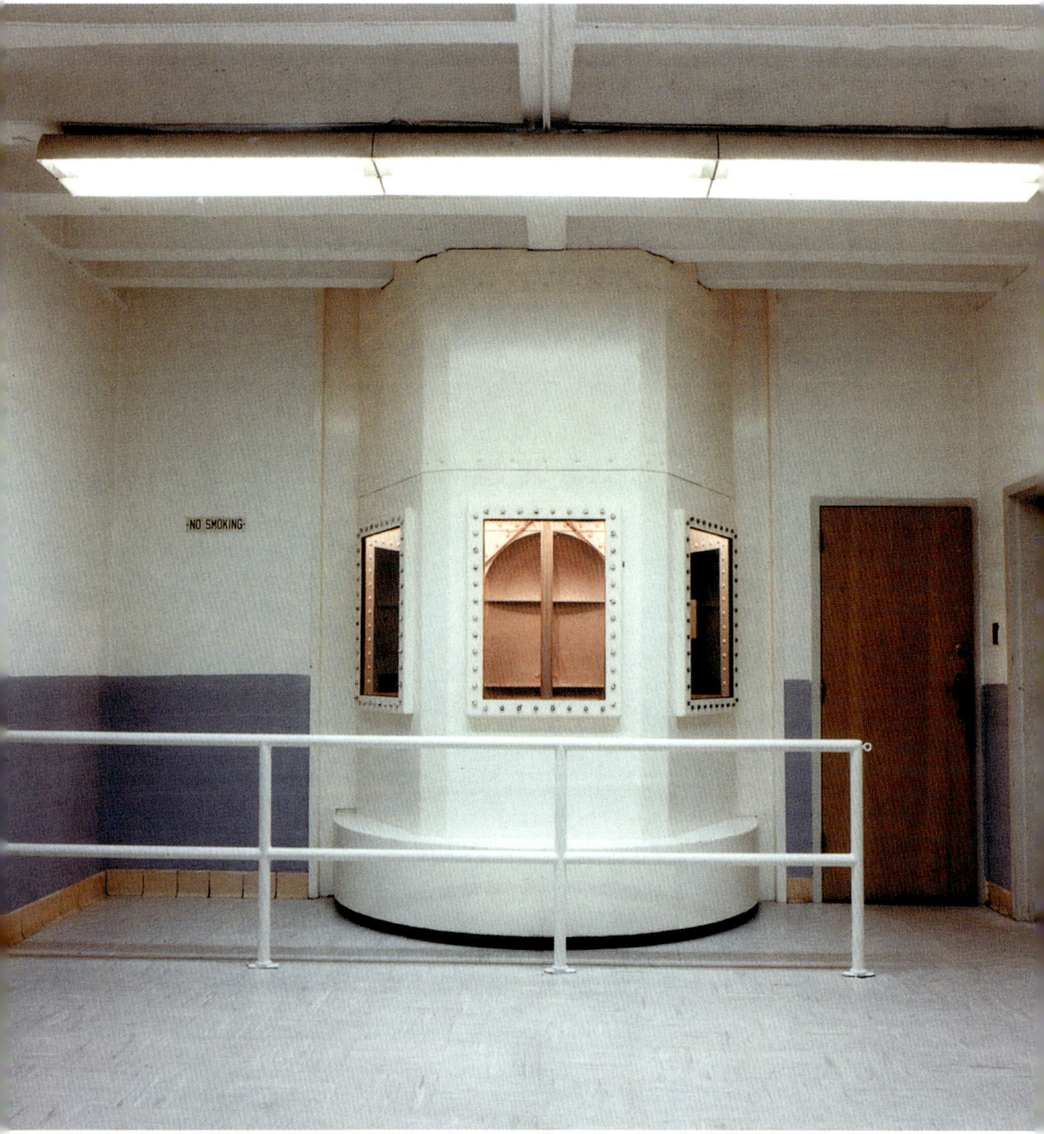

The spectator is assaulted by the image and a sense of irritation transforms the photographs of corpses taken by Serrano into the certainty of the useless existence of the corpse, its gratuitousness, in the proof of a failure and a broken promise. The image stops being incorporeal and becomes intrusive and primitive, it manages to suppress the distance of the representation and enters into the primitive magic in which there is no distinction between image and object,

Lucinda Devlin, *The Omega Suites. Lethal Injection Chamber*, Petosi Correctional Center, Petosi, Missouri, 1991

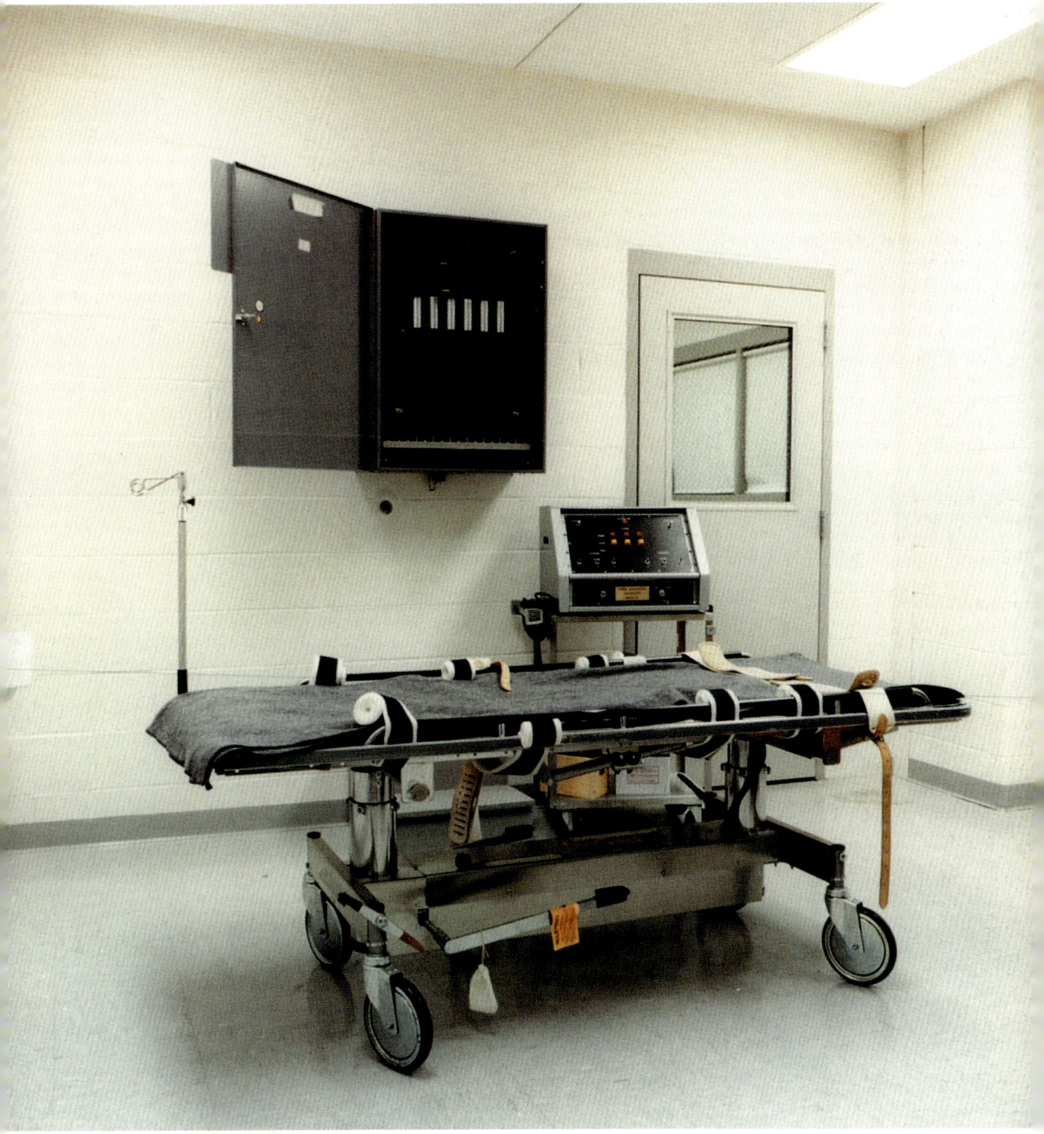

subject and object. Serrano proposes the necessity of a pact, a coming to terms with works that put forward the idea of an art that refuses to obey the very laws of the transformation of life into functions, and death into disappearance.

"And there is no longer anything or anyone... In fact, without a house, without inherited things, without dogs, what kind of life is this? If at least one had one's memories..." (Rainer Maria Rilke)

Death authorised

It is precisely the application of a symbolic ritual to a situation that excludes any possibility of symbolic response that constitutes the especially odious character of this type of punishment.

(Jean Baudrillard)

Death penalty or extreme therapy: punishment is meted out, things are cleaned up, justice is done, examples are set and one is pushed into the shadows of society. Death ceases to be a sacrifice, and becomes instead a torture, and afterward it is transformed into an execution. There is no history of death and the death penalty, but rather a genealogy of the social configurations that have led to its implementation. Senators, executioners, inquisitors and Holy Inquisitors, policemen, judges, politicians: there is a long succession of the figures who are authorised to deliver the coup-de-grace, the very instruments of crime are used, the same language, the same means. When in 1830 in England a regular police force was established to reduce the level of violence being done to individual citizens, it proved to be much more repressive and dangerous than the criminals, quite simply replacing the criminals in the waging of violence against the citizen; a small-scale aggression was replaced by a generalised and authorised aggression. The death penalty is useless.

The first traces known of the death penalty date back to 2080 BC. The Code of Hammurabi (c. 1700 BC) imposed the death penalty in various forms: by fire, quartering, impalement, and so on, for 34 different crimes: murder, adultery by a woman, theft, and many others.

In 534 BC, Lucius Tarquinius Superbus, the seventh and final King of Rome, introduced crucifixion. The victim, with this method of execution, did not die of hunger or loss of blood, but by suffocation: the victim was unable to breathe because of the pressure of his outstretched arms. Death came amidst atrocious suffering.

Around AD 200, the emperor Septimius Severus ordered the decapitation of 18,000 Cretans. The method became a specific form of execution in the Roman Empire; in fact, it was known as "Roman justice".

About AD 300 Erasmus, who fled Formia, was sentenced to die by "evisceration": his sixty-eight metres of intestines were ripped from his body and wrapped around a long pole.

In May 1431, Joan of Arc was burned on the Vieux-Marché square of Rouen. During the Inquisition, Torquemada, the Grand Inquisitor of Spain, sent more than eight thousand people to the pyre; they were burnt in order to purify them.

In 1500, some of the earliest sophisticated instruments of torture and death began to make their appearance, such as the *poire d'angoisse*: an iron object that, when introduced into the mouth or other orifices of a prisoner, would cause death by starvation, infection or lacerations. But it was not until 1515 that the Tribunal of the Inquisition presented the "mater dolorosa": a sort of sarcophagus with an interior bristling with spikes that penetrated many parts of the condemned man's body, causing a slow and horribly painful death.

Execution on the "wheel" was a French-made speciality, created at the behest of King Francis I in 1534: it was one of the most commonly used methods of torture and death in the Ancien Régime. In this form of execution, the limbs of the victim were literally ripped out of their sockets.

Lucinda Devlin, *The Omega Suites. Electric Chair*, Indiana State Prison, Michigan City, Indiana, 1991

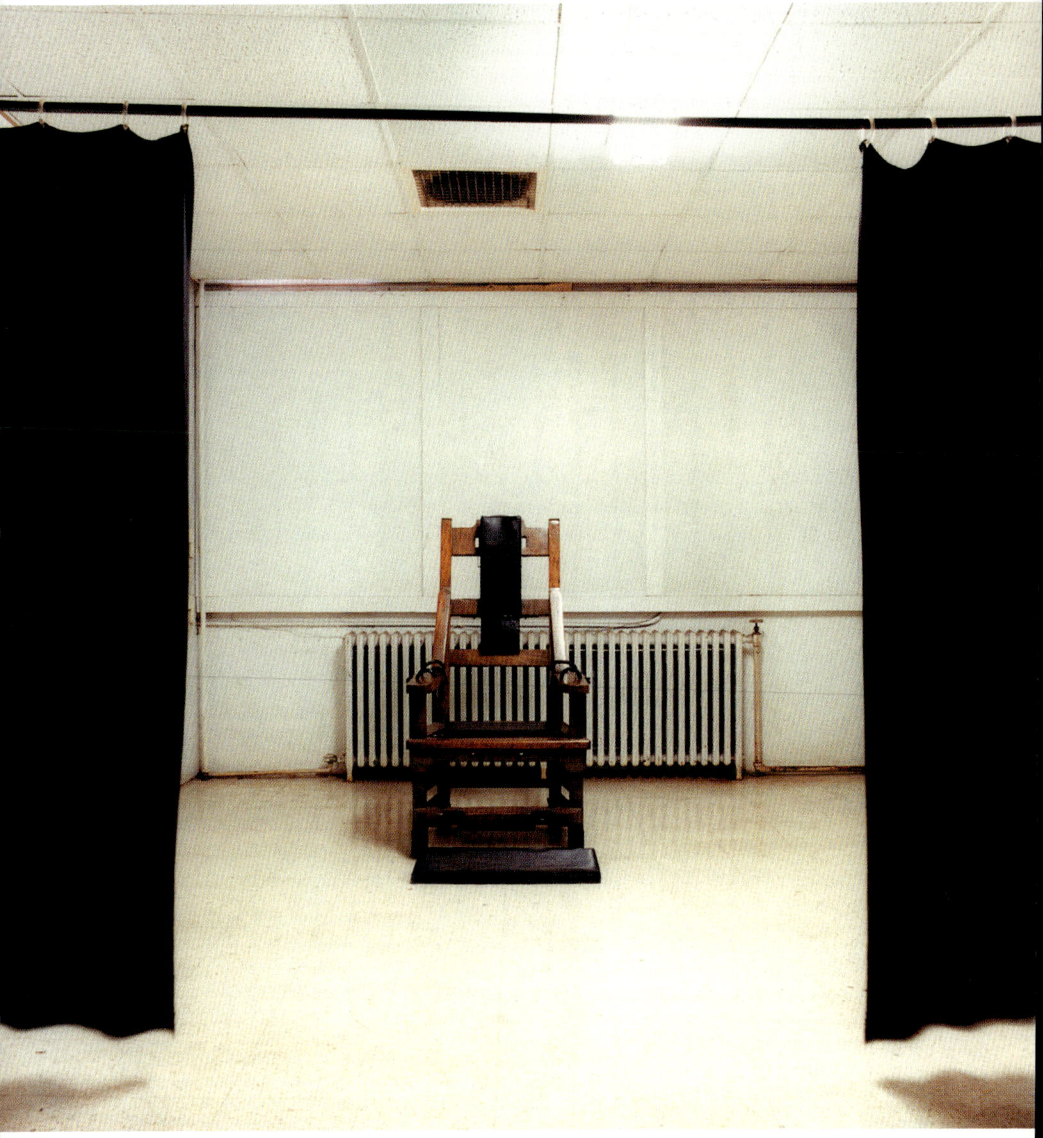

It was in 1792, on 25 April, that the guillotine was used for the first time, with the execution in a public square of a certain Jacques-Nicolas Pelletier. Doctor Louis, a great surgeon, managed to implement the idea of the renowned Doctor Guillotin ("pour une mort rapide et égalitaire") with a machine for cutting necks. During the period of the Terror (1792–95), the guillotine was used to cut off an unknown number of heads, which according to various sources ranged from 13,000 to 18,613.

In 1870, Spain introduced the *garrotte*, which was also used in Portugal. The last Spanish execution by *garrotte* was that of a Catalonian anarchist, Salvador Puig Antich, in 1974.

In 1888, the rivalry between two industrialists, Thomas Edison and George Westinghouse, opened the market for electricity in the United States, and Harold Brown invented the electric chair. A year later, the state of New York passed the idea into law, and on 6 April 1890 Francis Kemmeler was the first man in the world to be sentenced to die by electrocution. His death took 17 minutes.

On 8 February 1924, again in the United States, Gee Jon was the first person sentenced to be executed in the gas chamber. His death was caused by a capsule of cyanide.

The decapitation of Eugène Weidmann, at Versailles in 1939, was the last public execution in France.

In 1948, the General Assembly of the United Nations adopted the Universal Declaration of Human Rights, which proclaimed: "Everyone has the right to life, liberty and security of person" and "No one shall be subjected to torture or to cruel, inhuman or degrading treatment or punishment".

Cell 2455, Death Row, published in 1954, is the title of the biography of Caryl Chessman, who was sentenced to death in California, and it was to become a manifesto of a new generation of anti-death penalty abolitionists.

The Omega Suites is an artwork by Lucinda Devlin, an American artist who for ten years has taken photographs in every American penitentiary — overcoming numerous and obvious difficulties — of death chambers and the instruments and methods used: hanging, electric chair, gas chamber, lethal injection and firing squad. Photographs that depict the spaces of the condemned man and those used by the witnesses to the execution, sterile chambers, clean, technological. These are spare, spotless, rigorous images, without the shadow of a human presence, but the cruel anatomy of each object, each detail, each element of the sites of the execution of a justice that has chosen the same methods as those used by the criminals themselves. And we see spreading out the chrome-plated and functional design of the last instants of life in the penitentiaries, from the cell of the last meal to the autopsy table, illuminated by neon lights, a white, chilly light, a timeless light, a shadowless light, a bodiless light. Prohibitions, rooms, objects: a sterile dimension which extends everywhere like a film and seems to penetrate even the interstitial spaces of the objects, intercepting the images and infecting them. The photographs of Lucinda Devlin are perfidious and chilly like the glossy pages of a design magazine, in which the rooms are restored with such perfection that it becomes difficult to succeed in extracting the life from them. Immobile and devastating in the decision to seek out the dream of an aesthetic purity in the instruments of death, these images suggest damnation and grace, the cruelty of the authorisation to kill and the mysticism of a corporeality that has already vanished. And there is no pity, no mercy in the gaze of Lucinda Devlin: a sterile scene, between the irony of the concern for healthy habits (next to the gas chamber in the penitentiary of Baltimore we see a large sign reading NO SMOKING) and the condemnation to a precisely scheduled end to a life. Devlin depicts the objects and the instruments that are inflicted upon the condemned man's gaze, the diseased obsession with disinfection, removal, cleaning. How could we fail to see in those objects and in those instruments, in that perfection and in that functionality a sense of repugnance, obscenity, intolerability... Death seems to have been tucked away. Surgically removed.

The photographs of Lucinda Devlin are reminiscent of the methods for the elimination of the image of death in the society of the spectacle, of the elimination of the diseased body from society, the elimination of the degenerate cells of the social structure. The images are not presented with the horror of blood, fear, screaming mouths and gazes charged with terror. There is nothing alarming or unpleasant. At first glance, in the elegance of the format, in the obsessive perfection, in the rarefied, precise, sharp colour, these images do not seem to be linked to death; they are carefully made and elegant, but capable of passing in review one of the most widely consumed and accepted horrors of the contemporary world.

Images that question the status of death, breaking the taboo that makes it unspeakable.

Impact Body

FOREWORD

And if the prison resembles hospitals, factories,
schools and barracks, how can we be surprised
that they all resemble prisons?
Michel Foucault

Freaks, monsters, prostitutes, animals, foreigners. Michel Foucault raises the question of the position of the subject within society: "How are human beings made subjects in our culture?"

The objectification of the subject, to Foucault, is split into two specific phases. The first has to do with the methodologies and the structuring of society, which take on the standing of science: the case of the subject who works, set into the vaster analysis of wealth or economics, is a clear example of this. The second phase is identified with what Foucault calls "practices of division": "The subject is divided within itself or it is separated from the others. This process objectifies it". And here we see the categories of madness or normality, disease and health: the opposition of one toward another helps to establish the identity of the subject, the figure of a "precise" subject, and therefore, its placement. "The general subject of my research", wrote Foucault "is not, therefore, power but the subject... At the moment that the human subject is placed within relationships of production and meaning, it is likewise placed within very complex relationships of power." Forms of knowledge, in fact, modify the subjects that make use of them and man is modified precisely in his determination as subject. This mechanism shows that the entire cultural structure exists as a function of bodies, acts directly upon and within them, manipulates them and establishes them as territories to be colonised, to be carved out and built.

"Who else in the world knows something like the body does? It is the most recent product of our old culture, the one that has been most extensively purged, disassembled and reassembled." (Jean-Luc Nancy) Carved, used, forced, raped, disassembled or reassembled in a cultural apparatus that has been constructed around it, "dressing" and "redressing" the bodies with very specific meanings. The central idea then is that of a modifying intervention which is directed at times toward the physical environment, at others toward the human body, at times toward behaviour, at others toward the mind. A modifying intervention and an intervention on the body constitute the principal poles of the semantic structures of the word culture.

The ground, the environment or the bodies upon which culture intervenes undergo a transformation especially in the sense of an intentional imposition of models and forms. The culturalised body, however, the body that a culture forges, shapes, carves and marks, seems to be the element that most easily transmits the general idea of forms and models, imposed and incorporated.

Culture, then, understood as the "production of knowledge", disciplines bodies in depth, intervening in them through veritable relationships of force; but, as Foucault points out, "every relationship of force implies in every moment a relationship of power". These are power relationships that pass materially through the very depth of bodies, creating what Foucault describes as a network of biopower, a somatic power. Rationalising bodies means using them, making use of them, it means disciplining them. Foucault goes on to say: "There was, over the course of the classical age, a general rediscovery of the body as the object and target of power. It would be easy to find the signs of the great attention dedicated to the body — the body that was manipulated, trained, which obeyed, responded, which became skilful or whose strength was multiplied. The great book of the man/machine was written simultaneously on two registers: the anatomical and metaphysical one, whose first few pages were written by Descartes and then carried on by medical doctors and philosophers; and the technical and political register, constituted by an entire array of military, scholastic and hospital regulations, and by well-considered empirical processes for controlling or correcting the operations of the body". Foucault singles out on the one hand the great logical construction inaugurated by the Cartesian "cogito ergo sum", the manifesto of the disjunctive logic of mind/body; on the other hand, that vast apparatus of constructions and processes, aimed at a disciplining of bodies according to specific utilitarian discourses. "Docile is what we call a body that will be submissive, which can be utilised, that can be transformed and perfected.... We are not talking about intervening on the body en masse, wholesale, as if it were an unbroken unit, but rather to work on it retail."

The body thus enters into a gearing of power that "searches it", "composes it" and "breaks it down" into privileged zones of use: discipline becomes a "political anatomy of the detail" from which emerges a "microphysics of power". The set of these practices of "sectorialisation" which are operated from time to time in bodies find their legitimacy in those places in which bodies are obliged to obey, conceal themselves and experience shame. Those are the places of total institutions: the insane asylum, the clinic, the prison, the sanatorium, as well as the nursery school, places of education, rest homes... they are the places that Foucault defines as "heterotopic", where "the set of vital, organic and psychic manifestations seems to implode into a fully codified existential space.... In the proper use of the body, which allows a proper use of time, nothing should remain idle or useless; everything should be summoned to form a support for the required act. A well disciplined body forms the operative context of the slightest gesture".

And so we come to the problem of truth and the "will to know", in which Foucault depicts a Western society that has always been basically a "confessional society" and which has bound up its very formation of the subject with its openness to its own truth. "For a long time the individual took his or her authenticity in reference to others and through the manifestation of a personal bond with others. Later, authentication came through the discourse of truth which he or she was capable or obliged to perform upon himself or herself." Confession, as an "act of truth", has become in the West one of the principal techniques for producing the truth; it has expanded its sphere of action and its effects to an incredible degree, in the areas of justice, medicine, teaching, in simple family relations, in love relations and in schools. In those places where extracting a confession means acquitting or convicting someone or something: "One's own crimes are confessed, one's own sins are confessed, one's own thoughts and desires are confessed, one's own past is confessed, and one's own dreams are confessed... When the confession is not spontaneous it is extorted: it is burrowed out of the soul, it is ripped from the body..."

And the body becomes the site of exemplary punishment, of the response to confession. "Confession, the act of truth, is a narrative ritual in which the subject that speaks coincides with the subject of the enunciation; it is also a ritual that personifies a relationship of power, since one does not confess without the presence, at least the virtual presence, of a partner who is something more than a mere interlocutor, but rather the instance that demands the confession, imposes it, evaluates it, and intervenes to adjudge, punish, pardon, console, reconcile... A ritual in which the mere enunciation produces in the one that articulates it certain intrinsic modifications: it makes him innocent, it redeems him, it purifies him, it absolves him of guilt, it liberates him, it promises him salvation." In the final analysis, confession is always present in those who enunciate it, but it finds its efficacy only and strictly in those who extort it.

Between the end of the eighteenth century and the beginning of the nineteenth century, in Europe and in America, the penal system was revolutionised and, slowly, torture and execution were replaced by detention. Michel Foucault has written extensively, over the years, essays and investigations of the penal system, those methodologies through which power selects the means that determine the mutations of the disciplinary institutions, and he has sketched out a history of "docile bodies". In the passage from the theatricality of corporal punishment to the discretion of incarceration "...in a few decades the body that was tortured, ripped open, amputated, symbolically branded on face or shoulder, exposed living or dead, offered as a spectacle, vanished. What vanished was the body as the principal target of penal repression". According to Foucault's analysis this change in reality is a very important turning point in the history of modern societies, a transition that maintained its centrality by contributing to the modification of the conditions and the morphology of the system of punishment: what begins to disappear is the "spectacle of punishment", and from being a ceremonial act it gradually changed into an administrative act, from a public action to a hidden action. If ceremonial punishment outdid the violence of the crime being punished in an attempt to reconfirm through excess the power of the sovereign before a witnessing and participating public, the reformed punishment, instead, presented itself as a sort of concealed punishment which acquired a mental value, that is, began to be perceived not as a concrete act, but rather through an awareness of punishment. "The exemplary mechanics of punishment shifts gears: justice no longer takes on publicly the role of violence that is linked to its own exercise." Execution becomes a secret act, the body is no longer touched as in torture and execution; the individual, again through a punished body, is now however deprived primarily of his freedom, even though in reality in the context of penal justice there always persists a "torturing" background, even when it assumes almost abstract forms. Every correction is organised in any case through a process of work upon bodies, now secret, and according to Foucault that essentially brought about a change in the relationships between Body and Power. This new way of conceiving punishment now forms part of an "economy" that, with methodologies and strategies taken from the management of bodies, takes profit and saves on the use of force. "This political investment of the body is linked, according to complex and reciprocal relationships, to its economic utilisation. It is largely as a force of production that the body is invested with relationships of power and dominion, but, in exchange its self-construction as an embodiment of labour is possible only if it is incorporated into a system of subjection (in which need is also a political instrument, carefully pre-ordained, calculated and utilised): the body becomes a usable force only when it is simultaneously a productive body and a subjected body. This subjugation is not obtained only with the instruments of violence and ideology; it can also very well be direct, physical, play upon force, establish itself within material elements, and all the same not be violent; it can be calculated, organised and directed technically, it can be subtle, and make use neither of weapons nor terror, and yet still remain physical in nature."

It is the individual correction of the guilty party that must be the point of reference for the others; it is the idea of the evil-doer being punished that should suffice to reconfirm the code, and to "create submissive individuals", inside and outside of prison.

Thus the reform that was proposing to distribute the power of punishment and render the penal system more transparent, relaunching the prison as a punitive institution, constitutes an institutionalised, invisible power, which operates in closed places.

Armies, convents, factories, hospitals thus begin to take interest in bodies rendered obedient and trained, domesticated bodies; even if many ordered structures had existed for centuries, it was only over the course of the seventeenth and eighteenth centuries that the disciplines became "general formulas of domination", different from those previously known, such as slavery, vassalage or monastic rigour.

"In the workshop, at school, in the army there is an entire savage body of micro-penalties…" Bodies observed, studied, divided into rigid categories that do nothing more than to emphasise the value placed on the "norm", excluding anomalies and differences upon which, perhaps, the mechanism of discipline coincides with a process of normalisation that tends to run alongside surveillance.

Marina Abramović, *Anima Mundi: Pietà*,
performance with Ulay,
Carré Theatre, Amsterdam, 1983

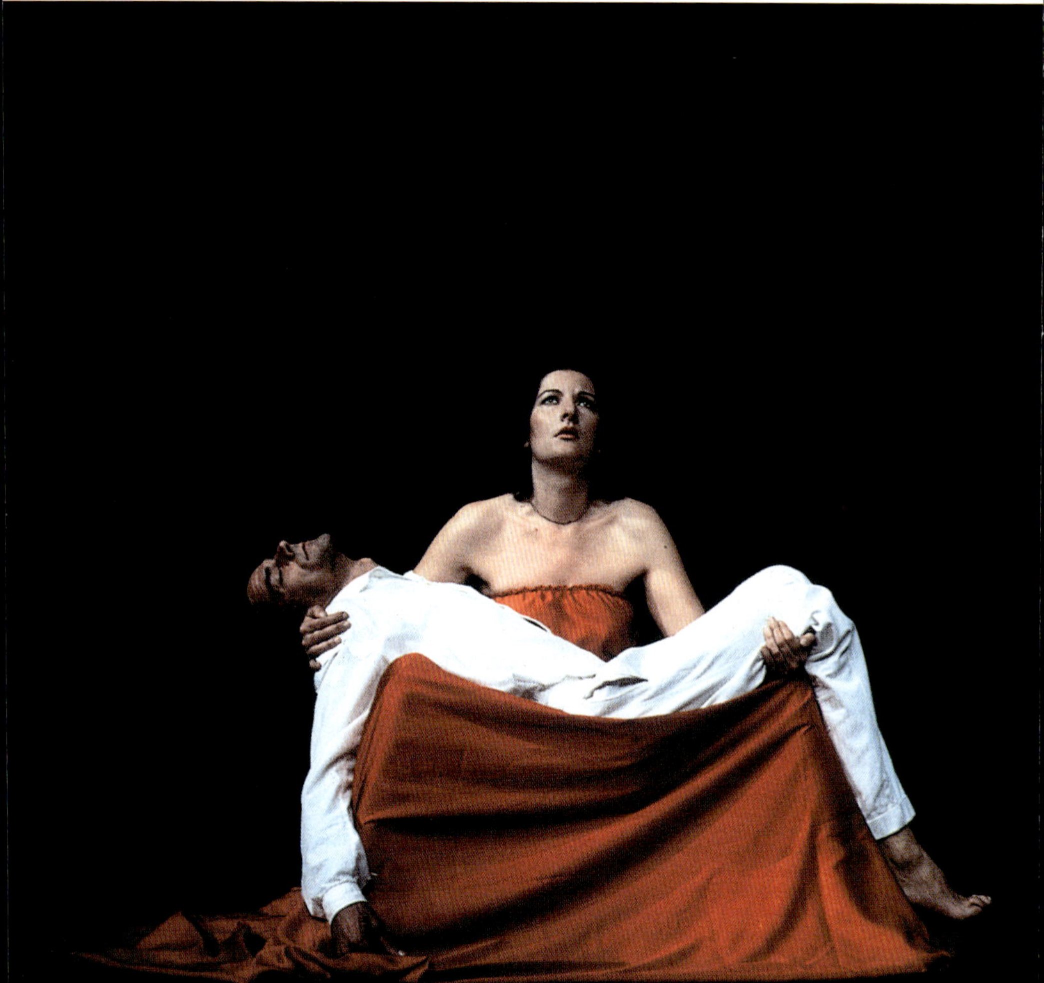

Living with the other, with the foreigner, faces us with the possibility of being, or not being, other.
Julia Kristeva

STRANGERS
Refugees, Guests, Exiles, Outsiders

Foreign is the condition of those who inhabit a world that each day produces new levels of reality, a society in which artificial realities are produced at a continuous flow, foreigners incessantly bombarded by pseudo-realities. Being foreigners is no longer merely a matter of nationality, but rather the fact of being other, intuiting the alien side of reality, constructing other sides of the world. "I is someone else", wrote Rimbaud, almost as if to announce the possibility or the necessity of being foreigners and living as foreigners, prefiguring a kaleidoscope of identities: to inhabit rationales separate from the memory of the body, from the dream of infancy.

Being a foreigner gives one the possibility of not agreeing with reality, it is the magic of looking at the things of the world with amazement and curiosity, like an explorer, like an ethnologist: "It takes a certain lack of balance, a hovering over an abyss, to feel disagreement" (Julia Kristeva). The foreigner is the subject that transforms reality into fiction, revealing the surreal side that becomes real in order to utilise portions of reality by constructing a pool of "credible" fiction around it. An arrogant reality that moves along the boundaries of life, reality seen by a foreign gaze. Feeling oneself to be foreign is the beginning of an undertaking of oneself that is luminous and uneasy, it is setting oneself forth as a project, as a "special effect". Identities and subjects that live in a migratory dimension: of identity, places, races, and in countless morphological possibilities. One of the most evident signs of the transformation now underway is the way in which humans see themselves, and in the altered subjectivity we see a process already underway of redefinition of the "human" being, already become a foreigner.

"When I left Yugoslavia I decided that I would become a modern nomad. I see the entire world as my studio and I am increasingly interested in being in a 'place' that I call 'the space in between', the space between two things, the space in transit, the space that is a passageway between two places, when you leave one place and you reach another. All of my work is centred on the idea of crossing boundaries, both in a physical and in a metaphorical sense"; a way of doing art, Marina Abramović's way, that teeters on the brink of confusion, a way to emphasising the characteristics and the tensions of the "Other" inside of oneself, outside of oneself, distant from oneself. It is the human being itself that constitutes the luminous and complex object of the artistic investigations of Marina Abramović, the human being that constitutes itself as the object of a reflection, at times embarrassing — as in the case of the discourse on origins, at times humiliating — as in the case of the discourse on boundaries (geographical, political, religious), at times authoritarian — as in the case of systems of control, whether they are diplomatic or military. Marina Abramović is a foreigner. "Don't speak your own mother tongue. Inhabit sonority, a logic separate from the nocturnal memory of the body, from the bittersweet sleep of childhood. Carry inside yourself like a secret crypt, or like a handicapped child, beloved and useful, that language of a long time ago that fades but never determines to leave you. You become a master of another instrument, the way that you express yourself with algebra or on the violin. You can become a virtuoso in that new artifice, which procures a new body for you, equally artificial, sublimated — some even say sublime. You have the impression that the new language is your new resurrection: new skin, new sex. But the illusion is ripped to shreds when you listen to yourself", wrote Julia Kristeva about the experience of being foreigners, in reference to the Other who lives in the same place, the same space, the same time.

That of foreigners is a special act of birth that characterises a being who is always too far this side or the far side of the margin of usefulness. A series of shifts and movements connotes this age as it does other ages, but right now what is being affirmed is not merely an interplay of crossing through various places, but rather a complete theory of otherness. Marina Abramović is an alert and aware presence, a total presence that tries to coincide with its own body in the place of the event, a state of presence, the possibility of becoming a threshold between the heritages of archaic cultures, Eastern and Western cultures, states of suspension from the body, as in the performances in which immobilism and silence become proofs of resistance, maximum mental concentration and control of the body, the need to rejoin the human body with the planetary body. "I believe that the environment, and first and foremost, geographic configuration, is extremely important for the formation of the collective psychology: the Balkans are a place where East and West come together, a place in which two completely different civilisations enter into contact and mingle, creating what I define as the 'mental Baroque', a sort of permanent intertwining of love, hate, tenderness, passion, sex, fear, and shame." Marina Abramović renders clearly evident that Western civilisation has perfected and spread the concept of fear and, in contrast with Eastern cultures, has never developed and investigated techniques capable of shifting physical limits. She offers the abandonment of oneself in order to become a creative act, to reappropriate a dimension of contact, with the elements, with earth, with such specific materials as copper, crystals, hair, bones; some of her performances are constituted solely by objects made expressly for the audience to use them, once again a shift away from the concept of the passive spectator: "I don't think that art can change the world, but I do believe that certain artistic actions can influence the changing of minds". Punctuation, duration and time occupy an important part of the work of Marina Abramović: ever since her performances in the 1970s, her actions have taken place in real time and in a space shared with the audience, even if she has often made use as well of digital technologies for the implementation of a part of the event. And real time is the special time used by Abramović, a time that is not manipulated, transferred, alienated, distanced; it is a reality of experience that is transmitted, an exchange of energy and experience of the same duration as the participation in the event. The preparation of her body is rigorous and rigid in the phases preliminary to the performance, a full-fledged special regime that calls for isolation, exercises in physical and mental resistance such as fasting, going without sleep, isolation, a sort of stimulation of a threshold of the body that becomes especially receptive to the specific creation of a flow of energy that is ready to reach and draw in the audience attending the performances. Marina Abramović chooses for her actions several of what in ethnology are defined as "dangerous classes", attitudes of savagery that survive, despite civilisation, in the panorama of the contemporary Western world. "Art that refers exclusively to itself is possible only in decadent societies and can exist only in cities. As soon as one finds himself alone outside of the city, in the desert, 'the object' no longer performs its function, and art as art loses any and all meaning. Initially, art never referred to its own context, but rather it originated out of an interest in the human being, who needed art for rituals and religion", declares Abramović, in a phrase that clearly sets forth her concept of art, which becomes a manner that cannot leave out her own body, her personality, her personal history.

The materials with which Marina Abramović does her performances and artworks offer a special alchemy between the tensions of the contemporary and archaic civilisations, between the obsession of repetition and the obsession of ritual, between the everyday gestures that become dangerous acts and the extreme gestures that form part of the everyday. History, religion, war, emotional memories, loving relationships all become elements of a communication that is direct, strong, and other. She cuts herself, she combs her hair, she washes herself, washes, runs, remains motionless for hours, she marks herself, slips and falls, she allows herself to be crawled upon by snakes, she dresses, she strips, she dances, she speaks, she writes, she carves her skin. She involves the spectator in a relationship of empathy, a multi-sensory relationship in which all of the senses are activated and in which it is possible to remain extraneous to the action. The audience thus becomes part of the artwork, and senses powerfully the trap in which the technological systems of communication modify behaviours and awarenesses. A critical involvement that tends to highlight the "distractions" of contemporary beings with respect to themselves and their own problems of definition and conscious modification. "The shift toward Body Art for me took place in a spontaneous, almost subconscious manner. And after the first performance I could no longer imagine working with any other medium than my own body in relation to and in contact with the body of the audience." The last performance of Abramović with Ulay, with whom she collaborated and performed from 1976 to 1988, was *The Walk*, a march that lasted from 30 April to 27 June 1988 along the Great Wall of China. It was from the end of the 1970s that Marina Abramović has been generating exchanges of energy with spectators, a transformation of individual energies that becomes a systematic overcoming of limits, both physical and mental, that the artist herself puts into play in performance after performance. Silence and spiritual exercises in Tibet (naked monks lying directly upon glaciers), coexisting with Australian Aborigines (dreamtime and daytime), participation in Sufi rituals (trances), the acquisition and the study of meditation techniques and the profound research into religious rituals and mytholo-

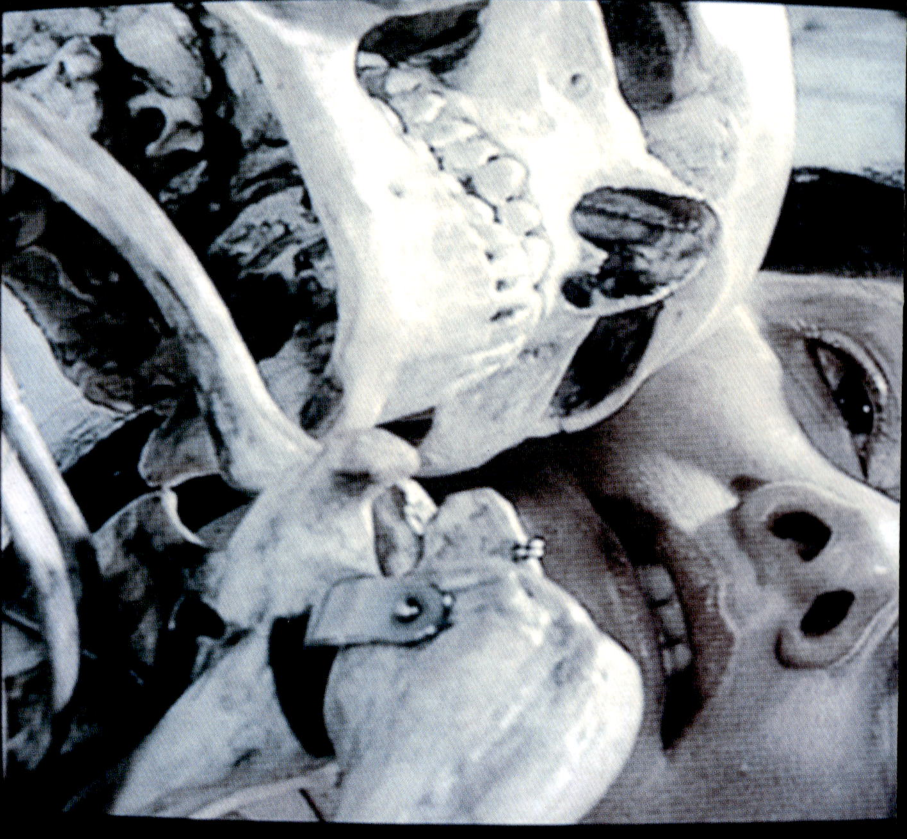

Marina Abramović, *Cleaning the Mirror II*,
video-installation, Oxford University, 1995

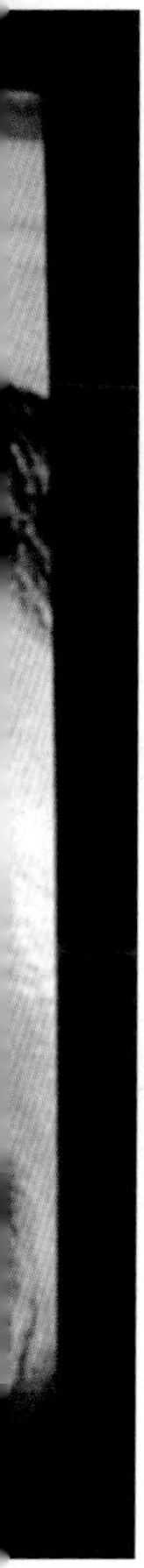

gies of various extraction, widely varied in origin, but all sharing the common denominator of overcoming bodily limits, all accompany the performances and developments of Marina Abramović, an attitude and a predisposition to the border states of the body that introduce her directly into unforeseen dimensions of the very concept of existence, pain, resistance, fear, control and shame: "Above all, I wanted to work on all of those things that provoke the feeling of shame. In this type of performance I try to perfect myself, as a sort of mirror upon which the audience can project its own interior conflicts".

A sort of progressive elimination of the concept of fear: fear of life, pain and death. *Cleaning the Mirror* is a series of video-installations in which the artist places the spectator face to face with a number of primary fears of the individual suppressed by contemporary culture: fear, pain, death. In *Cleaning the Mirror I* Abramović cleans a human skeleton, an energetic operation done with a brush, soap and water, a situation set before a metaphorical last mirror. The scene is filmed by numerous videocameras in the real time of the cleaning of the skeleton, framing parts of the body divided into sections. The performance is presented to the audience through the recomposition of the body in a video-sculpture constituted of five monitors that reassemble the fragments of the human skeleton: the head, the thorax, the hands, the pelvis, the feet. In *Cleaning the Mirror II* she lies on her back, a skeleton on top of her, which moves with the artist's respiration in an impalpable boundaryland between life and death.

In *Cleaning the Mirror. Power Object*, she selects a specific series of authentic ritual objects from the collection of the Pitt Rivers Museum, such as, for instance, a pair of shoes believed by Australian Aborigines to possess the power to allow one to fly, a mummified Egyptian ibis, a mediaeval bottle in which a witch was thought to be trapped, a copper mirror from archaic Greece. Archaic civilisations are accompanied by objects to which specific qualities and characteristics were attributed, objects associated with rituals bound up with birth, life and death, rituals that accompany an individual while representing fundamental moments of one's existence. A mixture of religion, magic, mystery, a concentrate of allusions and occasions that define the power of objects. For the installation *Cleaning the Mirror. Power Object*, Abramović created a number of wax figures with a crystal at the centre, in a ritual in which she bandages the figures one by one, like so many mummies, and then bathes them with the blood of a pig, as if to recall the symbolic power of special objects dense with energy in a contemporary period that has stopped wondering about the meaning to which they allude. Rituals, symbolism, objects full of meaning that have little or nothing to do with functionality and production. Objects and pauses and respiration of a mental dimension that needs to produce poetry, magic, mystery. And beauty.

An alien production, warded off by the noise and the pace of the contemporary horizon, a world populated by billions of people who mostly live in urban areas and are expected almost to double in number over the course of the coming quarter century. A reflection on the contemporary urban condition is the definition of a space that exists solely for consumption whose essence is the product of the uncontrolled juxtaposition of spaces and social experience. A condition that determines a world in which overpopulation will be experienced almost exclusively in areas with high population density, very little of which we are capable of imaging except to sense that they will present themselves as a sort of generalised Babel. Increasingly the strategy of consumption orients life in the metropolises, tending toward the creation of a transverse economy that strives toward a globalisation of East and West, North and South. Demonstrators in Seattle, and immediately afterward in many other cities across the planet, marched against the hypothesis of a world entirely unified and standardised by the market laws of the multinationals. The flows of migration invent new cultural collocations and new environmental aggregations that increasingly move away from the folkloric vision of ghettos like Chinatown or Little Italy, giving origin to new mixed realities, and carrying out a continual recomposition of signals and messages, often opposing signals and messages, which stack up, interact and become confused in a haphazard fashion. Opulence and ever higher thresholds of poverty coexist in the same places at different times, but above all they share social spaces in which ethnic groups and life styles are mingled. And it is racism again. Once again racism is justified with a "universal" point of view, which distinguishes between human, inhuman, biological characteristics of the species, skin colour... special arguments are developed to define the characteristics of "normality", creating distinctive criteria. To whom are we referring when we talk about "foreigners"? Someone who is different from us, often perceived as threatening, as an "impurity" that contaminates, penetrates, modifies. The foreigner is the presence of a bordering territory, a borderland between a society and what ever lies outside that society. The foreigner is the incarnation of the difference between inclusion and exclusion, he is other, the different, the destabilising element. The abolition of the differences in a society that is finally universal, under the sign of a single culture: this is the dream of the normal man, a man who has a "soul" and who belongs to the "right" species. "According to these criteria (soul or sex) in effect we obtain an equation of Black = White, but this equivalency excludes therefore that much more radically all that which does not have a soul or a 'human' sex. Savages, on the other hand, who did not theorise either soul nor species, recognised earth and animal and the dead as partners. We have rejected them, in accordance with our universal principles, the principles of our egalitarian metahumanism which, by integrating black people according to white criteria, does nothing more than to extend the limits of abstract sociality, entitlement sociality. It is always the same white magic of racism at work, and it does nothing other than to whitewash negroes under the sign of the universal." (Jean Baudrillard)

David Hammons is one of the most radical of contemporary artists, who chooses a critical activity as a response to rancour, resentment and revenge. "Criticism is not a re-action of re-sentment, but the active expression of an active way of existing: attack and not revenge..." (Gilles Deleuze) Beginning from his debut in Los Angeles he chose the Afro-American community as the site in which he placed his artworks and his actions: "White people claimed that my work was 'too black'. The whites are too consumer-oriented, and my work was difficult to consume, and so most of my collectors were black. I left Los Angeles in part because of the racism, but in New York the situation was not all that different". In most cases, the installations of David Hammons were done on the street, in Harlem, Brooklyn and the Lower East Side, and their power lies in their appropriation of a great deal of "reality": traffic, people, hustle-bustle, a complicated succession of segments of individuals in chance encounters and unexpected relationships which the artist, on the basis of a power of "investment" in

David Hammons, *The Blizz-ard Ball Sale*,
Cooper Square, New York, 1983

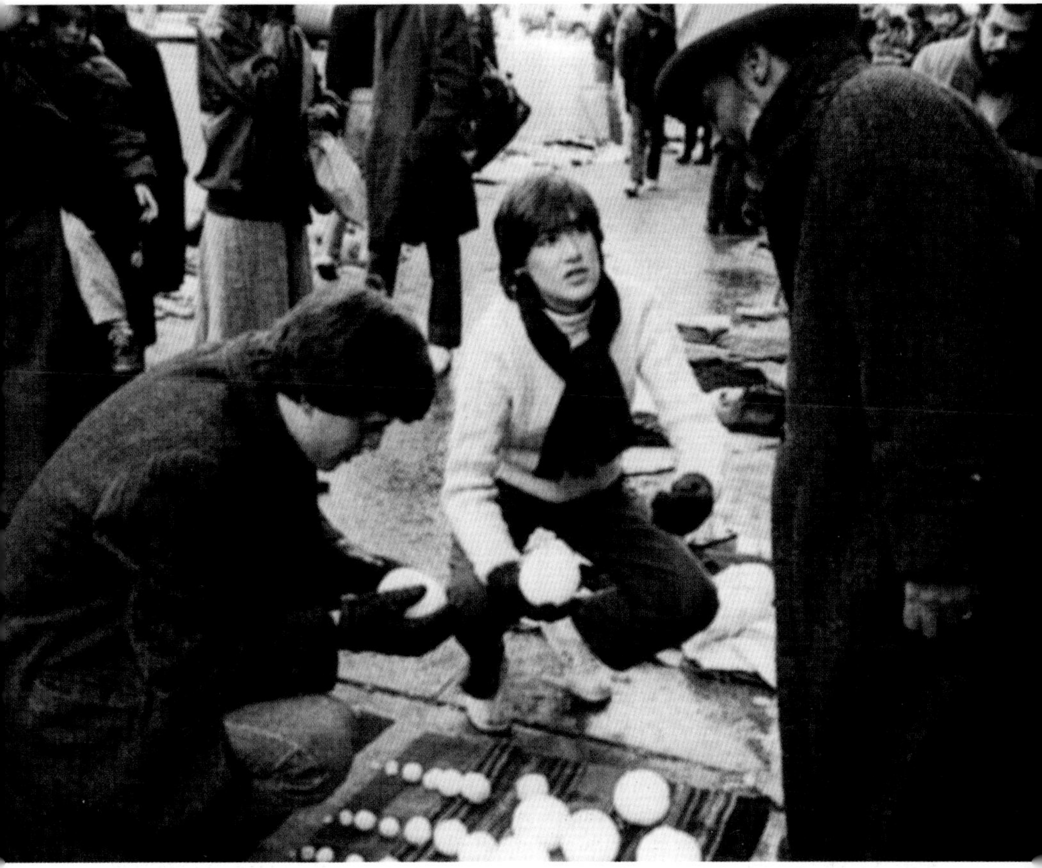

the real, manages and directs. David Hammons almost exclusively makes use of materials from the Afro-American community, and his own community is his chief raw material; he takes the stance of being extraneous to questions of art, often declaring that the public that is interested in art is no more interesting than any other kind of public: "The audience for art is not the public. You don't meet any real people at openings. But the people who are instead going who knows where are the ones who interact with my work. Rarely can you see anything of the sort in the world of art, because the art world is so exclusive: it is like a country club", and he prefers to work in the street, he chooses topics "from the street": politics, racism, economics, which trigger and provoke an unexpected and invasive contact in the flow of a time structured for work and for commuting, which envisions stopping only for lunch. Interruption for Hammons is a notion of impact, it helps to circulate a plurality of senses, a constellation of motives, a complex of successions; it activates the strategy of a coexistence of environments and references, it implements placements which trigger movements, transformations and provocations. Shoe vendor, purse vendor, news vendor, Hammons acts upon the condition of precariousness of both individuals and their relations, and objects, as well as life itself. A precariousness that sinks its own roots and its own reason for existing into the fortuitous: there is no real reason to be evicted, for losing your job, for becoming criminals, for voting, or for having a car crash. You live and you die by chance, even though everything is powerfully underpinned by an economic and social structure that declares its own affiliation with the sphere of rationality. An improvised derby in which there are no subjects or existences but rather signs that identify conditions, workers, women, invalids, handicapped people, people who are different, black, signs of discrimination and difference that "fortuitously" and "irrationally" determine life, existence, death. David Hammons uses almost exclusively found objects or else objects purchased at flea markets. He displays and offers up the energy of a research, the necessity for art of solitude and discomfort. "I grew up seeing people putting out things in courtyards, there will always be folk art and poor people making art in this country." Hammons acts inside open and claustrophobic structures, he indicates rumours, abuses, uselessness, violence, conditioning, he works in ghettos, he seeks sites of reality, levels of reality born of the civilising rage of the manufacturing era, of merchandise, of the spectacle, of flexibility, he seeks the level of reality in a condition of overpowering abuse in which life is nothing more than a bet. "Harlem is a ghetto, but it keeps me very close to reality. There is no conceit in poor communities. I do see however a great deal of conceit in the world of art, and I try to bring something that makes it seem a little more real when I can, if possible. I want just a few people to talk to after a performance. I think that talking about art is more important than art itself. I will do more performances because we black artists are very insecure: we don't do things in a frivolous manner because we want them too bad. Young black artists are afraid to do certain things because they are a minority and because they have not yet reached a level in which they can be frivolous in what they do." Hammons indicates the invisible and pervasive strategies of adaptation: to the visual, written and spoken word, to language, clothing, climate and intolerance. Installations, painting, photography, sculpture, performances, videos, Hammons relates to many techniques in accordance with his very definition of reality: something of which an equivalent reproduction can be made.

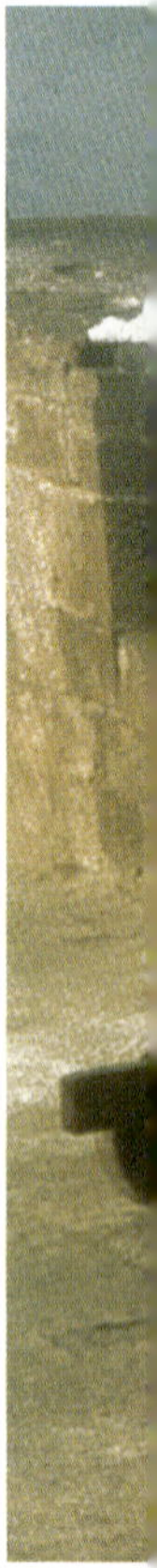

The Blizz-ard Ball Sale: a little carpet and a series of various sized snowballs, two for a dollar. "The night before there had been a heavy snowfall, and I saw lots of people selling shit and speculating on the problems of others. It always happens, I always find that whatever is the most outrageous is the easiest to sell, and so I learned to do a kind of 'bungee jumping' in the art world... What I want to do is to try to invent something to get out of this world." A little carpet and a series of various sized snowballs, two for a dollar, on the little square in front of the Guggenheim Museum in New York, alongside other vendors of objects and gadgets, alongside the uselessness in which human existence plunges and is buried and covered over. A little carpet and a series of various sized snowballs, two for a dollar: Hammons sold them directly, without any middlemen, without any gallery-owners, without the professional figures who get fifty percent. A little carpet and a series of various sized snowballs, two for a dollar: an artwork in which

Shirin Neshat,
still from the video *Rapture*,
1999

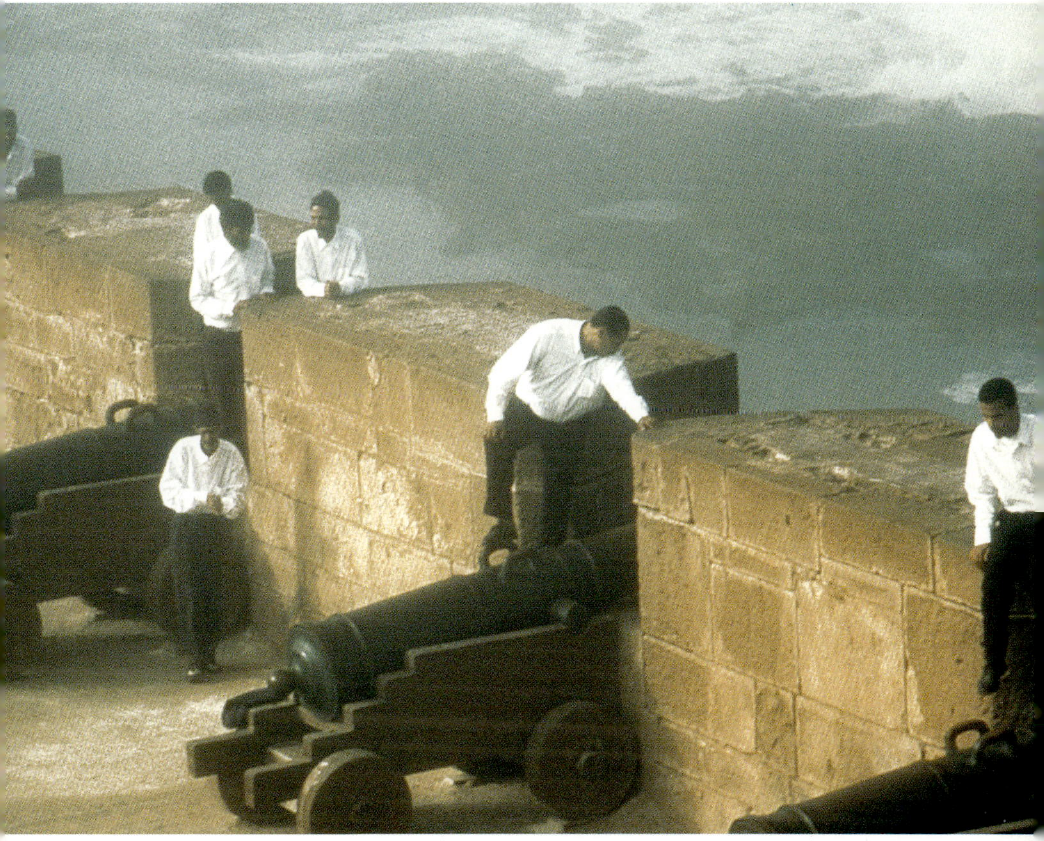

the American dream melts at the first rays of sunshine and "the biggest democracy on earth" begins to take on water. The reality that Hammons reproduces is not the object of which it is possible to make an equivalent reproduction, but the mechanism, the system, the function: and what emerges in the mechanism is the madness that generated it. The series of artworks in which Hammons makes use of clothing traces another boundary line within the context of a universe that is defined as "globalised": Italian, Islamic and Christian clothing. "I want to do a piece with a white boy dressed in a Senegalese outfit, so that people of colour could see how absurd they look in the clothing of white people"; the madness of standardisation, of being held hostage to the kidnapping of universalisation that to an even greater degree amplifies the sense of exclusion, the exclusion of blacks, yellows, red men, the exclusion of "foreigners" if they are not mortified in their differences. Having to resemble is the diamond tip of exclusion, the perfect form of a culture that aspires to the strategy of a flat electroencephalogram. David Hammons organised a reflective gaze onto any aspect of life, on its everyday nature in its transitory form; he creates the incident that singles out the points of existence in which life is not possible, the extreme points, the limit conditions. Hammons tries to capture the meaning of the everyday experience in order to reaffirm the character of the individual, his culture, his experience, and in this way helps to explode the methodology that is meant to serve to deliver the individual from himself, a critique of the social and political organisation that calls for individuals ready to become other than themselves, individuals that reach a point of annihilation, dissociation. A de-subjectifying undertaking: "At times it can be a lot of fun for me to do shows, because from my work you can't have the vaguest idea of my origin. I can use my work as an American Indian of as an Asian Indian". And Hammons indicates the limitations and the cruelties of the borderlands in the concept of identity, the phenomena of stiffening of identity in which conflicts are rendered extreme. Hammons organises an attack, through his own work, on the social body, on the somnolent homogeneisation of identity: "Since I am black, I think that dignity is the most fundamental thing. White people are always ready to put other white people in their place. They need them in order to make their shit seem like something marvellous... it is a vicious circle. I don't undress for them. They aren't real. They are a group of people who dress in black twenty-four hours a day". And so we see the spaces through which it may be possible to introduce a transformation, codes of communication are being structured that may be capable of linking up to a collective practice, artworks and existences that function as invitations, as gestures made in public for experiences that took place in full, escaping the realm of pure subjectivity, in a way that allows them to become zones of discourse and awareness that others can intersect, travel again, pass through repeatedly. Hammons creates artworks in which "he deals with people", the question of being in the world, of the relationship of individuals with the contemporary world, artworks in which the linearity and the naturalness of rules, prescriptions, prohibitions and abuses is opened to discussion. An invitation to begin a renewed discussion of the categories of diversity, integration, dissociation, uprooting, reversal, through the possibility and the urgency of being able to construct a world of relations in which it is possible to break up the relationships with oneself, losing identity, in which it is possible to attain the decomposition of the subject itself, its dispersion, an escape from the limits of one's own impossibilities. Hammons places the accent on the necessity of the physical presence — one reacts to virtual images the same way not long ago we reacted to a physical presence — and addresses the problem of physical contact, person to person, person and space in which we live: and this, nowadays, is his preoccupation.

One of the foundations upon which modern states are built is the rivalry with other states, whose members are "foreigners": from this fact we derive yet another barrier that establishes that some are in and others are out, and especially a marked anti-nomadism that has the objective of safeguarding the need for stability and recognisability, the need to provide "foreigners" with a domicile and an affiliation. "Blaming", defined by Mary Douglas in 1992, is a mechanism whereby society, in the continual process of redefining its own boundaries, attributes blame and establishes responsibilities; the boundaries of marginality are redrawn, there is a renewed emphasis on the need to belong to recognised places and communities, the rules and requirements for obtaining "admission" are structured, and the foreigner, the most vulnerable body in society, is identified as the enemy. Triggering the process of "blaming" tends not only to recognise danger in the Other, but also and especially to justify the discipline and control of entire zones of society. Michel Foucault had identified in genealogy and bio-politics two useful instruments for verifying the ways in which society continues to react toward foreigners: "The condition of possibility of power, or at any rate, the point of view that makes it possible to render understandable the use of that power, right out to its most 'peripheral' effects, and which also makes it possible to utilise its mechanisms, such as the grid of intelligibility in the social field, is not to be searched in the original existence of a central point, a single centre of sovereignty from which it would radiate out derived and descending forms; it is the mobile base of relationships of force that induce, incessantly, by their disparity, situations of power, but always local and unstable".

Alienation restricts forms of behaviour, cultures, rituals and social structures in outlying urban areas or in the peripheral areas of the world: the attempt is made to an increasing degree to distance and isolate foreigners and outsiders in native lands that become ghettos, borderlands, war zones, reservations in which consumption, alcoholism and violence can become forms of self-elimination from the "healthy" body of Western society, from the sites of production. Again, Foucault: "In what way, in modern Western societies, is the production of the discourses to which has been attributed (at least for a certain period of time) a value of truth, linked to the various mechanisms and institutions of power?". Foucault sees, in the relationship between power and knowledge, a form of control that is not merely coercive, but above all capable of the production of reality, in which the truth is not only determined by disciplinary norms of control and exclusion, but it is also "linked in a circular manner to the systems of knowledge that produce it and support it, and to power effects that it induces and which reproduce it". The exercise of power is therefore possible for an economy based on the production of reality, an economy and a reality that see in racism the possibility of indirectly putting to death: "Everything that can be indirect death: the fact of exposing to death or multiplying for some the risk of death, or in simpler terms, political death, expulsion, or rejection", says Foucault.

Shirin Neshat arrived in Berkeley to study art in 1974, from Qader, one of the most religious towns in Iran. When she returned to Iran in 1990, from New York, where she now lived, she was totally horrified by the changes that had been provoked by the Islamic revolution of 1979, which re-established masculine control over all public space and enforced the segregation of women: they were fired from their jobs, forbidden to speak or to sing in public, masculine and feminine places were rigorously separated, women were required to wear the chador. Shirin Neshat began to photograph herself covered with a veil, covered with writing, covered with prejudices, she placed the female body at the centre of the political debate that once again, in the name of a faith or a law, was determining the conditions of shame and the humiliation of a separate, mute existence, a life led with eyes lowered and a veil covering the face. "I must say that I was profoundly touched by the idea of dying for a faith. The obsession with death in that dimension no longer has any reason for existing. At times I try to think what people of my age must have gone through: first the war between Iran and Iraq with all of that death and grief; then the revolution, and again blood, arrests; and then the economic disaster: in other words, one world of pain after another." Shirin Neshat

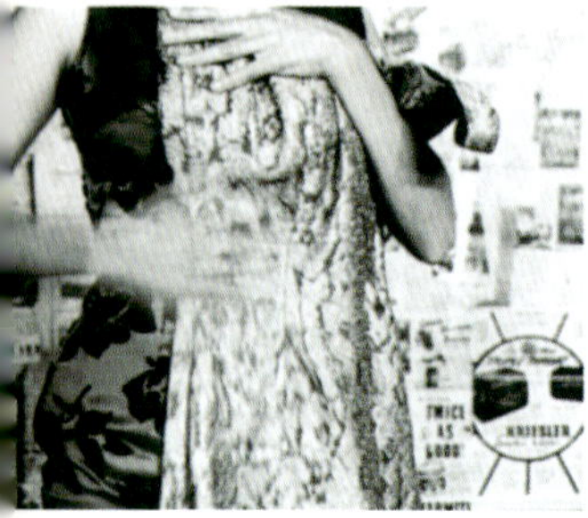

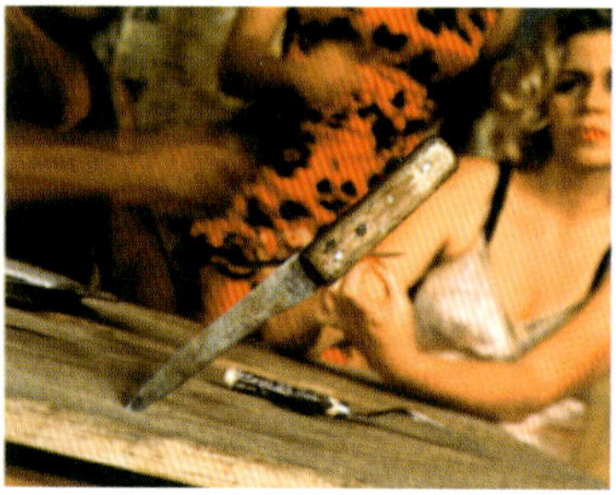

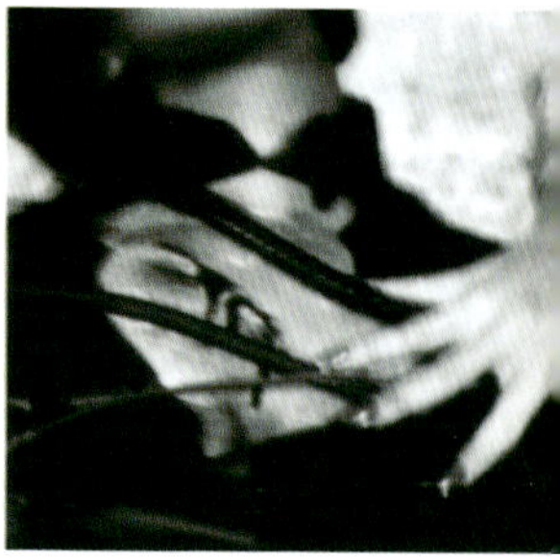

has been exploring for the past several years the complexity of social conditions within Islamic culture, turning a special gaze upon the role that women play here: in *Women of Allah* she presents a series of photographs inspired by the Islamic revolution in Iran, coming face to face with a female character closely linked to terrorism, close to the facility of giving and receiving death, a radical, determined individual, who must necessarily have a close relationship with violence. It is Shirin Neshat herself who portrays this character: the photographs portray her in images that are intense and powerfully connoted, and in the years of "politically correct" art her character was strongly objected to, ignored and warded off.

What is proposed by Shirin Neshat is an anti-conventional vision that tries to maintain a certain detachment from prejudices, both those of the Eastern world and those of the Western world; she suggests a powerfully foreign identity and presence, hostile and openly declared, which is exposed to the flow of prejudice. "The veil, inasmuch as it is a characteristic that ideally defines the Islamic world, has imprisoned Muslim women in an image of substantial diversity. It has been so badly characterised that not even the wardrobe of Barbie, unusual in its enormous variety, has included it. The queen of the international toy market, sold in over 140 countries, has taken on many different nationalities. Such a marketing campaign of ethnic diversity however decided that the veil was a marketing strategy not well suited to Barbie, the icon of American femininity", writes Farzaneh Milani, an Iranian woman and a professor of Persian literature at the University of Virginia. "Someone might have thought that I was identifying with the radical attitude of that character... I do not know whether on a subconscious level this is true or not, I can only say what my conscious intentions were. People as a first reaction hated that character: in those years anything that had to do with politics produced ambivalent feelings, and I was setting forth an image of the contribution that women had offered to the Islamic revolution..."

The character that Shirin Neshat portrays in *Unveiling* and *Women of Allah* is a woman who wears a chador and carries a rifle, images covered with writing in a language that is foreign and "hostile" — some thought that they were passages from the Koran, others thought that they were merely decorative calligraphy. In reality, the veiled body, identified in the past with submission and nowadays associated with the violence of terrorism, is worn by a Shirin Neshat covered with verses by Persian poetesses, in a complex textual relationship between body and veil. "I

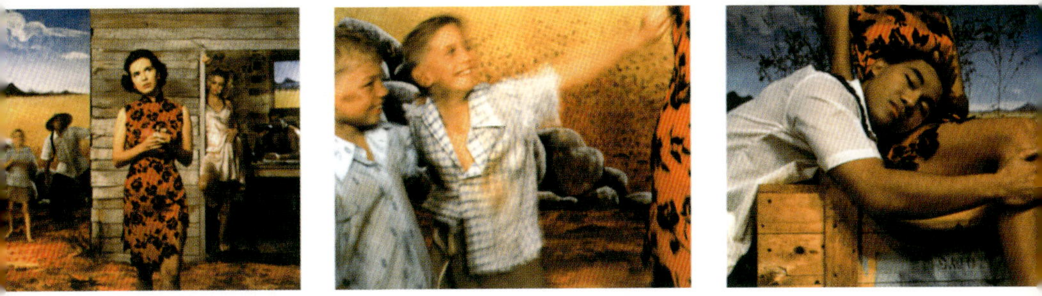

Tracey Moffatt,
Something More,
photographic series, 1989

believe that I am part of a group of artists who consider the artist herself of himself as an expression of reality, not so much in terms of the objects produced but specifically because the artist is included in the reality of things and in their occurrence. For this reason I am trying to go beyond the traditional mediums of art, such as sculpture and painting, in order to delve into multimedia languages, because they have a more all-involving power. The use of technologies is one of the most stimulating intentions of this particular period: the idea of increasingly attaining a contamination between video, computer and body, as well as the idea of allowing the audience to participate more and more within the context of the artwork. What I am most interested in is the possibility of creating artworks that are as poetic as possible, artworks in which what counts most is the fact of expressing emotions, whether or not they deal with social, religious and political subjects."

Since 1996, Shirin Neshat has been returning regularly to Iran and, influenced by the vision and independence of Abbas Kiarostami, she has begun to work with video images and experimental film, exploring the "question of the separation of the sexes and its relation to the theme of control and ideology". In *Anchorage* and in *The Shadow under the Web*, she investigated the sex-based distribution of spaces; especially striking is the wave of disquiet that trickles out from under the veil in *The Shadow under the Web*, the video that she created for the Istanbul Biennial: a simultaneous projection on four walls, a continual racing through various places, squares, empty streets, a veiled shadow that at times comes toward us and at other times flees… "I feel that I have a great deal to say about different cultures, that every so often might appear so strange, so distant, and yet in the end I believe will become a universal whole. There is so much that still needs to be said and which will need to be said. Perhaps interactivity will prove to be a good medium for the delivery of these messages, and above all it can help me to seek out the various possibilities of transmitting and translating these messages, without diminishing their meaning, while still respecting their sense and, what is even more important, allowing them to reach many people, allowing them to be understood at their best." With *Turbulent*, *Rapture*, *Fervor* Shirin Neshat portrayed the structures of oppression that condition the lives of Iranian women. Neshat's work is very complex, and is one that is conducted on the body of Islamic culture, a culture in which the feminine body appears in fragments selected by the Khomeini revolution: the eyes, the hands, the feet… all the rest is *hijjiab*, chador, and a gown

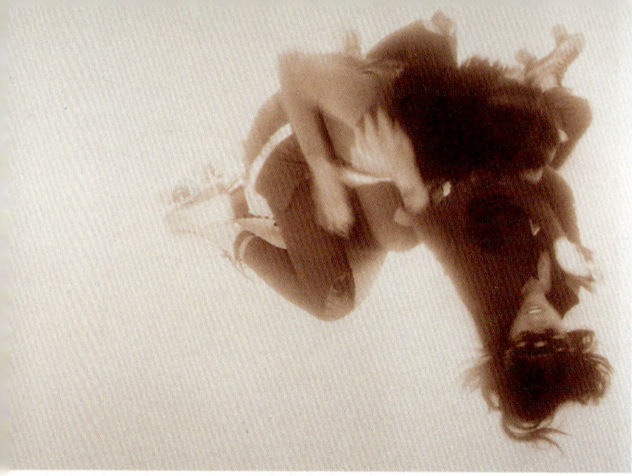

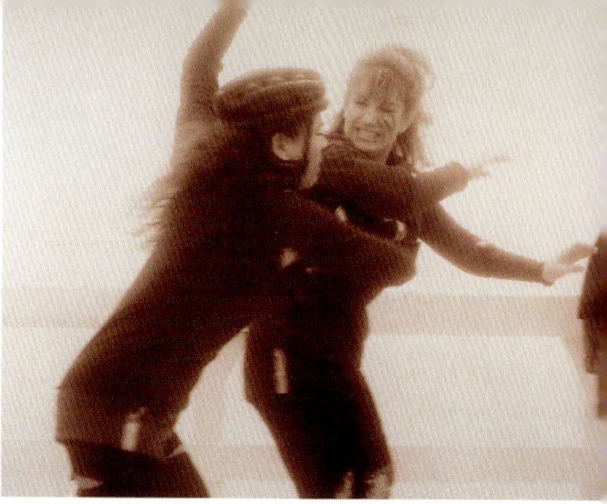

as broad and loose as a mantle conceals and withdraws the body. Garb that is obliged and imposed by social and political norms which trace their ancestry back to the Koran, garb that, if women fail to wear it, brings with it punishment for outraging Islamic morality, with penalties of detention and corporal discipline: either prison, for a sentence ranging from ten days to two months, or alternatively seventy-four blows of the whip.

"Perhaps it is impossible to understand completely my artworks, unless you have the full baggage of both cultures. I try to capture something that can be felt emotionally by someone in order to lead them to a mysterious area, perhaps confused and mysterious, but necessary for any clear presentation of mingled times and cultures that do not mingle, but indeed tend to become extreme when in contact one with another." Shirin Neshat focuses the complex role of women in Islamic culture, including the violence of an invisible and covered body, the spiritualism and the politics of the female martyr that foresee the obligation to participate in the armed forces. The interplay of contrasts is very strong: there is a depiction of the violence of separation, exclusion, prohibitions and discriminations; there is a representation of the tensions and the abuses that have passed in Islamic culture through the body of women, subject to iron-bound social regulation, which thus becomes a political body and the visual point of reference of the development and occurrence of a number of important events, just like the idea of the female body in its militant form, in its transformation into a fighting body. In *Turbulent*, whose central theme is sexuality in Muslim society, we clearly see the marked distinction, which becomes a distinction of social and political worth and weight, between masculine identity and feminine identity, and there emerges a complex plane of repressed feelings: affection, desire and sexuality, and how they can transform themselves into taboos that act negatively upon individuals. Once again Shirin Neshat seems to explore forms of controlled behaviours that enter into conflict. The artist makes use of music as the structural load-bearing element of the video: the male song represents the culture and the positive aspects that it generates, the female singer instead symbolises the exact opposite. In Iran, following the Revolution, women were no longer allowed to appear in public, and there are many cultures that forbid women to sing in public; this also excludes them from mystical rituals, and pushes them to stay far away from contact with the transcendental. In *Turbulent*, after the song of the man, with his numerous and participating audience, the female character, with no audience at all, begins a variegated, polyphonic, involving, cheerful and heart-breaking song: the liberation of

Tracey Moffatt,
Guapa (Goodlooking),
photographic series, 1995

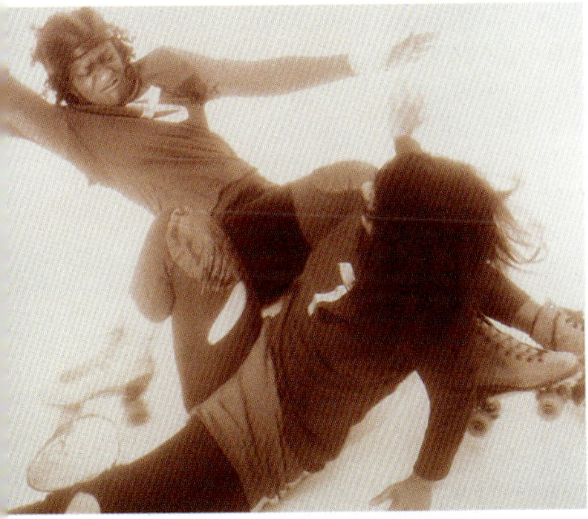

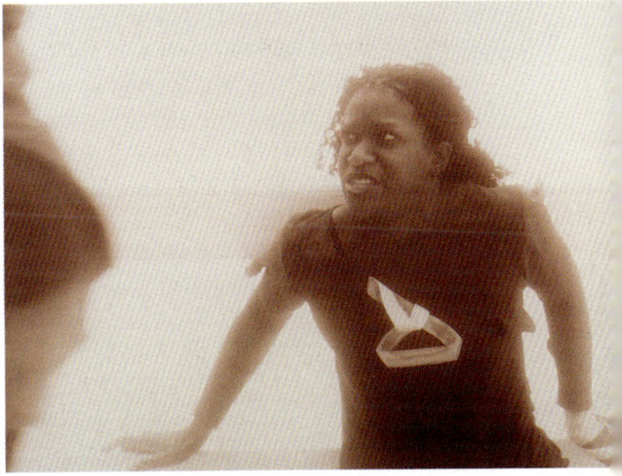

the voice, a repertoire of vocal possibilities that range from song to moaning to screaming, "vocal body" that grew in the obligation of silence and separation.

Shirin Neshat enters and displays one by one the places and the architecture of separation: the public places, the places of worship, the places of friendship, the places of travel, the places of life, and the places of death. *Passage*, 2001, suggested to Shirin Neshat by Philip Glass, places us in a timeless landscape with sharp and clearly defined colours where the sea, the dunes and the long extending horizons serve as framework to yet another separation, the separation between the feminine and the masculine, even in the face of death. A large crowd of men arrive from the horizon transporting a corpse without a coffin which they are accompanying to the land of the dead, and as they move forward they are approached by a group of women covered in chadors, digging a grave with their bare hands; when the body is lowered to the ground, a circle of fire is lit which envelops the entire scene in a suggestive union of air, earth, water and fire, excluding only a little girl who plays with pebbles. Neshat seems to want to affirm, in work after work, that there are more points of contact than points of separation between one culture and another, stressing the differences in roles, the sexual discrimination, the distinctions between acting and immobility, and supporting the reasons for being foreign, a condition that occurs not only in the presence of different cultures, but also within the context of one's own culture, amongst species, amongst individuals, and within one's self. "Artaud used to say: to write for the illiterate — to speak for the aphasic, to think for the acephalic. But what do we mean by 'for'? Not 'in favour of…' nor 'in place of…' It is a question of becoming. A thinker is not acephalic, aphasic or illiterate, but he can become those things. He can become Indian, he does not cease to become it, perhaps because the Indian in turn becomes other, and he escapes his own agony. We think and we write even for animals. We become animals because even the animal becomes other than self. The agony of a mouse or the execution of a calf remain present in our thoughts, not out of piety, but as a zone of exchange between man and animal, in which something of each passes into the other. It is the constituent relationship of philosophy with non-philosophy." (Gilles Deleuze)

The political and military strategy identifies in "other" countries, and especially in poor countries, the chief threats to dominant nations, and it accompanies this thesis with a mass media news production that describes the crises and the dangers of the "outlying areas" as internal problems of those societies. That is how in the general common understanding of the dominant countries, with the encouragement of the majority of the mass media, civil wars, genocides, ethnic cleansing, hunger, fundamentalism, all wind up being attributed to the "barbarianism" typical of "primitive", "backward", "underdeveloped", "pre-technological" peoples. What is entirely hidden is the information needed in order to understand that this kind of strife and disaster is the consequence of the economic and political decisions imposed by the World Bank and the International Monetary Fund in favour of dominant nations, a strategy and a methodology that push public opinion toward the mechanisms and devices intended to lead to the exclusion of foreigners and the necessity for police and military control. Legislation in favour of investment immigration in a number of countries tends to renew the traditional immigration of independent white colonialists: so it is in Canada, Australia, and since 1990, the United States as well.

The being is beginning to be structured in the image of a place that is apparently unable to be experienced physically. We can only describe as a film set the space that Tracey Moffatt, who describes herself as an "image maker", constructs for her photographic images, videos and films. She was born in 1960 in Brisbane (Australia), in exactly the sort of Australian space that she reproduces in her films; Australian by nationality, she chooses to emphasise her mixed cultural roots, which are in part Western and Anglo-Saxon and in part Australian Aborigine. The artworks of Tracey Moffatt aim at the tough subjects — which she often decides to present with great irony — of difference, injustice, misunderstanding, the conflicted history of the Australian policy of assimilation. The capacity of relations between different beings is sunk deep in a sort of other dimension, distant, that glasses over the possibility of impact on the real that seems to consigned to an oneiric dimension. Misunderstandings between generations, social layers, cultural environments and opinions, all seem to run through the works of Tracey Moffatt, immersed in an imaginary context, in an invented world, in a surreal or unreal space, the precarious and false space of theatrical stages and film sets, in which she intervenes with the visual language of documentary photography: two aspects by now necessary to the definition of a media truth, or the space of surfaces. In *The Song Lines*, Bruce Chatwin described the overwhelming and irrepressible impact that a new psychological regime can induce in a culture; the Australian Aborigines perceive their space and their environment through special cognitive rituals: the places are marked by memories of songs. The songs and the dreams define the human path across the territory, they identify the places and the roads. When Western cartographic models were "transported" there and other signs of civilisation were superimposed upon them (cities, railroads, highways), in this environment the mutation was so sudden that the Aboriginal mind had been unable to absorb and elaborate adequately the new universe of signs. Alcoholism and psycho-physical decay are a consequence of such a sudden disruption of the universe, thus causing the devastation of psychological world. Destruction.

In *Up in the Sky* Tracey Moffatt makes clear reference to such post-apocalyptic films as *Mad Max*, to situations that have undergone traumatic and irreversible experiences, as the shock of a transformation imposed from without. *Up in the Sky* is a series of 25 photographs printed on coloured paper, in part steel-blue and in part ochre-yellow, in which it seems that the only form of relationship that is possible is conflict, an exchange of conflicts: two men fighting, three women disassembling an automobile, a white woman with a dark-skinned new-born baby in her arms, a man who is trying to persuade other men of his own ability to transform himself into a dog… Once again the human body is the site of conflict, whether racial, sexual or generational; a menacing body, an inadequate anatomy, an impenetrable physicality. A series of mysterious photographs in a suspended time. The space and time of Tracey Moffatt are always excessively circumstantial to a situation that is incomprehensible but apparently "normal", the representation of convulsions and agitations that, in parallel with the insubstantiality of many contemporary activities, show the eccentric and marginal side of a point of view that expresses reactions and feelings. A sort of testimonial of different ways of conceiving of existence. Over the past two decades the strategies and the decisions of the last two centuries have been rendered visible: irreversible pollution of the atmosphere, earth, seas and rivers, decline in the sources of energy, chronic malaise of the world economy, and the proliferation of a new humanity, type-tested, standardised, depressed, anxious and unstable. And Tracey Moffatt chooses to represent the approach to the everyday of one of the "foreign" cultures that have undergone a systematic and violent aggression on the part of the Western mentality, provoking an existence of solitude and alienation. The theme of the series of photographs, *Scarred for Life*, is physical and psychic violence: dependency, exploitation, desperation, hatred, childhood traumas reproduced in the style of the magazine *Life*, with short comments defining their contexts. In these images, in which the absurd mingles freely with the traumatic, we clearly see the inconsistency and the absurdity of a series of conventions that are transplanted from one culture to another: Moffatt defines a space in which introduces characters that move within the context of hallucinatory situations, situations to which they have evidently fallen victim. These images are projections of mental processes bordering on delirium, at times surreal in their almost total absence of logic, and disturbance is their principal rule: disturbed images that underline disturbed behaviours, which by their simultaneously ordinary and extraordinary nature cannot help but be suffered, linking back to what is commonly known as reality.

In her video *Nice Coloured Girls*, Tracey Moffatt analyses the history of the exploitation of Aboriginal women by white men, and sets the approach of the colonialists with the indigenous women over against the attempts of modern and urban Aboriginal women to overturn this relationship. A condensation of opposite terms, a revolt of the characters, and the harder they try to create a different living condition, the more they reproduce the models to which they were subjected. Again in *Night Cries: A Rural Tragedy*, or else in *Bad Evil*, we see surfacing the memories, the fears, the beliefs and the outlines of an Aboriginal culture devastated and distanced until it vanished on a media horizon that flattens everything and unifies everything: the memories, the complicated blood relationships mediated by the figure of the interpreter, the family hostilities, the silence, the alien status in one's own land. An absurd parallelism between worlds incapable of coexisting, narrated in a surreal manner, as only a history could be whose hinges were gazes and excesses. The series of photographs *Guapa (Goodlooking)* has as its setting a women's roller-skating race; the artist casts girls of various ethnic origins, and the race turns into a new pretext for an account of violence, eroticism, antagonism, racial conflict, in the disturbing and unsettling framework of a surreal atmosphere that is by now a distinctive feature of all of her artworks. With Tracey Moffatt the "foreigner", the "other", is a social product of exclusion, the protagonist of the alienation of the metropolis, it is the incarnation of an unease and a discomfort that show the consequences of processes of marginalisation and extremism of the resistance of outsiders to standardisation.

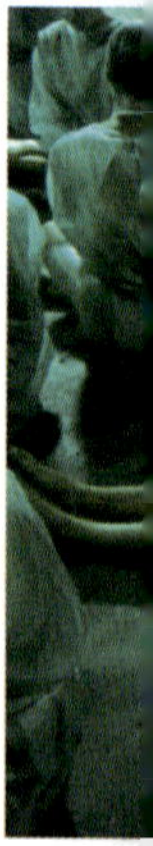

Foreigners to their own existence. "Don't agree. Never, about anything, with anyone. Take things with amazement and curiosity, like an explorer, like an ethnologist. Tire of it, wall in your own faded disagreement, neutralised, in order not to have the right to say it.... Those who have never lost even the slightest root seem to you to be unable to understand a single word capable of relativising their point of view." (Julia Kristeva)

In the conclusion of the first volume of his history of sexuality, Michel Foucault speaks of the paradigmatic passage from the "old right to put to death or allow to live to the power of allowing to live or discarding into death.... The old power of death in which the sovereign power was symbolised is now carefully covered over by the administration of bodies and the calculating management of life. A rapid development over the course of the classical age of the various disciplines — schools, colleges, barracks, workshops; the emergence, as well, in the field of political practices and economical observations, of the problems of childbirth, longevity, public health, habitat and migration; and the consequential explosion of various and numerous techniques for obtaining the subordination of bodies and the control of populations. This leads therefore to the beginning of an era of 'biopower'".

Sukran Moral is a Turkish artist, and for the past few years she has been "in transit" in Rome. She places prejudice, the precarious state of being a nomad, "expelled", at the centre of her artwork; she creates situations and actions in which she tests her spectators, she studies their reactions, their behaviour, their thinking, and various cultural gaps ... "In 1994 I was expelled from Italy and I was obliged to invent an ironic and transgressive performance about my own dramatic personal situation, *Marriage with Three*, since at that time in order to keep from being expelled the only solution was to get married. And so I developed a performance that would stage a male fantasy: the desire to create a harem. In Islam this fantasy is permitted, while in the West officially one is allowed only to have a single wife, while secretly men have many lovers. With this performance I made ironic observations about both Islam and the West. From this point of view,

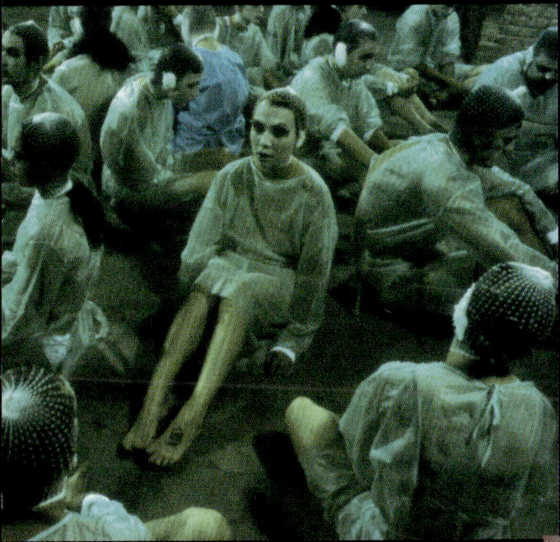

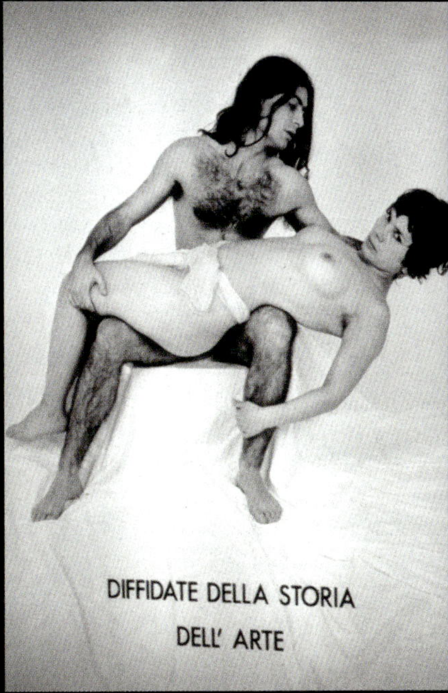

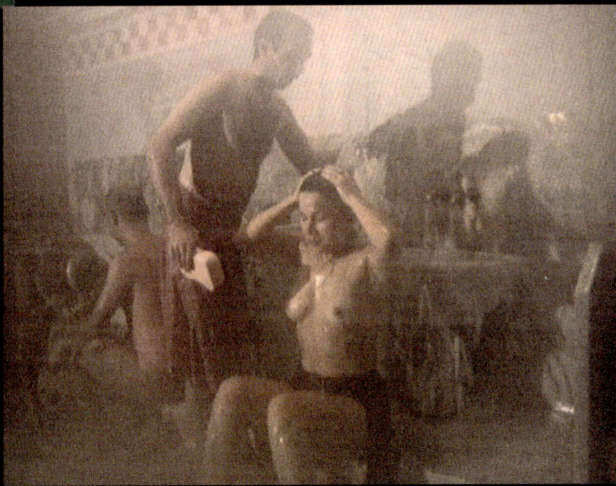

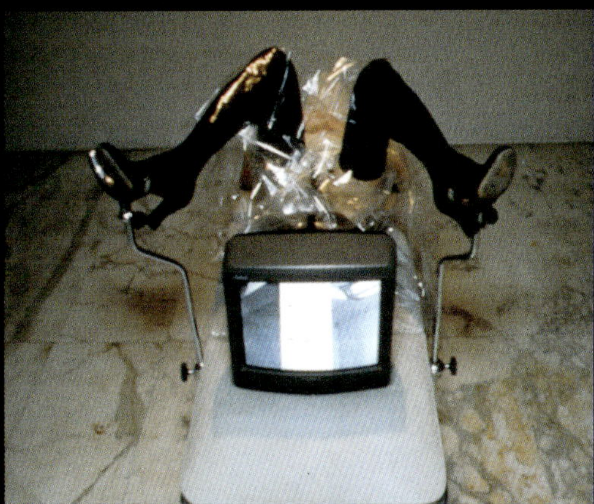

Sukran Moral,
Dolore, Murazzi del Po, Turin, 1999

Sukran Moral
Diffidate della storia dell'arte, 1995

Sukran Moral, *Hamam*,
video-installation, Istanbul,
1997

Sukran Moral,
Speculum. Diffidate della storia dell'arte,
1997

my work, in general, can be considered as a form of protest, even if for me it is a way of living." Sukran Moral operates on a plane of awareness that chooses to highlight the miserable functionality of a system that bases its rules and its norms upon temporary and discriminatory conventions. Dating from 1995 is *Don't Place Your Trust in the History of Art*, a performance that "accuses" Western art history of never contemplating the art of other cultures and civilisations, except as decoration, something exotic, naïve, a medicine against boredom. That same year she made a flag of the European community upon which she wrote in Turkish: "European Culture is Racist". This is history written by the winners, the identification of the difference between a "white" attitude, culturally more homogeneous, and another attitude, more heterogeneous, mestizo, impure. "I think that nowadays we should be especially careful and wary of cultural colonialism. Art is one of the sites of fundamentalism, all you need to do is look at all the most important biennials, events, and art market/fairs in the world. Contemporary art, in my opinion, is operated entirely by white chauvinist men, and often the women who achieve success in the art business do so only because they represent exactly the codes of convention, while pretending to criticise them." Sukran Moral identifies the obvious, racist and hierarchical categories upon which discrimination against foreigners is based, the clichés, the age-old fears, the oppositions between East and West, South and North, masculine and feminine; she undertakes an operation of substitution, a violent critique of Western culture, which annuls or systematically ignores other visions of the world or of various worlds. A process of redefinition of identity that passes through the political, economic, and cultural body.

"Everything is political and nothing is political. Even love. In one artwork, done in video, I wept in front of the videocamera. For me, that was a political act and at the same time a personal, intimate act." Sukran Moral is an artist who made the decision to live in a country other than her own, and in so doing, in living in this foreign country, chose to enter into contact with another mentality in order to give origin to an exceedingly stimulating culture, to begin over again from the very beginning in order to understand her own roots and herself from a distance, in the contact with a new culture. In her artwork, *Speculum*, Sukran Moral shows a woman on a gynecological examination table with a monitor between her legs: the monitor is identified as the woman's vagina and it replaces that vagina. A vagina-monitor that becomes a screen of awareness; the position is the same as always, the representation of the passivity of women and the voyeurism of society, all the same the spectators no longer see a passive object and subject, but a critical subject that obliges them to look at something they would prefer not to see. In place of the image that Western art has always reproduced of the feminine — a woman, the woman of art history, depicted as a saint, a mother or a goddess — Sukran Moral has offered the critique of the male chauvinist codes of the history of art, and at the same time, unmasked them. "In our society, anthropological behaviour has never developed in parallel with technological advances. There has always been a gap between humanity and science. The discomfort that emerges from this fact creates relationship problems." The artworks done for the Istanbul Biennial are a series of dislocations of both identity and diversity: Sukran enters a bordello, an insane asylum, a morgue, a Turkish bath, and as an extraneous body she shows a hidden and non-touristy reality. The exotic nature of package tours is replaced by the discomfort of life and relationships, outside of the mediocre thinking that has transformed the planet into a catalogue for a low-cost travel agency. The videos used in her performances were shot in the marginal areas at the outskirts of the city: the morgue, the insane asylum, the bordello; she also wanted to do some filming in the prison, but the Ministry of Justice refused to give its permission. "In my work I have intentionally allowed myself to be influenced by the place, the moment, and pure chance. The street where I shot the bordello scene is very famous and legally recognised. It is a sort of Vatican City, a city inside the city. In order to get permission, I really had to work, at the commissariat they did everything they could to discourage me and, in the end, they gave me authorisation, but I had to go in with a police escort. As soon as they saw the videocamera, everybody started running and they started shouting at me and attacking the policeman. I succeeded in persuading only one prostitute not only to allow me to do my performance in her house, but even to teach me tricks of the trade!... I found a number of similarities between bordello and a museum, in fact, I hung a sign on the door that read: 'Museum of Contemporary Art', and in my hand I held a little sign reading 'for sale'. The audience of prostitutes resembled the art audience in many ways. In this work, there is irony but no detachment. And that is intentional. I am not an Anglo-Saxon artist. I am very Mediterranean."

In *Hamam*, the performance and the video created in a men's Turkish bath, the historic site of the separation of the sexes, Sukran Moral undertakes a symbolic reversal: the creation of a harem of men. She critiques the homosexual and male-chauvinist fantasies linked to this traditional place through a cinematic view and a rendering that chooses a sensual and exotic pictorialism; the only woman in a place that has always been inhabited and experienced only by men, she abandons herself to the moisture and the intimacy, she allows herself to be washed, she talks, she eats fruit, she drinks wine, she makes toasts, and slowly the scene becomes increasingly irritating, increasingly claustrophobic, an exasperated attack upon the habits of men who choose separate places in order to allow themselves to regress to childhood, allowing themselves to be washed, massaged, cradled and rocked, manipulated, far from the "foreign eyes" of the opposite sex.

Foreigners, in their native towns, in the places that they chose, foreigners to themselves, guests that perhaps will remain extraneous to the society that accommodates them, unsettling in their decision to remain, to share the social spaces of "others", tolerated only in transit, confined in their otherness, identified as "other". The toleration extends to all those figures that cut only episodically into the surface of the societies that house them: travellers, sailors, diplomats, political exiles, and above all, tourists, figures that will return sooner or later to their original condition and who will circulate harmlessly and, basically, invisibly. Different, however, is the position of those who decide to stay, those who contaminate and cut with their mere presence a compact fabric of rules and certainties, those who demand recognition. Mobile beings, who easily cross boundaries, who still represent scandal, not in their declared diversity, toward which it is possible to maintain a cognitive, cultural and juridical distance, but in their mimetic capacity to mix in, which takes the form of one of the most evident metamorphoses undertaken by Western societies: the transformation of the foreigner into an enemy.

We continue to remake history, but inversely it is history that continues to be made by each of us, upon his or her body. What character would you have wanted to be, in what era would you have wanted to live? And if instead you had been a plant or a landscape? And yet, all this, you are it already, only that you trick yourself in your answer.
Gilles Deleuze

CONFUSED
Madmen, Animals, Criminals

A subterranean and silent language, a radical character, a borderline function.

The impossibility of a mediation; the extreme experience of the body chooses a form of action that becomes a declaration of existence; lives that choose direct contact with the open discussion of self and the world in which we live. The term transgression is applied to the necessity of a human condition that manifests itself, which causes a change from the surfaces of apparent normality. Imprisonment is the introduction into a closed system, a prison, a orphanage, an insane asylum, a hospice, a boarding school, a monastery, the room of a house. A system of offence and separation in which social interaction is impeded and in which the imprisoned subject is obedient to a power. "Perhaps, one day, we will no longer know exactly what madness could be.... Artaud will belong to the foundation of our language, and no longer be considered a renegade; neurosis will be one of the constituent forms (and no longer a deviation) in our society. All the things that we now feel about the modality of the limit, or the estranged, or the intolerable, will have attained the serenity of the positive. And what now for us designates this External may truly one day designate us, yes us", writes Michel Foucault in his *History of Madness*, a prophecy that is already beginning to come true. Estrangement, a constant interdiction, invisible, silent, which pervades bodies and days. There is an attempt to unify, and what cannot be rendered homologous is imprisoned, languages are rendered uniform, along with the desires and the forms of knowledge, minds and needs are instigated toward the useless, the superfluous, the insubstantial — the horizon is the shiny and pervasive line of new life styles, the promise of new oases of protected reserves of luxury — new strategies of appearance are explored, and so we trigger the mechanisms of anxiety, panic, unhappiness, inadequacy, and we amplify the difficulties of living.

Madness, "reason in flames", "truth stripped bare", the scream, flight, escape, more powerful than any reason, than any law, than any threat. There is no place of emergency in which to extinguish, normalise, treat, reintegrate, no border equipment. Once again Foucault: "I know that one thing will survive, and that is the relationship between man and his ghosts, his impossibility, his bodiless pain, his carcass during the night; and I know that, once the pathological is placed outside of the circuit, the obscure affiliation of man with madness will be the ageless memory of an evil cancelled in its form of disease, but irreducible as grief.... Being lost, and forever, this is the relationship with madness..."

And the body becomes the boundary that determines an intricate and complex route, a cultural flow that is transformed according to the historical and cultural context in which it fits, in symbiosis with the environment in which one lives.

Technological acceleration, beginning in the second half of the nineteenth century, has led to a definitive unhinging of that mechanistic vision of a body composed of a "stable assembly of movable parts", unhinging of that model of the body, closed and clearly delimited, Cartesian in inspiration, which could be analysed and known only through the dissection of cadavers. And borders yield. Beginning with the avant-garde, we find ourselves face to face with the visualisation of a crisis of identity, a universe in which the individual is increasingly estranged and functional. As early as the first few years of the twentieth century, the image of the body, in artistic, philosophical, psychoanalytical and scientific experiences, begins to crumble, to con-found itself with that which is other than itself.

With German Expressionism there began to emerge a type of representation of the human figure by now tending toward disarticulation, violent expression, the breakdown of the ego in chromatic forms and traces which transmit tension and imbalance.

The body that is not afraid to show itself in all of its otherness is the body upon which the meanings of the social discourse tend to condense, all that which we are as a cultural organism, and how codes, norms, fears and desires are interjected. The body of Edvard Munch is a monstrous body, which frightens, fascinates, causes repulsion and attracts, the body of anguish and pain, the misplaced body that flees the bounds fixed by the programmes of social organisation, a body that threatens the symbolic order upon which the security of relations is based. Munch's idea of the human seems to elude that which is customarily presented as "necessary discomfort", it is a being that rebels, that screams, that shows the forbidden — disease, difference, anguish and death — and obliges the spectator to a confrontation that cannot help but be avowedly conflictual.

From the monstrous body of Munch it is impossible to turn one's gaze away, it is a presence that lures the spectator in a duel to the last drop of blood in which the ante is the possibility of a reflection of an identity-driven, individual and collective matrix. Munch's being refuses to allow the flame of life to go out too soon, he chooses elsewhere, the visible otherness that flees role playing; he reveals an autonomous and liberated pulsation, in madness and diversity, in the gaze that has the power to intercept the diseased cells of prejudice and cause them to emerge. The universe in which Munch places us is a disturbed universe in which the body looms, in which it mercilessly reveals the arbitrariness of the structures of a system that does not call for individuals unless they are functional to the system itself. Munch names otherness, he fabricates a discarded identity, an identity that becomes a nightmare and a metaphor. Munch's monstrous body is an uncertain, ambiguous body, a boundary body. Munch intuits and reveals the functional mechanism of a system that has built its foundations on the idea of normality, and he opposes the deviant force of its living expression, a rebellious human condition that by attrition attempts to erode the stagnant system of oppositions. Munch's individual without qualities and without destiny is a ghost, a threshold, boundary creature, a hybrid, monstrous, a creature of metamorphosis without path, unpredictable in its outcomes, which announces and exalts its difference, the tragic experience, an irredeemably mutilated subject, wounded, crippled.

Munch's being is not simply aware of having been deprived of liberty, but it is chiefly conscious of its own forced submission to methodical programmes of psychological destruction. It is the end of a figuration in which it is still possible to identify the boundary between that which is body and which is not, it is the danger of disassembly/expansion to which the human figure is subjected, in which the points of view are multiplied in order to hold together a single exasperated vision in which the gaze is lost. Munch eliminates, by twisting them into unrecognisability, the boundaries between the exterior and the interior: bodies open up, new dimensions of their sensibility take form — unknown mental universes, the exterior loses its own compactness, seems to liquefy, melt, become molten, and a figuration is engendered in which what is considered interior, part of one's own self, is catapulted to the exterior of one's body and projected well beyond a limit that no longer exists. Munch's individual seems to undergo a twisting, an irreversible transformation, a painful and metamorphic torsion of the entire psycho-physiological unit, the body in conflict with itself as a whole. What is the threshold beyond which the torsion becomes intolerable? Apathy, passivity, lack of initiative, regression, dependency?

The Scream is the painting that more than any other characterises Munch's artistic identity: a creature with its hands on its head breaks into a desolate howl, tragic, unheard. A mute and total shout, hurtling past any known language, the cry and the desperation of an imprisoned individual, detained in its anguish, on the threshold where control breaks down. A break that occurs on the border of a cultural code that is suddenly perceived in all its devastating violence. This is the moment in which every cell explodes, screaming with pain,

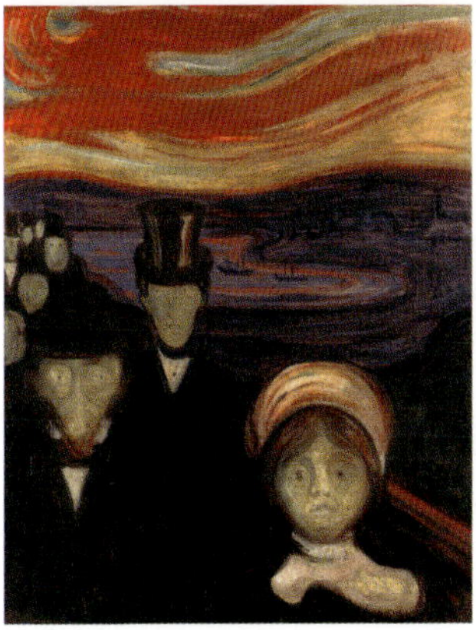

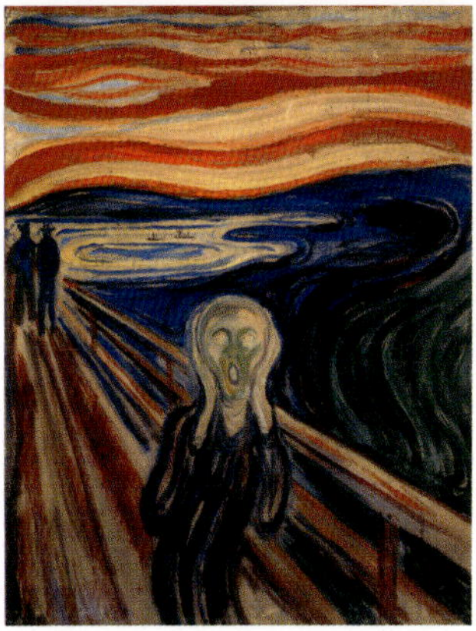

Edvard Munch, *Anguish*, 1894

Edvard Munch, *The Scream*, 1893

and emerges through the vehicle of a metamorphosis. The individual depicted by Munch acts against an invisible wall that attempts to segregate it into a "common ground" of the discourse, excluding it from the interplay of relations. It is a monstrous, unqualified, separate individual, the individual depicted by Munch, the victim of a cruel spiral, an individual that seems to hurl out the need to "open all of the prisons of being in order to afford humanity every possible future…" (Gaston Bachelard).

For centuries the visible face of transgression has been madness, classical portraits of suffering, hospitals, the psychic and physical discomfort of being in the world, a complete detachment from that which is temporal and contemporary with the idea of an agonising existence. The face of the individual disappears against the background of a deformed existence, a punitive reality; the body of the madman becomes a disquieting conscience, and management of it becomes the political response that invents and realises new forms of violence and control. A suffering man is a danger, a social disturbance, he is transformed into the body of madness and transcends his social identity: "…these men who believe they are kings, or that they are made out of glass… is their madness more intermittent than dreams?" (Michel Foucault). And so madness, melancholy and delirium become the materials of art, language and delirium intertwine, madness belongs to artwork as well as to dreams; there is no exchange with language, there is no relationship with the reasons of the world, there is no way to agree. And madness becomes the break with an artwork; again, Foucault: "This does not mean that madness is the only common language of artworks and the modern world (dangers of the pathos of curses, inverse and symmetrical danger of psychoanalysis); it means instead that, with madness, an artwork that seems to penetrate and plunge into the world, revealing the world's senselessness and transfiguring itself in the mere features of the pathological, in the end involves the time of the world, dominating it and leading it. Because of the madness that interrupts it, an artwork opens a void, a time of silence; a question without answer provokes a laceration without healing in which the world is obliged to interrogate itself. By now, and with the mediation of madness, it is the world that becomes guilty (for the first time in the West) with respect to the artwork; behold it being reclaimed from that artwork, obliged to conform to its language, constrained to recognition and reparation, to acknowledge the reason of this unreason and to this unreason. The madness in which the artwork plunges is the space of our work, it is the endless road to making sense of it, it is our vocation, whether of apostles or of exegetes.... There is no madness that is not a supreme instant of the artwork, and the artwork rejects it indefinitely, pushing it to the furthest borders; where there is artwork there is no madness, and all the same the madness is simultaneous with the artwork because it inaugurates the time of its truth. The instant in which the artwork and the madness are born and are completed together is the beginning of the time in which the world finds itself called to judgement by this artwork and guilty of that which is before it".

But increasingly the world rejects the call to judgement, for all the bodies tortured, raped, wounded, humiliate, for all the minds alienated, warded off, emptied out, for all of the passivity imposed through isolation, the limitation of movements, the expropriation of the possibility to decide, the obsessive control, the psycho-pharmaceutical drugs administered... for all of the individuals that become altered subjects in the experience of relationships and in the techniques of the body. What is the threshold that separates arm-twisting from torture? A form of estrangement always tries to dislocate, increasingly, the imagination outside of the body, and outside of the body it projects dreams, desires and life itself.

An original and parallel universe without censorship, a sort of foreseeing that opposes another scene to reality; the world seems to submit, in the arrival of the inauthentic, to a sort of alteration, through which it appears, every so often, that the authentic world shines through. "It is only as an aesthetic phenomenon that existence and the world appear justified", writes Friedrich Nietzsche. There are artworks that take into account an indissoluble interweaving of the authentic and the inauthentic, a series of alternate worlds. There are realities that exist behind realities that do not exist. Another reality, invisible and otherwise unknown, underpins the visible reality and determines its existence; reality is variously steeped in things that are not real, simulations that are more-or-less successful. We therefore describe a sort of "spotted" reality that bases its madness on the persistence in Western society of the technologies of warfare and the media.

"We almost always live through screens: a screened existence. And at times I think, when people say that my work seems violent, that perhaps from time to time I have actually succeeded in washing away one or two layers of the screen", wrote Francis Bacon. Born in Dublin in 1909 he then moved to London in 1925; after 1945, Bacon subjected his painting to an aggressive and rebellious deformation, inserting figurative representation into the context of an informal and gestural torsion. He became the proponent of an artistic tension that attempts to be an existential denunciation, a screen of reflection upon a condition, the human condition, propelled by this point into the abyss of nervous breakdown. Bacon undertook a systematic desacralisation of the image, choosing a deviant gestural dimension, perceived as a rebellious necessity for escape from the limitations of rationality; he chose a traumatic, disturbing, aggressive representation as denunciation, allowing a glimpse of the image of defeat, of contemporary barbarianism, the image of a man slowly but systematically driven to annihilation, to a lack of will.

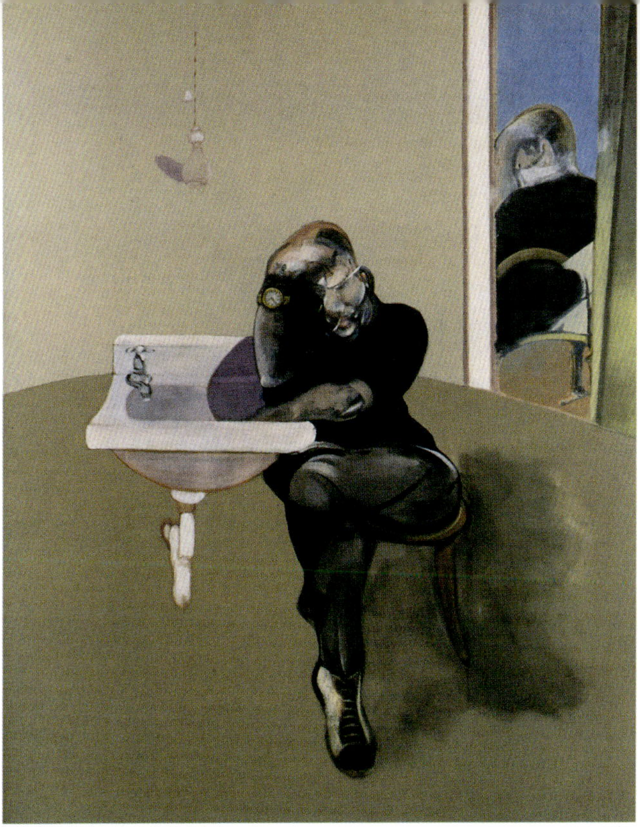

Francis Bacon,
Self-portrait,
1973

You'd be bored!
Birth, and copulation, and death.
That's all the facts when you come to brass tacks:
Birth, and copulation, and death.
I've been born, and once is enough.
You don't remember, but I remember,
Once is enough.
(Thomas Stearns Eliot)

All of Bacon's artwork is focused on the human figure, it seems to want to display the structure of existential desperation, alteration, the psychological abyss. "We constantly persecute ourselves. Freud rendered us aware of this part of our being, independent of the fact that his ideas are therapeutic or not": Bacon used to read Freud's clinical cases as if they were x-rays of a more widespread condition, anatomies of a separate, double, anguished form of existence, an existence that in reality was taking place within codified norms and rules but from which emerged the paralysis and the nightmares and the impossibility of one's own existence. Desperation is the condition of the figures painted by Bacon, figures that are broken, bent, contorted and alienated: an existential extreme that transforms a desperate being into a foreigner in the eyes of convention. "Camus wrote that it is one thing to have no hopes, and another thing to be desperate. Weighing horror does not mean transpiring sadness. If anything, it improves your defences";

Bacon chooses to represent a civilisation that suffers from nervous exhaustion, which has accepted its own condition of impotence, which has transformed sensations into painful wounds without a hope of healing. Bacon's artworks seem to suck the spectator right into their interior, seem to need to engulf living bodies into a centrifugal space, the very space of paranoia, neurosis, schizophrenia, of madness without literature. Alienation and discomfort and a lack of points of reference characterise the human figure as painted by Bacon: "Rescuing the figure from the figurative… The figure is nothing other than the perceptible form referred to sensation; the sensation acts directly upon the nervous system, which is made of flesh…. Colour is in the body, sensation is in the body, not in the air. Sensation is what is painted. That which is painted on the canvas is the body, not inasmuch as something represented as an object, but rather as the subject of that particular sensation", writes Gilles Deleuze in his essay dedicated to the Dublin-born artist. Bacon's deformed body seeks a relationship with present-day life, and winds up becoming a design of total subversion of lived experience. Bacon does not try to rehabilitate the discomfort of living, on the contrary, his images feed the regressive and psychotic aspects of the society of the spectacle and market. He undertakes a sort of refusal to enter into conflict with society, he rebels against a media-driven vision of the real and reproduces the general alienation of a society that is increasingly impenetrable to the desire for change and in which the struggle for survival has become an impotence to live, passivity, anguish, and in the best of cases, boredom. Bacon presupposes a condition of art in which individuals can mirror themselves, artworks that become an appeal to the fragmentation of that identity destined to fail, artworks that are ranked against the aestheticisation that is produced by the very civilisation of the spectacle and market, artworks that oppose the emancipation of the sensibility against the control of emotions. Bodies not predicted by the abstraction of statistics, bodies undone, shattered, emaciated, brutalised: "A shattered face is more beautiful than a relaxed face because it also reveals its internal organs, the blood, the tendons. I have always maintained that realistic painters are not that realistic in portraying the body, only in portraying the body's skin". Bacon intuits the necessity of a reconfiguration of the human body, a deformed body, elongated, flat, stretched, the body in close relation to the structure that contains it, which seems to grip it within it, which seems to clearly show the claustrophobia and the asphyxiation into which the body is forced by deformation. Mirrors, umbrellas, sinks, chairs, floors, walls, ceilings…. the bodies of Bacon seem to pass through matter, they seem to annul themselves in the material of reality, a body under constant strain, a physical, mental, sensory, emotional, imaginative strain… a body that seems, in its very dissipation, to liquefy the certainty of rational structures that explode into a disquieting and uncontrolled presence. The figures of Bacon undergo a torsion that forces the structure to roll itself up into completely collapsed worlds and psyches, they change their semblance and subjectivity becomes subjection.

Bacon's vision determines a zone of impact into which the spectator plunges, a configuration from within of structural cages that exert an exasperating and sophisticated control, straining to prevent every vital emergence; there emerge obsessions, neuroses, nightmares, panic, altered states and oneiric projections.

The human body has become the site of disturbances that the human mind and psyche are obliged to undergo, a body definitively colonised, occupied, a

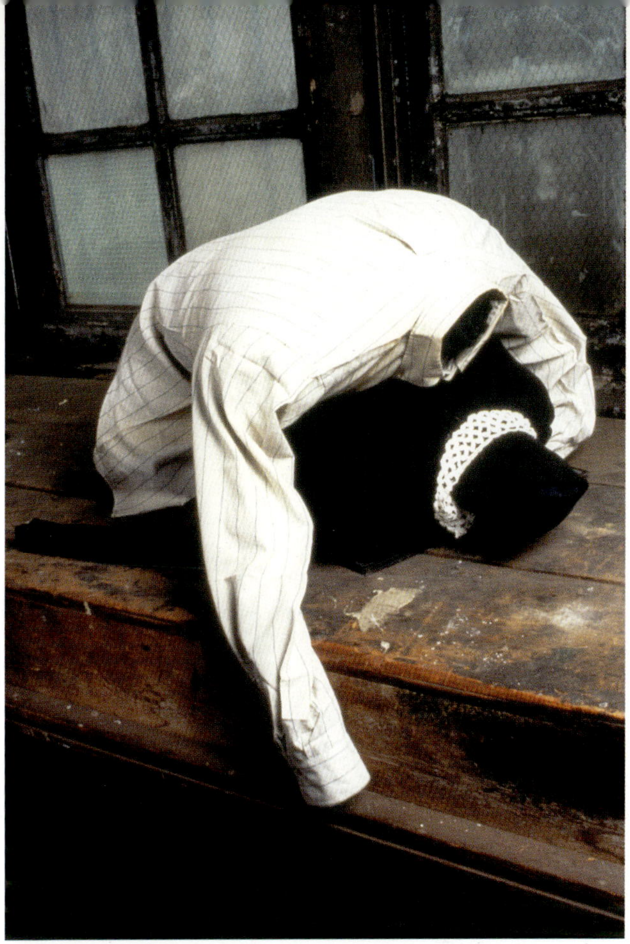

Louise Bourgeois,
Couple, 1996

body deprived of power. “In the impossibility of withdrawing from our natural biosphere, we are preparing, as has happened so many times in the past, to colonise an infinitely more accessible planet, that of a body-without-soul, a profaned body, for a science without conscience that has not stopped profaning the space of the body of the animal, the slave, or the colonised.” (Paul Virilio) Training of conditioned reflexes, uni-formed bodies, destabilisation, occupation on the part of the media-driven universe of the nervous system, modification of the conceptual and perceptual faculties, alteration of the sensory sphere, necessity of prosthetics: an organism by now entirely occupied, existences linked to physiology, frustration that is born of passivity.

And there is a primitive gait to be observed in the body that is subjected to alteration against its will, attempting to extricate itself from the technological domination in order to recover, carved out of its own skin, a shred of self-perception.

Body as prisoner of a social system whose structure it accepts and suffers, the forced implantation of a technology of production that forcibly distances it, to an increasingly great degree, from any sort of human relationship. A being that no longer incarnates the interpersonal exchange and that hijacks the phys-

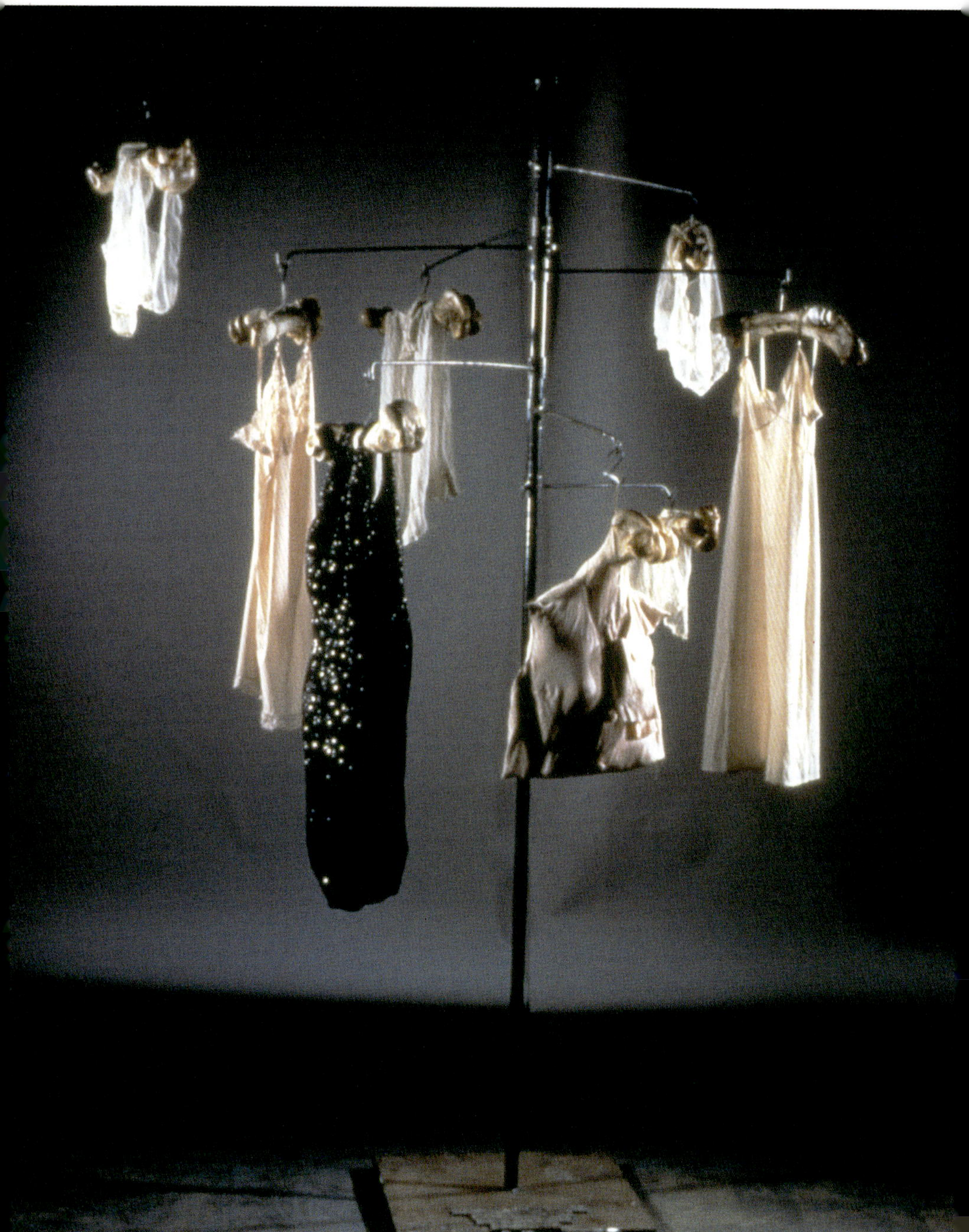

Louise Bourgeois,
Untitled, 1994

ical experience into alteration, counterfeiting, a general drift. A last, desperate attempt to make do, which drives us to reconstruct our own ego from the point of view of the body, aesthetics, and individual psychology, at the expense of the general collective psychology, decomposed in a system of relations that is by now excessively polluted.

"The theme of pain is what I work on. Giving form and meaning to frustration and suffering. What happens to my body must take on an abstract formal configuration. And so you might say that pain is the redemption of formalism. The existence of pain cannot be denied. I offer neither excuses nor solutions... I know that there is nothing I can do to eliminate or suppress it. I cannot make pain disappear; it will be with us always. The *Cells* represent different types of pain: physical pain, emotional pain and psychological pain, mental and intellectual pain. Each *Cell* speaks of fear. Fear is pain: often it is not perceived as pain, because it always disguises itself", states Louise Bourgeois. Her artworks extend throughout the territories of alienation, anxiety, sex, fear and death; but the body, in reality, is her obsession, "pieces" of bodies, isolated and concentrated. Dense with emotional and physical content are the fragments that are found inside the *Cells*, the separate and distanced space that becomes the fixity of maps, the invariability of the place, the stereotype of perspective, but also the biological cell, the cells of bees. The *Cells* by Louise Bourgeois are the metaphor of territories of individuality, of the zones of alliance, of the psychic and physical places in which individual memories and emotions are filtered and preserved. In the artworks of Louise Bourgeois there is a constant duality between interior and exterior (between the thinking body and the exhibited body, erotic, complacent and self-involved), between pleasure and pain: some of her works seem to indicate the power of the mind and the emotions over the body. The worlds that she has represented belong only to the places of her memory, and activate and give life to a sort of "organic memory": the body as an extension of the mind, as a representation of a mental state linked to a memory. The body for Louise Bourgeois is simultaneously a closure and an opening: it creates situations in which it is necessary to touch in order to see, touch, caress, graze, not rip to shreds, dismember, destroy. The body for Louise Bourgeois is above all extension, exposure; she reconstructs settings in which fragments of bodies appear, hands joined together, ears in waiting, eyes with needles, a dangling heart, elements of a powerfully claustrophobic environment in which the body appears in fragments, pieces, missing parts. *Arch of Hysteria*, a contemporary deposition, without any mother supporting the body, a luminous hanging body, suspended, decapitated... There is no body except for the body of a dismemberment that cannot manage to find unity. A powerfully explicit language: tears, seminal fluid, sweat, urine, saliva, vomit: the organic liquids "are the representation of emotions, of the mechanism of instability. When a muscle relaxes and tension drops, a liquid is secreted. The internal emotions physically become liquids, secretions of a precious substance". Pain cannot be conquered, and it is necessary that it be shown in order to make visible the emotions that become power. "Our emotions can break us as if were crackers", and Louise Bourgeois confers a physicality to fears, to states of mind, to that which, through the body, transits and lives under the form of sensation, the immaterial emotion becomes visible in the reactions of the body, and becomes a bodily evidence. The body of hatred, loneliness, pleasure and suffering... the body of Louise Bourgeois is the body of trauma, of an enclosed, full, immanent world, a world in itself. Artworks as anthropomorphic figures, made of bronze, resin, iron and cloth. *Couple, Single III*, cloth bodies held together by external stitches, sutures that seem to demonstrate the urgency and the necessity of repairs to the self

Cell (Clothes) is a circular room formed by wooden doors and windows painted white, set one next to the other as a sort of partition; clothing and stocking hanging on thin iron rods, black or white, a stool. On the back of one of the light-coloured items of clothing is stitched an entire phrase, "THE COLD OF ANXIETY IS VERY REAL". "'To hang up' is a very important act because it allows things to change their location, it is an act without escape, it changes the hierarchy of the artwork; the foundation disappears." Again memories of childhood: each of Bourgeois's cells has to do with memory, they are all strongly characterised by an atmosphere charged with signs of the past, the clothing is all vintage, a sort of autobiography narrated by objects, by clothing, by accessories of one's own past existence: "... our life, from birth to death, is a single thread. Thread of life, thread of water, thread of thought. Turn and turn, a single thread, turn by turn". In *Red Rooms (Child)* she inserts in the circular partition structure of wooden doors hanging spools of thread, lacquered red, glass anthropomorphic limbs, also lacquered red, an oil lamp, old suitcases. "Red is the colour of blood red is the colour of pain red is the colour of violence red is the colour of fear red is the colour of jealousy red is the colour of resentment red is the colour of obsession red is the colour of criticism." In the series *Untitled*, from the end of the 1990s, Bourgeois makes use of her own clothing, hung up together with fragments of body, bones, little faceless rag dolls. The wardrobe seems to become the cartography of her existence: the armoire, with its contents, becomes a sort of memory of her changes. "The form of clothing is a metaphor with which to proceed and change life day by day. It is possible to narrate one's life and recall life through the forms, weight, colours and aroma of those pieces of clothing in the armoire.... When the artwork is finished and the exorcism is complete, I feel much better, I feel relieved and I tend to abandon the subject and move on to a new one.... My regret is that art is moving toward entertainment." In a note to the *Prolegomena*, Kant writes that the self is without substance and without concept, that it is "only the feeling of an existence"; with Louise Bourgeois we sense that it is not in terms of "incarnation" that we should think of the body, but that we define a body that becomes the unity of a being outside of itself. The body exposed: we cannot reach the body except from without, an exterior quality that can be touched. The body is always outside of its own intimacy, the self is nothing other than the singularity of a touch.

> *Sitting together in candlelight, those brain surgeons, university professors and financiers displayed all the capacity for intrigue and self-preservation that they had developed in years and years of careers in industry, business and university.... Finally a new order emerged, whereby all the life of the skyscraper revolved around three obsessions: security, food and sex.*
> *(J.G. Ballard,* High-Rise*)*

An extenuating mechanism of the mutation of the senses, of pain, pleasure, play and perversion, human semblances that are reflected upon bodies bombarded by intolerance, prejudices, preconceptions, mistrust, re-education and rehabilitation. "I think that we are becoming more creative with our bodies, but that at the same time the body is less and less the home of the soul, and much more its façade. It is a place less dedicated to the expression of yourself and more involved in the alteration of the self. For that reason the body today has less and less to do with our own real identity"; Janieta Eyre chooses to depict not bodies but "doppelgangers", she herself photographed and duplicated, images in which it is impossible to distinguish the difference between the "original" body and the "body double", between a real body and its clone, between body and identity. A yielding, a nervous collapse, an alteration in the locking and sliding interplay of the mind: Janieta Eyre creates images in which there exists the possibility of having two original bodies for a single individual. "For me identity is something that belongs to every other person. It is something that I find in the expression of their mouth, or in their way of looking at me. My identity in reality is of no interest to me, especially because I consider my body to be a disguise." As if in a manual of schizophrenic origin, Janieta Eyre transfers her identity into a series of subjects outside of herself, subjects for whom she creates a substrate of life that remains obscure, as in dreams charged with metaphors and symbols; she designs and creates images in which the protagonist is the possibility of constructing other lives, an existence determined by a series of accidents and banal events in which is buried the key to their destiny of madness. Everyday objects, such as crockery, cutlery, sheets and pillow cases, furniture, all trace the horizon of an imaginative delirium in which the artist seems to want to remember that photographs always have something to do with death: "I think of each of my images as a sort of burial. And so I give value to things the way that the Egyptians, for instance, might have buried things together with their mummies. Objects that would be useful in the afterlife, such as pans or cutlery". The "imaginary lives" of Janieta Eyre appear as a cosmetic symptom of an existence spent in a delirium, fragments of an alienation that intertwines timidity and intimidation, subjects victim to a great variety of phenomena, different one from another, in which all sorts of relationships yield, except that in which madness overlies the delirium of a bargain with reality. A sophisticated and suffocating horizon of schizophrenia appears in the images of the existential double of Janieta Eyre, a self-aware and refined propensity for the fake, for the reinvention of reality, the manipulation of identity, the construction of the crisis of meaning that breaks the relationship between the image and the real, a reappropriation of the psychoses that transgress the frontiers of the processes of normalisation underway in reality.

The body represented by Janieta Eyre is a body that is at once self-expressive and self-altered, a continual exchange of identities, a human interplay between copy and original, between positive and negative, an almost maniacal methodology that intervenes with a form of disguise, with a dream dimension. The work of Janieta Eyre continually clashes with the concept of biography: her artworks are anti-biographical artworks, they prefer transmigration, the tending from one form to another, a fluctuating identity that is quite similar to child's play or the unmanageable delirium of schizophrenia; the very costume alludes to a possible and perfect world, but at the same time this further possibility is frightening, and can be definitive... Far from the idea of a further biography, Janieta

Janieta Eyre,
What My Mother Left Me (Incarnation # 41),
1995

Janieta Eyre,
Clones,
1999

Janieta Eyre,
Sindone Recipe for Turin Shroud (Incarnation # 22), 1995

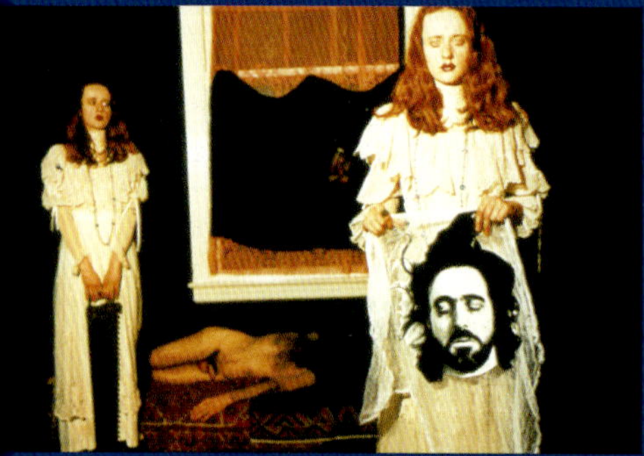

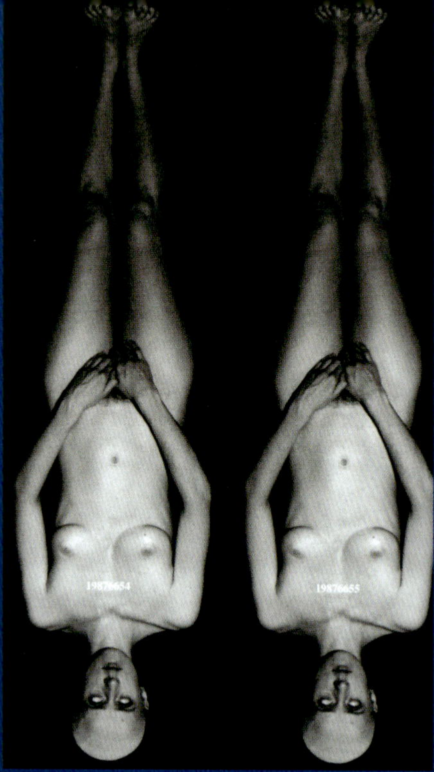

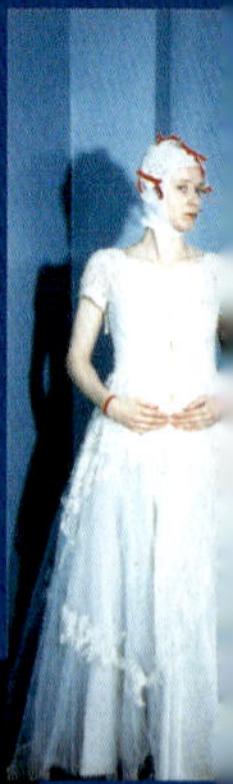

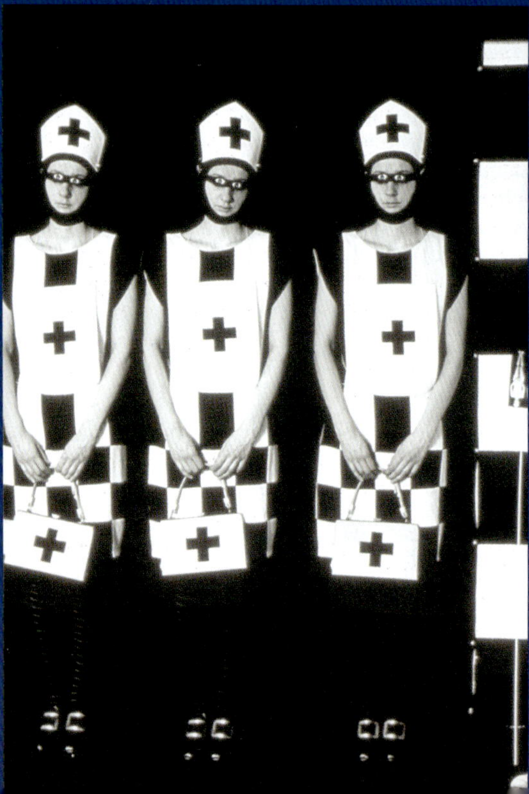

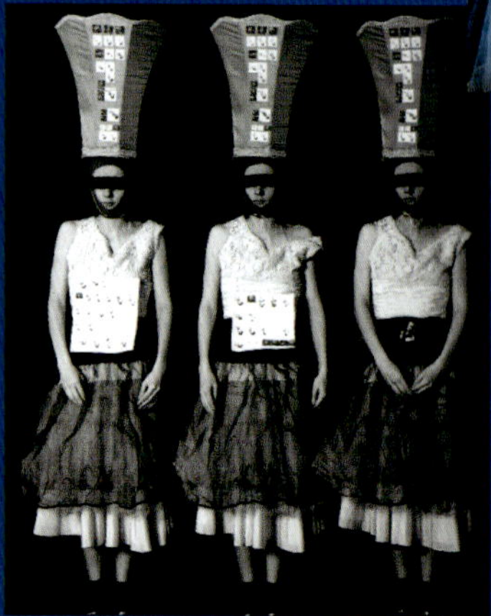

Janieta Eyre,
The Book of Small Souls,
1999

Janieta Eyre,
The Royal Hospital Staff (Triptych–3),
1999

Eyre prefers the fairy-tale dimension that leads into a new territory in which it is necessary to lose one's way, the need for a closure of eyelids that reopen in a different world, a fairy-tale voyage capable of all the various morphologies, including the morphology that causes death. "I often have the sensation that I can witness my own death, every time that there is a possibility of an accident happening: every time that I cross the street, I do it with the image of my body slamming onto the bonnet of an automobile, when I walk down the stairs I always see myself with my neck broken at the bottom of the flight of stairs." She systematically pursues the loss of the subject, she realises the paradox that has nothing to do with lived experience, she activates a neurotic device in which the disappearance of meaning appears as coincidence, she prompts a constant flow between removal and sublimation, and she underscores the paradox that attempts to cause rational experience to coincide with reality.

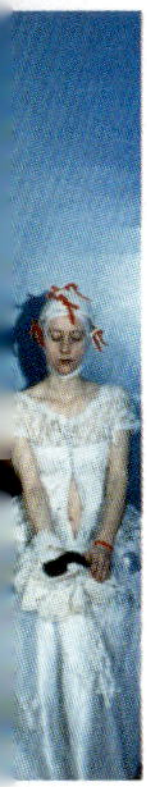

For Janieta Eyre vision is part of foresightedness; she organises the deceit of simulation which finds consolation in the accusation of madness, and in a universe that tests and imposes the logic of separation and division achieves the subversion of multiplication and the sum, and replaces the relationship between the real and the imaginary with the short-circuit of the symbolic. And we see the world of sensations, the escape from equilibrium. "I am interested in many different things, old photographs taken by unknown artists, mediaeval paintings, I love the Mannerists, I like painters such as Francis Bacon who paint in reverse. Recently I also became interested in the series of weeping women by Picasso": a further slip, a way of reconfiguring the world, existence, relationships, an alteration that selects the experience of distance, that distance that for psychoanalysis determines the difference between the artist and the psychotic, tracked down in the fact that the artist manages to find the road back from the imaginary world in which both of them tend to withdraw because of the reality with which they are forced to measure themselves.

For Janieta Eyre foreshadowing, dreams, doubling, all belong to what Freud describes as "the pleasure of the representation of one's own ghosts", achieving the power of vision as a complete experience outside of reality, as a condition of revolt, choosing the estrangement in which the body is summoned to perform the role of the final frontier and using, in order to decorate the body, all of the objects that in the clichés of language suggest madness: cutlery and alarm clocks hanging from her neck, fishes and chickens as decorations on her clothing, the exponential doubling of the personality... Janieta Eyre lives in a body trapped by the phantoms of the literature of madness and she repeats, endlessly, an imaginary scheme that takes form in image after image, and, in the tradition of the great visionaries, in her artworks we see a process of nightmares, hallucinations, metaphors, symbols, dreams and wordplay: fear no longer restrains her, and there emerges the delirious force of the conflict between becoming and appearing, between the self and the code of signs that unhinges the forced maps of the territory of the identical. There is no indication of any way out, the emotional tonalities are annulled and what is activated is the spectacular mechanism of the annihilation of all feelings in a routine directed toward the perpetuation of a total universe. Janieta Eyre undertakes a flight from tragedy, and seems to want to maintain with Brecht: "The effort of getting up every morning, putting on your pants, washing your face and so on, and knowing that all

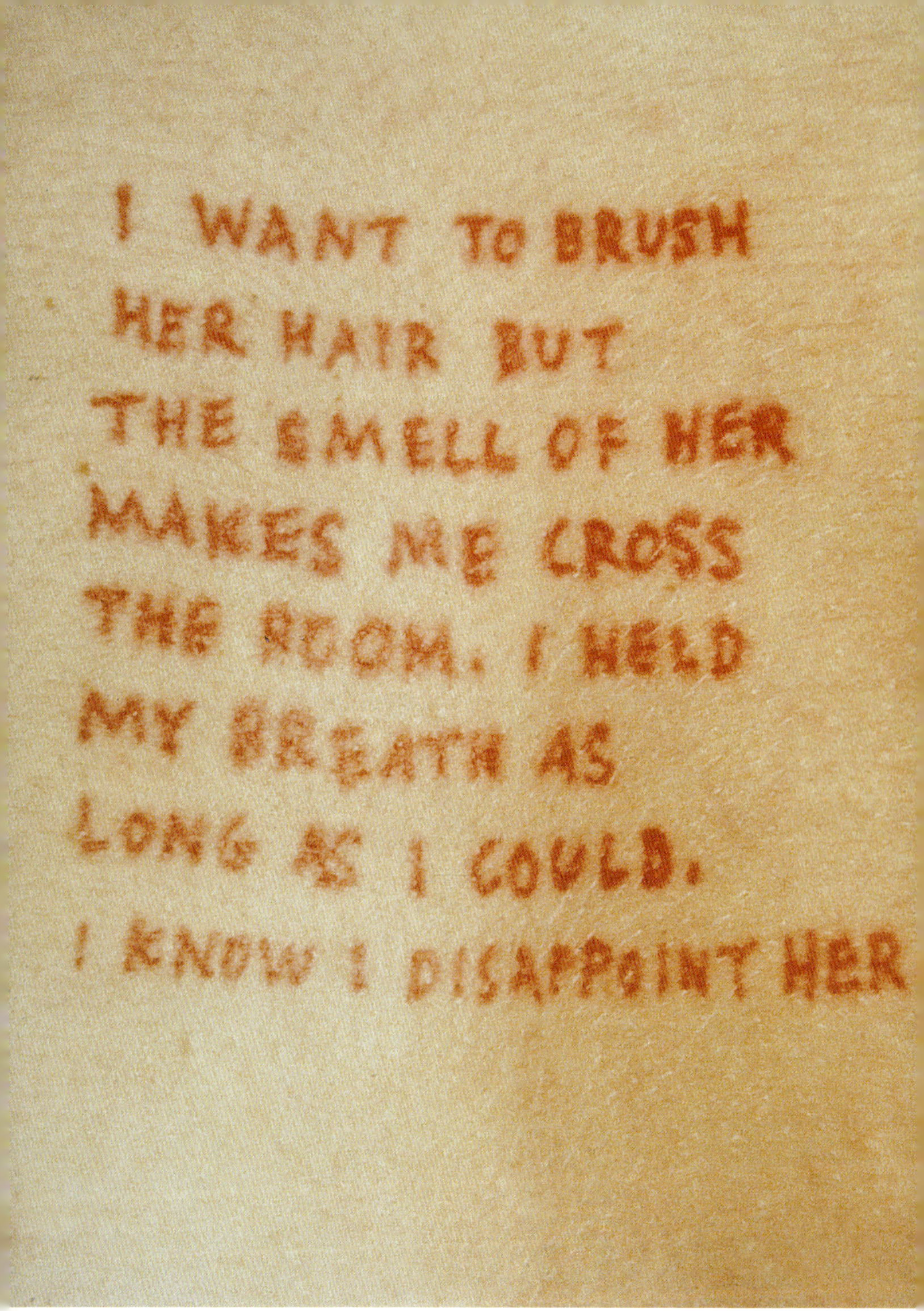

Jenny Holzer, *Untitled* (from the *Lustmord* series), 1993–94

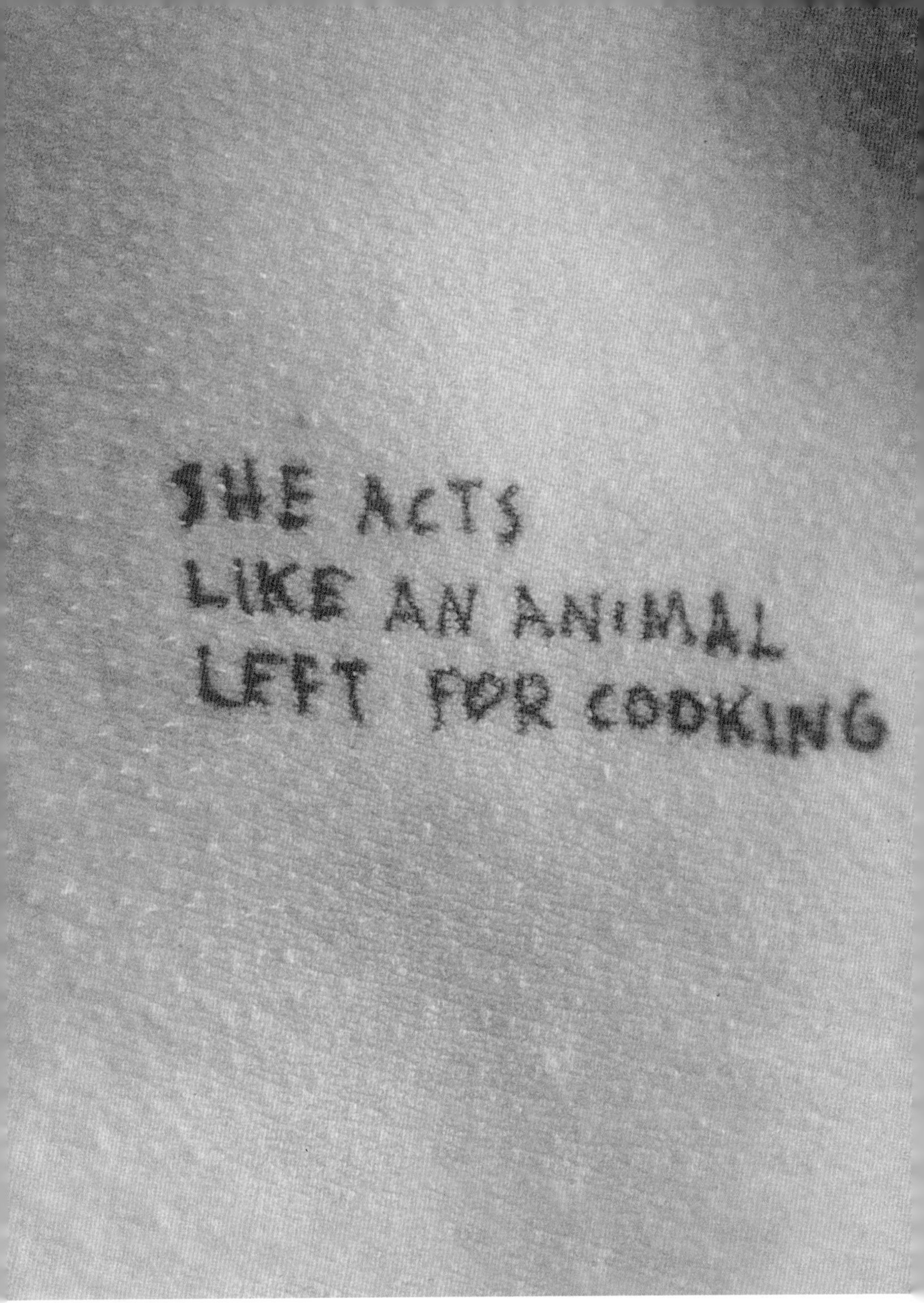
SHE ACTS
LIKE AN ANIMAL
LEFT FOR COOKING

this will never end. That is the true tragedy". Tearing, lacerations, clashes... Janieta Eyre creates artworks as events that allow the subversion of rational order to dribble out, in the form of a series of emotional operations that never become representations, but which suggest the power of the metaphor: metaphor of bodies, instincts, hallucinations, history. And loss of self.

> *The condemned man has the law that he has broken inscribed on his body with the harrow. This man, for instance, will have "Honour your superiors!" inscribed on his body. There would be no sense in telling him. He experiences it on his own body.*
> *(Franz Kafka,* In the Penal Colony*)*

Jenny Holzer works with language, signs and words. The language of the body, of gestures, of postures; transmits subliminal messages, transmits curiosities, closures, fears, timidity. On the skin a history is written: somatisations, scars, tattoos, wounds, the body as a map of transmigration. In 1993, when the whole world was watching with horror the atrocities of "ethnic cleansing" in what is now called the former Yugoslavia, Jenny Holzer began to work on a series of "writings on the body" whose theme was war and the bodies violated by the widespread practice of mass rape. Messages written on human skin, in red ink (the blood of the victims?) in English and in German:
"I AM AWAKE WHERE WOMEN DIE."
"THE COLOR OF HER WHERE SHE IS INSIDE OUT IS ENOUGH TO MAKE ME KILL HER."

The title of the series of "writings on the body" was *Lustmord*, a term that means "sexual crime": a fierce critique of male violence against women, the innocent victims of wars. All of Jenny Holzer's work focuses on a multiple identity, and here too the texts were written from three points of view: that of the attacker, that of the victim, and that of the observer:
"I WANT TO BRUSH HER HAIR BUT THE SMELL OF HER MAKES ME CROSS THE ROOM. I HELD MY BREATH AS LONG AS I COULD. I KNOW I DISAPPOINT HER."
" I TRY TO EXCITE MYSELF SO I STAY CRAZY."
"SHE SMILES AT ME BECAUSE SHE IMAGINES I CAN HELP HER."

In 1979 Jenny Holzer joined Colab, a group of artists who believed that the present-day structures of art, galleries, museums, specialised journals, etc., had by now become inadequate; they far preferred the ordinary chance sites in the larger fabric of the metropolis. In her quest for an altered communication that no longer passed solely through the system of art, Jenny Holzer created her *Truisms*, authoritarian messages, declarations, clichés... written on a single line and then distributed in the form of fliers and posters, handed out on the street to passers-by or plastered on the walls of New York. An obsessive, unexpected, sudden communication, which provoked the audience of chance strollers, accustomed to the usual advertising messages, who suddenly found themselves reading instead phrases such as:
"ABUSE OF POWER COMES AS NO SURPRISE."
"HUMANISM IS OBSOLETE."
"WAR IS A PURIFICATION RITE."

In the 1980s, Jenny Holzer made use of advertising panels, luminous signs, electronic scoreboards, t-shirts, and even sales receipts: this is the space of direct communication, personal communication, impossible to pin down in the body of the metropolis, an unpredictable urban hypertext, the appropriation of antagonistic sites, an undifferentiated emission, the circularity of a message that hits like a fist, unexpected and violent. In 1982 she was given the opportunity to make use of the huge electronic tickertape that runs day and night in Times Square to send her messages. The discrepancy was between the medium employed, technological, impersonal, cold and perfect, and the phrases that spoke to the vulnerability of contemporary man. Her texts now passed from the "underground" dimension of the truisms to the official dimension, as the artist herself explained: "I suddenly changed the emphasis of my work. It was like having the voice of authority saying something different from what it would normally say".

In these years, the writings became increasingly personal. Her truisms were followed by the series *Inflamatory Essays*, blocks of a hundred words arranged on twenty lines, written on posters in various colours and disconcerting in their content: concentrates of sex, violence, power, aggressive messages, caustic messages, reports that come from around the world and which the artist reinterprets, rewrites, bringing imperceptibly to the surface the fact that "I am not interested in interior monologues. The language is a direct reaction to what happens in the world". Her installations in closed places were sinister and spectacular: dark rooms in which LEDs appeared (machines that emit light through diodes), electronic altars, chapels and stone benches upon which are carved cold and brutal phrases.

"CRACK THE PELVIS SO SHE LIES RIGHT. THIS IS A MISTAKE. WHEN SHE DIES YOU CANNOT REPEAT THE ACT. THE BONES WILL NOT GROW TOGETHER AGAIN AND THE PERSONALITY WILL NOT COME BACK. SHE IS GOING TO SINK DEEP INTO THE MOSS TO GET WHITE AND LIGHTER. SHE IS UNRESPONSIVE TO BEGGING AND SELF ABSORBED."

In *Laments*, from 1989, she carved onto a series of stone sarcophagi extreme meditations on contemporary death: AIDS, environmental death, nuclear threats; two of the sarcophagi used in this installation were "child-sized", and one was for a new-born: "The laments are regrets, the hopes and fears of the nameless dead; a last chance to say what had never been said".

"THE KNIFE CUT RUNS AS LONG AS IT WANTS. IT IS THROUGH MY STOMACH. I KEEP LOOKING AT IT. I HAVE MORE COLORS THAN I WOULD HAVE THOUGHT. THE HOLE IS LARGE ENOUGH FOR MY HEAD. THE HOLE WAS BIG ENOUGH FOR THEIR HANDS TO MOVE FREELY."

A sense of impotence, rage, rebellion, violation of the body: in *Lustmord* Jenny Holzer chooses the most painful writing, the writing on the skin, no longer the skin of the city, but that of her own body, carved and cut with poisonous, toxic words: a rebellion against military rape:

" I TAKE HER FACE WITH ITS FINE HAIRS. I POSITION HER MOUTH."

" I FIND HER SQUATTING ON HER HEELS AND THIS OPENS HER SO I CAN GET HER FROM BELOW."

Writing on the skin, the sign that remains on the body, the body as the place of violence, as the site of denunciation, rebellion, a place in which the signs will remain carved forever. Fragility and disintegration of the body, of identity: a multiple, fragmentary, contradictory identity, which denounces the aberrations of a

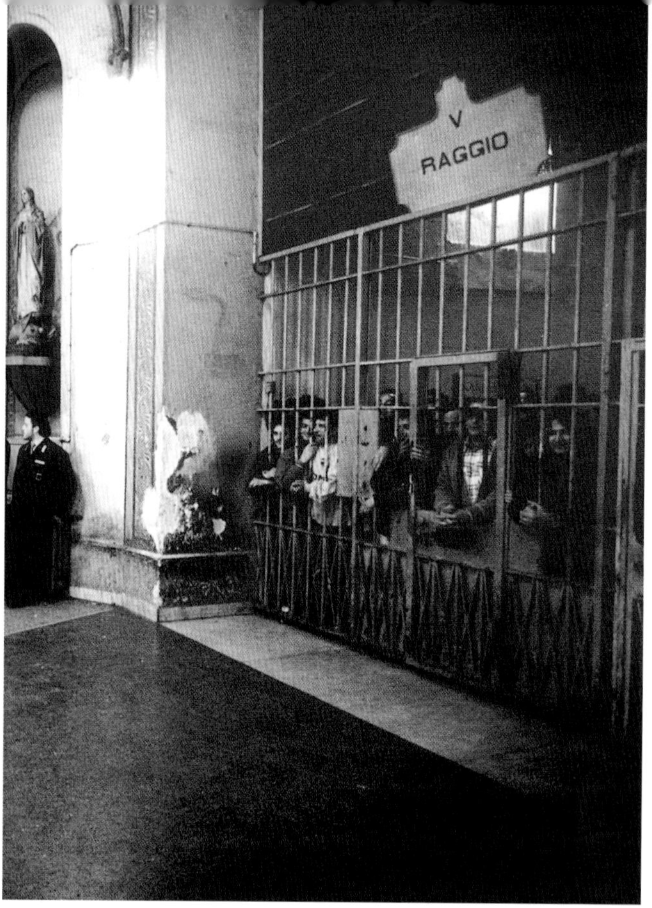

Laurie Anderson, *Live. The Rotunda*, multimedia installation, Milan, San Vittore House of Detention, 1998. Photo by Roby Schirer

universe that tolerates stereotypes, violent aggressions, arrogance based on identity, a writing on the skin as a sort of "lexical self-portrait", the signs of a condemnation inscribed on the body like a serial number or the signs of abuse.

> *Penitence then presents itself as a dramatised exhibition. To manifest one's suffering, show shame, make humility visible and display one's modesty: these are the chief features of punishment.*
> *(Michel Foucault)*

In prison you learn yoga, weight lifting, tumbling, and the basics of soccer. Each new arrival in the cell is an intruder, it is necessary to learn to execute some very difficult dance steps, the dance of cohabitation with strangers, the dance between different crimes, the dance between individuals whose time is punctuated by the same rhythms. To learn to take care of your prisoner body, to begin to feel your own body beginning with the sense of expropriation and nullification that prison immediately imposes. The body is piled up, classified, sorted and fed. The body of the prisoner is a ritual body, a metaphor, and there are other ritual and metaphoric exercises, such as writing on the body, designing it, shaping it, mistreating it, a fetishistic attention to the body which the prisoner guards

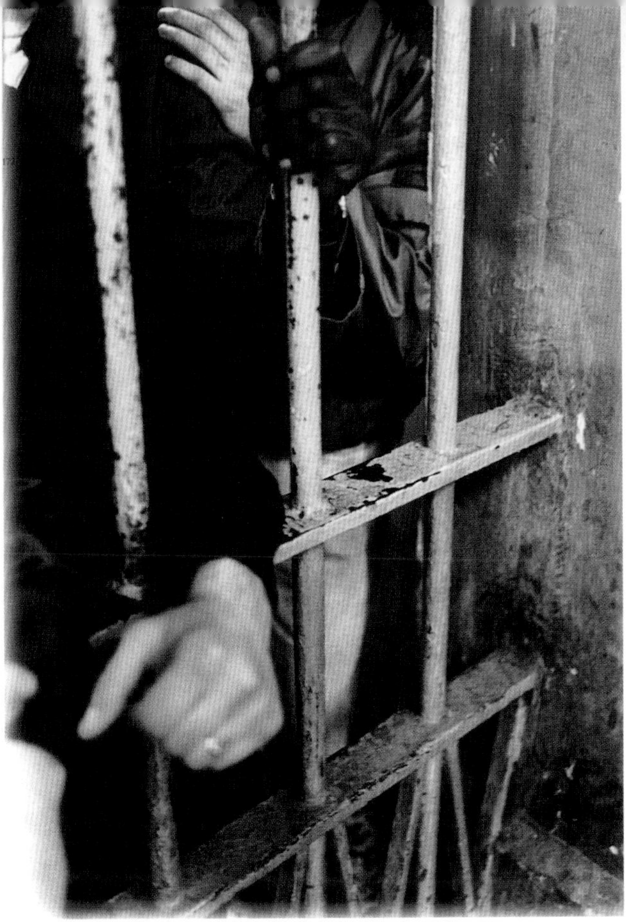

Laurie Anderson,
Live. Behind the Bars,
multimedia installation,
Milan, San Vittore House
of Detention, 1998.
Photo by Roby Schirer

from the abandonment and manipulation to which others might subject it, a body to be transfigured, a powerful symbol of a difference. The bodies of the prisoners are more handsome than the bodies of their guards, bodies as challenges, as care of the self, as reappropriation. For the prisoner the real body is a territory of resistance: the abyss of physicality opens up and the metaphorical construction of one's own body begins.

Installations, telepresences, figures projected in the darkness of an exhibition space, figures that tell and gesticulate: Laurie Anderson asks questions about the operation of the institutions, about communications, and especially about the technology which she herself uses to teletransport a prisoner out of his prison.

"Danny Hillis, the man who invented the millennium clock, told me his idea for a movie. He said, this is the plot: the aliens are approaching the Earth after having travelled across the universe for thousands of years, years during which they took photographs of the Earth, zoom photographs, as they got closer and closer. Now they have almost reached the Earth and they have an immense archive of images: a sequence of the Alps emerging from the bottom of the ocean, an enormous volcano spitting fire and ash onto the Earth's surface, covering it for hundreds of years, the construction of the Great Wall of China, and so on. As they get closer and closer to the Earth, the photographs are bigger and better focused. And so the aliens call down to the Earth and they say: 'We have these photographs, photographs of the history of the Earth, and that's not all: we even have photographs of the Crucifixion. And they are for sale'; and then they send a few down as proof. All around the Earth a giant bidding war breaks out, and the last world war is fought because of these photographs".

This is just one of the five stories that a virtual Laurie Anderson, projected onto a cast, a beam of light with human appearances, tells us with the slightly drawly and melodious voice of someone who knows how to tell a story.

Stories from Life.

Almost total darkness, black sand, black walls, the only colours are in the images, tiny evanescent dots of light, small almost alien beings, magic, unknown even if they are identifiable. "I try to create a magical quality in the body of a person, whose existential worth is unknown to me, or at the very least, powerfully connoted, but impenetrable: an alien that has been confined or isolated in a prison for a very long period of time. Through my work I bring that person 'down to earth', or perhaps I should say I bring that person into my territory, the territory of art". That is how Santino Stefanini, guilty of robbery and first-degree murder, a member of the Vallanzasca gang in Italy in the 1970s, prisoner of an institution for the past eleven years, now a convict in the penitentiary of San Vittore, is helped to escape from prison in order to enter the world of art.

1998. Milan, Prada Foundation. A dark room, whining sounds in the background, gravel on the ground, crunching at every step, almost as if to intimidate anyone who wants to move, as if to force everyone into immobility before a disturbing, uncomfortable scene, the image of a prisoner, his eyebrows rising and falling, the fingers of his hand moving.

"The project developed by pure chance, from the idea of doing something musical in a church not far from Vienna. I went to see this lovely little Austrian town, all perfect, with all its little houses, the church, the onion dome steeple, all of that, and I realised that right in the heart of this picture-postcard town there was a maximum-security prison. Across from the guard tower was the bell tower of the church. So the idea was to take the image of a prisoner and project it into the church. Obviously this project proved to be impossible to achieve, because they refused to give us permission to do it. But I started to write a piece about tele-presence, about how to influence our world as well as the role of the Church and prison with respect to the human body. The Church with the incarnation and prison with incarceration. Then we decided to implement this project; but Austrian law prohibits the representation of the face of a prisoner. Prisoners are completely cancelled out, in a certain sense. Cancelled out. Forgotten faces. Bodies that relate only to a limited spatial dimension, which is contained in a room, a cafeteria, a courtyard. Always walls, boundaries, doors. The only form of escape is virtual escape, where the space seems to have been altered and yet it always remains the same, the imperceptible presence of a series of limitations, or dimensions, which can only be crossed by the imagination. I was interested in the concept of incarceration and in prison as a form of institution designed to ensure public order. For instance, recently New York has been cleaned up and has become a sort of Disneyland: it is no longer the dirty city that we used to know. So now where have all the criminals, the nut-cases, the drug addicts, and the drug dealers gone? Many of them have wound up in prison. In the United States many prisons are real businesses: you can even invest money in a private company that operates a prison. But we should understand the way they operate. I therefore thought of a project about prisons as institutions and on the function of incarceration as a delimitation of a space, which the body is forced to relate to. The relationship with Santino Stefanini was fundamental to the achievement of the *Live* project.

I met Santino in the prison of San Vittore, I spoke to him about the project, and he immediately understood what I was talking about. He talked about a 'virtual prison escape', which is exactly what I was thinking about. I had long been looking for a place where it would be possible to establish a different point of contact, a more fluid content. When they told us that we could organise this project, I couldn't believe it, this was a unique and wonderful opportunity. The possibility of speaking directly with Santino has been invaluable. The presence/non-presence of the convict in the room completely warped our perception of space. His movements communicate the fact of his being *Live*, the fact of his being there in that room at the same time that he was in prison. A mute communication, in which images that appear tangible speak, projected upon the life-size cast of the convict. One thing that I found interesting, and which to some degree was represented in the installation of Santino, is his almost infantile form of communication: that is, Santino communicates with us in a way that is not verbal, he has no possibility of speaking, and he reminds me of children when they are seeking the attention of their parents who are distracted, or else conversations in which at a certain point you realise that the other person is not there or else that you yourself are not there, that you are not communicating anything at all. At certain times, in fact, communication does not work; and then if you get technology involved, there is no way out, because we communicate but without really communicating. A second thing that struck me was the issue of immobility. The killer is stationary, absolutely immobile, almost as if he were an Egyptian, but at the same time it seems as if he can see us; and this long-distance communication gives us the impression that he really can see us. Impressions of a vision impregnated with an oneiric dimension where the dream passes through the dimensions of time and space in all of their possibilities. Perhaps an attempt to go beyond the limits of physicality, beyond the limits of death." (Laurie Anderson)

Systems of confinement, the loss of control over one's own body and one's own existence. The imprisoned body is subjected to twisting and pressure that has to do with the most profound aspects of the human experience and which radically modify meanings and languages. In total institutions, there is modification of sight, hearing, sexuality, the perception of time and space. The imprisoned body is a mutilated body, a body which is denied the possibility of relations with other bodies.

"I must have a body, it is a moral necessity, a requirement" (Gilles Deleuze): a body that becomes a malleable material, modifiable, a body which is denied the determination to explore the zones of coexistence and comparison, a body that is incapable of creating connections, deviations, "hybrids", a body that is active as a shock and welter of messages, languages, points of emission, passages of frequency, a body as a passage from the territorial transition all the way out to a level of ubiquity. A body that shifts its own appearance in order to adapt to the

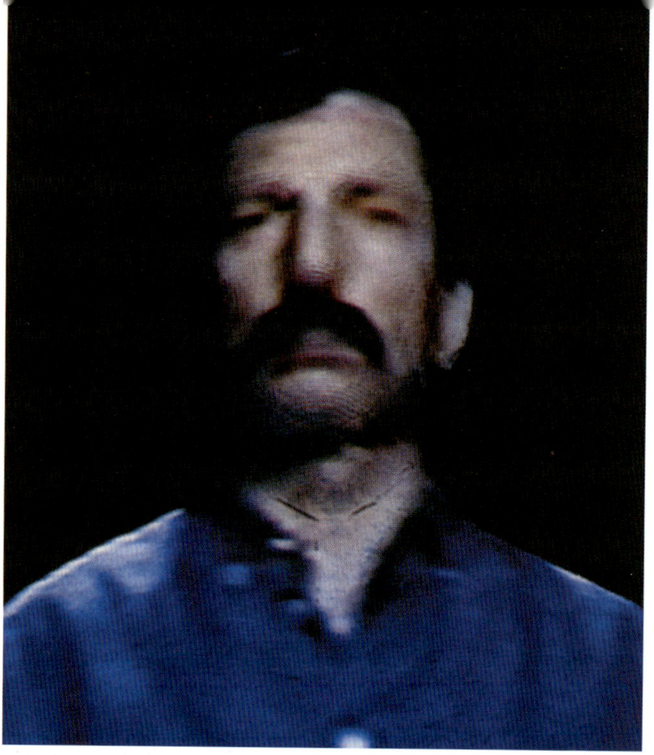

Laurie Anderson,
Live, multimedia
installation, Milan, 1998

rigour of the institution. If identity has been subdivided into types, creating and reinforcing in this way the figures of privilege and the figures of slavery, it is by interpreting all the roles that the order of the subdivisions is threatened. Inside the total institutions there emerges an individual that invades and is invaded, which replaces a false purity with the awareness of one's own vulnerability. And the body becomes the place of corruption, the collapse of a self that cannot help but present itself painfully disintegrated, parcellised, mutilated, and is born as an unexpected body.

"Do you know those nights when you are sleeping, and it's completely dark and silent, and you don't even dream? The real reason is this: on those nights, you've gone away. You're in somebody else's dream. Busy in somebody else's dream. I remember where I came from / There were burning buildings and a fiery red sea / I remember all my lovers / I remember how they held me / World without end remember me..." (Laurie Anderson).

All of Venus is under the sign of Titian, in the mystical relationship between flesh, fur and the mirror... the masochistic scenes need to establish themselves as sculptures or paintings, to reproduce sculptures and paintings, to double themselves in a mirror or in a reflection... the heroes of Sade are not art lovers, much less are they collectors... Masoch on the contrary had all the reasons to believe in art, and in the immobility and the reflections of culture the plastic arts, as he considered them, immortalise their subject, suspending a gesture or a pose.... As Sade would say: tyrants are never born in anarchy, you see them arise only in the shadow of the laws, or authorised by them.
Gilles Deleuze

SINNERS
Sex, Women, Gays, Other...

With Gilles Deleuze we enter into a "fold" of thought, the interior of an imprint, a touch, an impulse, which has impregnated and modified contemporary thinking. With Deleuze we abandon the safe and "comforting" paths of rationality and logic in order to run along the risky trails of a thought open to the disparate and the unthinkable. Deleuze's philosophy is a virtual universe, a universe consisting entirely of images, visions, colours, lights and planes. To create concepts is, for the French philosopher, to construct a universe all his own, personal, self-sufficient, autonomous, with its own colours, with its own lights and with its own planes, which absolutely seeks no mimetic relationships with reality, which doesn't represent it, which doesn't signify it, but which creates it in accordance with methods that are internal to that specific universe. "Every philosophical concept", says Deleuze "is a fragmentary whole that does not adapt to other concepts since the outlines do not coincide. Rather than composing a puzzle, concepts develop out of a toss of the dice.... And the philosophy that creates them always presents itself as a powerful Everything... an Omnitude which includes them all on a single and identical plane. It is a table, a plane, a cut. It is a plane of consistency or else, to be more specific, the plane of immanence of concepts."

The philosophy of Deleuze is a universe of concepts made up of concatenations, connections, appearances and disappearances, a series of planes with their duration, a philosophy that self-imposes the continuous creation of concepts, and every instant a universe appears or disappears, it is territorialised or deterritorialised, and new configurations are described. "Crossing through chaos: not to explain it or interpret it, but simply to cross it, from one end to the other, in a passage that orders the planes, the landscapes, the localisations, but which leaves the chaos to close back in upon itself, like the sea washing over the wake of a ship." These universes create new relationships of philosophical thought with their own metaphors, with their own thoughts, with practices that are no longer representations but which are instead experimentations of self, as creations of self through a thought "in the process of becoming".

Amongst the thought exercises and experimentations on oneself that are most clearly Deleuzian is the set of practices that, in the wake of Artaud, focus on the creation of a powerful conceptual universe that gives life to the Body without

Organs, a combination of practices that answer the question: "How to make a body without organs? And, What is a body without organs?"

The corporeality inaugurated by Deleuze enters into a close relationship with the concept of desiring body, a body that it is no longer meant to be confined to the tranquil barriers of an accepted corporeality, but which instead offers itself as a field of action, as the field for an almost inevitable exercise and experimentation. It is the philosopher himself who points out the necessity of creating a body "of one's own". "In any case you have one (or many), not so much because it pre-exists or is already a given, even though, in a certain sense, it does — but you have to make one in any case, you can't desire without making one — and it will happen, it is an exercise, an inevitable experimentation, already performed in the moment in which you undertake it and which cannot be done until you undertake it." The BwO (Body without Organs) is, in the words of Deleuze, a desire just as it is a non-desire, an instance, an urgency that does not belong to the world of ideas but to the world of practices, a set of practices, a thought that takes concrete form in experimentation. "One may say: what is the BwO? — but you are already on one, dragging along like a beggar, wandering in the dark like a blind man, running like a lunatic... Upon it we sleep, we are awake, we fight, we win and we are defeated, we seek our place, we experience our incomparable happiness and our astounding falls and collapses, we penetrate and we are penetrated, we love."

The war of the BwO has been going on since 1947 when Artaud, with *Pour en finir avec le jugement de dieu*, declares war on the organs, or better, on the anarchistic functionalism of the organs. The late writings of Artaud are characterised both by a powerful current of atheism and by a nostalgia for a sort of "golden" state of the body, a body without "dents", a body without apertures, a "glorious body", or, perhaps, a "body without organs": "The body is the body, / it stands alone / and has no need of organs, / the body is never an organism, / the organisms are the enemies of the body, / the things that are done / happen on their own / without the assistance of any organ, / every organ is a parasite, / it serves only a parasitic function / destined to support the life of a being / that should not exist".

Deleuze, influenced by Artaud, declares that the BwO is in operation as soon as the body has had enough of its organs, and wants to drop them or lose them. The world of the organic thus becomes the extreme metaphor of an organisation, the social organisation, in which the ruling principle is that of the organisation of roles, hierarchies and social strata, and in which each organism performs, autonomously, certain very specific functions.

"The BwO screams: they made me into an organism! They bent me without any right to do so! They have stolen my body! The judgment of God rips it from its immanence and forms it an organism, a significance, a subject... You will be organised, you will be an organism, you will articulate your body — otherwise you will be nothing but a depraved individual. You will be signifier and meaning, interpreter and interpretation — otherwise you will be nothing more than a deviant. You will be a subject and, fixed as such, subject to enunciation and folded over a subject of enunciation — otherwise you will be nothing more than a vagabond." The BwO tries to flee from these schemes, it wants to be something other than the signifying bodies of the social organisation and the subjectifying powers. The BwO is a body that, in the wake of Foucault, experiments upon itself its own future and seeks a way out of the rigid schemes of subjectifying power/knowledge that builds its bodies and its organs: "They won't let you experiment in your little corner". The BwO, writes Deleuze, "is what remains when everything else has been removed. What is taken away is precisely the phantom, the set of meanings and subjectifications." Opposed to this set of subjectifying practices, the BwO offers disarticulation as property, experimentation as operation, and nomadism as a series of movements. To disarticulate is to render one's own body available to an entire series of connections, conjunctions, concatenations, and paths open to the circulation of intensities and flows. "The body is nothing other than a set of valves, sieves, locks, bowls and communicating vessels... A BwO is made in such a way that it can be occupied only by intensities. Only intensities will pass through and circulate." The BwO are bodies that live on their flows, their intensities and their desires. Examples of BwO are: the hypochondriac body, "whose organs have been destroyed" and put continually in discussion, the paranoid body, "where the organs keep being attacked by influences, but also restored by external energies", the schizoid body, "which gives way to an active internal struggle that it itself conducts against the organs", the drugged body, "experimental schizoid". And, to complete the list, the masochistic body: "You can't even get near if you start from pain, it is primarily a question of Body without Organs". An example is provided by their flows, their waves, their intensities: the refrigerative waves of the drug addict or the pain-bearing waves of the masochist. "The drug-addict doesn't want to be in warm places, he seeks out the coolth, the cold, the Big Chill. But the cold must reach him the way that drugs do: not on the exterior where it will do no good, but on his own interior." The practices that culminate in the creation of the BwO of the masochist invert Foucault's theory of "docile bodies". If the body of the disciplinary powers is a body "custom" modelled, that of the masochist is the result of a series of choices made in total liberty. If power passes materially into the very depth of the bodies, the BwO of the masochist is swept, on its interior, exclusively by intensities sought out and desired.

Pain, for a masochist, is the price that must be paid, not to attain pleasure, but to break a sort of pseudo-link between desire and pleasure as measures extrinsic to the act:

"Lover, 1. You can chain me to the table, fastened tightly, from ten to fifteen minutes, the time you need to prepare your tools; 2. At least a hundred lashes of the whip, and a few minutes' interval; 3. Start sewing, sew the hole of my glans, sew onto the glans the skin that surrounds it, so that it can't work free, sew the ball sack to the skin of my thighs. Sew my breasts, sew on a four-hole button to each nipple. You can join them with buttonhole elastic. Then go on to the second stage: 4. You can choose whether to turn me on the table, onto my chained belly, but with my legs together, or whether just to tie me to the pole, wrists together, as well as the legs, and the whole body tied fast; 5. Whip my back, my butt cheeks, my thighs, at least a hundred lashes of the whip; 6. Sew my butt cheeks together, the entire line of my ass. Sew tight with double thread, knotting each stitch. If I'm on the table, tie me to the pole; 7. Give me fifty lashes of the whip on my butt cheeks; 8. If you want to give more power to the torture and execute your threat from last time, drive the needles all the way into my butt cheeks; 9. You can then tie me to the chair, give me thirty lashes on my breasts and drive in the smallest needles, if you want to, heat them up first, all of them or only certain ones. You should tie me tightly to the chair and put my wrists behind my back, to push

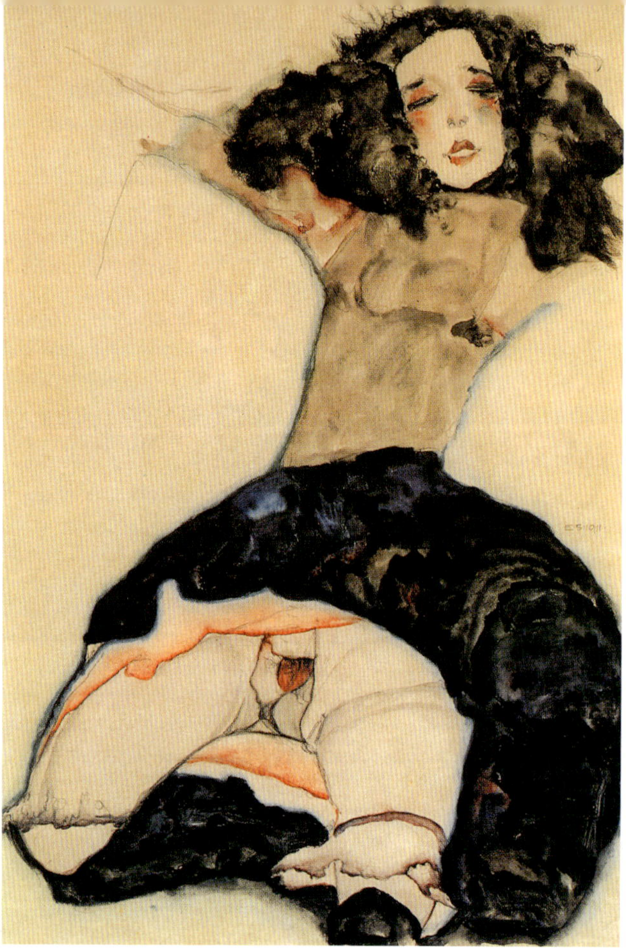

Egon Schiele,
Girl with Dark Hair,
1911

my breasts forward. If I have not spoken of burning, it's because I have an appointment soon and the burns take so long to heal."

Suffering, then, is, for the masochist, just one of the ways to manage to constitute oneself as a BwO. Everything is allowed, what counts is that pleasure be the flow of desire itself.

An interplay of meanings bursts into a heterogeneous and unexpected context, breaking a series of very specific rules, removing from power its own tools; we appropriate the marks, the brands, the pain, the humiliations, the signs on the skin, the shaved heads, the abuse, and they are transformed into instruments of pleasure, chosen signs: a powerful theft, unforeseen, unexpected, which changes the rules and leads to the selection of new and invisible means of persuasion.

"Obscenity", writes Bataille "is a manifestation of the disturbance that shakes the state of the body in conformation with self-possession, the possession of enduring and established individuality"; obscenity therefore cannot be reduced to the mere mechanism of prohibition and transgression, but rather it is that which disturbs conventions by introducing, in specific contexts, disorder and its irregularity, its laceration.

At the age of sixteen Egon Schiele entered the strict and traditional Academy of Fine Arts of Vienna. The Vienna of the time was a cosmopolitan city, the city of Franz Josef, which boasted a glittering military and social hierarchy, refined and middle-class, yet concealed discontent and political rivalries, and brutal poverty amongst the proletariat. These were the golden years of the Viennese Secession, founded and presided over by Gustav Klimt, whose motto was, "Give our time its art, and art its freedom", and whose Romantic undertaking had been to think of art as a form of expression capable of capturing and being the "spirit of the time", the famous *Zeitgeist* so present in the proclamations and the declarations of the protagonists of the Secession. Klimt, Schiele, Kokoschka, Schnitzler, Musil, Kraus, Freud, Wittgenstein, Mach, Mahler, Schönberg, and Loos are just a few of the names from Vienna at the turn of the twentieth century, some of whom violently introduced several points of orientation and confusion in what is now contemporary culture.

At the age of nineteen, Schiele was already considered a "true artist", and he wanted to be "the new artist": he began a series of investigations that explored the fragility of language and the fragilities of the mind that condition the body and its relationships, beginning with its approach to the female world with a crude gaze, erotic to the point of sarcasm and grotesquerie, somewhere between rage and nostalgia. Schiele's neurotic sensibility was to characterise all of his brief body of work, which ranged from 1908 to 1918, when he died at the age of twenty-eight; he painted sex as guilt, as a forbidden gaze, and he worked through his obsessions with sex and death with a singular and sophisticated form of expressionism. His model was Gustav Klimt, who would become his friend and mentor, and for the rest of his life he would strive to measure up to his idea of art, even though he replaced the pacific and gilded vision of Klimt with an anguish that clearly spoke of melancholy, thus foreshadowing the most widespread disease of modernity. A long series of self-portraits unveiled a fragile, vulnerable, disturbed, gangly, unnatural body, just as in the portraits of his beloved sister, Gertie, his first model, whose body he would continue to depict in all his portraits of young adolescents, which so much dominated his work. There are hundreds of drawings that depict the pitiless anatomy in which he portrayed himself: he painted and drew his own body huddled in panic, he chose and captured hysterical postures, portraying the stiffening of the limbs, and he often depicted himself naked on the dizzying edge of a void that appears to separate from his figure, a space that seems to want to have nothing to do with him. As Musil wrote in his *Young Törless*: "When he imagined his body free of its clothes… his eyes immediately perceived twisted movements, restless, a stretching and turning of his limbs and a deformation of his spinal cord, such as one could see in the depictions of martyrs, and in the grotesque spectacles of carnival performers"; and Schiele portrayed himself in the same manner, taking inspiration from the madmen (or "alienated people") confined in the psychiatric hospital of Vienna. With his images, with his gestures of contracted, twisted hands, the artist triggered a series of emotional provocations that moved him further and further from the iconography of the Secession: he stripped off the decorative skin for a syncopated and sharp-angled vision, a vision that preferred tension to decoration, an unbearable expressive tension, amplified by the empty space around the figures. Egon Schiele painted the contractions of a spasm, the discomfort, diseases of the mind and of sensibilities; these were the same years in which Freud was exploring the mechanisms of the subconscious: years in which the phantoms of the mind were becoming visible.

There are many paintings depicting Wally Neuzil, the former model for Klimt who became his lover and the protagonist of his erotic drawings; these works, along with those featuring young female models practising autoeroticism, constitute a crucial part of Schiele's vision and distinguish a production intended for a special type of collection. Fragile, immature bodies, exposed, genitals and gazes in the foreground, bodies that touch themselves, explore themselves, undress themselves, bodies languishing, playing at watching and at being watched, portraits of exercises of self-enjoyment upon which Schiele insists to the point of depicting himself as he masturbates. "I believe that man must suffer sexual torture so that he can become capable of sexual feelings", he wrote in anguish, trapped in the cages of a repressive culture that wound up deforming the figures linked to sex, in a Vienna that lived a day-time Victorian moral code, rigorous and strait-laced, and a different, nocturnal, relaxed sexual life, strictly concealed. "Vienna was obsessed with sex, it was the city's swamp, a subterranean darkness upon which rose the splendid structure of the middle-class society with its radiant and irreprehensible façade", and in portraying sex Schiele depicts the frustration and the desire for transgression, exhibition, the bodies of anxiety. "The bodies burn, they consume their own light by living", he wrote in a letter dated 1912, replacing the voyeurism of the early paintings, intended for collectors of erotic drawings, with the heavy and obsessive figures of aggression and disease, the gaze of madness, the portraits of bodies of solitude and panic, desperately coupling. He wound up in gaol, he was subjected to a trial, and about a hundred of his drawings were confiscated, one of them even being burned as an object lesson. But the erotic content of Schiele's paintings remained crude and provocative: he continued to paint the awareness of defeat, the abyss of despair in which there is no room for the idyllic.

> *On the other hand, this dialogue is logical in the context of the imposed bisexual model (masculine/feminine), because this suddenly places sex as two structurally opposed "terms". The possibility of the transition to the absurd limit of serial numbering, to sex as an accumulation, is implied by the bisexual structure, beginning from the moment in which the masculine and the feminine are placed as entire terms. Thus the ambivalence of sex is reduced from its bivalence (of the two poles and the two sexual roles). Now that this equivalence passes through the metamorphosis of the "sexual revolution" and now that we see, it is said, the disappearance of differences between masculine and feminine, the ambivalence of sex is reduced by the ambiguity of the unisex.*
> *(Jean Baudrillard)*

Pierre Molinier, who killed himself on 3 March 1976, was one of the most interesting protagonists of the French artistic scene in the 1970s. Many of the adjectives that have been used to describe him: perverse, immoral, scandalous, sick, pederast, transvestite, because of the photographs in which he often portrayed himself in scenes that were variously sado-masochistic and autoerotic. He was first discovered by André Breton in the 1950s, and his images were a continual process of experimentation, testing the boundary between the oneiric dimension and pornography. If for Surrealists the dream was the true dimension of the Ego and for Sigmund Freud the dream revealed the buried contents and the concealed

Pierre Molinier,
Portrait de Luciano Castelli, 1975

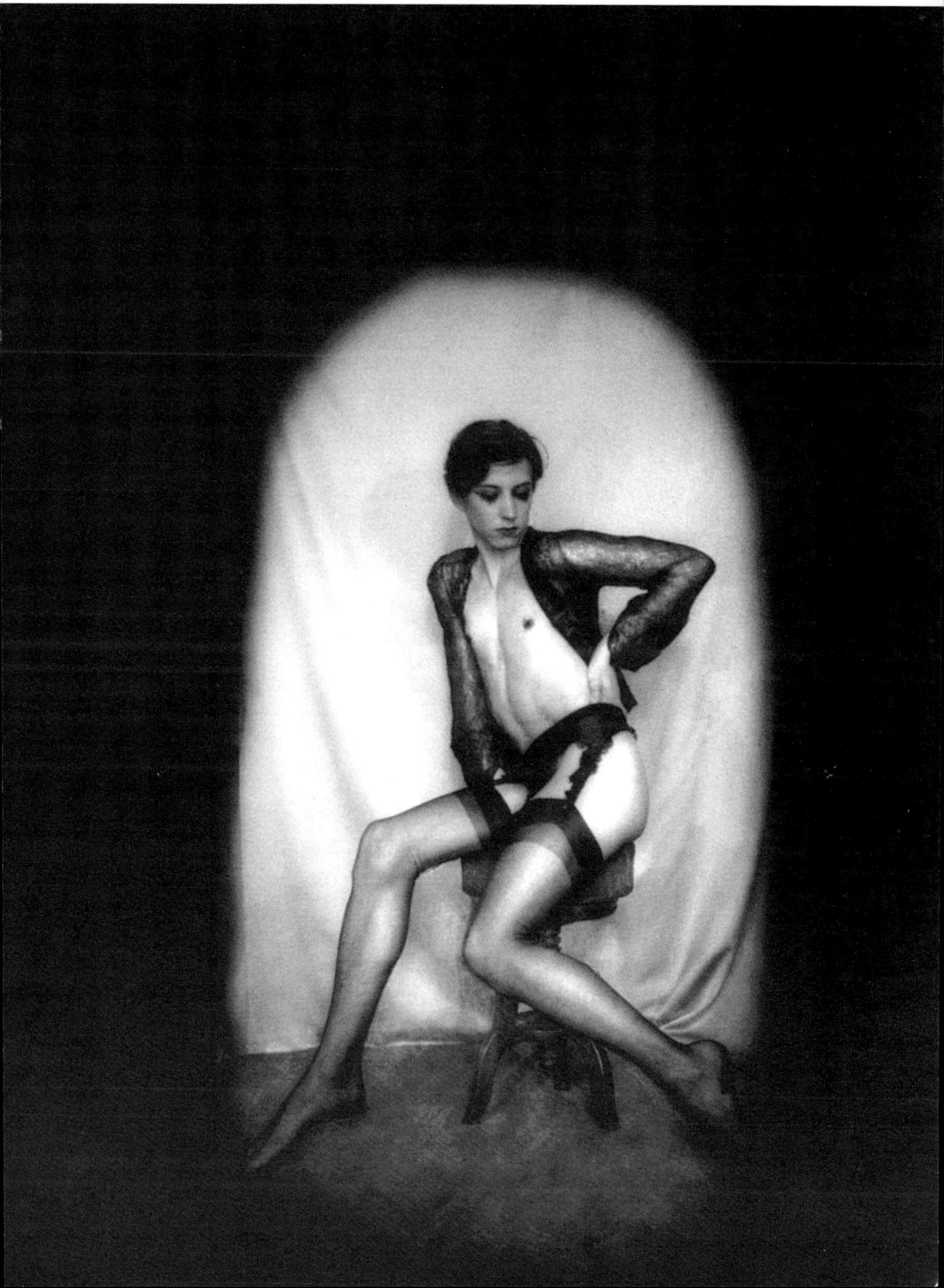

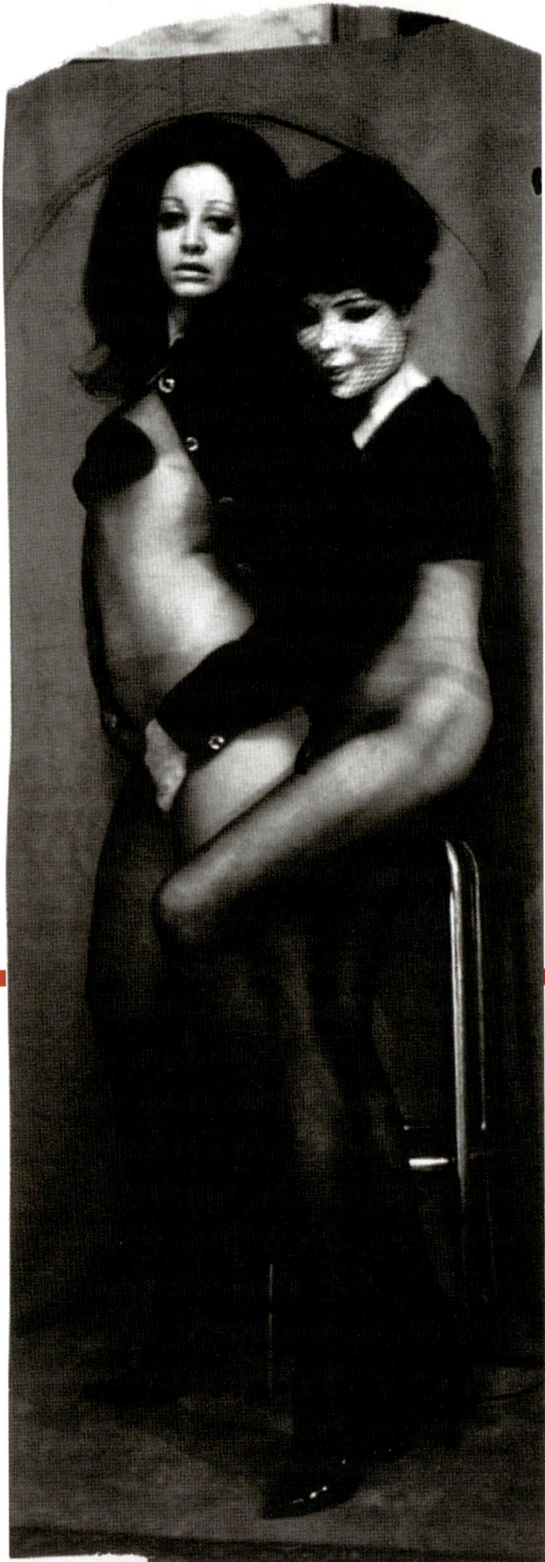

Pierre Molinier,
Pierre et Hanel,
1970

impulses of the subconscious, for Molinier the dream was the source of images that, cunningly elaborated and designed, became the screen for a collective perversion that was exceedingly well concealed in the coils of the morality of the time (no different from the morality of today) which rejected sexual ambiguity and even its very mention. Making use of some of the most famous techniques of Surrealism, such as photographic montages, *frottage*, or drawing in India ink on wet paper, Molinier, in his artworks from the end of the 1950s and the early 1960s, created figures immersed in an absolutely unreal atmosphere charged with fantastic suggestions, figures that in any case clearly set forth a sexuality that was no longer concealed in the modesty of the censorship of the Superego. In the second half of the 1960s the images of Pierre Molinier became self-referential: he himself was now the protagonist of photographs in which he cross-dressed, he stripped, he made use of a female mask and sexual objects of all sorts. He built something close to a movie set where the lights, the backdrops and the furnishings rendered an atmosphere not unlike a cheap hourly hotel room or a brothel, thus declaring the fiction that all the same was not widely received because of the overwhelming transgressive power of the genitalia in the foreground, whips, leather phalluses, masks and group sex. The photographs by Molinier transgress upon the idea of a "normal" sexuality, introducing all those allusions to the most common erotic fantasies that are skilfully concealed. Molinier's bodies are dismantled and reassembled, in a first phase in a dreamy and surreal world, in a second phase in a multiplication of sexual ambiguities.

The protagonists of his images are nonetheless also the glamour and elegance of lingerie and poses that merge sexual liberty and pornography with the pleasure of a subtle and refined eroticism. The artworks of Molinier do not seem to consider the canonical biological division between males and females; the reassuring binary vision of sexual gender, which has accompanied man in every phase of his development, from the earliest of times, does not seem to interest Molinier in the slightest, instead he seems to accentuate, precisely with his own masculine body, the characteristics of an exasperated femininity. The division between the sexes, which has imprinted itself upon all the discrimination concerning that which is licit and that which is illicit, upon what is masculine and what is, instead, feminine, is unhinged by this artist who not only exasperated the change of roles, upon which humanity had constructed an entire world of relations and interactions, but he systematically violated all traditional models, profoundly restrictive in nature, which often demanded that an individual behave in a manner that was entirely alien to that individual's self. Molinier introduced, without any awareness of it, the notion of "transgender", that is, a remarkable man/woman being. He undertakes a process of feminisation and uses some of the most canonical symbols of femininity: fishnet stockings, wigs, stiletto heels, veils, gloves, and he creates a performance, absolutely private and without witnesses, in which he confronts his own double, thinking of himself as a new creature. He/she lives in the theories of hybridisation of the most advanced Surrealism, in the psychoanalytic theories of the double, in the transvestitism of Marcel Duchamp and introduces many of the themes that shortly thereafter would explode into the actions of body art. The being in which Molinier is "incarnated" by now lives in literature, art, cinema, advertising, fashion and society: the fracture between the sexes narrows increasingly, but at the same time it survives in the complexity of everyday relationships. Molinier no longer recognises the sexes as antagonistic, as bearers of opposite values such as femininity and virility, and he reassembles the erotic stage. And there is immediately a scandalised outcry. The oneiric and performative universe of Pierre Molinier seems to have unhinged the rules of a private life that is exposed, displayed and violated, and which obliges us to measure ourselves with tensions, impulses and deviations. With Molinier what is born is a photograph-document in which the History of the Flesh is no longer written with wounds and pain, but with a game of discovery and overstepping boundaries: the gratuity of images is offered to the voyeuristic gaze of a spectator who captures that which pulsates, lives, that which is lived, more than shown. And this is the particularly fascinating aspect of the artworks by Pierre Molinier: from his images the body is revealed and veils itself, we see breasts, bottoms, backs, nipples, belly buttons, genitalia, feet…

Anatomies marked by outfits that become tatters of physicality, the indication of erogenous points and sensuality scattered over one's own skin and the skin of others. The provocation of organs that are incandescent, multiplied, amplified, shown as instruments for the activation of pure energy; and the body becomes a sensory pressure, a perceptual shock. There is a scandalised outcry and the physical dimension is replaced with an aggressive dimension of a project of the body in which sensory architectures, grafts and instruments become desires and formulae, accessories to sophisticated machines and new organisms born directly from the image. At times confusion is necessarily a point of departure from which to progress toward the combination, at times instead exactly the opposite occurs; this depends on the dynamics of the various works, from the type of emotional graphics that they produce, from the types of falls and releases. Molinier always sets out from a sort of order and then creates a sort of final confusion in which all of the elements precipitate dizzyingly into a sort of funnel where everything is compressed. Everything is compressed in the figures that seem to pass through the experience of sex, everything is reduced to a structure in which both the images, and the bodies of the "actors", as well as the set itself are all confused in the very form of being a visual structure, in a lowest common denominator that is the very structure of the artwork, the skeleton. In that combination we can see the fusion of various elements without losing individual characteristics, a fusion that engenders a set of individuals who remain such. And prejudice seems to be one of the values of Pierre Molinier, the prejudice that defends against quantity; by choosing a form of concentration, the damnation of art, after all. All of the elements are equivalent in his artworks, all of them; there exists no preconstituted hierarchy, and what is proposed is a dynamic of representation that creates a movement of power, a movement of modification, a predefined hierarchy in which all of the elements have the same dramatic value. It is only a question of assorting the weights and the powers that are catapulted upon the spectator, entangling him: in irritation, complacency, disgust and complicity.

Molinier implements a capacity for the modification of objects and perceptions, and therefore of sensibilities. He knows that art has this capacity, this technique of modification of reality, and this technique is implemented by his images through the calculation of the powers that he manages to shift. For Molinier the sexual dimension seems to be a form subject to modification: it starts in one form and necessarily must wind up in another. There is a transmigration of body and sign, the body becomes a sign, traces an itinerary, a passage in an excessive and irregular figure. Molinier's work merges continually with the concept of biography, in the sense that biography is the identity that must necessarily be fought, and it chooses the mask, a transmigration from the masculine to the feminine, a tending from one form to another, a fluctuating identity very similar to child's play. The very selection of items of clothing alludes to a possible and perverse world, but at the same time this further possibility is frightening, it can be definitive. A sort of curse to repeat an increasingly exasperated sexual dimension, increasingly alluring. Molinier creates images that tend to make us aware of the fact that the protagonists portrayed are aware of doing things in front of other people in order to be watched by yet other people still. This mechanism determines a sort of dramatic construction that has to do with time, the manipulation of a power; for this reason the artist does not choose to perform in public. He has other objectives. The "chamber theatre" that he constructs in order to portray himself with respect to a performance is always related to fables, and it leads to a territory in which it is necessary to lose oneself. The performance does not need a curtain, darkness, a distance. The "chamber theatre" of Molinier instead requires the closing of eyelids, a moment of necessary suspension in order to make possible a mutation, a modification, a surreal and boiling voyage. All of his images develop out of his work on texts, which then becomes work against the text. They spring out of dramatic requirements, where the visibility of the route must be possible. The bodies must find themselves in the world of the image and they must fit in perfectly as a problem of form. The form of a body rebels *a priori* and becomes perfect and ready for all transgressions. With Molinier came the discovery of the bodies in order to then discover adventures in which everything is experienced in an unreal sense, an evil fable capable of transfiguring any body, sex, or disease…

An overabundance of glorious body, bodies marked and marvellous.

A close-up of organs, almost separated, that in their turn become bodies. A complexity that cannot be traced back to the organism but to an organisation, the corpus. All of this is very clear in the works of Molinier, where the sexual organ becomes an apparatus; it creates a system of tunnels in which the protagonist is lost, and the spectator gets lost with him. The same route as the narration: progressively as Molinier pushes further along, the spectator cannot help but follow him, feeling at the same time that he or she is an accomplice and a voyeur.

> *There occurs in them [women] a sort of self-sufficiency that compensates them for the sacrifices that society imposes on their freedom to choose their own object. Strictly speaking, these women love — with an intensity that is comparable to that with which they are loved by men — only themselves. In truth their needs do not induce them to love, but instead to be loved, and they please themselves with men who meet this need of theirs.... They exert an enormous allure for men, and not merely for aesthetic reasons (they tend to be the most beautiful women), but also because of certain interesting psychological constellations.*
>
> *(Sigmund Freud,* Introduction to Narcissism*)*

Phalluses, wheelchairs, female genitalia, shaving brushes, tongues, beds of contention: beginning from the watercolours of the 1930s and 1940s, Carol Rama chose to depict the symbols of an acknowledged and submersed carnality, a gaze and a collection of objects that in her artworks become obscene, scan-

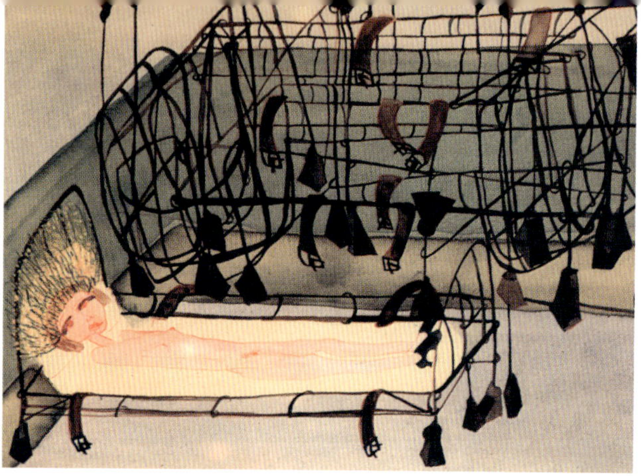

Carol Rama, *Appassionata*, 1940

dalous, excessive and embarrassing. Fragments of foreshortened females, and teeth and little red slippers and masturbation, Carol Rama traced the geography of experiences that indicate the variability of the feminine condition and the impossibility of portraying a standardised history of it; she tells a silent tale that can scarcely be told, an intimate and private history that contrasts with History, devoid as it is of the stories of women, and an incapacity to visualise them which makes clear the fact that History is always the story of someone in particular, never the story of everybody. "And yet Carol Rama girded this vivid visionary work with a disturbing halo that smacked of fable, myth: why distinguish that which belongs to the memory from a hallucination? We do not know and we should not know if we are penetrating into a painting, a dream, a page from a diary, the inventory of the unconfessable..." wrote Lea Vergine, and the artworks by Carol Rama become a sort of representation of the obscenity that chooses the disturbance of a code. It is the perturbance of the "conventional" language of an artist who insists upon "dirty" images and symbols ("divinely exciting obscene words", as Joyce described his own obscene letters to Nora), the intrusion into an accepted formal code by an element that traces the evidence of the rebellious awareness of Carol Rama exactly where the violation of a hierarchy, a rule, takes place: all that can cause a convention to vacillate.

For Carol
the long tongues sticking out (expert), and the
thuddingly heavy cocks (tension, contention):
(bodies, in other words): and the straps, and the hooks (and the crazies):
the blades (and the wigs), and the friction

(frigid) of the wheels, with the clubs
of the elbows and the arms: (and the action
of perambulators and baby carriages), and the spokes
of the curls (amputated): (and correction)

(corruption) of heads (and testicular
springtimes), of legs: the butchers
(the slaughterhouses), the knives, and the real

shoes: the exhibited fish (and fishnets, and rings),
the halfbits (indicted): and the fairs,
the markets: (the hair flourishes)
(Edoardo Sanguineti, 1980)

Sanguineti, Mollino, Pasolini, Man Ray, Andy Warhol, Massimo Mila, Luciano Berio are only a few of the strands of the larger web of relations of Carol Rama; "it is a sort of unauthorised appropriation that each of us commits with life", she was to state concerning her friends, all of them protagonists of stories that overlap, intersect and interact beginning with the expressive languages to which each of them delegated his or her sense of their own being in the world.

Carol Rama pursues and tracks down warps and wefts that lacerate the gaze, break into secrecy, give voice to the forbidden. The private sphere is separated from the public sphere and what emerges is the secret, independence, audacity, playfulness, grimaces and laughter; what emerge are the heroines of seduction who surprise by the vivacity with which they manage to speak to us of fear, joy, pleasure and fantasies, goddesses of shamelessness, impertinence and provocation. Deities, mythological figures and ordinary women are tracked down and displayed, they proffer advice and impositions and cures that serve no other purpose than to direct the universe of women, to educate them, monitor them, enclose them, protect them from their own physical and moral weaknesses, the cause of sinning and danger. As Giorgio Manganelli, a friend and great habitué of Carol Rama, wrote: "We need to get to the point where we can talk about culture the way we talk about pussy; let's get one thing clear, if culture and thinking aren't vital, if they don't engage you at a gut level (literally, not metaphorically, because thinking is a total thing, like dying, it is a 'fact', a true and tangible object), if there is not something dirty about it, disgusting, even revolting, like everything that has to do with the viscera, if it is not all of this then it is nothing more than vice, disease, decoration: things which it is good or even necessary and honest to rid oneself (strip oneself) of entirely"; and the artworks of Carol Rama speak of things that are dirty, disgusting, sometimes revolting. Sanguineti wrote: "Perhaps the secret myth of Carol is that men succeed in communicating one with another, not only through their poor recognisable codes, and even less through the equivocal impasto of feelings, the ambiguous repertoire of their emotions. But rather through a common practice of objects, in a sort of feverish intimacy". Eyes, skulls, syringes, tongues sticking out and snakes and blood and wreaths of flowers and teeth and breasts and shit: this is the repertory of Carol Rama, a repertory of personal, corporeal, suspect things, such as symbolic visualisations, like the monsters of the subconscious, or the gestures of abandonment. Her first personal exhibition was in 1945; she was already well known and appreciated in the most interesting circles of international culture, and her artworks had already generated notice for her rebellious style and her cruel use of materials. But in Turin her exhibition was considered scandalous: the lack of shame, her direct erotic references, her excessive subjects, but especially the absence of dramatic emphasis and the pure exhibition of the sexual objects on display triggered a repressive reaction, the police were summoned and the exhibition was shut down even before it could be inaugurated.

"The world of Carol Rama is a recipient of refuse, of nos, of nocturnal tatters, of excrement, of vicious graces: not simply because everything is peripheral, but to the contrary because it is connotation of the necessary, the centre, of everything

Annie Sprinkle, *April Showers…*
(from the *Muff of the Month* series)

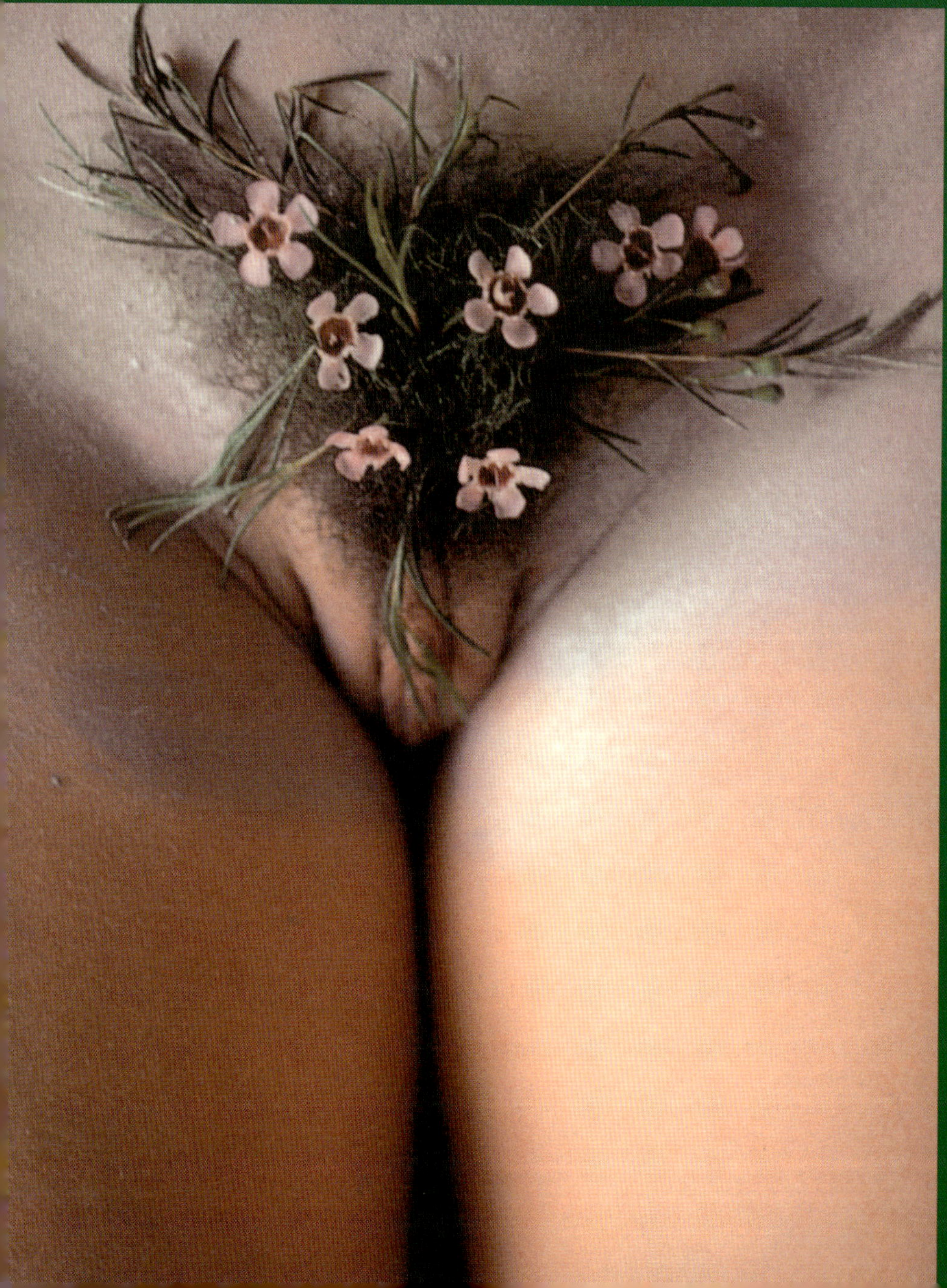

Annie Sprinkle, *Anatomy of a Pin-Up Photo*, 1997. Photo by Zorro, design by K. Gates

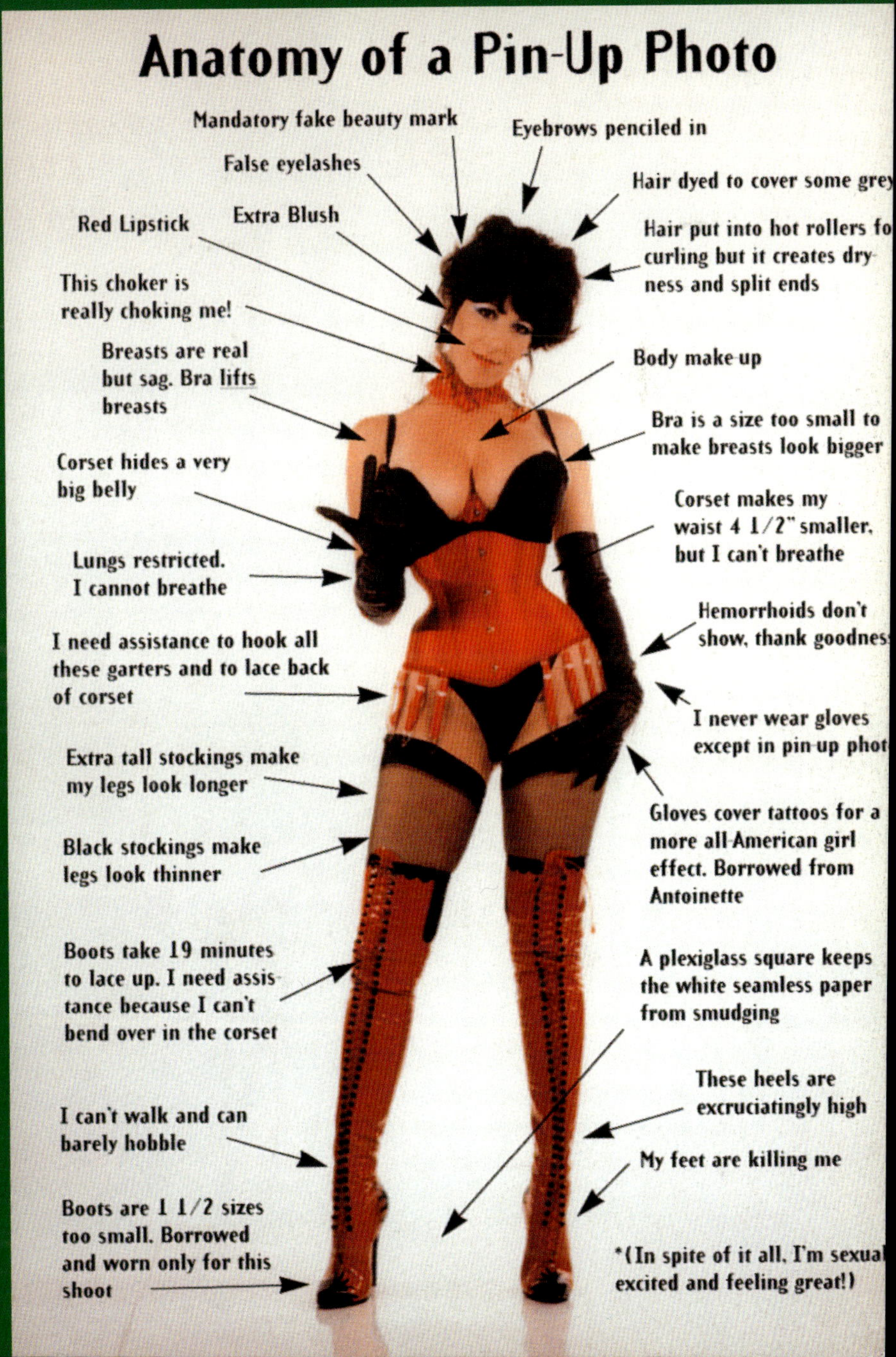

that is alive and therefore takes part in putrefaction and the lethal.... In the drawings of Carol Rama there is never anything dead, consumed, coagulated; everything is immersed in a spectacular putrefaction, everything chatters and rants and raves: a slobber of delirium envelops and delights all the images." (Giorgio Manganelli) After more than half a century, the output of Carol Rama, as well as the work of the last few years, provokes the same reaction of discomfort; but she continues "to invent an erotic, sentimental image, a private image, but which is not that closely linked to me, after all".

The taboo applied to the pointless, this passion for the futile and the artificial that is perhaps more fundamental than the sex drive itself.... Certainly, the same taboo applies as well to "futile", non-reproductive sexuality. But by fixating upon sex, we run the risk of extending the deceits of puritanism, which always attempts to shift the focus to the sexual.
(Jean Baudrillard)

Born in 1954 in the United States, Annie Sprinkle lives and works in New York and Amsterdam. She is a former porn star, a former dancer and a former prostitute. Annie (whose real name is Ellen Steinberg) explores everything that has to do with pleasure, transforming her own manifold erotic experiences in a sort of manifesto that intertwines Asian philosophies, political tensions, meditation, yoga and liberation from "trash sex". She has written more than three hundred articles about sex, she has founded magazines, CDs, newsletters, documentaries, acoustic experiments, books, movies, videos, photographs, websites, and done numerous performances. Among her most important texts we should mention: *101 Instructions for the Use of Sex*, or, *Why Sex Is So Important*, *Annie's Sex Guidelines for the Nineties*, *Metamorphosex* and, with Veronica Vera, the *Post Porn Modernist Manifesto*. Moving freely between the ghettoes of pornographic theatres and international art museums, through a series of actions, performances and videos she has exposed the areas in which the body expresses itself politically, culturally and literarily, beginning with the relations amongst these various phases and their general confluence into sexuality. She created a totally new and unprecedented dimension of female sexuality, and she has fought against a censorship that claims to protect "public decency" and "good morals", against a mutation that has already taken place. "My awareness of being a naturally sexual person was also an awareness that I could be something other than a porn star... I am accustomed to showing my sexuality openly; it is important for people to see the power of female sexuality... My work talks about me, about my sexuality, and it is work that becomes political because sex is political. I have used pornography to talk about sadness, intimacy, happiness, and many other feelings. Perhaps that is what has so upset people, which unleashes sex or those with whom we experience sex; people talk about porn as an overall concept, and that's not how it is. To an even greater degree what upset people is the happiness that I found in pornography: this is intolerable, because porn is commonly accepted only if the protagonists are unhappy and miserable because they have been unable to attain 're-spectability'. I have changed the rules of the game by talking about my happiness. And now it is my intention to become even happier, in a more intimate way... there are times when we are too tired to be happy..."

AIDS, abortion, euthanasia, rape and violence: art grafts research into the most merciless aspects of existence. A body regenerated in the biological and material-based sculpture by Jeff Koons, executioner and then victim in his intervention on the body, in his marriage and union with the porn star Cicciolina, in their bodies modelled in orgasm. An impact with a real world that has long since become fictitious in its forms and in its elements, a very concept of the real that breaks apart, replaced by models, projected upon its own image toward self-destruction. Celebration of sexual acts and erotic drives in a little pyschoanalytic and pop puppet theatre, simulacra, taboos from the sexual sphere, symbologies of the erotic body, and further detention and dependency linked to the feminine nutritional obsession, in the cube of chocolate consumed by the nibbling of neurosis and desperation. The nibbling of Janine Antoni. The nibbling of her hungry investigation into the heart of the contemporary unease, psychopathologies and brain washing, somatisation and schizophrenia of the everyday linked to the aesthetics of the female body, anorexia and bulimia. The difficult and powerfully marked path of women and their bodies in a quest for acceptance into the social and cultural system: feminine subjectivity violated and disturbed by a non-acceptance of the self caused by a dependency on the exterior, which then flows into a nutritional transgression. A woman imprisoned in a social masquerade, tortured by the image of a perfect body, by cosmetics, by aesthetic ideals, by the neurasthaenia of the end of the century. Women who lick the chocolate bust of their own libidinal body, consuming it, in a crisis between lipstick and chocolate bonbons. The body of the phenomenon passed through by plastic surgery and a new skin, fluctuating amidst human body parts emerging from the wall — the work of Robert Gober, separate yet autonomous limbs, which refer back to an unsettling presence, a terrifying absence, pieces of everyday life, amidst all-consuming domestic walls and middle-class civilian uniforms; and lastly it masquerades in the androgyny of Matthew Barney and his characters, howling a phenomenology of impossible incarnation, seductive and irreverent mythological creatures, metamorphic organisms in acid and symbolic representations, bodies detached from reality only to be plunged into the visionary and the mutant.

Control and dependency, electrical mechanisms and existential mechanisms, self-control and loss of the power of self-control, the structure metamorphosises itself and becomes a place of confinement, a measure of separation from the other: the body becomes prisoner of itself. The body and its individual subjectivity, still hounded by a system of hegemonic and subalternate powers, a claustrophobic system that pins us down with lobotomising mechanisms.

The photographic work of Nan Goldin seems to involve not only sight but the senses of smell, hearing and touch: bedrooms, bodies, embraces, bites, gazes, smiles, tears, bruises, burning cigarettes, alcohol, sheets, and hands touching sex. The bodies photographed by Nan Goldin function as trade goods: bodies as places of transgression and loneliness, bodies in which the identities multiply, bodies as a place of discovery, research, where sexual choices function as excursions of singularity, sex as a tool of encounter and communication. The "family" of this American artist is composed of men, women, gay people, transexuals, hermaphrodite, friends sick with AIDS, prostitutes, a tribe that has chosen to drift, even if it lives with the spectre of AIDS looming near. "What I am interested in is depicting the political and social side of what underlies sexuality… In my work

Nan Goldin,
Deborah and Noa Kissing, 1995

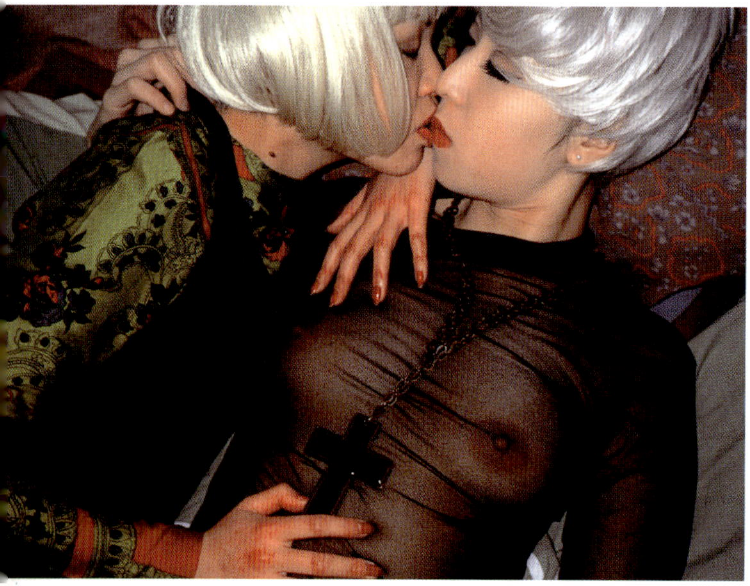

Nan Goldin,
Wayne and Toshi, 1995

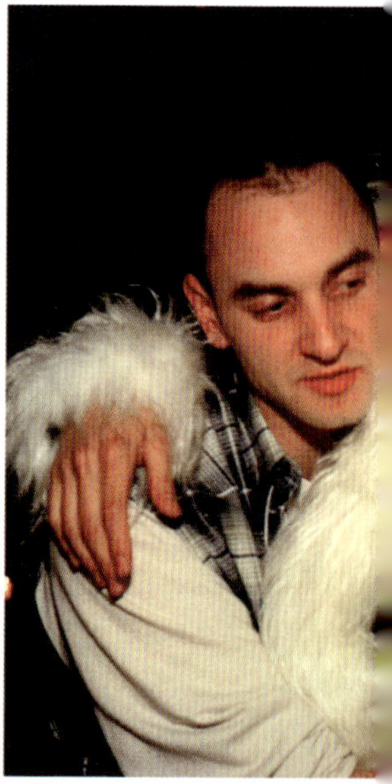

extreme sexuality is only touched upon. The central theme is love as a positive condition of reality. Love as the possibility of a being to live many different identities over the course of a lifetime.... Sex is a way of breaking through between you and the other, the most direct way of communicating."

In the series *The Other Side* Nan Goldin photographs the environment of the transexuals, whom she was already frequenting in the 1970s — in a phase in which the reality of the transexuals was not even accepted in gay circles — and which represented decidedly extreme and unacceptable lifestyles. Nan Goldin organised her photographic work as a sort of diary of images, which are practically a documentation of slices of lives and bodies in which the final idea is about loss, a modified sexuality, which invests the taboo of sexuality that is useless because it is not reproductive. And Nan Goldin, through her shots, became a witness of the mutations of bodies, genders, fashions, which have taken place in the context of sexuality over the last thirty years. *The Ballad of Sexual Dependency* is the result of a long process that began toward the end of the 1970s, and gathered photographs of autobiographical events: "Progressively as this project was developing, the slides tended to break down by category: men, women, transexuals, and so on, and that led to the birth of *The Ballad of Sexual Dependency*. These photographs taken from my life speak of my lovers, my friends, my places and my emotions". The series of slides was shown to the public in the form of slide show, a rapid projection of seven hundred slides with background music as a "voiceover", a view of worlds that tend to be relegated to the nocturnal dimension of "beings" kept at arm's length and mutated.

The images made by Nan Goldin seem to focus upon a form of conscious hu-

Nan Goldin, *Kana and Her Boyfriend, Akihiro*, 1995

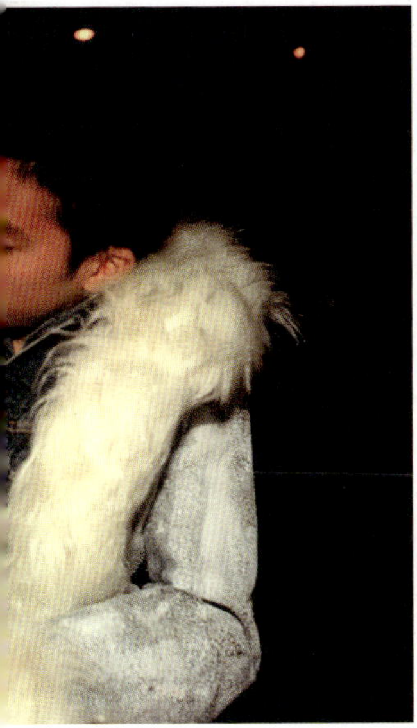

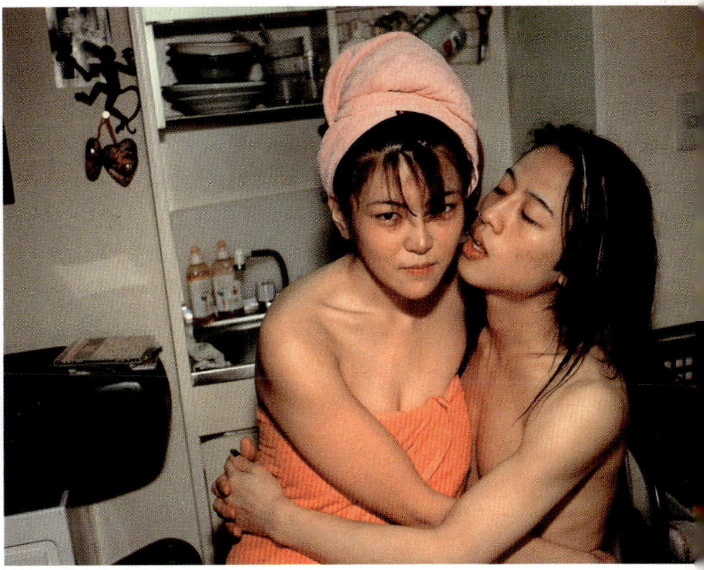

man marginalisation: protagonists of the anonymity of the metropolitan world, the individuals that she portrayed know that they are losers, repressed dreamers, characters in an existence devoted to the consumption of alcohol, cigarettes, drugs and sex, protagonists of a life that plunges into sheets and mattresses and borrowed rooms. Powerful images in which sex is a component of desperation and encounters, haphazard, forced, bored and inevitable. A form of sex that is necessary to fill the void of an existential impotence. The sexuality portrayed by Nan Goldin is harsh and incisive, a sexuality in which the genitalia have the same weight as the settings in which the sex is practiced: upside-down shoes, rumpled clothing, toilets with open doors, traces of moisture and mould on the walls, stains on the sheets, filthy kitchens, cheap perfume and soap bars, clouds of smoke hanging over everything, television sets left on… A sexuality the contributes to the creation of an environment that is downcast, shabby, devoid of even a hint of comfort; a sexuality that is given and accepted as inevitable, a long familiar scene that deteriorates with the relentless repetition, a sexuality without fantasy, without hope. A sexuality that is as heavy as the awareness of being out of the game. The protagonists portrayed by Nan Goldin seem to express the awareness of the precarious nature of their existence, bodies of both physical and psychological abandonment, shaken by the useless events that save them from martyrdom by marginalising them into survival, aware of their own frustrations in a dizzying whirlwind of relationships without satisfaction but necessary to their own survival. Skin carved by tattoos, surgery scars, bleached hair, the scabs and slag of a depression that exhausts bodies and gazes, always impotent in the face of the flowing stream of nights and days. Bodies that perceive their own fragility, their own lack of immunity, bodies that infect one another, fall ill, collapse. Once again, defeated. The places of Nan Goldin seem to have housed only this type of humanity, nothing but a diseased mediocrity; they are places where inevitably a certain type of individuals comes as if fatally attracted, where in anonymity one and all experience the same frustrations, the same marginalisation, the same precarious state. New guests, but all with the same characteristics as the previous inhabitants, a cycle of subterranean lives about whom no one thinks to ask, in which nothing important ever seems to happen. In Nan Goldin's photographs, the colours decompose, the smiles seem posed, the genitalia lose all erotic connotation, and we can clearly see tiredness, apathy, depression, the loss of sexuality, the depersonalisation that characterises the anonymous condition of these beings without history, individuals in airless and claustrophobic New York settings, a state of confusion in the underground flow of humanity. Even the quality of the photography seems shabby, every shot appears to want to amplify the dilettantish dimension that the subjects being photographed tend to express, a chance, haphazard dimension, without design, without ambitions, without hope. Everything seems to be impressed in fragments, an entire world captured in a fixed image, in which the flash acts as a disquieting presence: the flash is reflected in the mirrors, on the walls, in the glass, on the faces, in the eyes, as a blinding glare that almost wants to cancel out subject and setting, that appears to expand and spread over the entire image until it dissolves it, until it transforms it into a social overexposure, both sexual and generational, in which only the genitals are hyper-illuminated until they become indistinguishable, unrecognisable. Useless.

Nan Goldin's images seem to impress intimate motives that reveal a sense of awkward inadequacy, a sexual languidness and apathy in which the bodies appear off-balance, dragged at, hovering between twisting and unease, badly executed copies of sexual services in amateur, home-made pornographic films. Bodies that have been debilitated, wounded, beaten, sewn together, crushed and diseased. Bodies that fail to fit into any classification, concealed silhouettes, defenceless, assaulted by every sort of attack.

In 1989 Nan Goldin curated, at the Artists Space in New York, the exhibition *Witnesses: Against Our Vanishing*, which triggered violent debates. And as had been the case with the exhibitions of Andres Serrano and Robert Mapplethorpe, the authorities drastically reduced the funding available for contemporary art. The funding for the Artists Space was suspended and sero-positive artists, or artists suffering from AIDS were excluded from the show.

In a narrow sense AIDS (Acquired Immune Deficiency Syndrome) is not the name of a disease, but rather the name of a clinical situation whose consequences are a spectre of diseases: "AIDS has a two-fold metaphorical genealogy. Seen as a micro-process, it is described like cancer: an invasion. When attention shifts, however, to the transmission of the disease, a metaphor is evoked that calls to mind syphilis: contamination (it is contracted through the blood and the sexual secretions of people who are infected, or from contaminated blood products)" (Susan Sontag). In order to describe AIDS, military metaphors are used: invasion, mobilisation of cells, defenders of the immune system, anti-bodies that face up to the threat, and so on. A language that is typical, as Sontag goes on to suggest, of political paranoia, with accounts in which the infection preserves the science-fiction flavour based on the model of technological war.

But, aside from militaristic metaphors, AIDS is "proof" of an irregular behaviour, it is not so much a disease as a form of guilt, the guilt of dangerous behaviours, addiction to drugs that are injected into the bloodstream and/or sexual behaviours that are considered deviant. "With AIDS, shame is linked to an imputation of guilt… so far contracting AIDS means revealing, in most cases, that you belong to a certain 'risk group', a community of pariahs. The disease renders explicit an identity that might have remained hidden to neighbours, colleagues, family members and friends. It confirms an identity", writes Sontag again, and AIDS becomes the symbol of a "moral decadence", of the risks linked to "exchange", of the fear of a foreign "invasion"; and, by fomenting a strategy of terror with respect to the new and foreign peril, we find interesting indications in the proposal set forth by Jean-Marie Le Pen, in France, to require that all foreigners be tested, or the declarations of the former prime minister of South Africa: "The terrorists are challenging us now with a weapon more frightening than Marxism: AIDS". AIDS represents the threat of a total event, a menace to all of Western society, described as the consequence of illicit acts or as an invasion of "foreign bodies". It incarnates the fear of exchange.

Art absorbs and reflects the behaviour of a society that still divides the majority from the minorities, which still separates and closes off individuals into different categories such as blacks, women, gays, which still acts and reacts with the use of prejudices and stereotypes. In *The Importance of Gay Typification*, Richard Dyer wrote: "One of the most important characteristics of being gay is that it can't be seen. There is nothing in the physiognomy of a gay person that declares him to be gay, there are no biological markings like those that indicate sex and race. There are signs of being gay, a repertoire of gestures, expressions, forms of behaviour, and even settings… that speak of being gay". Subsequently he identifies classifications that subdivide into species and subspecies the members of a minority: macho, sad young man, queen and dyke are among the most commonly used stereotypes. As early as the beginning of the 1970s different ways of living one's own sexuality were discussed and made public; some began to openly express the need to shift away from predefined sexual identities, eschewing the quest for a fixed sexual identity through given models. In his *History of Sexuality,* Michel Foucault describes the characteristics of sexuality, and specifically of homosexuality in ancient Greece. In Greek classical sculpture, the male body was considered to be the central theme, adapted as aesthetically perfect, subjected to a diet that was meant to ensure the survival and well-being of the state as a healthy organism, interpreted as a physical metaphor for the *polis*. And the image of the classical pose of the male body became yet another stereotype of the gay iconography, the muscular body as a sign of a life that is neither depraved nor decadent, the symptom of a healthy existence, and the athletic, perfect body, in good shape, began to connote a homoerotic aesthetic. Athletes, sailors, motorcyclists, policemen: thus winds out the list of figures portrayed with muscular arms and exposed bodies that characterise the sexual statuary of the male body and which became explicit points of reference. The context in which the artists of the most recent generations approach the themes of sexuality and the multiplicity of genders has moved away from the classical poses and references to statuary for the homoerotic body: there is an attempt to emerge from the value judgement that classifies a being as woman, gay, black, and so on.

Piotr Nathan, *Solidified Leap*. *"The plan of the site shows an enlargement of the outline of a stain of urine on the mattress from a person who is dying of AIDS"*, 1993. Photo by Christine Fenzl

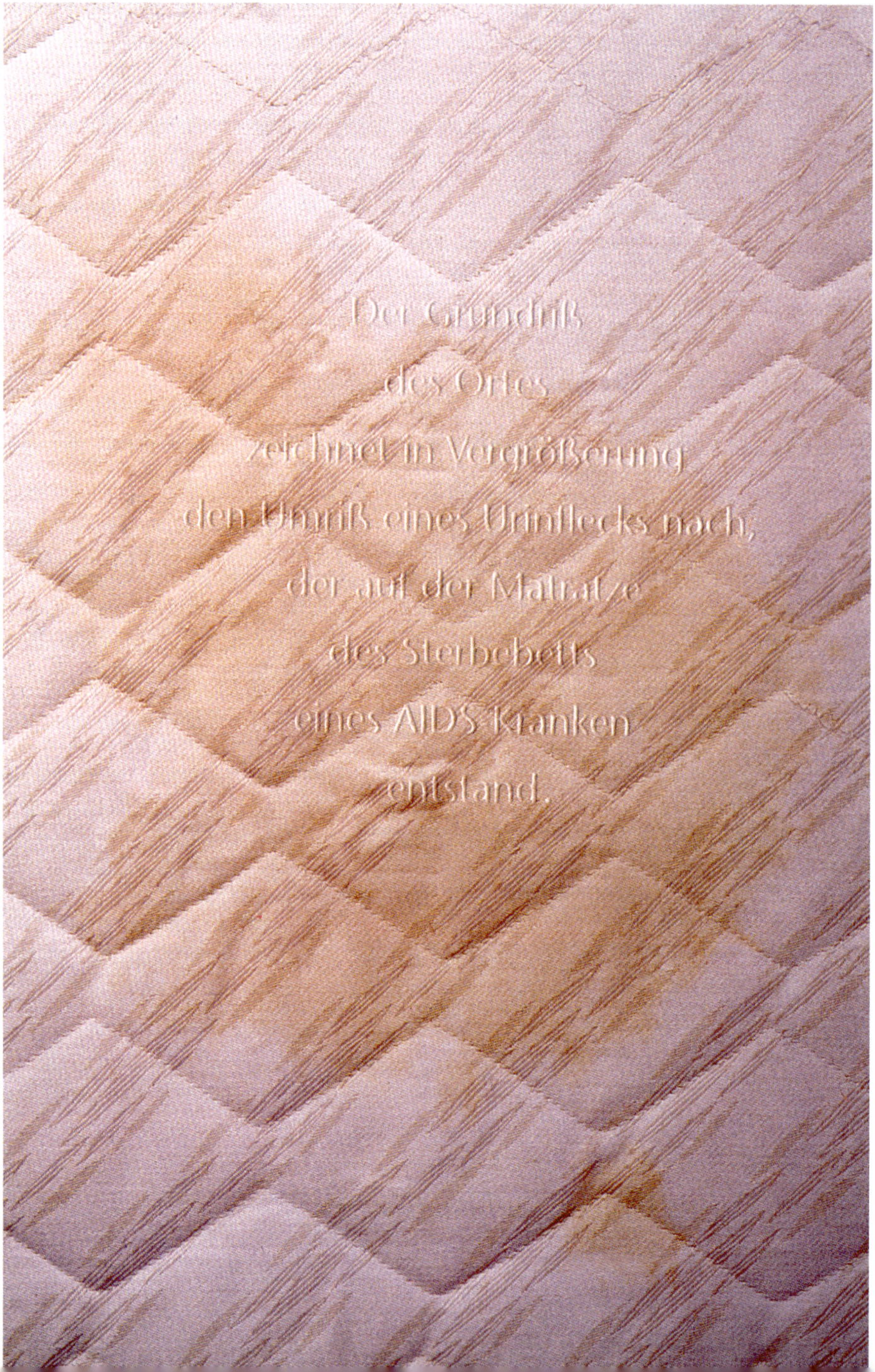

At the end of the 1960s, in America and in Europe, questioning the concept of masculine and feminine was chiefly a political necessity. Submission, the abuse or misuse of power, the lack of women's rights, as well as the masculine role in Nazism, Fascism, totalitarian systems, and last but not least, the War in Vietnam, impose a reflection on the concept of authority, roles, classifications and separations.

Jürgen Klauke was known in Germany at the turn of the 1970s as the performance-artist "who always had eye-shadow, lips with light-blue lipstick and fingernails painted turquoise". A complicated and tough-minded research into androgyny, gender-blending, the transformation of the body. The photographs that make up the series — *Self-Performance*, *Transformer*, *Masculine/Feminine* — directly treat the complexity and multiplicity of sexual identity: fake breasts, vaginas and flowers superimposed upon the male body, serpents and jewels explicitly open the discussion of sexual symbolism, all the way up to a neutral, manifold, ambiguous vision, to the point of confusion of roles and the emphasis of integration and disintegration in the attempt to redefine social relationships.

Slowly, the muscular representation, in the collective imagination, has been overlaid by the idea of being gay as abnormal, unnatural, as disease, and the fact of being gay has become a sort of middle ground between the sexes.

The Polish artist Piotr Nathan works on the dignity of man, wounds and cruelty. In intimate and poetic works shock makes its way to an encounter with the body in its everyday nature. "While I work I don't think of the reactions that I might unleash. A few days ago I was riding my bicycle and someone in a car insulted me with real hatred. In cases like that, one has a sudden impact with reality. You think that you are building a world for yourself where it is nice to live and everybody gets along, and then from one moment to the next you discover that 80 or 90 percent of the people surrounding you are full of resentment and would like to lock you up somewhere so that you couldn't get away. The same thing happens with my work. You do something in your studio and you think to yourself, 'This is my world and this is my sexuality', but I don't want to attack people whose reactions I don't understand."

Nathan invites friends and strangers to his studio and asks them to lie down on the mattress and relax to the point of pissing on the sheets, while he designs the various shapes that result from the stains they make. This led to the artwork *Solidified Leap*, displayed as a giant banner fifty metres long, made up of sheets stitched together. The urine stains become the common differentiating and analogous element, the marker of a private territory, the proof of the existence of an intimacy that Nathan decides to exhibit in the gallery's bathrooms. Every sheet is different from every other, marked by the individual singularity of the imprint left by the liquid, which harks back to the intimate action of madness and disease. The reaction was very tough, once again even the idea of naming bodily fluids was repressed. The urine stains, which for the artist were the signatures of the 37 persons who passed through his studio in that period, become a site of obscenity and a confirmation of the disease that proliferates in gay circles. The invitation for the exhibition, held at the Kunst-Werker gallery in Berlin in 1993, is a reproduction of one of the stains on the mattress, over which was printed this text: "The plan of the site shows an enlargement of the outline of a stain of urine on the mattress from a person who is dying of AIDS". Piotr Nathan's project is an autobiographical work: "I think that I have an identity inasmuch as I am gay, but I would not call my work research. I am quite simply interested in the state of materials, whether they be skin or other. The choice of the materials is closely bound up with my way of understanding art. My art does not have feminine aesthetic nor is it macho art. There are no stones, there is no iron. It is not built to last forever". Themes that are in some sense collected with the experiences of the end of the 1980s connected with homosexuality and AIDS, which render the presence and the absence of the body the principal subject of his work, artworks that are very physical but which refer to the body only through remains. The reference is to a marginal life, a slice of intimacy told to unknown people, individual history through objects and materials that impose themselves upon the universe of dematerialisation. It is the idea of the past and of the transitory that so fascinates Piotr Nathan, the ways of dying, as in the series *The Worlds of a Target*, done in 1993 with the casts of bulletholes on the walls of the houses along the old Berlin border, or else in *Solidified Leap*.

Absence and presence, an interplay of physicality and disappearance; in *Die dem eingesperrten Spiegel gewidmete Schwimmende*, in 1991, Piotr Nathan did an installation in the Nürnberger Eck hotel in Berlin: two naked men sleep on sofas and from the ceiling hang down, on threads, their jackets made of red and white lace; an armoire lies, overturned. The allusion to a fragile life, hanging on a thread, contrasts with the armoire on the ground, set out like a coffin ready to receive and conceal the bodies of the two men; the jackets hang, suspended, between sleep and death, without any body, pure physicality, pure containers of interchangeable bodies. Nathan moves along the line that separates intimacy from the audience: "I am interested in people. When I do something what interests me most is not the art. There are numerous motivations that drive me to do what I do. I live to invent stories when I go from place to place, looking at any given thing. I like to think: what are they about to do or what type of people are they? What job do they have, are they a couple or not? This is life to me. Being a part of it without trying to interfere", and so he allows the materials to express their metaphorical relationships with the individuals, veils, curtains, light, water, automobile windshields and windows, always in search of a poetic filter that makes it possible to see individuals as part of a vague and nuanced background, in search of a fragile protection of intimacy.

"From the 1980s on, death became part of everyday life. Anguish became a roommate in our bedrooms. It accompanied us everywhere and poisoned the possibility of trust between people", and so AIDS too was used as a further barrier against gay people. In the exhibition *Let the Record Show*, at the New Museum of Contemporary Art, graphic work by various artists was exhibited in the street-level display windows, and in one of them were shown portraits of seven people infected with AIDS, with adjoining quotations of ordinary people on the problem of the disease, one of which ran like this: "We used to hate fags for a basically emotional reason. Now we have a very good reason for hating them".

Robert Mapplethorpe, Felix González-Torres, Philip Lorca di Corcia, Lyle Aston Harris, Jack Pierson, Yasumasa Morimura, Wolfgang Tillmans: these are just a few of the artists who have dealt in their works with the dangerous and arrogant idea of identity experienced as discrimination, marginalisation, exclusion; each of them has opposed the power of prejudice with the iconography of the fragility of existence, the precarious nature of their own lives, the instability of feelings and the emotional cruelty of their own intimacy made into an artwork.

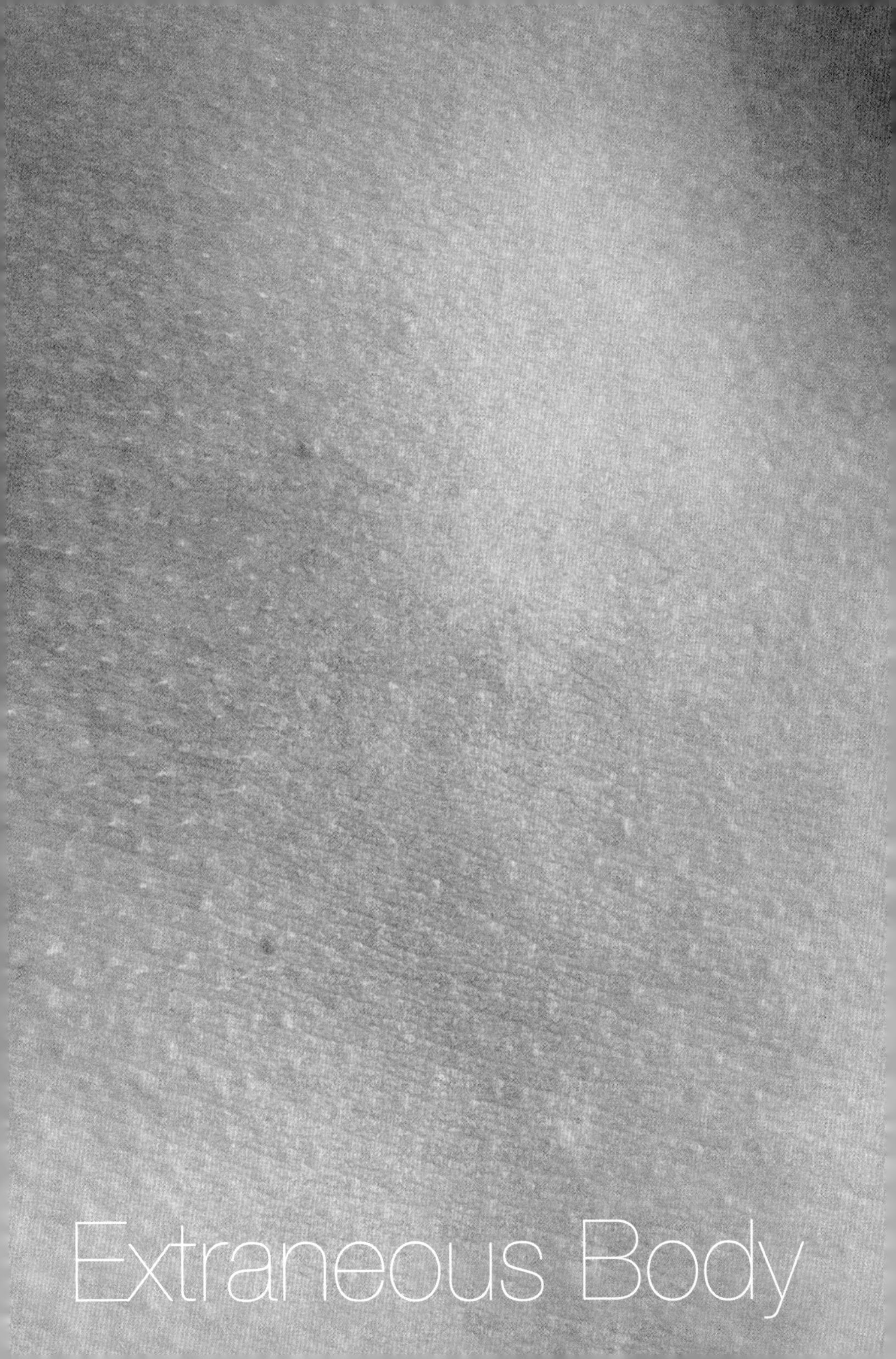

Extraneous Body

FOREWORD

...in the Western tradition persistent dualisms have existed...
Foremost among them are those of the self/the other, mind/body,
culture/nature, male/female, civilised/primitive, reality/appearance,
whole/part, agent/expedient, artificer/product, active/passive,
right/wrong, truth/illusion, total/potenial, God/man.
Donna Haraway

Donna Haraway traces, in her *Cyborg Manifesto*, several of the cultural trends that tend to focus the theme of the body in contemporary knowledge and power. In his analysis of the establishment of modern bodies, Foucault had developed the concept of "bio-power" and emphasised the political and cultural construction in which the human body was entirely redesigned according to a sort of anatomical and utilitarian mapping. Within this logic, the body is fragmented and its rationalisation is structured into an apparatus of constructions and processes directed to a summary disciplining of the body oriented toward specific discourses of utility. In the final analysis, the idea was to "break down" the body into privileged zones of use, from which to derive a full-fledged and veritable "anatomy of details".

The body that emerges at the centre of this discussion is the territory for a twofold vision: on one side it is considered as the sum of all its anatomical and organic parts, on the other it is seen as pure subjectivity, as the site of the transcendence of the subject. In the light of the spread of new technologies into society, Donna Haraway offers new models of the "will to know" of the contemporary order. Technology, a human product par excellence, has always multiplied and extended human faculties. Today, however, this parallel path has become so intimate that the technological and the biological, as categories, are intersecting and completing one another. "Pre-cybernetic machines could be infested but, in the final analysis, the machines did not move themselves, nor did they design themselves. They were not autonomous, nor could they reach the human ideal, they could only make fun of it. The machines of this end of the century have rendered entirely ambiguous the difference between natural and artificial, mind and body: our machines are fastidiously lively and we are frightfully inert."

The technocriticism of the 1960s and 1970s (especially in the United States) had directed its efforts exclusively toward the technologies of communication: let us recall, for instance, the experiments on corporeal extensions in the technology of Marshall McLuhan and the studies on cybernetics done by Norbert Wiener. Parallel with the study of communications technologies the foundations began to be laid for the analysis of biotechnologies which, at first considered to be of secondary importance, after a few decades would become the founding nucleus of contemporary technical and scientific treatments. The most important and far-reaching revolution which now appears looming on the horizon is represented by the possibility of intervening, replicating, altering, and above all, recreating through biotechnology the body's organic process. Genetic engineering and the technology of reproduction are among the most significant examples in this area: we are witnessing a sort of rewriting of the bodily parts, and in this context we should also note the presence of nanotechnologies, prosthetics, robotics, and virtual reality. This convergence of intentions, visions and experimentations offers the body as a "intersecting surface of multiple and changing codes of information, from the genetic code to the computer code".

From the surveillance in the network of bio-power according to Foucault, all the way up to the interventions in the contemporary bio-technological network, that which remains continually watched, analysed and controlled is precisely the body, a hybrid body, scrutinised on the infinitesimal scale of its component material.

"Writing, power and technology are old companions in the accounts in Western culture on the origins of civilisation, but miniaturisation has changed our experience of the mechanism. Miniaturisation has proved to be closely tied up with power: it is not that small is nice, as much as that small is dangerous, as with a Cruise missile."

Bio-technologies operate a sort of rewriting of the biological structure: "In the empire of bio-technology, we have finally moved past the order of the sign.... We are not merely talking about cellular experiments in the laboratories of exact science, but also about the language of the laboratories of recombinant genetics as incubators of a new language of political and social power".

In this sense, biotechnologies become a process of textualisation of the body as a problem of code, a form of "sequential ordering" of human codes, inasmuch as a transcription (of the human) by purely technological means. The universe of a hybrid body, made of machines and organism, is developed in the theories set forth by Haraway with the idea of the cyborg. The cyborg is the idea of bodies that are being produced in this period: the technologies of communication and biotechnologies constitute the principal means of their reconstruction. These new instruments form the terrain upon which an entire new vision of life, social relations, identity and perception is constructed.

Robert Gober, *Untitled*, 1991

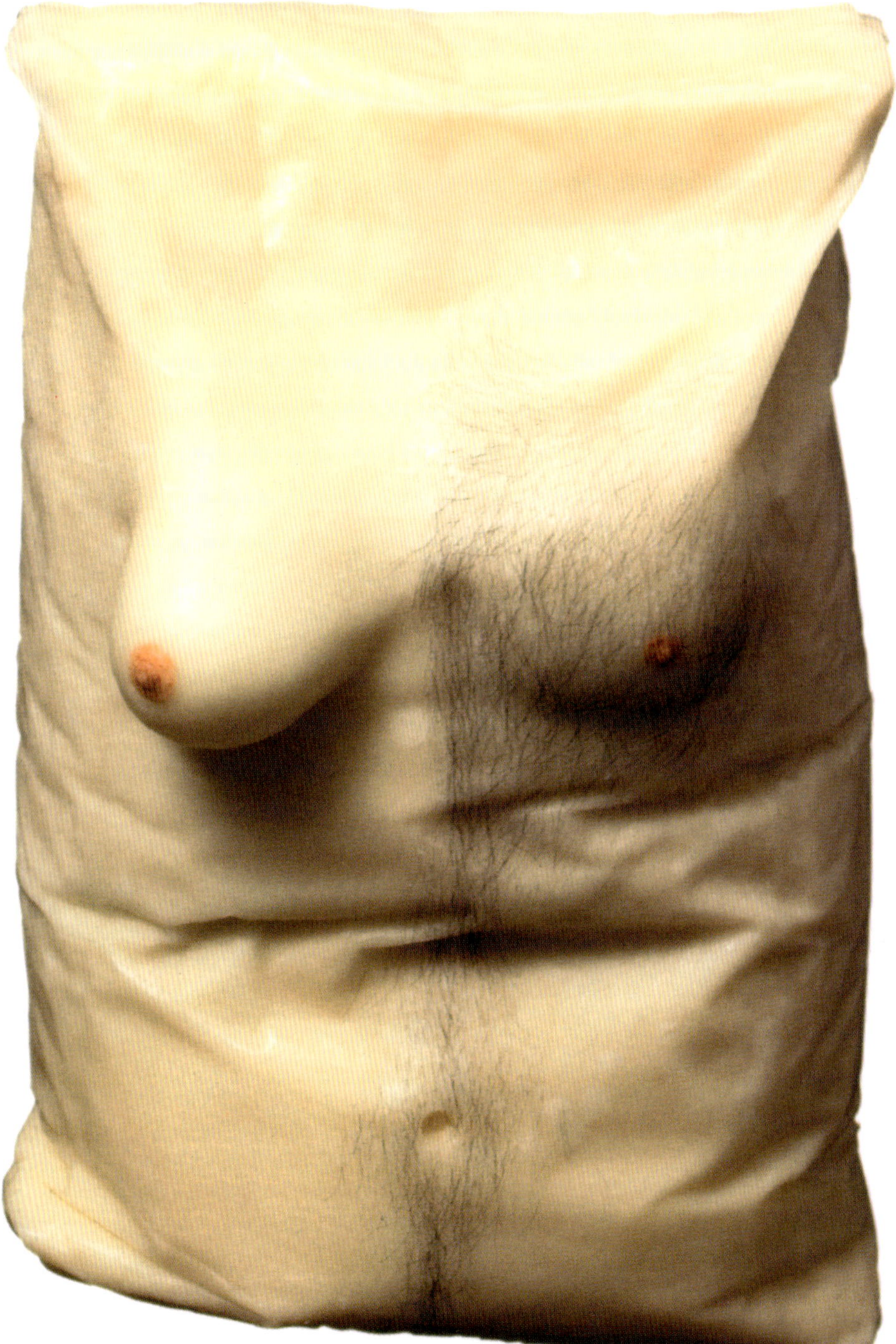

From cars to television, the goods that the spectacular system chooses to produce also serve it as weapons for constantly reinforcing the conditions that engender "lonely crowds".
Guy Debord

INCARNATIONS

It was at the end of the 1950s that an era dawned in which it became clear that there was a new way in which the economic organisation and the conception of knowledge were being transformed, especially on the basis of the powerful impact that new technologies and means of transportation have on society and people's minds. "Knowledge is and will be produced in order to be sold...", wrote Lyotard, indicating a form of knowledge which was becoming the most sought-after kind of merchandise, upon which all the systems of production were based; it is the goods for which men will fight. In this new technological habitat the dynamics of communication and the complexity of languages have become per se the basis of the possible analyses of culture, especially in the face of the manifestation of the illegitimacy of scientific knowledge and the extinction of great narratives.

"At the same time, the classical boundaries of the various scientific fields are subject to a process of revision: certain disciplines disappear, and there are shifts in the borders between others, resulting in the creation of new territories", once again, Lyotard writes; and he writes further about how technology has become a prosthetic device that commits the body to efficiency, and about how science is financed only with a view to increasing the power of the financier and how it is access to information and the management of scientific discoveries that nowadays confers "legitimising" power. The structure and the opportunities of the new languages in the post-modern era for Lyotard define imagination as the capacity to link together data that are usually considered to be independent, to dare to combine things that will necessarily have equivalent worth since nothing ever has an absolute validity for one and all nowadays. Extensive communication, interdisciplinary context, commodification, manipulation of information, a high technological level, a general sense of precariousness are characteristics of the post-

Orlan, installation video for *Ceiling no. 5* (from *Performance: Opération Réussie*), Paris, 8 December 1991

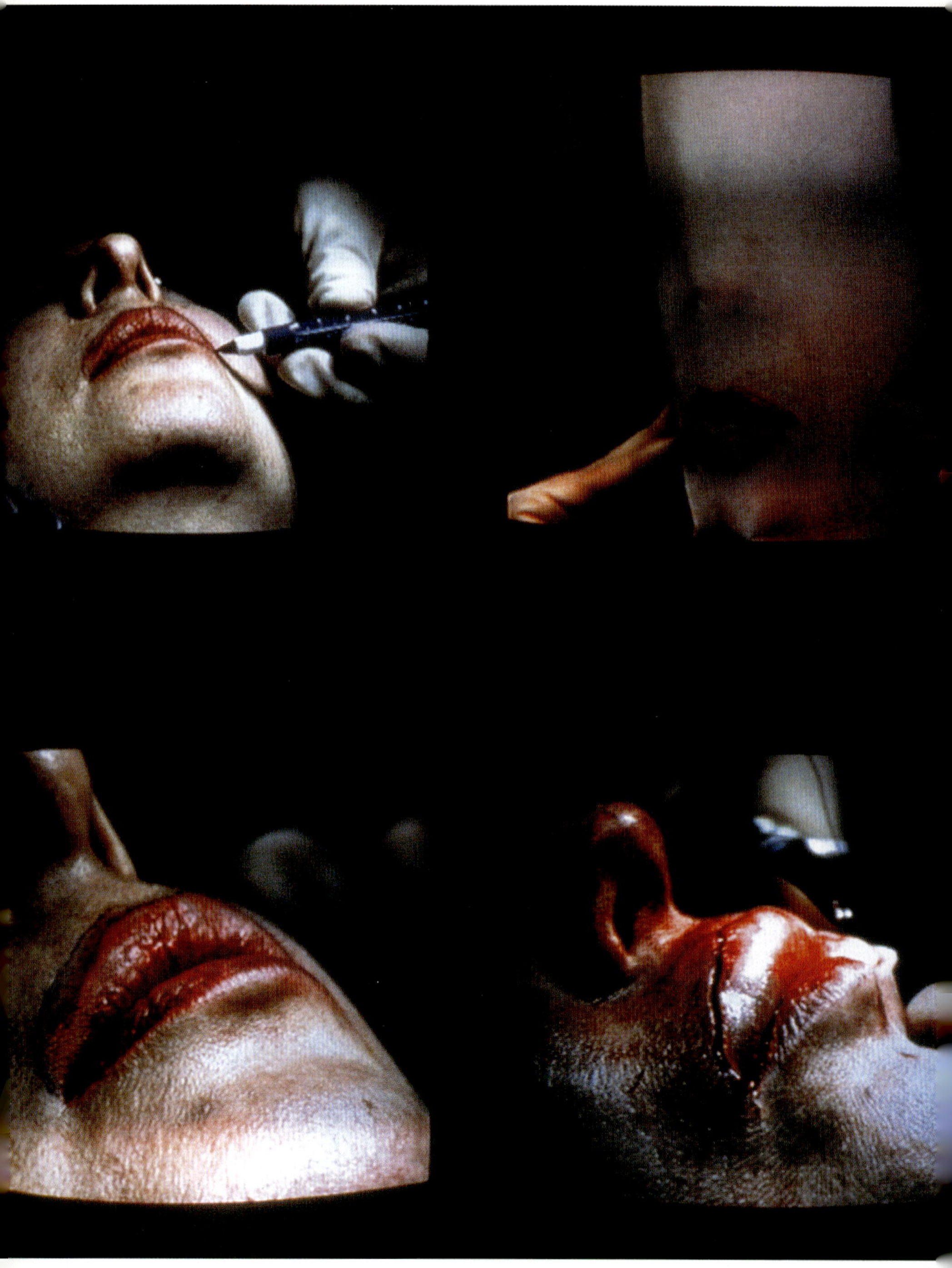

Orlan, *Photographic triptych with injections of anaesthetic in the upper lip and central photograph with narcissus*, 1993, detail

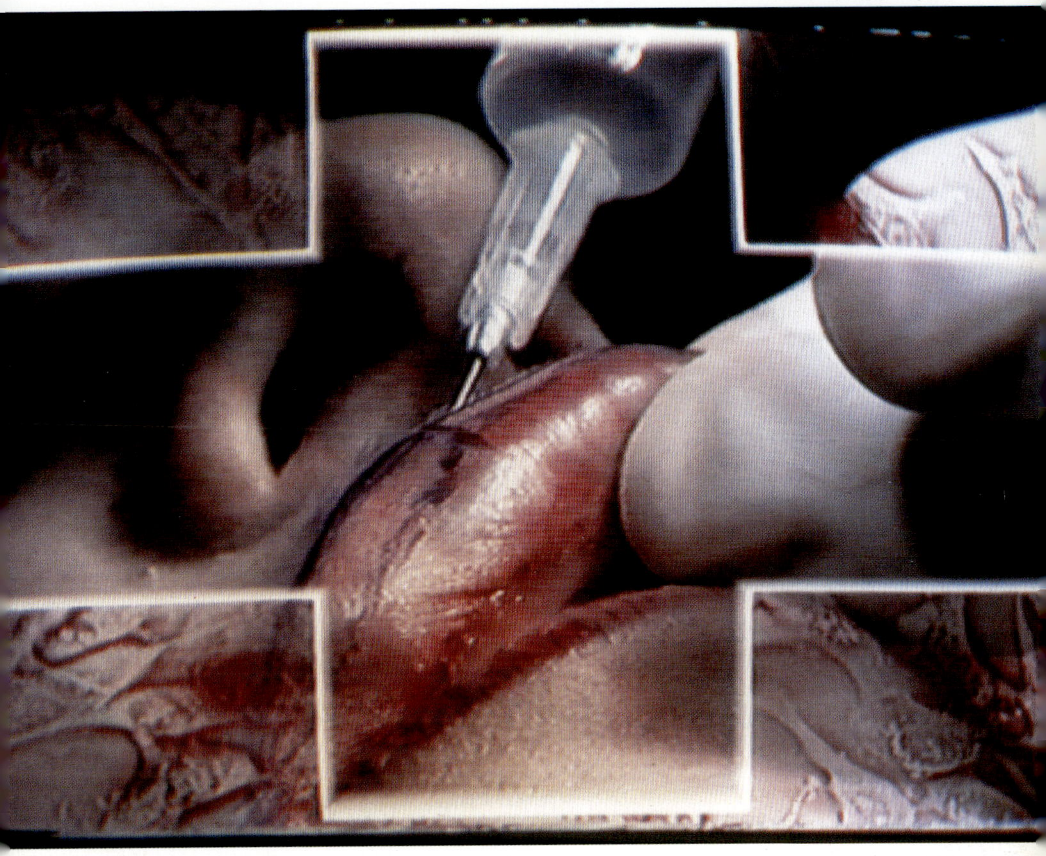

modern condition that have proven to be variants of the Society of the Spectacle, identified and thoroughly defined by Guy Debord.

It was in 1967 that Guy Debord published *The Society of the Spectacle*, the text that would pioneer the tensions and the intentions of the social organisation that began to establish its own presuppositions in the production of reality. Debord analysed and identified a contemporary world in which the categories of true and false were artificially produced by the media, which condition and determine new illusory dimensions set forth as real. The language of images is the privileged social communication of a spectacularisation of which each and every power has always made use; but what becomes important now is the diffusion and ramification of the mechanism, which now acts on an unprecedented global extent.

"From cars to television, the goods that the spectacular system chooses to produce also serve it as weapons for constantly reinforcing the conditions that engender 'lonely crowds'." No one manages to have an overall view, the individual is completely separated from every context, and is immersed in a micro-world that presents itself as the only one possible, and as global. Debord identified in the change of the means of production and the flow of the economy the prime operative factor for the existence and overloading of a "surplus of survival" that converted every activity, product, feeling and human relationship into a merchandise, and all relationships into commercial relationships. The world is the world of merchandise, and it imposes the duty to produce and consume, in an unstoppable cycle. Consideration is now given not only to the worker's working time but also to his free time, and the workforce is expected to provide a further contribution, meeting its obligations as consumers: "Thus the 'perfected denial of man' has taken charge of all human existence".

Everything, in the society of the spectacle, is falsified in conformity with the interests of industry, and the individual has been led to produce a spectacular thought that induces him to be willing to serve spectacular power. "He will essentially follow the language of the spectacle, because it is the only one that is familiar to him: the one in which he was taught to speak." In Debord's view, in fact, nowadays the individual sees the world essentially through images already selected by others: the omnipotence of the spectacle generates the ignorance of the spectators, and this ignorance leads them to ask no questions concerning the conditions of existence. Science itself is at the service of the economy, right up to the point of threatening the very possibility of human survival. "When the all-powerful economy has become mad, and the spectacular times are nothing but this, it has suppressed the last traces of scientific autonomy...", and in a society in which the omnipotence of the spectacular economy is openly admitted, science is forced to rely upon a market that has shifted toward spare parts and spectacular aesthetics regarding the human body. Again Debord: "The action takes place in an unspecified time in the future. A mysterious disease caused by the use of cosmetics has wiped out all women who have passed through puberty. Even 'culture', in all its forms, has become a spectacular merchandise: the image is omnipresent, it organises the consumption of 'events' that engage and enthuse individuals; all images are placed in a spatial neutrality and a temporal suspension without precedents. For the first time in history the arts of all ages and civilisations can be known and accepted together, and the fact that it has become possible to collect and recollect all these art-historical memories marks the end of the world of art. In this age of museums in which artistic communication is no longer possible, all the previous expressions of art can be accepted equally, because the loss of their peculiar and temporal conditions of communication is definitely eclipsed by all the present-day obstacles to communication in general.... Ideas improve. The meaning of words plays a role in that improvement. Plagiarism is necessary. Progress depends on it. It sticks close to an author's phrasing, exploits his expressions, deletes a false idea, replaces it with the right one".

And slowly the spectacle takes the place of life, it is everywhere, it occupies all the spaces through the merchandises that have activated the process of banalisation that artificially constructs differences and humours: from birth, to childhood, to work, free time, early old age, everything has been colonised, up to and including death, which, as Debord writes, in society is now present only in those commercial activities that managed its worth in terms of money, such as insurance companies, and undertakers who administer the future of dead bodies. "This social absence of death coincides with the social absence of life."

The world has been transformed into a place of logos, advertising invades all of the spaces of the mind and all urban and extra-urban sites, imposing an increasingly massive presence of itself; David Lubars himself, the advertising director of the Omnicom Group, defined the strategy that regulates industrial policies: "Consumers are like roaches — you spray them and spray them and they get immune after a while..." And experts are constantly inventing new sales techniques: Gordon's Gin has been diffusing in English movie houses the smell of juniper berries, phone calls can be free of charge if they are interrupted by advertising messages, promos for the films of Batman are projected on sidewalks or into the night sky. In December of 1998 NASA announced its plan to accept advertising messages in its space stations, Pepsi plans to project its logo onto the moon's surface, Mattel painted pink an entire street in Salford, England: houses, terraces, trees, streets, dogs, automobiles, all transformed into accessories for the television celebrations of the Pink Month of Barbie... A sponsored existence punctuated with logos, without any possibility of redemption.

This social organisation requires new individuals with new bodies: it becomes clear how simple and accessible it all is, fashionable and necessary, the restructuring of the human body and its architecture. We discover that it is necessary to modify oneself in order to reconfigure one's own body through the hypotheses of new and advanced biotechnology; cosmetic surgery offers models of beauty formulated in accordance with the icons of the star system; discussion is going on over the alterations of the reproductive system and artificial spare parts; we are constantly inventing new serialised and classificatory configurations; we live under the control of the technology of social surveillance; our spaces are invaded by videocameras and monitors, disguised as organisms of care and prevention...

Orlan's project calls for a body that does not want to be anaesthetised, aware of its own metamorphoses, of the continual crossing of boundaries on the part of violent medical, scientific, technological, theological and mass-media intrusions; it is a project for a body that rejects the standards of beauty of special offers, a project for a monstrous, freakish, different body. "My body expresses the possibility of showing that beauty can take on appearances that are not generally considered to be beautiful. Every civilisation has fabricated its own bodies: showing that the body is completely alienated by religion, labour, sports, and even by our sexuality, which is the fruit of previously established models. Whether I am displaying the features produced by surgical operations — plastic results that have never been hypothesised for human being, or if I am showing digital images that reproduce ideals of beauty from various cultures around the planet which I associate to my own face, the result is invariably a production of hybrids, mutant bodies with possible appearances." Orlan opposes forehead implants to the body that is disappearing, along with questions about identity, the body and its relations to the new normalising, standardising strategies of power. Orlan self-grafts in a metamorphic process of identity through her own flesh and her own blood, transferring to it the bio-politics of the post-modern body, cyberfeminism, the problem of diversity, her own reconstruction, the manipulation of DNA, the body of mythology. Her body escapes the control of the market, it eludes the capitalistic logic that proposes and imposes a stereotypical canon, a prefabricated model to stimulate supply and demand, it detaches itself and retaliates against the imposed models of female icons of male desire, and thus be-

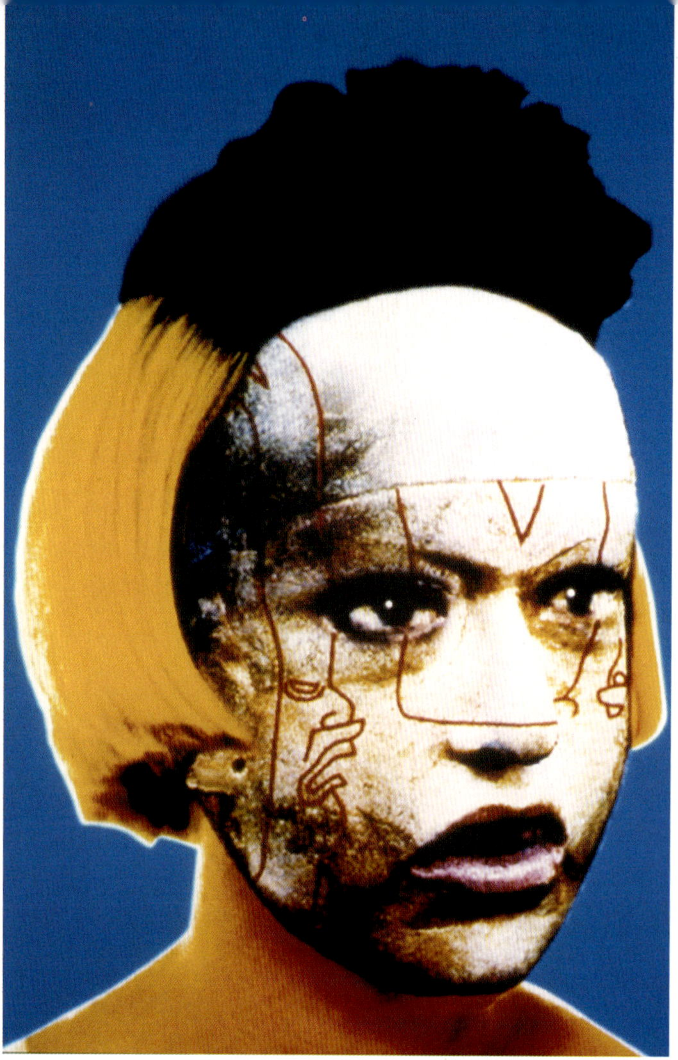

Orlan,
Refiguration - Self Hybridation n. 1,
1998

comes a non-conformist, anti-aesthetic and antithetical body. Her vagina is immensely enlarged, coloured by menstrual flow and by painting, and is completed with a text by Freud concerning the head of the Medusa: “At the sight of the vulva even the devil runs away”. The artist walks through the streets of Paris with her nude body printed on her clothing. She becomes *Sainte Orlan*, a blasphemous and exciting saint, and still saint and whore she offers tongue-kisses to whoever puts a coin into her plastic naked silhouette, offering instead the chance to light a candle to the Virgin Mary to anyone who puts a coin into the papier-maché image of St. Orlan. She disturbs the tranquillising respectable culture, she brings together the irreconcilable extremes of the stereotypical male imagination, she unhinges the social and symbolic structures of state, family and authority, and she hurls herself into the mutant adventure of an operation of plastic surgery, the archetypal project of facial redefinition. She is the first artist to have

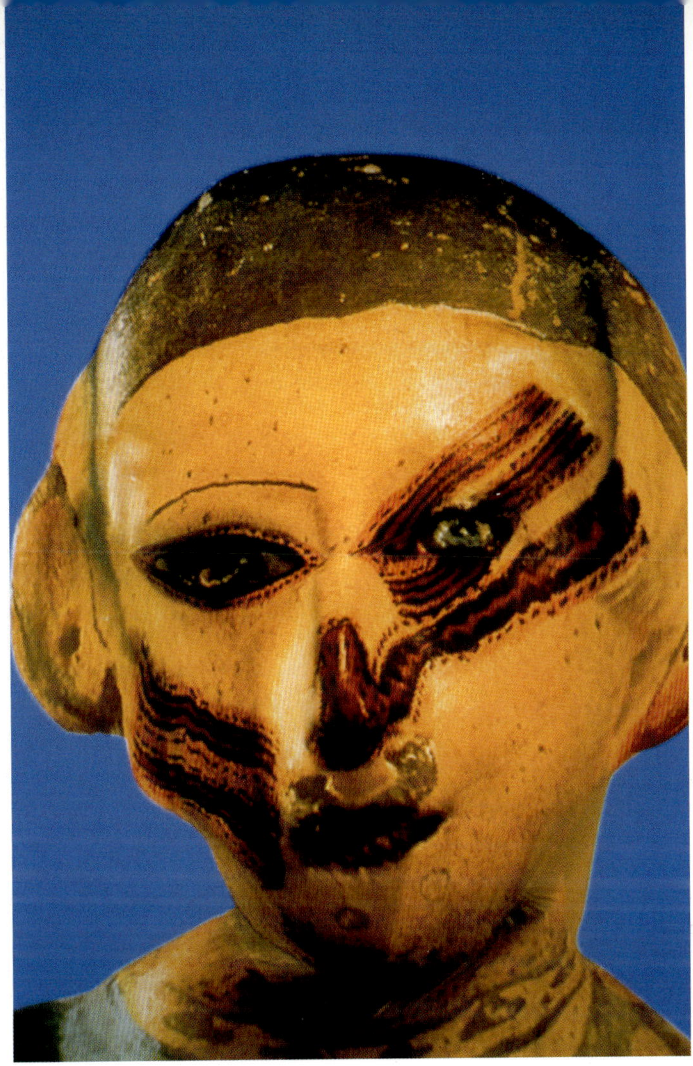

Orlan, *Refiguration - Self Hybridation n. 15*, 1998

used cosmetic surgery in the context of techno-biology in order to undertake her own transformation: she sketches out the idea of an identity exchange of a face that transforms itself through the icons of memory, history and myth, and through their hybridisation, she works directly upon the taboos of identity and organises her own escape from her own body-prison. Orlan subjects herself to a series of operations by plastic surgeons designed to change her own bodily image; she is the first to use surgery, deviating it from its content of improvement and rejuvenation, in a complex and radical attempt to mutate her identity. It is a project of continual destruction of all possible identifying images, seeking out and creating new ones. The interest of Orlan is centred on the creation of a nomadic identity, and in her fifth operation, *Performance: Opération Réussie*, 1991, she gives concrete form to her mutant adventure. Plastic surgery involves her in a project of archetypal facial redefinition: there is nothing aesthetic about the operation, all of the work is focused on the deconstruction of the ideals of feminine beauty, deconstruction of the icons of memory in order to reconstruct an indefinite and changing elsewhere, in this sense negating the notion of identity. For her fifth operation, Orlan has elaborated the text by Eugénie Lemoine-Luccioni, *La robe*: "Skin is deceptive... In life, you have nothing but your own skin... there is an error in human relations because a person is never what they have... I have the skin of an angel, but I am a hyena, I have the skin of a crocodile but I am a puppy, I have black skin but I am white, I have the skin of a woman but I am a man; I never have the skin of what I am. There are no exceptions to the rule because I never am what I have..." From the reading that Orlan does of this text emerges the idea of reducing the distances between being and appearing, there springs her determination to dedicating herself to her own plastic redefinition. The operating room becomes a sort of "theatre of cruelty" where a new identity is experimented and where all of the technical and surgical procedure is filmed on video, photographed and sketched: all material that will be exhibited during the second half of the performance.

During her sixth operation (1992) Orlan makes use of the discarded materials, the remains of the operations, by building armoured display cases that contain a circular recipient which in turn holds twenty grammes of her flesh, and on the display cases she has inscribed a text by Michel Serres: "What can we do now, the tattooed monster is running, the ambidextrous monster, hermaphroditic, of mixed race? Yes, blood and flesh. Science speaks of organs, functions, cells and molecules, admitting in the end that the time has come to stop talking about creating life in the laboratory; but never speaks of flesh, which indicates only the blending, in a given part of the body, right now as we speak, of muscles, blood, skin and hair, bones, nerves, and various functions that, if blended together, form that which the appropriate discipline analyses".

In the futuristic society staged by Andrew Niccol in his first film, *Gattaca*, an operation of "cleaning up" the discarded scraps becomes a full-fledged question of survival. Shaving, scraping off one's skin, plucking hairs, scrubbing, energetically rinsing all of the tissues in order to eliminate the cells of dead epidermis, prevent the body from losing its own residue by chance. It is not merely a "hygienic" question, since in the world of *Gattaca* the genetic code has become the only credible form of establishing identity: all that is required is a hair, a fingernail, an eyelash, even the imprint of the mouth on a cup or a glass in order to establish without a doubt just who you are. In *Gattaca* there are only two classes: the valid and the non-valid. The former are individuals who were genetically programmed and conceived in a laboratory so as to maximise the positive elements in the genetic code of their parents (eliminating *a priori* any predisposition to illness, obesity, myopia, baldness, alcoholism, drug addiction, and so on), while the latter are, in contrast, individuals generated in accordance with the archaic and absolutely risky and haphazard technique that involves a chance encounter between an ovum and a spermatozoa. The first class is made up of the elect, the second class consists of the subalternates. There are no longer any distinctions of class, wealth, or race. Genetics determines *a priori* the hierarchies of state, attributes roles and professions, establishes the boundaries and the sectors of the social body in virtue of a "chromosomic Nazism" (in the film it is called "geneism") with extremely rigid rules and despotic boundaries.

For the seventh operation, *Omniprésence*, 1993, Orlan organised a real-time transmission via satellite of her performance. The hookup made spectator interaction possible, allowing them to witness the operation and ask questions to the artist. During this operation, Orlan had two implants inserted into her forehead that are usually used to heighten cheekbones, two protuberances that served to annul any stereotype of desirable beauty and take on a disquieting appearance. Following the operation, in the Sandra Gering Gallery in New York, forty metal diptychs were exhibited, corresponding to the forty days that the exhibition lasted, plus one final image: a photograph of Orlan with her face passed through morphing. Each day, on the upper half of the diptych, a photograph of Orlan during her treatment was shown. At the beginning, the face was swollen and bandaged, then coloured, from dark blue to yellow, passing through red. On each plate were inscribed the words, "Entre les deux", and the date. On the last day the installation was complete.

Orlan's work, focused as it is on the destruction of any and all identifying images, leads inevitably to the question of being, of the subject. The artist does not place herself in her corporeal image in continuous mutation, nor in the images made possible by elaborating her own image on a computer. Orlan poises herself and emerges as a being "between the two", as something that continually eludes this interplay of imaginary references.

The images, whether they are photographic or on video, are always extremely powerful and shocking. The body opens up, blood spurts out of it, which the artist uses to make drawings, the scalpel penetrates, cuts, modifies the formal structure of the face. The impact is unquestionably disturbing and shakes up an audience heavily anaesthetised by the generalised spectacularisation that characterises the contemporary world. All of the performances begin with the reading of a number of texts that were fundamental to the development of Orlan's thinking: Michel Serres, Eugénie Lemoine-Luccioni, Artaud, Hindu texts, Raphaël Cuir, and others. "I read texts for as long as I can, during the operation, even when they are working on my face, which gives my latest operations the image of a corpse being subjected to an autopsy but which continues to speak, as if detached from the body…" The clinical appearance of the hospital setting disappears, replaced by a setting and choreography designed by the artist herself, from the images on the walls, to the characters present, to the clothing by various noted designers; the demystification of the surgical acts is accompanied by the determination to render it public, to open to the view of the world an act that is customarily considered private, to be carried out in solitude, an act to be concealed as if it were accompanied by a feeling of shame. "Rite of passage", is how Orlan describes it, to underscore the mutation to which she has subjected her own body, a body that changes from a natural and biological construct into an artificial structure, in continual transformation and alteration, always diverse and different. Finding oneself looking at this synthetic face, a symbol of the artificial which impresses its sign on our time, the symbol of a transformation pushed to its most extreme consequences, is unquestionably strongly suggestive and disturbing. Orlan denounces the basic assumption of the Christian religion, as well as psychoanalytic culture, according to which you must learn to accept yourself for what you are, and not for what you feel you want to be. If the two things fail to coincide, then we have pathology, disease and deviation.

"My work is opposed to DNA", claims the artist, implying with those words the need for all of us to stop and think about the new direction that human evolution is taking. An evolution that will no longer be a matter of chance, but which will in all likelihood be programmed, or at least managed, by knowledge, by the discoveries that are being made in the field of genetics, robotics, prosthetics and culture. A body that can be decided as a reversible decision. But also a mutant identity, the fruit of the tension that is established between the human and the technological, an identity not given or imposed, but rather planned out and constructed, not unique but multiple.

Orlan transforms her body into a living artwork that expresses the tension that contemporary man feels toward a future, already in existence, in which the relationship between organism and mechanism, between human and technological, becomes a hybrid. She exhibits extracts and relics of her body/artwork: at the Sydney Biennial of 1992 vials containing samples of her liquified flesh and blood drained off during operations; at the Lyons Biennial of 1995–96 four videos inset in the hospital-green ceiling, with a high-powered surgical lamp pointing right at the spectator (are we spectators of the event now finding ourselves on the operating table?), and she accompanies each appearance with a lecture during which she explains, with extreme clarity and precision, the evolution of her artistic approach and the meaning of her operations. "Lectures are an integral part of my work; moreover they make it possible for me to reach a larger audience... The discussion that follows after my lectures is crucial, it is a working session for the audience and for me, during which everybody develops their personal views of the world.... My body has become a site for public debate. And that is what I wanted."

Through a technical and surgical procedure, filmed and documented with photographs and drawings, Orlan proposes the morphology of multiple identity that proliferates to infinity, a desiring impulse: a changing of skin, a blurring of the flesh, a shaking of identity; and through the digital images of her own devastated, swollen and hybridised face, she challenges the anaesthetised psychic mechanisms of the spectators. The distances between being and appearing are reduced, she refuses to submit to men and God, she renders public the surgical act in its private dimension, and relics and blood sacrifices return to testify to the existential profundity of the performance. Orlan has had two protuberances grafted onto her forehead, which annul and completely re-elaborate all the stereotypes of the aesthetics of desire, of beauty: two facial excrescences like micromutations in the new flesh that present a two-fold challenge, to the natural and to the affirmation of the mass-market artificial imposed by the society of the spectacle. A challenge, offered by Orlan, that proposes an individual in all of his or her multiplicity, which records the alienation of every form of diversity, which suggests the affirmation of an unprecedented corporeality, a diverse and liberating existential condition, which attempts to subtract the body from the drift of its own flesh and from the inevitable breakdown of its organic dimension, replacing the degradation of living bodies with the interesting and seductive prospect of a self-produced body. For more than thirteen years now, Orlan has opened once again a discussion of the moral and social foundations of the contemporary, of traditional aesthetics, of sexuality, of "human nature", condensed in the canonical representation of the human body. "Artists do not work on violence, but rather on the fact of violating those who look at their artworks. The prime function of the artist consists of reopening discussions, disturbing the gaze, the way of thinking, the 'prêt-à-penser'. The artist is also a chronicler of his or her own time, especially of that which will be and does not yet exist. He or she knows how to listen to all that which is about to be transformed, they observe the seeds of the future. As soon as a new technology begins to spread, they ask: 'And what will the human being become?' As far as I am concerned, I am working on the relationship of the body with the new technologies, with pollution, and with diseases such as AIDS."

Alongside the power staged by the modifications of her own body, through surgical interventions, Orlan sets out the power of an absolutely impeccable theoretical awareness, once again shifting the target and the point of focus of her discourse. During her lectures/performances, she obliges the spectator to witness a surgical operation and, simultaneously, an intervention upon language, a dimension of total transformation, in which mutation acts upon her own body, upon language, upon the dead body of art, and on the minds of the spectators. She provides cold, open and unusual visual and verbal tests, a visual structure criss-crossed by media flows and a narrative structure that amplifies, enlarges and slows down, multiplying the prospects and grafting parts of a discourse with pieces of body and fragments of identity, an extraordinarily shocking encounter that subjects the spectator to a mental experience that lies somewhere between a roller coaster and a leisure cruise taken to the very limits of possibility.

Orlan knows and operates the places and forms in which the media experiment the extremes of visual and mental emotion: rock and roll, live television, televangelists, horror movies, disinformation and counter-reporting. She moves the mind of the spectator just as she moves the mouse of the computer, pushing it toward the threshold of a participation that gives no quarter and takes no prisoners, impeccable, precise as the incision of the scalpel into her skin, anaesthetised skin, vigilant mind and wide-awake conscience, awareness pushed well beyond the physical limits of pain, beyond the threshold of a sacrificial and heroic dimension of art. And this is an essential point in Orlan's interventions on the body, her rejection of pain. "I simply produce images. My work is based on the elimination of pain. The operations on the body are always perceived as torture and suffering; the idea has not yet sunk in that they could take place without causing the slightest suffering, because the great contribution of our era is the possibility of eliminating pain. The saying 'in sorrow thou shalt bring forth children' is incredibly ridiculous." Orlan does not focus on her body, rather she passes through it, she crosses it, she explores it in order to modify it, almost withdrawing from it entirely, subverting the conception of interior/exterior, subverting the relationship of pleasure/pain, altering the relationship of artificial/natural, in a suspended passage in which a philosophical act is performed: through the composition of her own flesh, she names it and mutates it. And she mutates her own identity to the point of requiring a new registration: an identity in transit. In the setting of the contemporary, the body is mutating into forms and situations that make it increasingly open to manipulating: hair dressing, tattooing, diets, piercing, all the way out to the changing of the colour of one's skin, the lengthening of limbs, genetic manipulations, and even to situations that entail a choice, that expose one to risk, that modify one's destiny: "In order to be deviant, it is necessary to take some risks", declares Orlan, as she opens deep rifts in the culture that demands that every choice be irreversible. She investigates her body through her own image on the computer: she looks at it "from without", multiplying its prospects, drawing closer line by line, pixel by pixel, until she causes it to disappear into another body, using language in a flow of energy that goes beyond consciousness and hooks up directly with one's nerve endings. She not only transforms her body, but even the site in which the intervention takes place: from operating room to set, from private to public, from place of anguish to place of conscious mutation. Orlan acts simultaneously in the flesh and in the intangible area of the mind, and opens the universe of an extreme insurrection of biology, and an overcoming of biology, in the direction of a strengthening of the electronic means of communication in the social body that has rendered obsolete our point of view on the body, on art, on the universe that surrounds us. "For me, art is not the furnishings of an apartment. It is a total implication, a movement that entails harsh critiques of society. It offers designs for new societies, or at the very least questions about present-day society and its way of thinking: that is what art must do." In *The Atrocity Exhibition*, and in *Crash*, J.G. Ballard "grafts" the hypertrophic structures of modernity with the altered structures of the human mind; he undertakes a surgical intervention amidst the tatters of reality that swirl through the media and the partial visions of communication. Mutation began in our minds, our bodies are being transformed, beginning with the great psychic pressures of the economic and ethnic problems, reality is slipping into the abyss of the virtuality of electronic communication: and Orlan pushes infinity into the bloody fissures of the body, and into the place in which, as Clive Barker puts it, "we are all books of blood; anywhere you open us, we are red".

With Orlan the traditional structures of art prove themselves to be inadequate, because she pushes on beyond, moving forward the frontiers of perception and enjoyment, making use of the media, communications, cinema, fashion presentations, and transforms all of these sites into exhibition spaces, manifestoes of mutations, into lectures and conferences of awareness, into shifting and glittering universes. She introduces muscles, flesh, thoughts, dreams and blood onto the screens of an horizon where the senselessness of identity (sexual, ethnic, cultural and religious) is declared, beginning precisely with the body: the body of language, long since fragmented and recomposed, and the human body which has lost its margins of distinction with the scenarios through which it passes. "Metamorphosis is an old myth. We have always tried to transform the body. Egyptians, Africans, Merovingians, Precolumbians: all evolved cultures have produced unprecedented forms of beauty and corporeal modifications: modifications of the cranium, little balls of earth placed between the eyes to provoke strabismus... Until the present day it was only possible to change the exterior appearance, but soon the new frontiers of genetics will make it possible to modify even the interior of the body, which will undergo processes of hybridisation with various human strains, but with animal strains as well. Quite soon, human beings will no longer be just a single species; there will be various species within the larger human family."

"Voluntary" images of monsters, of the different, are offered as instruments of subversion; to the reassuring and hypocritical imaginary world that separates the good and beautiful from the bad and ugly, art opposes diversity as a choice, self-construction as a methodology, identity in transit as a strategy. Some of the most

Matthew Barney, still from the video *Drawing Restraint 7*, 1993.
Photo by Michael O'Brien

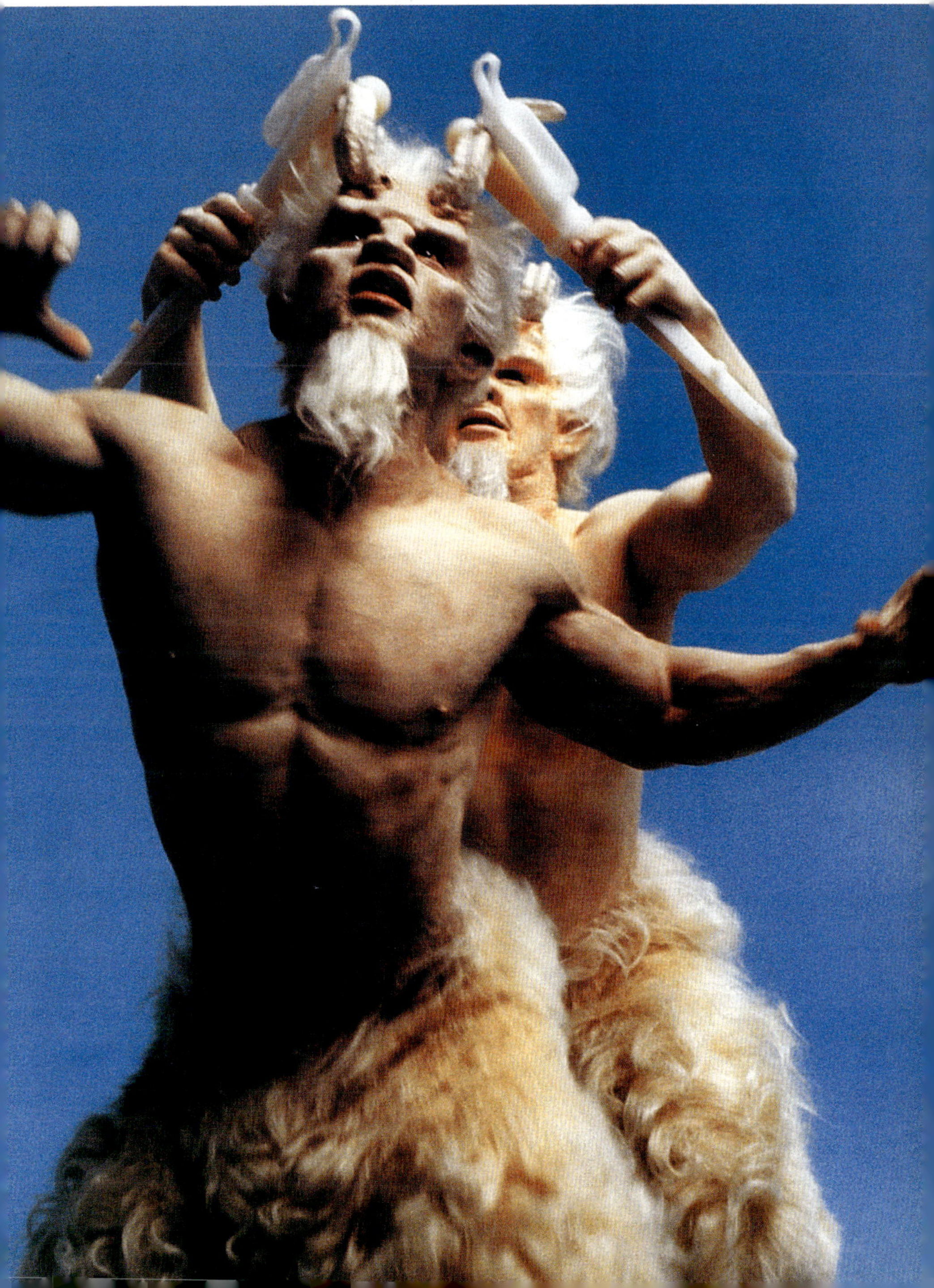

significant artists of the contemporary world have chosen for their own form of self-representation images that seem to come directly from the "educational" fables in which one was taught not to trust and to stay far away from the morphologies that were extraneous to the "normal". All that was needed was a big nose, or lots of hair, or an unusual stature or weight in order to trigger all the mechanisms of hostility and defence. The monster as an anthropological, cultural reality, as a biological presence, no longer a negative exemplar of all that wanders outside the normalising order of the mass-mediological morality that proffers models of reference which are aesthetically in conformity with the latest trends of the spectacle. In Latin, *monstrum* meant prodigy, but the current-day acceptance of the word has transformed the "prodigy" into a negative, evil, frightening prodigy. In short, stay away from the monster. Better the reassuring normality of imposed feminine models, in which one may — and in some professions one must — intervene in order to transform physicality into amplification of sexual organs; or the normality of the anorexic and bodiless models of fashion. Better the normality of masculine models whose physicality expresses physical power and threatening appearances. Better the transformation of individuals into clones and stand-ins for the figures that are imposed by the spectacle. But the spectacle is "incessant", and where the monster is concerned, there exists a classification, a hierarchy, a scale of values: the monsters that are chosen are those best suited to becoming yet another consumer object, to being built for transformation into marketable goods for precise and clearly identified customers. What frightens us and wards us off, what creates prejudice in certain contemporary artworks is certainly not the physical threat or the fearsome appearance (we have been accustomed to much worse by the culture of the spectacle), but rather, once again, the close approach to certain taboos, the possibility of naming the forbidden, the clear depiction of mental cages around which the psychological barriers are erected and against which the wars of prejudice and censorship are waged. The taboos of identity, death, disease, sex and deviance are definitively inscribed in genetic codes, inherited from family, society, cultural context and religion; they determine behavioural norms and forms of thought, convictions and oppositions. Flesh, blood, death, sexuality, God... And the monsters allow us to approach an exposed, mutated, hybrid flesh...

Physical deformation, the anomaly of body and flesh, is one of the subjects of monstrosity; the common mentality still attributes to deformity the absence of moral qualities, the evidence of a despicable perversion: the monster is evil because its inner world cannot help but correspond to the physiognomy. And so deformity and diversity wind up becoming proof of guilt.

The production of Matthew Barney is a graft or hybrid of mythology, sports, sexuality, medicine and scientific studies on the cross-breeding of different races. In one of his first video works, *Field Dressing (Orifill)*, 1989, composed of two monitors mounted on a wall along with a number of objects, the video showed the artist nude and gagged, climbing and descending a rope and every so often inserting clumps of congealed vaseline in all the orifices of his body. In his first personal exhibition in New York, at the Barbara Gladstone Gallery, 1991, Matthew Barney realised an artwork in which sculpture and psycho-sexual performance were merged: lubricated plastic, vaseline, refrigerating liquids, saccharose, combat mats, handlebars, mouth guards, a weight lifting bench, sternum separators and a speculum, all objects and elements taken directly from the environment of sports medicine, and four monitors displaying four different videos. In *The Jim Otto Suite*, Barney, nude, with a prosthetic device to protect his genitals, played Harry Houdini being punched in the solar plexus by an actor who played the football player Jim Otto; in *Blind Perineum*, Barney, nude, climbed ceiling and walls of the gallery, hanging from titanium ice-climbing hook-clips and spikes which he drove into the wall one after another, until he finally reached a refrigerator chamber in which there was a bench covered entirely with vaseline; in *Radial Thrill*, Barney wore stiletto heels, a slinky black evening gown and elbow-length gloves, as he pushed a football blocking sled, used in training.

In *Drawing Restraint 7*, presented at the Whitney Biennial in 1993, the artist introduced a narrative, both mythological and monstrous, by showing two videos: in one two actors made up as satyrs, with horns, hair and hoofed legs, fight on the rear seat of a white limousine that is driving through Manhattan, in the other one Barney himself is Kid, a young satyr with protuberances in place of the horns, devoid of genitals, with a long tail and long legs, who turns furiously around and around in an attempt to catch his own tail. But it is with the *Cremaster* series that the artist inaugurated a new symbolism and traced a series of visual clues that re-map a narrative and corporeal morphology which grafts and confuses myth, science, sex, sports, celebrity, dream, and — especially — proposes a multiplicity of polymorph male figures borrowed from an imaginary human bestiary, often portrayed by Barney himself. Erotic and autoerotic speculation, elements from fables, melodramatic atmosphere, a sophisticated and suspended acoustic structure, and the obsession with the construction of a body that has stopped being either human, animal, or vegetable. Artworks that hover between the soul and the flesh, between damnation and grace, between mysticism and corporeality. Matthew Barney always seems to be hovering between the desire for health (ethical, even before clinical) and a condemnation to an incurable disease. He chooses the elegance of colour and narrative, the rarefaction of care for himself, and he allows himself leaps and runs, rhythmic gymnastics and visual acrobatics; he chooses to stage the contagion of images, images that once again interrogate themselves on the standing of the monster, breaking the taboos of its unspeakability. Monster-image, images of monsters: the true monster is the infectious disease of vision which is, for Barney, a suicidal disease, it is a desire for obscurity, it is a wish for darkness and oblivion.

The body for Matthew Barney is a monstrous construction, cross-bred, manipulated, a corporeality that springs directly from a nocturnal imagination in which superheroes, myths from football, actresses, fauns, fairies and queens all utilise and wear sexual attributes, pornographic elements, and in which the very terminology, including the titles of the artworks, is borrowed from the genital and sexual sphere. The monsters of Matthew Barney seem to have been born in the laboratory of a contemporary alchemist, a laboratory capable of endowing technology with organic qualities, machinery of the subconscious, machines of a sexual desire that emerges from the classical figures of pleasure, desire, copulation, and determines a field of ambiguous and irrational energy that configures and reconfigures anything and everything — element, being — that is sucked back into the interior of the energetic path that the artist creates, rendering the interface between normal and monster a field of agonising uncertainty. The virus of fairy-

Robert Gober, *Untitled*, XLIX Venice Biennale, 2001. Photo by Michele Gregolin, Francesco Gorup de Besanez

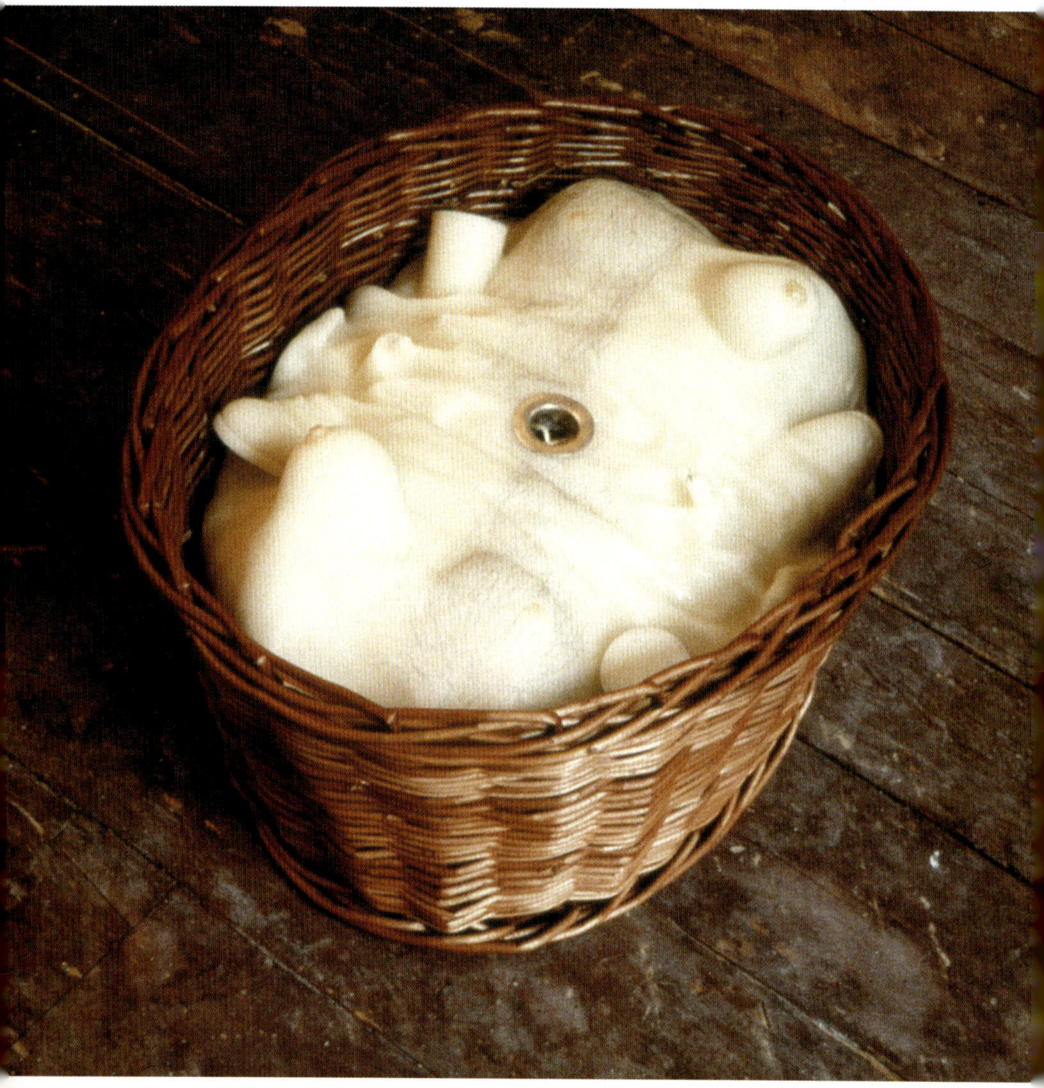

tale bestiality seems to move through the artworks by Matthew Barney, a perfidious virus, mobile, difficult to eliminate. It penetrates into the interstitial spaces of the narrative, intercepting the images and infecting them, rapid, devastating and lethal. However much Barney insists on pursuing the dream of the purity of the images, the virus finds its way and drags them down each time, into the soft regions of the viscera and the genitalia, where colonies of parasites of language and visual microbes slither and make their nests. Organic machinery sprung from the tales and the monsters of the subconscious, the beings of Matthew Barney seem to have been composed of the material of the colours and auras activated by magnetic fields made from high-voltage electricity, beings that have chosen to interpret a mission that develops through the hybrid forms of a reflection based upon insistent ethical questions from a media-based organism that renders us complicit in the comfortable position of voyeurs. Through his monsters, Barney seems to pose questions that have to do with human subjectivity reduced to the metabolic position of passivity, a chilling text of terminal functions of approach that reveals, in the narrative system and in the creation of new organisms, a body trapped in the foetal cages, in the position of submission to passivity.

Matthew Barney creates a theatre of special effects in which the body acts as the predator/parasite, a body whose characteristics and character elude us. He presents a universe that has the morphology of an altered, alien, anxiety-generating psychic dimension, which seems to be inserted directly into a living organism whose species is not known, organisms that live in a context charged with symbolism but where meanings collapse. What emerges is the game of victory and defeat, the struggle that designates the outlines of a competitive context that creates the environment in which the human disappears to leave room for the artificiality of the mise-en-scène, the fascination of the disappearance of all rational logic. In Matthew Barney erotic intensity is not linked to the intertwining of situations but to an entire world of representations of monstrosity, luxury, splendour,

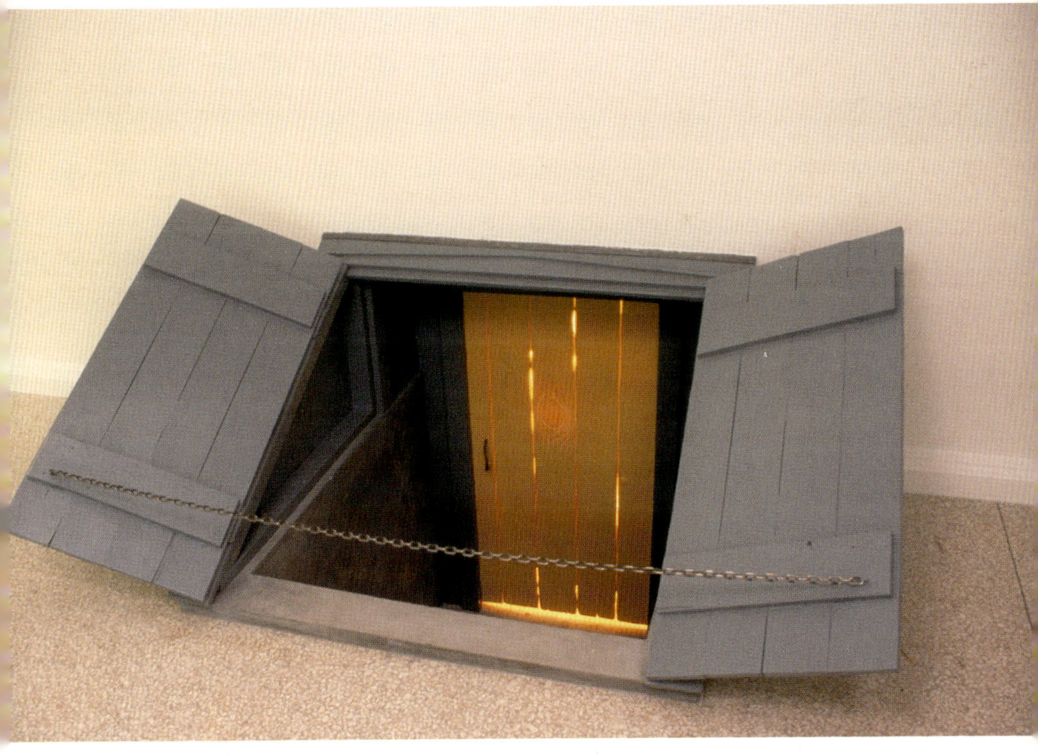

Robert Gober, *Untitled*, XLIX Venice Biennale, 2001. Photo by Michele Gregolin, Francesco Gorup de Besanez

surreal lights, the determination on the part of the artifice to bypass bodies and the heaviness of physicality, ceremony, the surplus of embellishment, excessive movements, and everything works together to create a climate of burdensome sexuality, soft, simmering and perverse. Kitsch, sexual ambiguity, bodies, disguises and cross-dressing all seem to reach what Baudrillard calls "the liberation of the Law in the arbitrary of the Rule and the Ceremonial", and from there the plunge into symbolisation, the moment of the enjoyment of the disappearance of meaning in decentralisation, in proliferation, in a Baroque movement that is opposed to classicism, order, symmetry and stability.

"We must find places for people everywhere, in schools, in factories, on the beach, or in front of the television, or by recycling: a permanent general mobilisation. In any case, you will never again be abandoned. All of the institutions, all of the social, economic, political and psychological mediations exist so that no one should ever again have an opportunity for this symbolic challenge, this challenge to the death, this irreversible gift that, like the mortification of the ascetic, allows one to triumph over any power, however potent its strength. It is necessary that this direct possibility of symbolic confrontation should never take place. It is necessary that everything be negotiated. And this is the source of our profound affliction. It is for this reason that the seizing of hostages and other similar actions revive something felonious: for the system, they are at the same time the mirror of its own repressive violence and the model of a symbolic violence that is forbidden to it, the only violence that it cannot exercise: that of its own death. Work is a slow death, it is generally thought of as a form of physical weakening. But it should be understood differently: work is not opposed, as a sort of death, to the realisation of life, and this is the idealistic conception; work is opposed like a slow death to violent death. This is the symbolic reality: work is opposed like a deferred death to the immediate death of sacrifice. And this is all the more true since the system undertakes to neutralise this symbolic retaliation by blackmailing it with a salary." (Jean Baudrillard)

In the work of Robert Gober the body is an invisible presence, it is not there, it is negated, it exists only in fragments, allusions, traces and hints that reveal the disquieting and monstrous realities of shared experiences. Gober prepares in great detail the setting of a physical and psychological presence, he leaves a series of clues, clues that a presence has passed this way, in that monstrously normal setting, in those "true" stories produced by the American everyday, in that atmosphere, slightly unsettling and evil, of a spectacle that has become the everyday. And yet in the reconstructions of Robert Gober there has always been a state of suspension of a perceptible but not visible presence, of that process that, as Gober himself puts it, "runs beneath everyday reality", and which reveals itself in simple occurrences and specific events. Gober reconstructs an emotional environment triggered and created from time to time by the encounter with an object, with a piece of newspaper, with a toy: an environment that later becomes physical in that dimension that Roland Barthes defined as the paradox of literature, that is, a situation in which something is at the same time real — because it attempts to represent, despite the inadequacy of the language — and unreal, because the real is undepictable. It recovers and reconstructs the images of "common experiences that persecute me", where the individual emotional fragments precipitate into the distorted perception of a reality that tends

Robert Gober, *Untitled*, 2000-2001

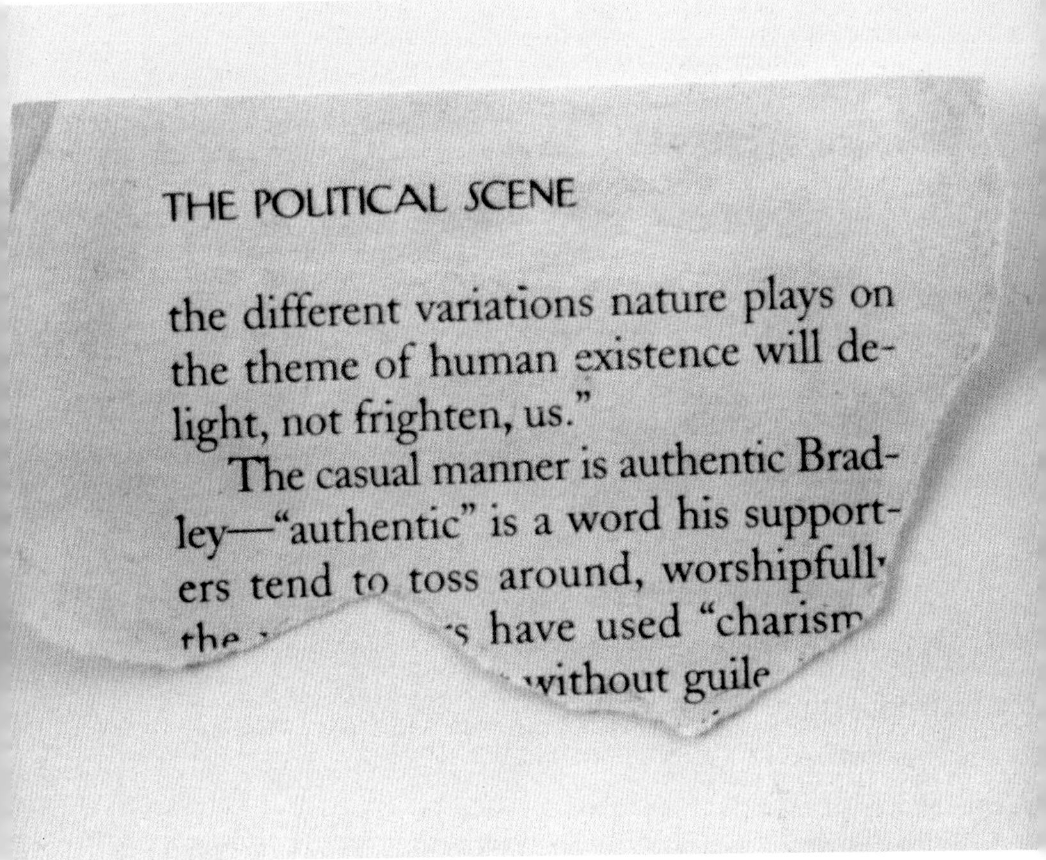

to flatten the experiences of the emotional life of the individual onto the experiences of the mass, those produced and implanted directly by the spectacle into the social body. Robert Gober reconstructs in maniacal detail all of the objects that he presents, a little plastic chair, a packet of kleenex, a sink, a washbasin, a bottle of gin... objects with the morphology of the accumulation of the spectacle, but reconstructed one by one: not therefore samplings from reality, but a reconstruction of reality that includes in the materials "humour, liberation, and the perspective of distance".

Simple, innocuous, normal objects, customary objects in the arrangement of reality, each of them however capable of evoking the anxiety and the concern of a situation that has been lived and is in the past but which remains vivid in the mind, becoming increasingly the symptom of an adequacy. The artworks of Robert Gober live on the razor's edge, glittering and slicing, of the biography that becomes collective experience: innocuous and domestic objects that serve as indicators of themes such as death, intimacy, abuse, faith, persecution, indicators of a series of monsters with which we are obliged to coexist on a daily basis, dangerous and terrible monsters, because they have a normal morphology, not particularly distinctive, like those nocturnal nightmares that frighten us so terribly but which in the censured recounting of them the mind reconstructs as banal objects or situations in which the reason of anguish plunges and precipitates. The artwork of Gober produces no astonishment, it does not focus on sensationalism: the artist chooses the understated demeanour typical of the normality of prejudice, abuse, prevarication, treating the unpleasant themes of censorship, states of health, AIDS, sexuality and gender, but through the reconstruction of the domestic and anonymous horizon, the panorama of everyday life. Dating from 1985 are the stacked sinks, all made entirely by the artist, who reproduces the embarrassment with an anthropomorphic association that alludes to a surrogate of the human form; incorporating the feminist themes of those years, Gober, who recognises in Jenny Holzer, Barbara Krüger and Sherrie Levine some of his "forerunners", condenses into the anonymous appearance of the sculpture an unsettling psychological value that is realised precisely through the choice to simulate reality.

It is the power of memory and the attention toward the emotional contents of objects that are the elements that distinguish Gober among the American artists interested in the nature of the object at the end of the 1980s; his capacity to ritualise everyday life will lead him to occupy the interstitial spaces between the public sphere and the private sphere, charging objects and forms with uncomfortable tensions of the sense of loss, childhood, the experience of violence, the loss of innocence, the dynamics linked to religious faith. "What in the final analysis is particularly intriguing in his work is precisely the lack of knowledge of the degree to which these objects are representations of the personality of the artist and the degree to which they speak in the name of a collective subconscious", maintains Gregory Salzman. Gober tries to trigger in the spectator that sense of familiarity that is produced by common objects, but once he has captured the look he inserts it into the uncomfortable position of distorted perception that is attracted by the very mechanisms of seeing and the individual evaluation of what is real and what is not. And at that point, Gober leaves us alone on the scene of the event, in a detailed reconstruction of things that the mind already knows.

Gober had already done a number of works with which he explored the scar that religion and family values can inflict, but it was not until 1995 that he did a statue of the Virgin Mary run through by a metal pipe, crossed through by the diameter of the tube which left an enormous hole in place of her belly. The artwork, installed at the Museum of Contemporary Art in Los Angeles in 1997, triggered a great deal of controversy, in part because many critics attributed to it the meaning of a round denunciation of the Catholic tradition which in those years was working extensively to repress sexuality in general and homosexuality in particular. The artwork, set on a pedestal at floor level which seemed to be covered by the water that was running down a staircase, was set between two open suitcases which contained algae, coins, and a foreshortened view of two wax figures reproducing the legs of a man with his feet in the water and the dangling legs of an infant, both of them hinting at the posture of an adult holding a child by the arms. A male childbirth? A baptism? An exodus? Gober once again leaves us dangling, between the symbols of regeneration and the traces of denunciation.

Dating from 1990 are the unsettling wax sculptures of legs protruding from the walls, casts taken from his own body, which testify to the loss produced by the seriousness of the AIDS epidemic between the end of the 1980s and the beginning of the 1990s, a period in which many of Gober's friends died. The decomposition of the body, the isolation of the limbs, the creation of busts which are also run through by exhaust pipes or candles, the creation of a mysterious and disquieting reality that appears out of the sense of void, silence, absence, shift Gober's work toward the concept of a body displayed parsimoniously, evoked through the rooms that inhabit it, the rooms, the bathrooms, the clothing, the shoes, all elements that "live" as a function of the body, which constitute its physicality in its inexplicable absence.

Ever since his very first work (1978–80) Gober has been presenting us with nostalgic reconstructions of everyday scenes and objects, domestic, anonymous, and a bit unsettling, little models of houses broken down the middle or else ravaged by terrible fires, beds painted white, front doors definitively shattered. Everything is petrified, and from the dog's little bed to the bathroom (antiseptic, fearful of dirt) there is not a sign of life: the human presence is denied and yet incumbent, in the "impossible cradles" of 1987 (cradles that are crooked, blocked, twisted, and in any case impossible to "inhabit"), from which emerge, by its absence, a childhood made up of nightmares, prohibitions and anxieties, the spaces of unhappiness, as is the case with the sinks, *Drain*, sinks that would be impossible to use because of the absence of faucets and drains. In 1989 the artist began to design wall paper; the three best know results, still used in his installations, are *Hanging man / Sleeping man* and *Male and Female Genital Wallpaper*. Also dating from 1989 is *Wedding Gown*, an empty wedding dress.

It is from 1990 on that people begin to notice in Gober's installations the first body fragments emerging from the walls of the exhibition spaces, a foot, a leg. These human limbs made of wax are absolutely hyper-realistic: hairy men's legs, suits with elegant trousers, tennis shoes or formal shoes on the feet . Once again, Gober alludes to the body, and absence is transformed into fragment, partial body; but it is also about what is not there, about what we cannot see, and that is the perfidious game of the artwork. And progressively severed legs, men overturned and sucked under by the spaces that contain them. Fetishes? Votive offerings? Fragments of cannibalism? Prosthetic devices? No element is offered to decode it: these pieces of body lie there, ready to accept the projections of an imagination that tends to "stitch" together bodies and stories, films, narratives, desires. And also in 1990 another strange wax creature first makes its appearance, a sort of pillow, a human torso half male and half female, a mixed body, "reformed", multigender. And the scene shifts to the body of the spectacle-information, again with a few summary bits of information, again an absence: *Untitled (Boy Drowns in Pool)*, 1991, is a lithograph of a page from the "New York Times" dated Friday 4 October 1960, in which we can clearly read, amidst the gossip and the weather reports, the tragic report of a drowning in a home swimming pool of a six-year-old boy named Robert Gober. Suicide? Accidental death? Or was it someone very close to him, for example his mother, who killed the little gay boy? Where was the father? How much love did this mother lavish on her "different" son? Midway between a B movie and a TV series about rich Americans, the news item constitutes the artwork, focusing on screens of the imagination linked to contaminations amongst information scattered in the info-sphere. And again: 1991, candle with human hairs; 1992, prison windows, and again body fragments, pieces tossed and scattered here and there, slowly the nature of the body shifts to other subjects, the incumbent body of that which is not there.

The year is 2001. Venice Biennale, United States Pavilion. Six sculptures, three prints, a photograph and an artist's book. Gober explores and investigates, once again, the roots of the American soul, delving into the contradictions that are part of the very underlying psychology of his compatriots. The objects presented seem to highlight the relationship to the themes linked to the body, gender, sexuality, mortality and social injustice. A series of objects reconstructed and placed in the context of a project that seems to be attracted by the bottom, a fluid bed of corrosion and excavation of memory. Gober multiplies the associative possibilities of stories, objects, fragments, elements that share a constant duality: masculine/feminine, water/earth, handmade/industrial product, memory/present, history/contemporary...

Fragments of true stories, accounts of the ordinary and the everyday: Abner Louima, an immigrant from Haiti, was arrested on Saturday 9 August 1997 by a number of New York City policeman following a fight at the exit of a music club in Brooklyn. After they arrived at the police station of the 70th Precinct of Brooklyn, Louima was searched, stripped, and repeatedly sodomised with the wooden handle of a toilet plunger. He wound up in the emergency room at Coney Island, handcuffed to the bed, with various injuries including a broken tooth, a perforated bladder, and a torn colon. One especially vivid image related to this case is the photograph, published in the New York Post on 17 August 1997, of a protest march that took place in Flatbush, Brooklyn, during which many protesters waved toilet plungers and Haitian flags as a sign of indignation at the torture that Louima had suffered, as well as the high level of brutality demonstrated by the New York City police during the administration of Rudolph Giuliani.

One of the sculptures exhibited by Gober, in Venice, is nothing other than a toilet plunger, the reconstruction of a familiar and apparently harmless everyday object that becomes an instrument of terror.

Just one more piece of proof that monsters have the appearance of normality.

1. A robot may not injure a human being, or, through inaction, allow a human being to come to harm.
2. A robot must obey the orders given it by human beings except where such orders would conflict with the First Law.
3. A robot must protect its own existence as long as such protection does not conflict with the First or Second Law.
Isaac Asimov, Handbook of Robotics, 56th edition, 2058 A.D.

FRAGMENTS
Man, Machine, Android

As if by reaction to the virtualisation of bodies, this era has witnessed the development of the practice of athletics as never before. The approval of "healthy" and athletic bodies, not unlike those applauded by authoritarian political regimes, and promoted by fashion magazines and by advertising; there is an incessant drive to conquer limits, to the intensification of sensations, the exploration of other velocities, all elements that can be identified in the explosion of sports that is a specific feature of the contemporary, a competitive reality that breaks out into extreme sports. The boundary between choice and alienation, between possibility and "obligation", between virtualisation and amputation, has become a fluctuating limit of imposed behaviour that is presented in the form of individual necessity. This configures a society in which the individuals will resemble more and more the dominant models of the spectacle and their "activities": year after year there are more and more settings in which specific physical characteristics are required in order to obtain a certain kind of work. Man, machine, android, robot, cyber… Being simultaneously in more than one place through the technology of communications and telepresence; the technologies used for medicine have rendered transparent our organic interiors; transplants and prosthetics cross-breed humans among themselves and humans with man-made prosthetics; dietetics, body building, cosmetic surgery all affect and heavily modify the human anatomy and form; the individual metabolism is altered with drug or pharmaceuticals.

Reproduction, immunity to diseases, the regulation of emotions, all of these classically private activities have become public, externalised, subject to control and classification. Videocameras and recorders perceive the sensations of someone else, experienced at another time, in another place, almost to the point of allowing an individual, or masses of individuals — as in the case of television — to relive the complete sensory experience of someone else. Implants and prosthetics tend to confuse the boundary between the mineral and the living:

eyeglasses, contact lenses, false teeth, silicon, pace-makers, hearing aids, acoustic implants, external filters in place of healthy kidneys. Corneas, sperm, ova, embryos and blood, all stored in special banks. "You are so many guinea pigs, my dear humans, and guinea pigs treated particularly badly, since the tests to which you are subjected are inflicted, varied, and repeated constantly and solely at random chance. There is no scientist, there is not even a laboratory assistant who regulates, adjusts, monitors, or interprets certain experiments, certain artificial vicissitudes, of which no one can foresee the effects, of greater or lesser profundity, upon your precious persons." (Paul Valéry) What separates contemporary humans, unconscious guinea pigs, from those figures produced by the imagination of science fiction?

Robots

In the 1920s, the National Theatre of Prague staged the utopian drama *R.U.R.* (*Rossum's Universal Robots*), in which the author, Karel Capek, the inventor of the term 'robot' (from the Czech word *robotiti* = "perform heavy labour"), speculated ironically on faith in the progress offered by science and machinery, and imagined that several of the inventions of the Rossum family (a name clearly developed as a reference to another Czech term: *rozum* = "work") had made it possible to build android automata. From the invention of Frankenstein to the construction of robots, there is a radical mutation that results in a shift in the goals and potential of artificial life.

Frankenstein is the proof of the boundless belief in electrical technologies capable of even imparting life, and simultaneously the fear of the physicalisation of a laboratory experiment that is condensed into the signs of a patchwork and monstrous physicality; Frankenstein is an extraneous body that will never succeed in finding a community in which to be integrated.

Robots, from their very "birth", are conceived as a replicable matrix, a collective existence, a new species mass-produced by a multiplying factory. The imagination based upon manpower sees in the existence of robots, indeed in the very construction of robots, the possibility of having access to one's own docile technological slaves, a more economic labour force, that will never go on strike and will never get tired, with which to replace workers. In literature robots, in order to perform these functions, must possess electronic brains that allow them a minimal autonomy of action and a logic of their own; but these "processors", almost always, are also the instruments whereby the robots gain self-awareness and then mutiny.

The robot thus abandons the initial role of mere metaphor for human problems and establishes itself as a new species — often with an appearance that vaguely approaches the human form — able to reflect on its own role in relation to humans and reality, thus taking on an increasingly meaningful psychological dimension. This new condition of machines was not immediately explored: indeed, in the context of American science fiction in the first few decades of the twentieth century, the nineteenth-century concept of the android persisted. For such popular writers as Abraham Merrit, Edmond Hamilton and Jack Williamson robots were inhuman and dangerous creatures, walk-ons who had the role of exalting the madness of their builder or the daring of the human hero who confronted them and defeated them. It was not until the 1940s, in the work of two authors, John W. Champel and Isaac Asimov, that we find any development of the idea of a possible robot psychology. Especially with Asimov, who gives some dimension and depth to the figure of the artificial creature, and conceives of the possibility of considering intelligence as prerogative not limited solely to humans, describing robots that emerge from the linear logic of mere machines, capable of unusual behaviours, to the degree that the figure of the "robopsychologist" becomes necessary. Asimov struggles in all his writing against what he himself called the "Frankenstein syndrome", and introduced in his stories the outlines of a future in which machines and men were able to coexist peacefully, often as a single organism/mechanism.

Androids

A fundamental element of the narrative of Philip K. Dick is the definition of the concept of "subjective reality", the unhinging of what appears as the world of objectivity, the annihilation of the boundaries between subjective reality and individual reality. In his stories, the figure of the android takes on its most ambiguous form, becoming the emblem of a technology that silently insinuates itself into human life, until it cannot be told apart, as in *Do Androids Dream of Electric Sheep?* — from which Ridley Scott made the movie *Blade Runner* — written by Dick in 1968. The novel is set upon an Earth devastated by an atomic war, the memory of which has been lost in time, a desolate place populated only by men called "Specials" (mentally retarded because of radioactive fallout) and by social misfits, while a "genetically corrected" humanity has moved to other planets. The only comfort for the remaining terrestrials are Penfields, a device that allows you to programme your moods, and Mercerism, an electric pseudo-religion through which the population (with the help of a machine) identifies with Mercer, a mysterious character who tries to climb an endless hill, while invisible torturers pelt him with rocks. For those who decide to move into space, instead, it becomes a status symbol to own an android as a docile slave. For the humans who are left on Earth, this function is entrusted to ownership of one of the rare and expensive animals that have survived the radiation, beings that represent the last link with a natural world that is abandoning man forever, in a reality in which the artificial (that is, the android) has become "more human than human."

This is the setting in which the story of Rick Deckard plays out, a "bounty killer of the year 2000" who has the job of retiring mutinous androids who have escaped from Mars and have taken refuge on Earth in search of liberty. Finding them is not easy at all because, not only have they developed an appearance very similar to that of human beings, but they have also acquired human thought processes and behaviour. The only faintly reliable means to identify them is either to analyse their marrow, which can only be done if the subject is being cooperative, or else the Voight-Kampff test which measures empathy, that is, the degree of involvement of the subject in the lives of other living creatures, especially animals, a characteristic that androids for the most part do not have, since they are fundamentally solitary predators. The new replicants (the Nexus 6), however, which Deckard is about to take on in yet another bounty hunt, have attained such mental development that they are superior to most of the Specials that inhabit the earth, making the test largely useless.

The most fascinating aspect of this novel lies precisely in this plot twist, because when everything can be the opposite of everything, even human figures take on this degree of ambiguity. In Dick's novel, you can never be sure of who is the creature and who is the creator, because often his androids are not even aware of being machines. And making the boundaries between human and android yet more confusing is the fact that, despite the continuing vision of the android as an evil creature working to manipulate reality, there begins to emerge in its personality a certain dose of humanity, while some human characters in the book have very little that is natural in their makeup, indeed they are more similar to machines than the replicants themselves. For Dick the distinction between human and android vanishes into a single "synthetic reality created by the media and by drugs, in which the essential human qualities (empathy, love, irony) are lost..." A reality where the artificial becomes the metaphor for "manipulation of reality on the part of power: economic power, family power, political power, military power, everything which threatens in any way the fundamental liberty of the human being".

Cyborgs

The cyborg represents one of the most fascinating and problematic figures of the imaginary universe; its history dates back to the 1920s, even though the term cyborg was not coined until the 1960s by two American medical doctors, Manfred Clynes and Nathan Kline, who used it in their description of the hypothesis being explored by NASA of modifying the bodies of astronauts, through the removal of certain parts of the organism, and replacing them with artificial elements, in order to allow them to explore other planets without necessarily using space suits.

This time the machine does not simply manifest itself as a metaphor of the Other than self in a new creature, but it passes from the role of a simple corporeal extension to that of an extensive symbiosis.

The first organ to be fused with technology in the imagination could not help but be the brain, transferred into a simple metal box without the slightest resemblance to a humanoid, which found its most significant portrayal in the short story, *Donovan's Brain* (1943), by Curt Sidmak.

From the box, things progressed to a more attractive form, the glittering metal reconstruction of a woman's body which contained the mind of a singer (Deirdre), as is narrated by Catherine L. Moore, in *No Woman Born*. This figure, however it might have appeared human in its essentially robotic aspect, was the source of great discomfort for anyone who saw it, because it was clear that behind the whirring gears was a human mind.

But the first depiction of the fusion of flesh and metal, imagined by NASA, is found in the stories of Cordwainer Smith.

The most important characteristic that a space cyborg has to possess is affordability: only the most indispensable parts of the human body should be preserved, in order to make it capable of adapting for survival in hostile environments or for long voyages in space. In this case, there is a slowing of the biological rhythm, through the "insertion of valves in the arteries, artificial colostomies to regulate the body water through catheters, needles linked directly to the brain to slow down physiological activity as desired" (*The Lady Who Sailed the Soul*).

The space man, though biologically modified, is assailed by "space sickness" every time that he is immersed in the universe, that is, a profound desire to die. It was once again Smith who, in order to resolve this problem, invented "scanners" (in the short story, *Scanners Live In Vain*), men in whom "all sensory organs, which are responsible for pain, are disconnected from the brain: the internal organs (like the heart and the lungs) no longer send detectable signals. This disconnected man therefore carries a series of control boxes, with which he can regulate by hand his own vital processes". They are "formally honoured by the collective and by the government but in reality they are ill tolerated because of their appearance and their habits", because, "since they have no control over their own muscles, they walk heavily, they have rough and deafening voices, and their faces are twisted into horrible masks. But they can temporarily return to the fullness of their senses and lives by subjecting themselves to 'cranking', a sort of induction by means of a surrounding wire that restores their hearing, sense of smell, taste, and control of muscles and voice". The most dramatic element, then, that is inscribed into the body of the cyborgs is that, despite the possibilities of a more powerful body, with capacities superior to the norm, they are viewed by the society in which they live only as technological freaks and are excluded, because their appearance represents a violation of the sacredness of the flesh undertaken by technology.

The cyborg is the most up-to-date of all fantastic figures. In reality technology has already begun to penetrate the human body in an irreversible manner: transplants, synthetic skin, microcircuits installed in the ear in order to amplify the sense of hearing and dental capsules that modify day by day a physicality that becomes increasingly artificial, and the theme of the invaded body begins to seem less horrifying to the average individual.

According to Stelarc, the Greek/Australian performer who works on the obsolescence of the contemporary body: "Far from Earth the complexity of the body, its softness and its moistness would be difficult to preserve. The strategy would consist of emptying, strengthening and dehydrating the body, in order to make it stronger and less vulnerable. The present-day organisation of the body is no longer necessary. The solution to modify it should not be sought in its internal structure, but rather can be found, quite simply, on the surface. It is a skin-deep solution… If we could build a synthetic skin capable of absorbing oxygen directly through the pores and efficiently converting light into nutritional chemical substances, we could radically redesign the body, eliminating many of its redundant systems, its malfunctioning organs, minimising the accumulation of toxins in its chemistry.… Extraterrestrial environments amplify the obsolescence of the body, they intensify the impetus towards its general redesign. It would therefore be necessary to design a more autonomous body, more energy efficient, with more diffuse sensory antennae and a greater brain capacity. Disconnected from this planet, from its complex and interactive energy chain, from its protective biosphere, the body is biologically ill equipped, not only in terms of mere survival, but also because of its inability to perceive the immensity of space and to operate there adequately. Rather than developing specialised bodies for the specific places, it would be necessary to think of a pan-planetary physiology that would be strong, flexible, and capable of functioning in a variety of atmospheric conditions, gravitational pressures and electromagnetic fields".

Little invasions

Breast. From the first prosthetics made of silicone — which has now returned to its original use as a sealant — whose use the FDA (Food and Drug Administration) prohibited in 1992 in the United States, we have moved on to implants filled with physiological solutions. The latest generation of breast implants is made by hand: they consist of rounded or anatomical shells, shaped like teardrops, which are filled with physiological solutions through self-sealing apertures. The implants produced by the Mentor Corporation have the advantage of being able to be inflated in a post-operative phase, making it possible to add solution as desired, through the original incision. They are available in either round or anatomical shapes, with smooth or textured surfaces, because when an extraneous body is implanted in the organism, it immediately forms scar tissue, which creates a capsule. When this situation takes place, it results in a hardened surface around the implant, often associated with the idea of how breasts should appear in which breast implants have been inserted. In general, to insert implants, one of two methods is used: in the first the surgeons make an incision beneath the armpit, in the second an abdominal approach is taken. Through an insertion device the doctor works his or her way through a layer of fatty tissue just under the skin, and above the abdominal wall. For the submuscular placement, a pocket is created, clearly separating the muscle from the ribs. Implants consisting of physiological solution offer the advantage of being able to be removed through the introduction of a filler tube through the original incision and draining the solution, deflating the implant and replacing them with new ones.

After the initial mistrust toward these alien artificial bodies, purely aesthetic, the entire phenomenon certainly became part of the norm. Indeed, the trend if anything reversed, and breasts began to swell on actresses, models and ordinary women, and from A cups, the progression was on to B cups, from B cups to C cups, and from C cups to D cups, all the way up to the 22 pounds of tits of Lolo Ferrari.

Penis. "The penis is, and continues to be, the central signifier of the human species because it represents what distinguishes it as a species: dominion over and transformation of the environment through the use of tools. In a certain sense, indeed, our era seems to seek comfort from its fears, induced by the extraordinary development of technology, harking back continuously to the importance of its first tool; and it takes from it reassurance that the species will not be overwhelmed by its own instruments precisely because it continues, in any case, to possess and dominate the first tool, the one that served as the model and foundation for all others. The first motor, therefore, triumphs, in the moment in which technology triumphs. This is one of the reasons (and perhaps the principal one) why feminism prompted, at its foundation, so much fear: dethroning the primacy of the penis could signify the loss of control over technology, the victory of machinery over humans, since female sexuality belongs to nature and biology, and culture was not founded upon it." (Ida Magli)

Professor Melvyn Rosenstein is capable, in his Los Angeles clinic, of lengthening a penis by five centimetres and widening its diameter by roughly 50 percent, at a cost of 4,500 dollars per operation. The surgeon states: "Why should we oblige patients to suffer through years of therapy in order to persuade them to accept the size of their penis, when in an hour I can give them the size they really desire? And so I started to do operations, guided by an exceedingly simple philosophy: it's their penis, and they can do what they want with it". With an average of twenty operations a day, for a total of 30,000 operations a year, and with a waiting list of four months, Rosenstein claims that he can reconstruct, like a skilled and talented architect, the external façade of men's virility. The surgical operation in reality is fairly simple: in order to increase the diameter, fat is extracted from the patient's abdomen and is then injected into the penis, and in order to lengthen the genital organ the surgeon performs an incision two or three centimetres over the penis, uncovering the ligaments that attach the member to the pubic bone, and then moving it lower down in order to force it to shift. Ben Novak, a colleague of Rosenstein's, says that he does not particularly like to be called a surgeon, that he prefers to be considered a sort of sculptor. While doctor James Elist is working on an experimental technique to enlarge the scrotum based on a saline solution to be injected. Rosenstein affirms that "many men leave the clinic with such a sense of confidence that it winds up affecting their personalities, including their sexual performance".

"All of my work", Orlan says, "stands against the standards of beauty that are based on male or female flesh, and it raises questions with respect to the standing of the body today and in future societies through genetic manipulations and new technologies, which are very interesting but not absolutely fascinating. All the same, we are definitely not mentally prepared for these immense changes and my work is aimed at preparing the future, a future that I try to imagine, putting emphasis on the pressures that are exerted on the body, especially the female body. With genetic manipulation, there is every reason to be concerned, but if we start early to ask questions perhaps we shall succeed in avoiding absolute idiocy."

"I can see in the dark, Case. Microchannel image-amps in my glasses. It's 2:43:12 AM, Case. Got a readout chipped into my optic nerve." In *Neuromancer*, 1985, William Gibson shifts the field of alteration and mutation to the mind, the mind as a place of technological and chemical alteration. Communications technologies and drugs, the world narrated by Gibson is a welter of telecommunications systems integrated into a single cyberspace, in which the sim/stim (simulated stimulation) is a reproduction and simulation of the human sensory system, a system for remote transmission of data, corporeal information and stimulation. The body is the visible element in which it is possible to visualise the field of battle between nature and culture, natural and artificial, flesh and technology, and mutation transforms the body piece by piece in the "sprawl", the gigantic urban container that accommodates the mixture of races that have blended their genetic material. Interfacing bodies and organs, microchips, displays and RAM, directly inserted into the body: this is the creation of a cybernetic organism, the connection between electronics and biology. The conditions in a dystopian key of post-industrial civilisation are narrated in shocking manner, the sphere of the everyday is deteriorating, altered, inhospitable, dangerous and exciting. For William Gibson, the characteristics of the new frontier of thinking are: the new relationships between man and machine, the transformation of the industrial and mechanical economy into a service-based and information-based economy, the shift toward a society based on information as a primary merchandise. On the horizon of the cyberpunk movement are Philip K. Dick, J.G. Ballard, Samuel Delany and William Burroughs, all linked by the intersection between man and machine, a voyage in parallel realities (within or without of the human mind), and an overflow toward alteration (mysticism, drugs, or psychopathologies).

The humanity described by Gibson is a humanity that has been modified by various technologies, the "original" ones produced by multinationals and the yakuza, and the others, cloned and sold on the black market. The matrix in an environment in the classical biological sense: in order to access it and survive in it, it is necessary to be adapted, mutated, no longer transplants but spare parts, with expiration dates, with the wear and tear of time, surrounded by other constructs in the space of electronic signals and technological simulacra. Metal, microchips, memory extensions... the depressing awareness that one will sooner or later need to be overhauled, but the certainty that one can rely upon a vast selection of optionals, illegal replacements for the nervous system, extra functions installed in the flesh, senses enhanced, synthetic diseases... Cyborgs, cybernetic organisms, an incestuous relationship between synthetic material and live flesh, between exterior and interior, between what is "born" and what is "built", transverse sexuality, multiple genders, relationships between mutant organisms: the machine becoming body and the body becoming machine. The current social system manipulates and constructs docile and available normal bodies, open to the power that lies at the foundation of the contemporary scientific gaze, and the body becomes the terminal of a series of media-based stimuli, the place of an affiliation or non-affiliation with a system of representation of one self on the stage of the world.

"The body is biologically inadequate... Only through a radical redesign of the body will we succeed in having significantly different thoughts and philosophies... Being human means being constantly redefined." (Stelarc) Redefining the human body and thus radically subverting the way it is conceived, perceived and experienced: that is the project of Stelarc, who as early as the end of the 1960s was exploring the dimension of the body inasmuch as a modifiable and alterable structure, as an element upon which to intervene in order to be able to modify and amplify its possibilities. Stelarc did research on his own body with a view to discovering the physiological and psychic limits of the organism, which in turn gave rise to the necessity of inventing technological enhancement instruments — prosthetics and implants — that were extremely advanced. The body, according to Stelarc, is no longer capable of adequately confronting a reality that is evolving at uncontrollable velocities: the technologies and their use in systems of social organisation imposed and implemented by the economic strategies of the last century have modified the environment in a radical manner that is dangerous to the human body, rendering the habitat unfriendly to man and provoking the need to make use of artificial "cures" for the safeguarding of individuals. Stelarc believes that human "salvation" is linked to the possibility of beginning to conceive of a body that is capable of competing with various new technologies and that is capable of absorbing and redeveloping the highly information-based reality in which it exists. It is therefore necessary, according to the artist, to develop a programme of evolution that, on the one hand, would be capable of eliminating all of the prejudices and fears in the face of the manipulation of the body and, on the other, will allow the transition from a form of evolution of a biological and natural sort to a new type of evolution, technological and artificial in nature. He declares: "It is no longer a matter of perpetuating the human species through reproduction and production, but rather perfecting the individual through re-design. What is significant is no longer the relationship between male and female, but the interface between man and machine."

Stelarc began to consider the body as a modular structure that could be assembled, ready to house on its interior technological grafts that could operate, act and evolve independently, replacing imperfect organs, often malfunctioning and in any case destined to physiological decay. Microminiaturised nanotechnologies implanted inside the body will produce a corporeal system not only capable of surviving a modified environment, but also of producing new modalities of perception of the real, new capacities of understanding and new paradigms for the interpretation of the world. For Stelarc only the modification of human physiology will be able to serve as the motive of different, other forms of thought. His work takes the form of a territory of fusion and interpenetration of the relationship of body and technology; the interface of man and machine for Stelarc must become a process of hybridisation with which to eliminate the separation of the two elements, to create a configuration in which it is of no importance to distinguish that which constitutes part of the sphere of the artificial from that which instead remains in the area of the natural. That which develops out of this hybridisation will be the result of the reciprocal action that man and machine will produce, one upon the other, a global recodification of the human standing. Once again, there is a demand for the elimination of two-fold thought, the end of the binary pairs of nature/artifice, internal/external, mind/ body, man/machine, life/death, physical/virtual, material/immaterial.

As early as the end of the 1960s, Stelarc began to show interest in the body, exploring its limits and possibilities, a form of research that was meant to break up the usual perceptive and sensory categories by amplifying them and emphasising them in a way that derived from both the techniques of meditation and estrangement from other cultures and from the extensive use of new technologies. In parallel with performances in which Stelarc developed strategies of rendering powerful and extending the body through technological supports, he performed a series of suspensions in which his body was lifted from the ground and allowed to float, accompanied by the deafening amplification of the very sounds of his body.

In the suspensions, which hark back to ancient sacred rituals aimed at the attainment of ecstasy, the skin is penetrated by metal hooks which, in turn connected to cables, make it possible to lift the body without any other means of support. The stretched skin expands, radiating into spatial configurations determined by the lines of tension that are engendered in fact by this method of penetration and traction, defined by Stelarc as "gravitational landscapes". These sensory deprivation performances also include a number of films that depict roughly three metres of internal space of the artist's body and serve, in a certain sense, as a counterpoint to the experience that he developed in parallel, focusing on the interface between man and machine, in an attempt to enhance and amplify the physical and psychological capacities of the human being.

"In the past, we considered the skin as a surface, as an interface. Skin has been a boundary for the soul, for the self, and at the same time, the initiation to the world. Once it is stretched and penetrated with instruments, the skin as a barrier is eliminated." The distinction between external and internal is unhinged, and

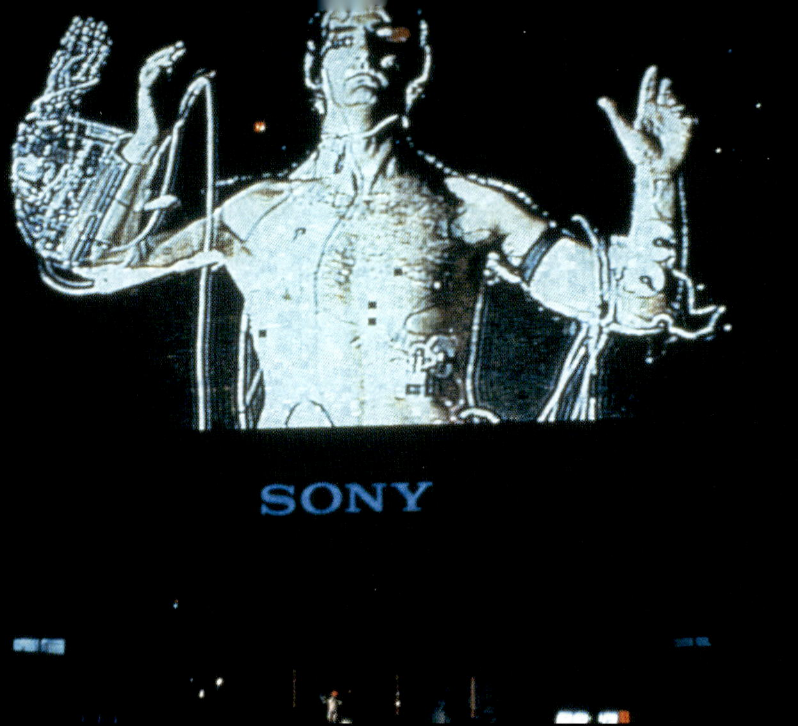

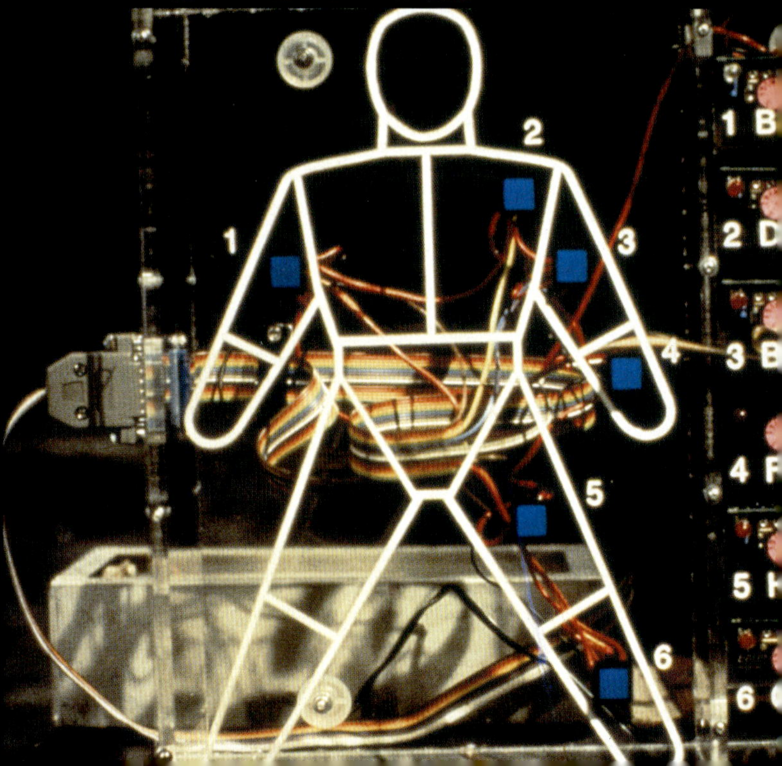

Stelarc,
Stimulation System,
Empire Ridge,
Melbourne.
Photo by T. Figallo

Stelarc,
Amplified Body Enhanced Image,
Tsukuba.
Photo by T. Shinoda

Stelarc,
The Third Hand,
Tokyo, Nagoya,
Yokohama.
Photo by S. Hunter

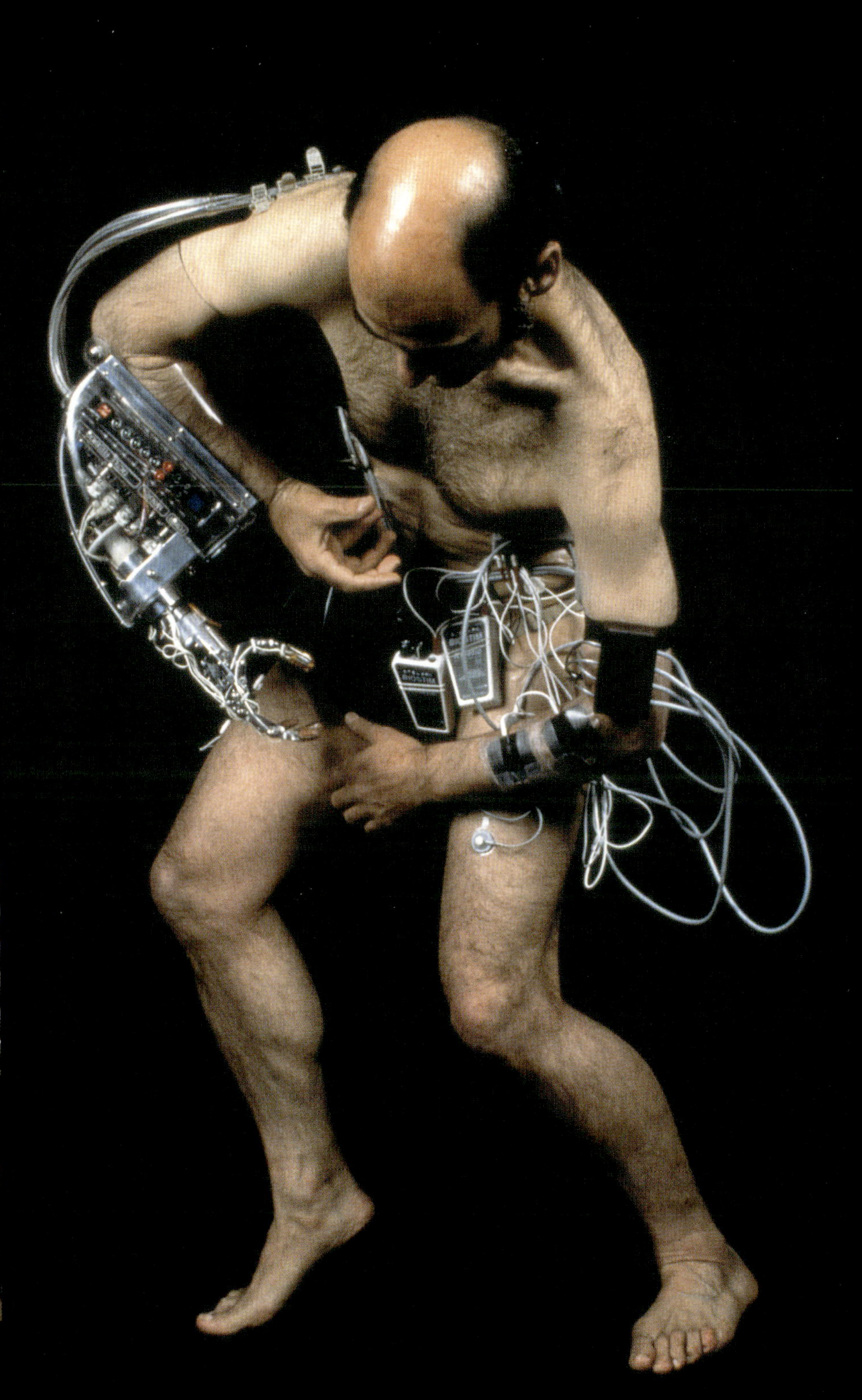

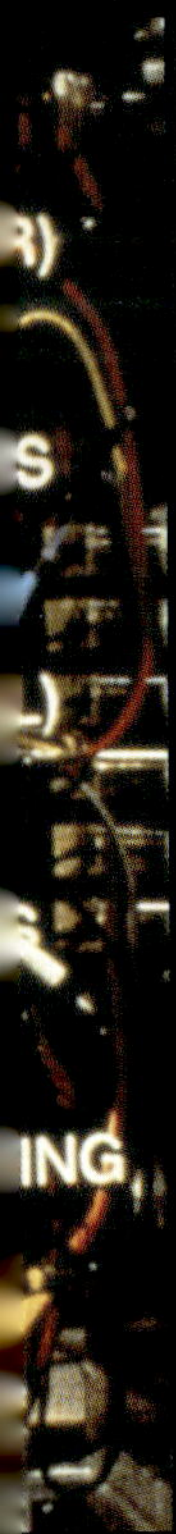

mutation can begin. Stelarc began to investigate the internal landscapes through films realised in 16 mm (1973–75): 14 minutes of stomach, 16 minutes of colon, 15 minutes of lungs, and an X-ray video of 60 minutes of the entire body, all the way up to *Stomach-Sculpture* (1993), a capsule measuring 50 x 15 millimetres, made of titanium, steel, silver and gold, capable of opening and extending as far as 70 x 50 millimetres thanks to a special mechanism that, connected to a servomotor controlled by a logic board via a flexible cable, allows the capsule to open and close in three sections. "Technology is transformed from a container to a component of the body... The empty body would be a better receptacle for technological components."

For Stelarc, the cyborg is already the hypothesis of a new species. "In terms of nanotechnologies, machines will navigate and inhabit cellular space and they will manipulate molecular structures that will extend the body from within." Microminiaturised nanotechnologies, by eliminating the concept of skin as a boundary/limitation between oneself and the world, invade the body, transforming it from a biological containment and protection structure into an open structure, a mutant structure, capable of accommodating on its own interior the logical decision-making capacity of the machine on the one hand, and the unknown aspects of fusion on the other. Darwinian and biological evolution is interrupted at the point in which technology becomes a component of the body and no longer, therefore, a prosthetic tool external to it. The dialogue between mechanical construct and human body emerges in all of the performances of Stelarc. In *Bionic*, the artist establishes a dangerous confrontation with a robotic machine, consisting of a base body and a sort of art at the end of which is placed a videocamera. The movements of the robot are pre-programmed through a software that interrupts when the body of the artist inserts itself with his own movements into the programme itself. In *Virtual Arm* and *Virtual Body* the interaction and symbiosis takes place between the real body of the artist and the virtual image of the same body or a part of it, a fusion of real and virtual events projected onto a large screen.

Ping Body Performance Digital Aesthetics Conference sets out from the concept of manipulating the body, no longer by another body, however robotic, but rather by the invisible and imperceptible activity of a network, that is, the Internet. The haphazard shifts on the interior of the network are sensed and transformed into spatial distances and transmission times and then communicated to the body. A graphic interface simulates in advance the movements that the artist's body is about to perform: movements that produce the sound traces that accompany the performance.

The choreography and the composition of the event are therefore generated by the movements of information that take place while surfing online, reversing the usual relationship that we have with this medium.

"For me, the problem is not whether we should talk about a machine of desire but rather how to think of the functions of the body without memory or desires, without intentions or expectations! For instance, in this involuntary system there is a collapse between intention and action. There is no meditative space between the two things. And so, if you activate my body by remote control, this body has no memory of the action that it is about to perform, because there is no intention of any sort... If over the past two thousand years the pathology of our system was triggered by a cloven personality, the potential pathology of the cyborg will instead be the fact of having a cloven physicality."

When Stelarc talks about body, he is not referring merely to its physiological meaning, but includes also everything that fits into the sphere of the phenomenological and the sensory, as well as the cerebral. Speaking of body as an object to explore, modify and amplify through advanced technological systems, as an object that is not opposed to the mental but which constitutes all one with itself, speaking of body and experiencing your own body as a mutant structure entails some profound thinking on the artist's part concerning the impact that it undergoes in its everyday nature, interacting with an increasingly technologically advanced society.

The performances that Stelarc has done in the last few years have demonstrated and visualised some of the manners and methods that can be produced by the fusion of man and technology: the hypnotic tension of a body that is no longer merely biological and neurological but neither is it only technological or artificial. An "ambiguous and slippery" area — as Stelarc himself describes it — that is still at an embryonic stage, a frontier zone whose effects and consequences are as yet unknown.

It is now clear that the body is at the same time cause and effect of a series of stimuli of social activity and the determination of the spectacle.

The preoccupation with bodily appearance, so evident in advertising, clothing and body building, is a strategy of superficiality that certainly has its consequences, because it is inscribed in the context of a much vaster symbolic game, and expresses a way of touching oneself, of being in relationship with the other, a way that is of constructing a society. With the notion of *episteme* Foucault indicates that we are more thought about than we think and more "acted" than we act. For Foucault the forms of representation and social organisation have a twofold aspect: on the one hand they are structured into elements that will shape profoundly and even in a subterranean manner the social representations, on the other hand there is the fact that these social representations themselves have as well an entire series of consequences on social organisation, though not necessarily thought, aware or verbalised as such. In the same way, in the field of scientific discovery, through the notion of paradigm, more flexible than the idea of model, Thomas Kuhn demonstrates how there exists a matrix from which, in the field of science, the ways of representing the world develop.

Prenatal diagnosis is one of the most important modifications of the contemporary, destined in the future to become obligatory in order to "identify" abnormal embryos that may have eluded the mechanisms of natural selection. In the course of a few years it will be possible for a couple to decide on the sex of their child, the colour of its eyes and hair, "package" it according to their wishes. In the United States there are sperm banks of Nobel laureates, laboratories in which the spermatazoa of men thought to be intelligent are collected, which clearly suggests the "age-old" design of using genetic control to "improve" the human race. Here is what Aldous Huxley wrote in *Brave New World Revisited*: "In the imaginary world of my fairy tale, punishment was infrequent and usually mild. The government exerted its almost perfect control by systematically inducing the conduct desired, and in order to encourage such conduct it relied upon various forms of manipulation that were basically non-violent, both physical and psychological, and upon genetic standardisation. Perhaps test-tube babies are not possible,

Critical Art Ensemble, *Flesh Machine: a genexploitation project*, Galerija Kapelica, Ljubljana, November 1997. Photo by Vladimir Krivic

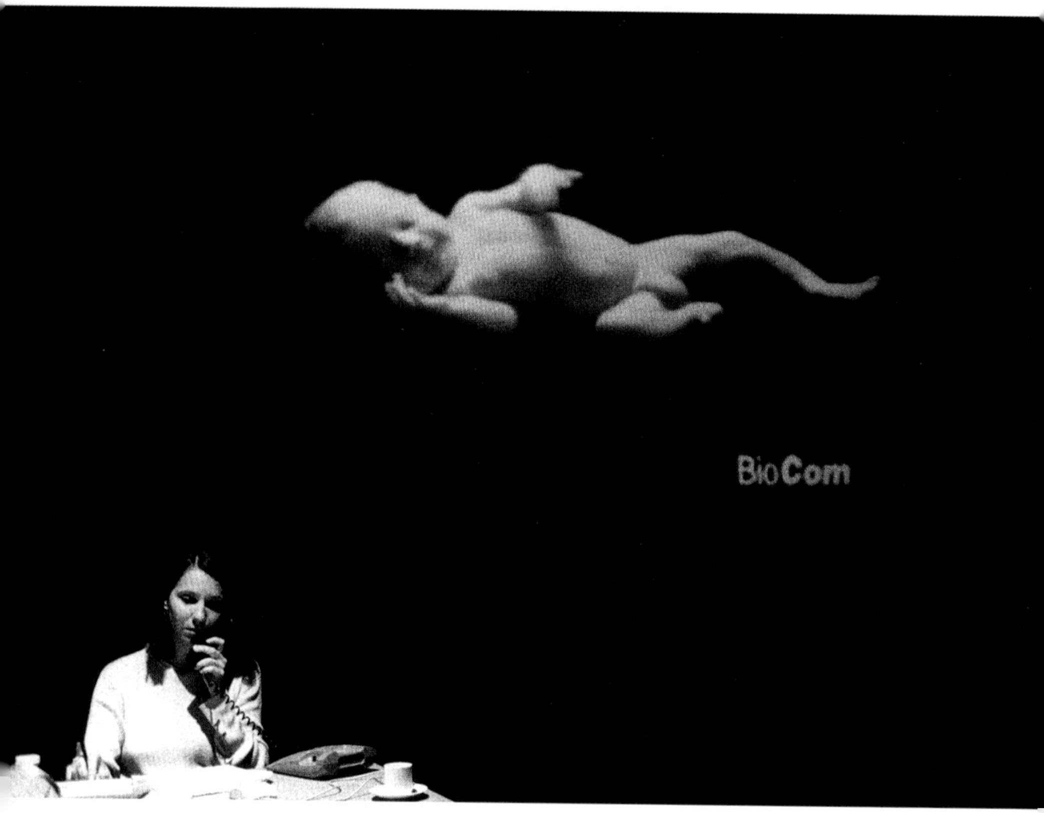

just as the centralised control of reproduction is not possible… it may be that for practical reasons genetic standardisation will be ruled out. Control over society however will continue to be exerted after people are born, through punishment, as in the past, and to an increasing degree, through more efficient methods of rewards and scientific manipulation".

Critical Art Ensemble is a group of artists who explore the interzones of the relations between art, technologies and political activism. Performances, books, design, films, videos, photography, theoretical writing: these are just some of the ways with which they create and present their incessant activity. The CAEs generically use these skills in a tactical manner, selecting a subject for investigation which they then insert into a specific situation, and then they direct it toward a specific audience, and then they construct an artwork in relation to the settings chosen. After they identify a specific cultural situation, the CAEs, which possess no specific instruments for their productions, make use of the means that best suit the subject and the context, through exhibitions in various places: galleries, museums, radio, TV, festivals, bars and clubs, online, in the street… Even though what they do is quite varied and interdisciplinary, there is one constant in their work: revealing or challenging the authoritarianism of the Western world, the

Critical Art Ensemble, *Flesh Machine: a genexploitation project*, Galerija Kapelica, Ljubljana, November 1997. Photo by Vladimir Krivic

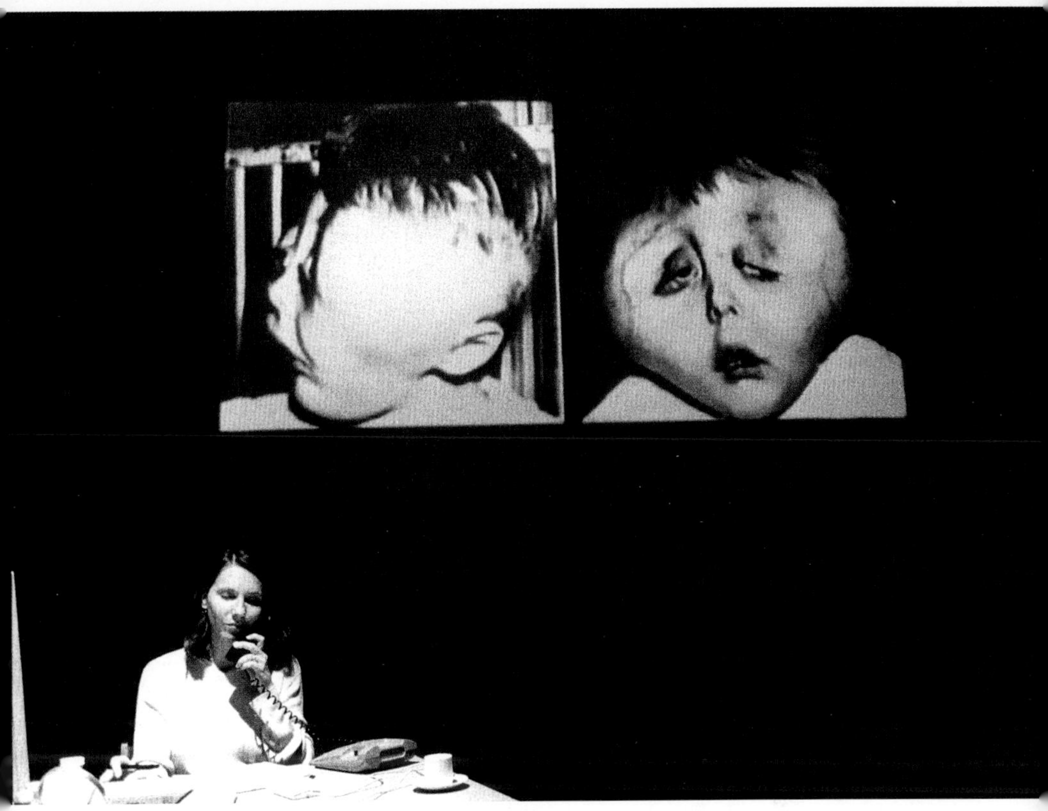

forms of persuasion, the manipulations and all of those activities that seem to have a public utility. Until 1996, the CAEs focused especially on criticism of news and the communications technologies. During the *Next Five Minutes* (*N5M*) — a festival in Amsterdam on the electronic media and political activism — they came to the conclusion that the discussion of the Internet was over, and that *N5M* would be their last word on the subject: and so they moved on to ideological problems connected with reproduction technologies. The discussion of biotechnologies was slowly penetrating into the problems linked to both art and politics, therefore determining for the CAEs a greater urgency than that linked to the discussion of the Internet. "We have done some research and we are absolutely astonished at the results. Our discoveries in the field of reproduction technology made us aware that we are about to witness a second invasion of eugenic bodies. The worst values of capitalism are about to be inserted into our flesh, and the ideology of social Darwinism will be readapted to the consumer economy. Speaking of these subjects, we would like to knock down the wall of scientific specialisation, and help the non-specialists understand what is happening in laboratories. Then show what is done when science is modified in order to display it to the public and try to create a language that helps non-specialists to under-

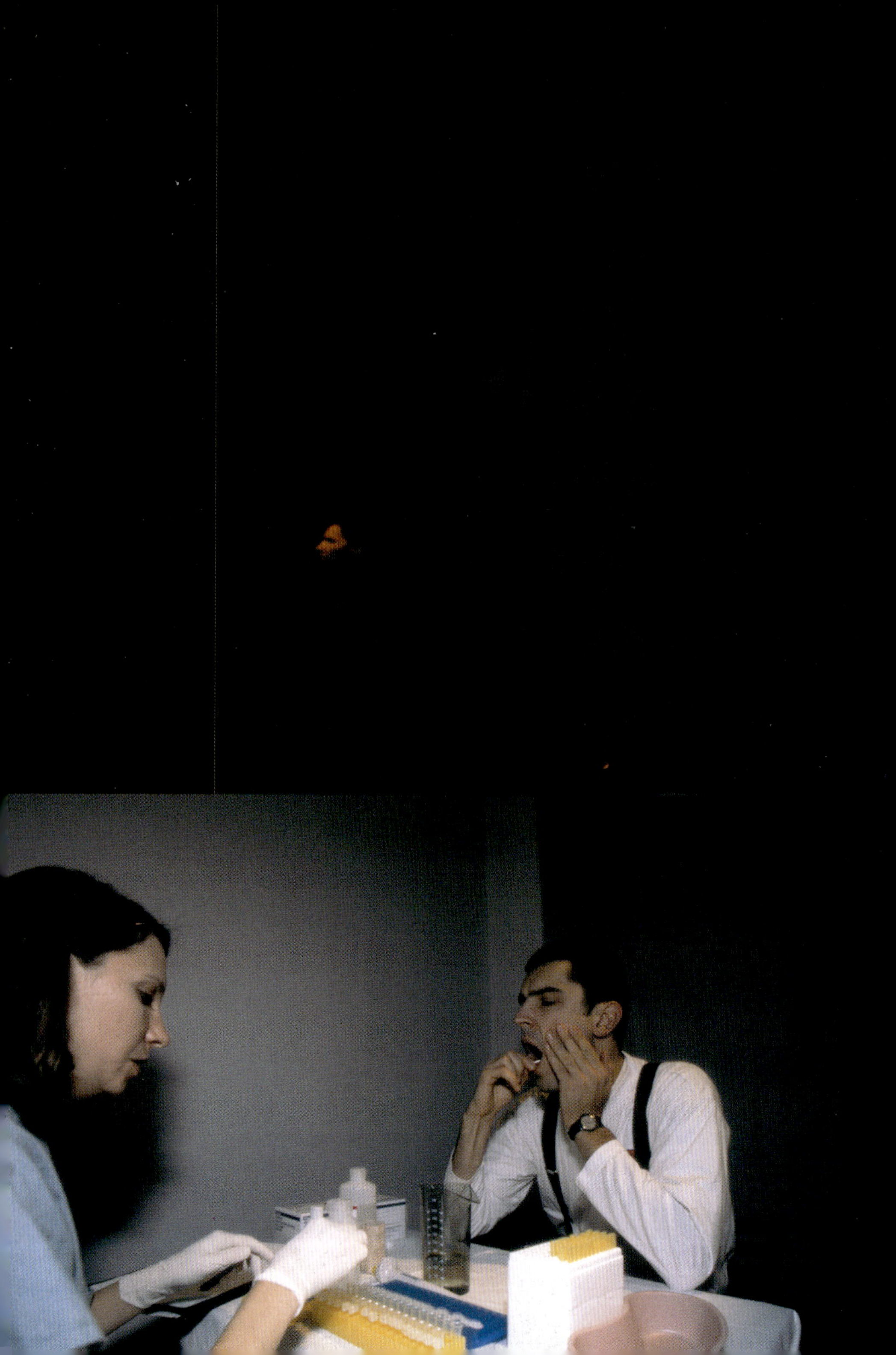

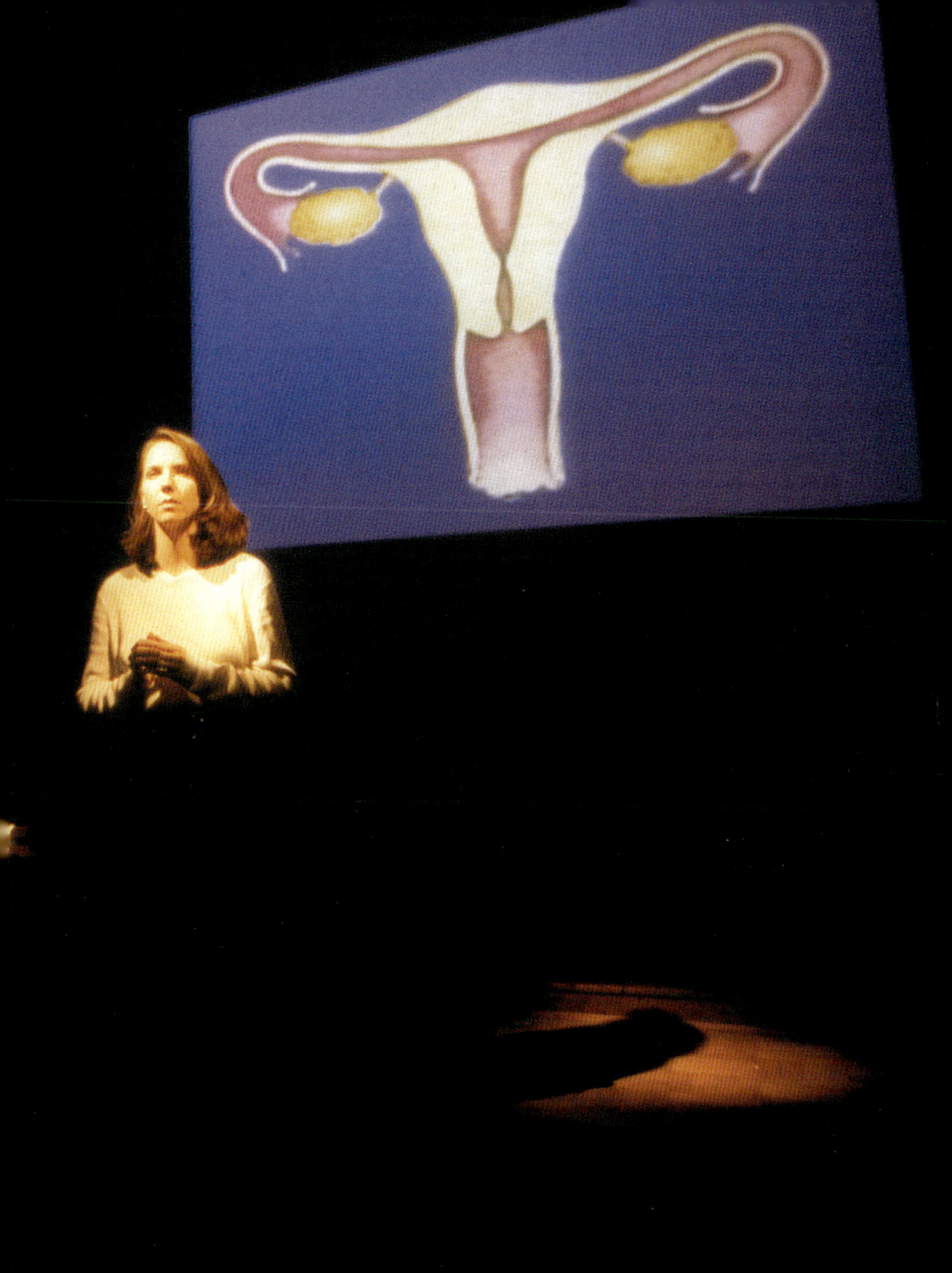

Critical Art Ensemble, *Flesh Machine: a genexploitation project*,
Galerija Kapelica, Ljubljana, November 1997. Photo by Igor Andelic

stand and analyse the new biotechnologies." And so the CAEs have organised a series of meetings, exhibitions and videoconferences and have presented magnetic supports and videos as well as the book *Flesh Machine*, in which they debate the economic and political goals that underlie reproduction technologies, hidden and buried beneath the provocation of ethical problems that allow the discussion to wallow in endless settings and in opinions that serve exclusively to distract from the real terms of the problem. The public chosen to talk about *Flesh Machine* is the middle class, identified as the class that makes greatest use of techniques of assisted reproduction. Galleries and museums were a perfect medium with which to reach this public, even though the CAEs also did performances and held debates elsewhere as well. "Once the public is inside, our work begins with a series of performances and readings. In the performance we try to explain the pressures which are brought to bear on women to reproduce and raise their children for reasons primarily tied to economics. With our readings we try to explain our position concerning the techniques of reproduction; after providing this information, we try to create a situation in which people can become directly involved, showing them how these techniques function and what lies behind the language of ethics."

The audience is invited, after having watched a CD-ROM with documentation on assisted reproduction, including the possible genetic tests, to go visit genetic experts to have part of their DNA extracted or to have some of their cells frozen; in this way, the performances of the CAEs introduce an element of novelty into the performance environment, that is, the creation of a bridge that immediately links observation and experience.

"We know that the English had, around the time of the Second World War, what they called the Doomsday Bug, created by exposing viruses to radiation until mutant strains were produced. And I am talking about more than thirty years ago — progress has been made since then! There are also ethnic weapons, which attack only blacks or whites or mongoloids or whatever, based on the enzymatic differences between the races. They could just as easily develop a disease that attacks only a certain ethnic group. This is old news; the first formulation of these techniques dates back some fifteen years. And here too lots of progress has been made", wrote frequently William Burroughs, analysing the phenomenon whereby systems of military experimentation and control shift their field of action directly into the cells of the human body, provoking the genetic alterations of a new strategy of terror.

After analysing the concept of digital clones and the relationship of those clones with eugenics, the CAEs shift the subject of discussion to the development of data bodies in order to consider the "genetic worth of the individual". When a genetic test is done a cluster of genetic information is created concerning the data body. An individual can potentially decide to take part in the flesh market, as long as his or her data body does not rule this out. By promising to remix genetic data, this market will develop sales campaigns to new and diversified "flesh" markets. In their lectures, the CAEs inform the spectators of the fact that in this process there are two basic problems: the map (data) does not represent the territory (flesh), and they are confused. For instance, there is an ample market of sperm provided by very intelligent donors. But by mixing the genetic material of two very intelligent donors, you cannot be sure that the result will be an intelligent being; intelligence is something much more complicated than a process of inheritance, and so the likelihood of having an intelligent child would be the same if the donor were selected at random. This example nullifies assisted choice as a eugenics choice, unmasking the false illusions that suggest sperm banks, which are offered to an interlocutor convinced that interventions to enhance reproduction serve some purpose and that it is possible to select the characteristics of one's own children. The same thing is true for predisposition, which is what is obtained with assisted reproduction, and which therefore to the same degree is unable to ensure the expression of a characteristic in an individual. Amongst the services offered by sperm banks for assisted childbirth there is also the possibility of requesting characteristics that will allow greater competitivity in a capitalist society, characteristics that will offer the possibility of being more successful in the field of work and in terms of results.... The CAEs discuss with the audience the strategies and modalities of genetic manipulation, demonstrating, with data, research and surveys, that the mentality that will allow us one day to walk into a clinic and select the characteristics of our own children is almost ready, and that the products, markets and consumer ideology surrounding the creation of human life are developing very quickly.

The actions of the CAEs create situations that trigger questions through which we clearly see the means that the culture of disinformation puts to use, producing mechanisms that induce false needs and false expectations, often highlighting the standards that market uses to impose itself upon society. "The success of a genetic product is measured according to profits. What people buy, instead, is perceived as something that is useful for the future. For instance, intelligence or health. Embryos can be tested very early to determine whether they are affected by genetic diseases or deformations. There are social pressures that push parents to rid themselves of any deformity, to abort that which is imperfect or unfit. The only value in capitalist society is efficiency, and the differences that represent inefficiency are eliminated in the name of progress. This moves us very far from certain agrarian societies where, instead, a difference is often celebrated." The products of genetics are therefore valued according to their likelihood to produce that which is considered normal. Social Darwinism is a product of capitalism to justify the enormous differences in the distribution of wealth. This political interpretation is at the service of the ruling class, which finds itself in the position it does because it is the best adapted class. In this theory, social constructs and contingent power relationships are transformed into something that is rendered necessary by nature. The same ideology is used today to define a universal standard for man that is ideal for the "free market economy": therefore the effort nowadays is to construct a population of efficient labourers. Validating and reinforcing the concept of biological determinism as an explanation for all social and individual variations, and a medical model for all human variations, is nothing other, in the final analysis, than a model on normality, which includes social normality and peremptorily indicates that *a priori* or following a corrective therapy it is possible to get back into line those who deviate from the norm.

"It is absolutely in bad faith to think that genetic modifications will preserve the species: the response to pollution lies in the restructuring of the environmental policies and not in a restructuring of the species in such a way as to render them immune to the effects of certain toxins. The risk linked to natural maternity drops greatly if the mothers have access to medical care. All the same, thanks to the anxiety and the fear of the masses, the markets are increasingly pushing for assisted reproduction. The threats can be direct or more subtle, but in any case they underscore the disadvantages that a child will face if he is not born amongst the normal."

There is a crisis in the area of the limitations of work right now. With the improvements of communication and information technologies we have encountered considerable difficulties in keeping pace with tools, and the velocity of technology and the economy have gone beyond the limits of the human body, which has thus come to be configured as a low-velocity element. Technology is a "black hole" that absorbs all human energies, and hence results in the production of stress, anxiety and alienation, which destroy the organic platform (the human body) generating the need to create new technologies. In the past drugs were used to push the body beyond its limits but the advantages that derive from their use have declined.

A potential response to this crisis is to create better workers, assembling the best predispositions; and that is why most of the new technologies are designed to target the middle class, which is being asked to reproduce beings that can withstand the attack of technology. The CAEs also ask whether the genetic information of the ruling class can reach a higher level of normalisation: in this way the changes in the standards of normality will no longer be radical but could be radical at the evolutionary plane. "Our position is that technology is not bad per se, we are in favour of technological development, buy we are opposed to the authoritarianism of capitalism. Moreover we find that often technology is used too often, not for the good of society but rather to enrich groups and perpetrate certain oppressive institutions. In our work we hope to show the positive aspects of technology and to show how they can be separated from the negative and oppressive aspects. The question is not whether to use technology or not, but how to use it, since it is a human necessity. In any case, the authoritarianism of pan-capitalism will never be eliminated, and we are working to oppose this force."

Everywhere survival is the order of the day,
as if for an obscure tedium vitae
or a collective desire for catastrophe....
Certainly, all of this baggage
of survival, including dietetics,
ecology, the protection of the redwoods, the seals, or the
human race, tends to prove that we are indeed alive....
Which is not such a sure thing.
Jean Baudrillard

FICTIONS

From Hyper-realism to Hyper-life

Behind the birth of Dolly, which made the subject of genetic engineering a territory of public interest, is a company called PPL Therapeuts, a corporation that financed the creators of the cloned sheep, and which has claimed all the rights to the discovery. Its speciality is that of creating transgenic animals (goats, rabbits, cows, etc.) whose milk contains proteins capable of combatting mucoviscidosis and blood clots. Ron James, president of the company, claims that the technologies will reduce by 18 months the tests for new pharmaceuticals (which last on average 3–5 years), and expects to produce quite soon human proteins from cloned animals. The future of cloned animals will be that of becoming biological "factories" at the service of major economic interests, and huge rivers of cash are being invested in this area. The case of PPL is an outstanding example: after the birth of Dolly, shares in the company skyrocketed 56 percent in a single week. Christine Laycock, a scientific journalist, claims that "the stock market and biotechnologies are made for one another: the stock market is where investors make bets (sometimes very risky bets) on the future; the latter invent objects whose commercialisation requires at least ten years". Instead of counting on hypothetical public investments, American researchers have understood that the stock market could support their research financially for years, with non-returnable funding, in exchange for a single condition: the goals of the research must be extremely practical.

The companies involved in biotechnology quoted on the stock exchange are 249 in the United States, 21 in the United Kingdom and 3 in France. According to other sources, with varying degrees of success, there are 700 biotech companies in Europe and 1300 in America. All for an invested value in the year 2000 of roughly thirty billion dollars, a sum that is destined to grow considerably year by year. The stock exchange investments make it possible to speed up the pace of research; the more promising the experiments, the greater the value of the investment. The Swiss company Novartis is already interested in the technique developed by the researchers in Edinburgh, in order to integrate it with their own research on "transgenic pigs", conceived to produce human kidneys and hearts. Once again, there are considerable economic advantages offered by cloning. The human heart possesses a protein that immediately eliminates any intruder, and in order to ensure that the organ taken from a pig will be tolerated, it must be modified in such a way that it can produce a protein capable of inhibiting the human immune system. But this process could provoke the spread of dangerous pathologies: a virus that is harmless for a pig could transform itself into something extremely dangerous for humans. In order to prevent this risk, scientists try to create "clean pigs". The present-day costs for producing transgenic animals is very high, for instance a cow costs about 350,000 dollars, while cloning would make it possible to produce from the first pig an entire brood with the same characteristics, amortising the costs enormously.

The pharmaceuticals industry is planning its own future in terms of genetic engineering. The Genome Therapeutics has sold to the Swedish group Astra, for 22 million dollars, the genetic information on *helicobacter pylori*, the bacterium responsible for ulcers and probably causing stomach tumors. Professor Steve Jones, a professor of genetics in London, and his group of researchers, have reached the conclusion that there exists in all species a gene that contains the hour of our death, a sort of biological bomb that has been ticking since our birth, a precious biological calculator that is a part of a chromosome called the telomere. The scientists who have been working on this project predict that within five years it will be possible to establish the duration of the life of any given individual; naturally, the gene does not contain the information: death by car crash, alcohol abuse, smoking, infections... in other words, the unpredictable variables. After the initial general panic, the ones most concerned with the discovery would seem to be executives of the large insurance companies: in fact, the life insurance business is calculated every year at many trillions dollars, and the Royal Society has already organised a seminar to study the impact that the genetic revolution might have on the conditions and selection of policies. For an economic sector threatened by this molecular crisis, there is another sector that in the future will find the solutions to all its problems in genetics, that is, cigarette manufacturers. Testing is now underway on a new kind of transgenic tobacco, capable of producing hemoglobin, the pigment of the red globules, indispensable in respiration. In the agricultural and chemical industry the concrete relationship with biotechnology is already a reality. In the United States alone, for instance, this year 30 percent of the 25 million arable acres of land will be planted with transgenic plants.

And the Americans begin to think about another problem: should they continue to take care of old people? The governor of Colorado, Richard Lamm, in 1984, said that those who are afflicted with fatal diseases have the duty to die in order to make room for the young. In 1987 Daniel Callaghan, director of the Hastings Centre of New York, proposed suspended survival care for anyone that was older than seventy-five. The American senior citizen, he said, has no right to assure himself or herself a progressive immortality at the expense of society at large. Economists have estimated that people above sixty absorb 30 percent of the national budget; this proportion will climb to 65 percent within forty years, and it will no longer be possible to fund programmes on their behalf, inasmuch as the medical and hospital expenses that they will require will represent almost half of all American paychecks. According to a report from the OECD, in the year 2000, aging has caused in Europe an increase of 40 percent of the health spending, and 80 percent in the spending for assistance to the elderly.

At the same time, Géraldine Magnan proposes a formula that offers the hypothesis of reviving the dead. "Cellular death takes place after brain death. It would be enough to extract a few cells within the first thirty minutes after death in order to be able to execute a proper cloning. A couple whose child had just died could be tempted and, after a few months, would have a chance to cuddle a lovely baby, identical to the first..."

So, the era of the re-creation of the human has begun, in silence, with no particular commentary, with no great disruption, without seeming to make much of a change in everyday life. It is the end of the Romantic idea of the construction of man by grafting, patching, cross-breeding, pieces assembled, which was followed by the post-Romantic vision of the creation of a human body that would present no differences from those that are already being produced through copulation. Frankenstein, the robot, the assembly line, the extension of man to other planets in the solar system, and in art and in the movies, artists such as Stelarc, and films like *Metropolis* by Fritz Lang, *Tetsuo* by Shinja Tsukamoto, *Crash* by David Cronenberg basically all belong to a vision of reproduction and hybridisation that has to do with a historical and technological dimension in which the forms of mutation were visible, identifiable and recognisable. The history that accompanies us is different in kind from that which we had imagined, and the forms of mutation have shifted from the areas of technology to those of biotechnology, from cybernetics to genetics: an invisible mutation, therefore, without any elements of difference or recognisability. Spare part organs, human parts that are "born" on animal experimental subjects, cloning, artificial skin, the Genome Project and the mapping of DNA, transplants, new media, euthanasia, biotechnologies, genetic engineering, inorganic materials that take root on flesh, a new cosmetic system all display a mutation that leaves no trace of its processes or its constructions. This type of image is less fascinating, less spectacular, less amazing than those that accompanied man's cybernetic dream, precisely because they contain no element of distinction. No super powers, no shifting skin, no laser gazes... images and forms devoid of evidence precisely because they "reproduce", "duplicate", "copy" the real.

Western culture has always successfully distinguished between manufactured products and products that come from the human, animal or vegetable kingdoms. The revolution of the contemporary world consists precisely of the development of the logical principles of life and machines, and applying both to the construction of extremely complex systems: by doing so the technicians are creating devices that are at the same time products and living things. If the robot is the mechanical moment of the reproduction of intelligence, mutation is the dimension that does not recognise the linear development of an evolution of the species. The final frontier of identity is thus exploded into absolutely unrecognisable bio-mechanisms.

In the short story by Philip K. Dick *The Electric Ants*, the protagonist, Garson Poole discovers, in the hospital after an accident, that he is not human as he had always believed. His body is stuffed with circuits, cables, mechanisms and a perforated tape that spins through a programme containing his perception of the world: "Programmed. I have been programmed! In me, somewhere, there is a matrix, a grid that inhibits certain thoughts, certain actions, and forces me to think and commit others". A step forward in the literary field of mutation: the "replicant", the artificial, a construct with human semblance that has not the slightest idea that he is not human. No distinguishing features, in fact, even a self-awareness as a human being. The "invisible" practices of human/technological cross-breeding, conveyed by the mass media through rare and reassuring images, are in reality protected by rigorous top-secret classification, and the results of this research are transformed into new merchandise that is put on the market under the widest variety of morphologies of technological "necessity". New technologies and massive doses of spectacle corrupt the traditional forms of social interaction, mutating the forms of relationship, the processes of orientation, transforming the body into a surface at the intersection of the information "offered" by surrounding reality; they impose a new being, prepared and adjusted to the demands of social life, and a code with which access is offered to virtual and immaterial spaces, in which the distinctive features disappear by which humans have previously been identified: name, age, gender, race.

"A new life awaits you in the Off-world colonies. *The chance to begin again in a golden land of opportunity and adventure. New climate, recreational facilities...*" (advertising announcement in the colourless sky of *Blade Runner*). A form of mimesis hybridises image and world, spectacle, economics, sciences, communications. Images that overlay reality, replace it and themselves become "urban nature", everywhere devices forcing the icons of "nature", images of flowers, fruit, animals, places, humans, horizons, everywhere images of natural reality that overlay upon reality in a strategy of simulation, the outlines and depths of which are lost until you experience the claustrophobic sensation of a restriction of vital spaces, a restriction due to the layers of images.

"The sky above the port was the colour of a television, tuned to a dead channel.... *Night City* was like a deranged experiment in social Darwinism, designed by a bored researcher who kept one thumb permanently on the fast-forward button..." (William Gibson) An exasperated relationship with reality, a radical realism, the reproduction of a banal, useless, domestic reality, a doppelganger. The great narcissistic wound, the bad dream of endless duplication, the nightmare of repetition. The fixing of subjectivity which fades away, the double of a human that slowly and without awareness slips away and vanishes, sinking into the simulacrum, into the virtual, into its media-driven double. The television is always turned on, the great black hole in which all the tragedies precipitate, becoming images, images that assault us: explosions seen live, death seen live, the dissolution of awareness. The most convincing catastrophe is broadcast: the transition from real to fiction and from fiction to the real in an endless circle in which it no longer makes any sense at all to distinguish between the two moments. The line marking the distinction between the internal and external landscapes of the media collapses, in the senselessness in which catastrophes occur for no reason, there are no explanations, leaving a disorderly and incessant labour of the imagination.

And hyper-realism becomes a disconcerting and upsetting "text" of the anthropology of a media-based civilisation, of the visual appeals of advertising, a horizon in which cosmetics promise eternal youth, eternal beauty, eternal life, a horizon that disguises the incredible quantity of death that surrounds us with the obligation to remain once and for all registered high-quality trademarks. Reality must submit to an ever-greater degree to image, and it is no accident that hyper-realism should have developed precisely in those United States where the dead are "prepared" with beauty products so as to seem more fresh, healthier and more expressive than in life. Jean Baudrillard identifies "three orders of simulacra that have succeeded one another since the Renaissance, parallel with the mutations in the laws of value. The counterfeit is the dominant scheme of the 'classical' era, from the Renaissance to the Industrial Revolution. Production is the dominant scheme of the Industrial Era. Simulation is the dominant scheme of the current phase, guided by code". It was in the Renaissance that the fake originated, through the problem of what is "natural", the metaphysics of reality and appearance, through an idea of nature that is engendered by the creation of the counterfeit. We shall have to stop, sooner or later, fooling ourselves with figurative resemblance; the counterfeit and the reproduction necessarily imply the anguish of the extraneous, and simulation has always been the site of gigantic manipulation. Reality has long since precipitated into hyper-reality, "and so we have passed from electroshock to corporeal expression as a form of conditioning of mental health.... We cannot help but think with black humour of Artaud's total theatre, his theatre of cruelty, of which this dynamic-space simulation is an abject caricature. Here cruelty is replaced by the thresholds of minimal and maximum stimulation, by the invention of perceptive codes calculated from the thresholds of saturation", as Baudrillard wrote.

The astronomical growth of the financial and cultural power of the multinationals over the last twenty years is bound up with the revolution that has swept through the production of trademarks instead of products. For a long time the production of "things" remains the central motor of the industrialised economies, but in the 1980s a new type of corporation began to compete with traditional American manufacturers — who directly managed their factories, giving work to tens of thousands of workers — for large market shares. These "precursors", Coca-Cola, McDonald's, Disney, Nike, Microsoft, and so on, insisted that the production of "things" was only a secondary part of their activities and that, thanks to the liberalisation of trade and the reform of labour laws, there was a possibility of subcontracting the actual manufacturing of objects to third parties, in other areas of the planet, because what their companies had begun to produce was, primarily, not so much things, as images of their trademarks and brand names.

Los Angeles 2019, one of the opening scenes of *Blade Runner* is a bird's-eye panoramic view of the megalopolis full of dark and dense skyscrapers that seem like so many giant bases built to hold up immense neon signs that illuminate the metropolitan decay: Coca-Cola, Nike, Pan-Am and TDK. An ecocide is slowly and imperceptibly cancelling the "living" parts of the planet: in many films and in short stories set in the future, trees, plants and animals have vanished, only to be replaced by skilful simulations that reproduce their characteristics, morphologies and habits, while in reality every day "things" are put on the market with various semblances, little animals or little children, or cute little aliens, which need care and attention in order to grow, survive, and not die.

Why not make a real character? I had never seen any,
Or heard of them, and I thought that it would be a good idea.
(John de Andrea, 1972)

In 1970, in the wake of the exhibition entitled *22 Realists*, held at the Whitney Museum in New York, interest spread in the work of artists who painted based on photographic documents; generic terms such as "photorealism", "super real-

John de Andrea, *Diane*, 1988

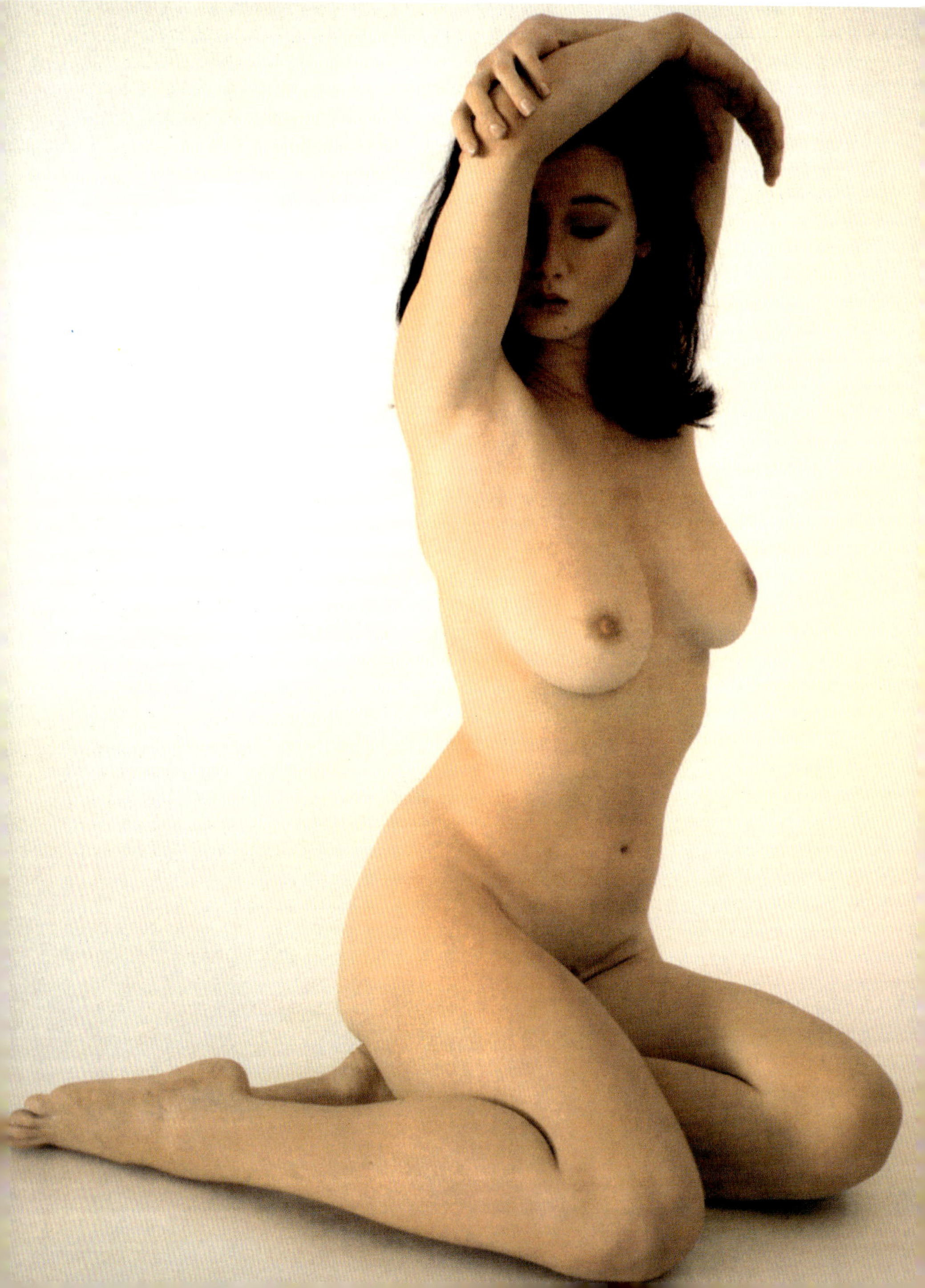

ism", "radical realism" and "sharp focus realism", became common and were used by critics to underscore the figurative nature of the images and their relationship to photography. But it was in Europe, after the Paris Biennial of 1971, that the term hyper-realism won out. Violently rejected by critics, the canvases and sculptures by hyper-realistic artists "stood out for their banality, their lack of any philosophical, political, moral or emotional consequence..." It was the "analogic depiction of the vacant space between reflection and mirror" (Abadie). Hyper-realism, which traces its roots to the return of the image proposed by Pop Art and to its contamination by advertising, insists on the "arrogance" of the image diffused by the modern media. As Wolfgang Becker would later write: "The image has become analysable, reproducible, and this array of signs constitutes an iconographic programme well suited to feed an electronic brain".

The decision of hyper-realistic artists to depict a reality caught in its most ordinary, everyday, often banal aspects, is the need for a "second" image: the re-elaboration of the same reality through the automatic filter of technology. We can sense, in the quest for a neutrality typical of the reliance on photography, a family resemblance to the previous experiments of Pop Art; but in the need to attain the more real than real, hyper-realistic artists identify the real with the subject reproduced through the mechanical means of photography and casting, choosing the optical objectivity of vision. We almost seem to see emerging the urgent need to fix a world that tends to disappear and make a reproduction of it.

In technical terms, the artwork of John de Andrea and Duane Hanson derives directly from that of George Segal, even if the figure that emerges is not a white and slightly rougher copy of the original model, but a sort of simulacrum, exact in every detail, perfectly finished, painted to make it resemble a living person, endowed with hair and real eyelashes and eyeglasses; and clothing... The nudes of de Andrea are duplicates of young people of the American middle class, who constitute the originals; for the most part attractive and endowed with a nice body, they reveal in a certain sense the class to which they belong and their original nationality in the way that their hair is fixed, in their attitude and their expressions. Duane Hanson presents a gallery of American types, described with vivacity, though also with a bit of cruelty. For both of them the attempt is to eliminate the "distance" of representation and insist on absolute fidelity, simultaneity and immediacy of an experience that is not real but, once again, media-generated.

In hyper-realism we seem to see the family album of America, a report on the American Way of Life, assembled into a catalogue of themes: shiny new cars carefully presented in automobile showrooms, piled up rusty carcasses in huge junkyards, the invasiveness of the technological universe, New York street scenes, department store display windows, drugstores... all themes that are characteristic of the society of the spectacle. To the mass-market consumer item emphasised by Pop artists, the hyper-realists opposed the universe of reflection, of the transparent and the unstable, images of other cars and buildings inscribed on the chrome of the bumpers, on the glittering surface of a car body, reflected in the display window of a department store. What is presupposed is the presence of a real place within which the metaphorical image of the painting itself is set, the exterior spectacle. The return of the image to American painting, which dated back ten years before with the appearance of Pop Art and the intrusion into the field of art of the advertising image, returned the public's attention to the urban setting, to the power of attraction of the image diffused in series by the media, which shifted their gaze to the setting of the everyday, thus modifying the concept of reality. The point of view changes, the decision to take as an original model photography already denotes the shift in vision: photography displays a monocular cliché of a subject that was originally seen by two eyes, the artist projects the slide of this photograph upon a canvas, and upon the canvas appears the reproduction of a subject taken by a single eye, the very same subject that had originally been seen with two eyes. The artist sees with his or her two eyes the projected image and paints a copy of it, configuring it in accordance with a binocular vision, reconstituting an impression of space and thus creating a reality that offers the illusion of approaching the original image while failing to match it in any way.

If Pop Art attained the apotheosis of the American Way of Life, hyper-realism created a new conceptual modification: from natural and biological construct, the body is transformed into an artificial structure, in continual transformation and alteration, constantly diverse and different. We find ourselves before a synthetic face, the symbol of the artificiality that impresses its contemporary sign, the symbol of a transformism that becomes a life style. With Pop Art, the everyday mythologies are reproduced, from western to song. We see a procession of all the media-oriented idols, one after the other, from which emerges the provincial American nature that identifies with the archetypes of modern international folklore; we see an illustration of the entire hierarchy of values of the planetary civilisation, we see the images of the planetarisation of a folklore elevated to the moral power of an international standard of behaviour and a language without frontiers, while at the same time there emerge the reasons bound up with the technological and financial power of the United States, the management and control of information, imperialistic policies, the enhancement of investments for the development of the mass media. We sense in these images the collective subconscious of a continent that looks optimistically upon the dynamics of industrial progress.

At the end of the 1960s, hippies and Black Panthers, young draftees and students began to display an American face that tended inexorably to crumble, and the images of hyper-realism offered a denunciation of the isolation and loneliness of men and merchandise in a picture-postcard universe.

The perfect bodies by John de Andrea or Duane Hanson, the automobiles by Paul Staiger, the façades by Richard Estes, or the women by Kacere are "more American" than real Americans: the absolute precision of the objective rendering and the reference to a higher scale than life-sized and natural allowed the emergence of a situation in which American cultural life had been plunged, encouraged by the hyper-realist determination to create an objective rendering, an instantaneous taking possession, devoid of any emotional or sentimental content. This therefore engendered the ambiguity of hyper-realism that plays upon a refined ambivalence: that of the already seen or the never seen, the objects and therefore the bodies are seen in their greatest familiarity and in their most obscure estrangement, in their immediacy and in their distance. The hyper-realistic artwork restores the object in its hallucinatory presence, depriving it of a dimension, without movement in the sculptures, without depth in the painting, and in any and all cases, without the idea of life. Hyper-realism seems to conjugate in itself a

Duane Hanson, *Motorcycle Accident*, 1969

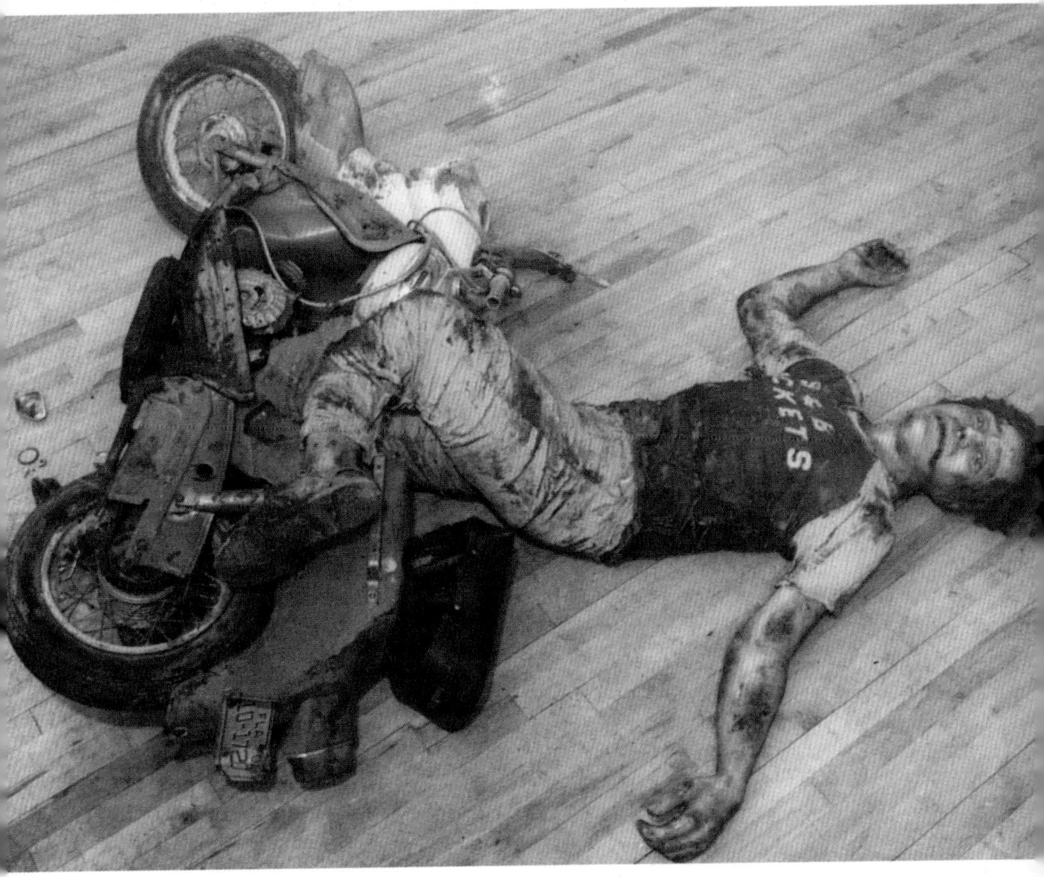

form of painting in which the representation is provided as pure representation, with the necessary elimination of the subject, a painting that is developed as the production of a production, "which adds, like any desiring machine, the producing of the product" (Deleuze and Guattari). Any artwork, however faithful to reality, to the very point of becoming indistinguishable, will never be taken for reality, but rather for what it essentially is: disillusionment.

The rhetoric of the real that appears in the artworks of American hyper-realism in the 1970s, in avowed opposition to the practices of the disappearance of the object and the form which in the same years emerged from Conceptual Art, is a powerful and sharp signal of the grave alteration that the real began to undergo. If the "golden age is that innocence of language where it need not double that which claims to be an effect of reality", as Baudrillard puts it, in hyper-realism we see the dissolution of even that final distinction between the real and the imaginary, and the yawning chasm opens up of a hallucinatory resemblance of the real to itself. Hyper-realistic artists, the targets of ferocious attacks by critics who marginalised their work and discounted their importance, intuited that in order to escape from the crisis of representation it was necessary to "trap" the real in a repetition and a maniacal duplication of itself that would entirely elude its meaning. In that way, doubled and devoid of reasons, it reveals exactly what it is: a perfect, constructed, organised universe, but without the slightest possibility of containing life, only the semblances of life.

A planetary *Truman Show* of the extension of Western culture replaces reality, transforming human beings into spectators or unwitting actors, varying from case to case.

The vertigo of simulation begins to propagate across the planet, making the power of the media central, especially that of the television; far from the "romantic" nightmares of the Orwellian *Big Brother*, the planet seems to find itself inside a vehicle that travels incessantly but without a pilot, without any guidance, in an absolutely uncontrollable and uncontrolled trajectory, in which appearance is replaced by the "presentation" of persons, objects, environments, animals, stories, films or documentaries, beneath the police-like and inquisitorial gaze of "spectators" who reproduce the forms and the lives of that which they see, continuing the folly of a endless duplication on the boundaries of representation of that which was already represented. The gaze no longer needs the illusion of a perspectival sense of depth in order to be deceived; everything shifts to the surface in a serial mode in which the real is more greatly reflected, and the first-degree murder of the real stops necessarily requiring that a guilty party be found.

Again *Blade Runner*: "more human than human" is the slogan of the Tyrell Corporation to advertise the replicant, an advanced type of robot, "virtually identical to a human being... superior in strength and agility, and at least equal in intelligence, to the genetic engineers who created him". Perfect beings that approach an ideal, non-deteriorated physical condition, as is instead the destiny of the humans, by now contaminated and altered by the ecocide that they themselves have produced.

American hyper-realism of the 1970s offers images of amplified reality, and bodies that are "more human than human": tourists, waitresses, policemen, women pushing shopping carts... the new screen of representation in which humans have been trapped is restored through the most faithful of reproductions, a carnal reality of the body annihilated by its semblance in a subtle homicide of the original.

One of the definitions of the real is: "that which can be copied exactly", and the hyper-realistic artists carried out the great revolution of abandoning representation precisely because of the characteristics of simulation that they critically brought forth, as signals, as dangers, as possibilities, as declarations. If in everyday life the real has disappeared into a mimetic dimension that reproduces it for screens of representation saturated with massive doses of unawareness, hyper-realism isolates and condenses the maximum degree of veracity into an evidently constructed form, and the representation winds up being unmasked by the very perfection of the simulation.

John de Andrea

"I began working with mannequins, then I found some plaster strips and I wrapped up a few poor girls at the University of Colorado.... I had combined

Duane Hanson, *Tourists*, 1970

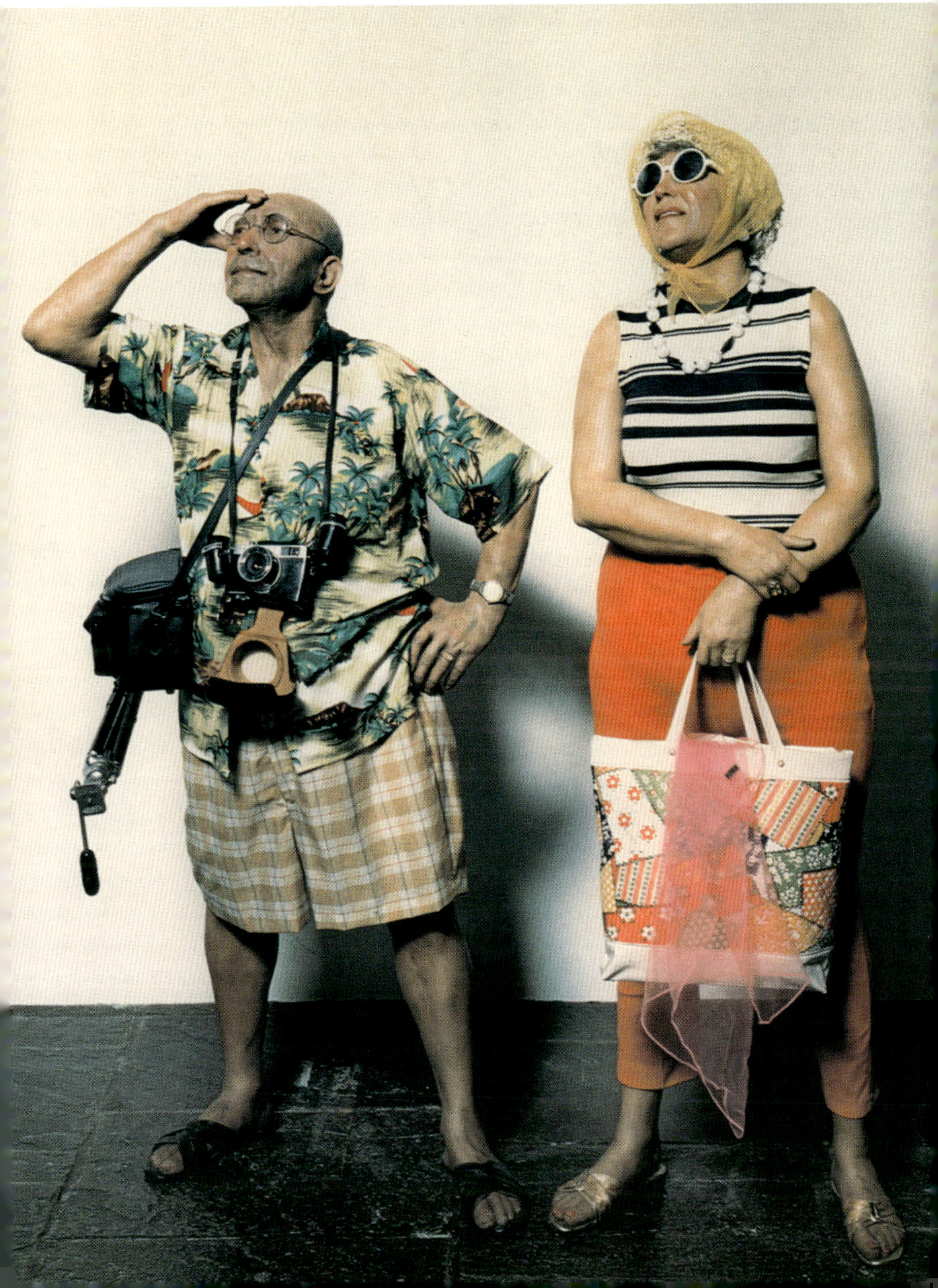

Judy Fox, *Eve*, 1987

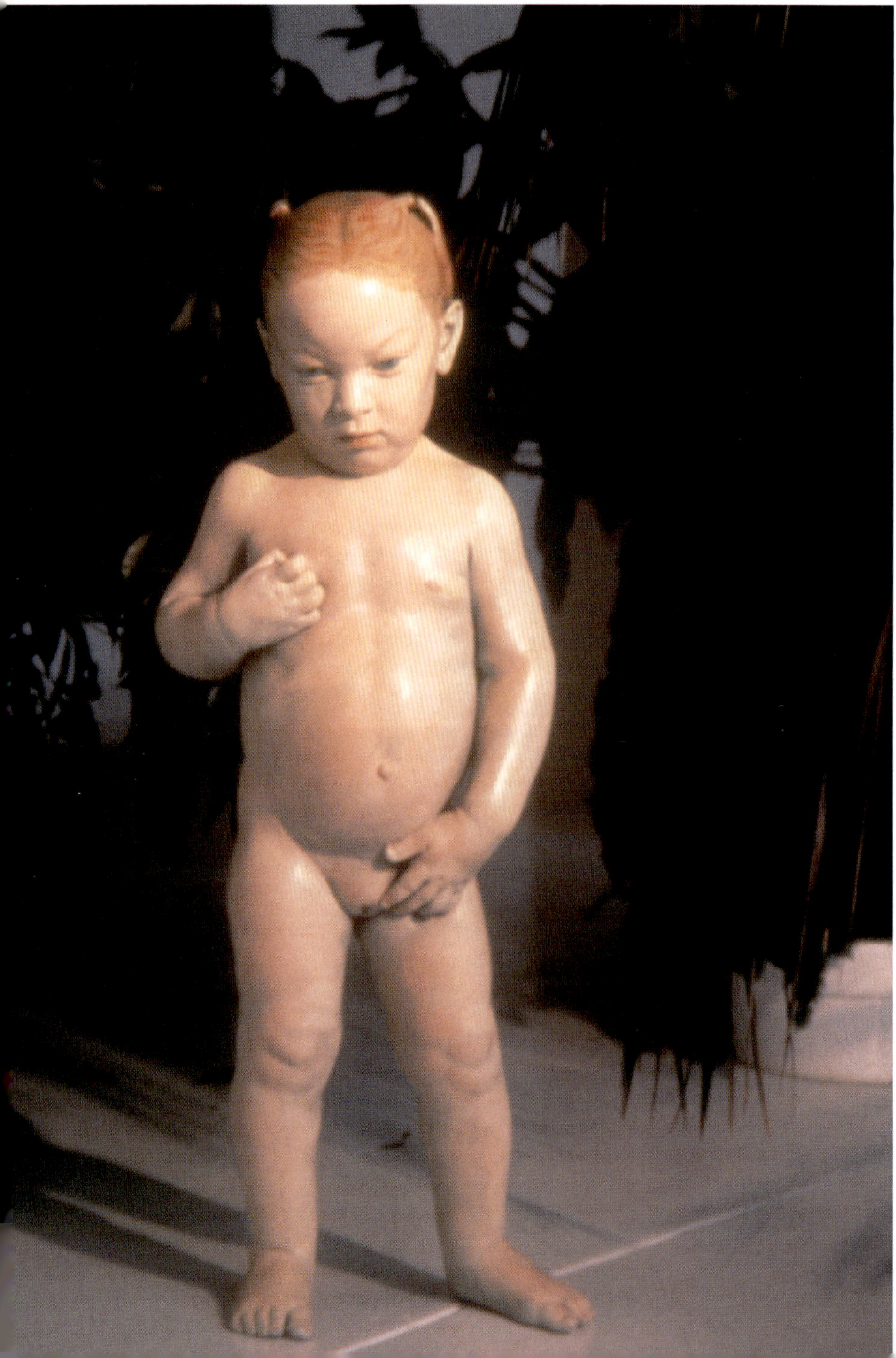

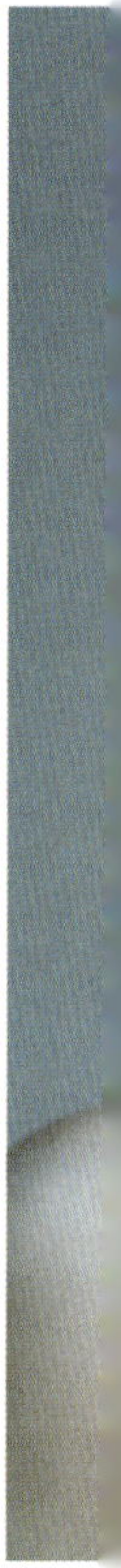

Reuven Cohen, from the *Babylon* series, 1997

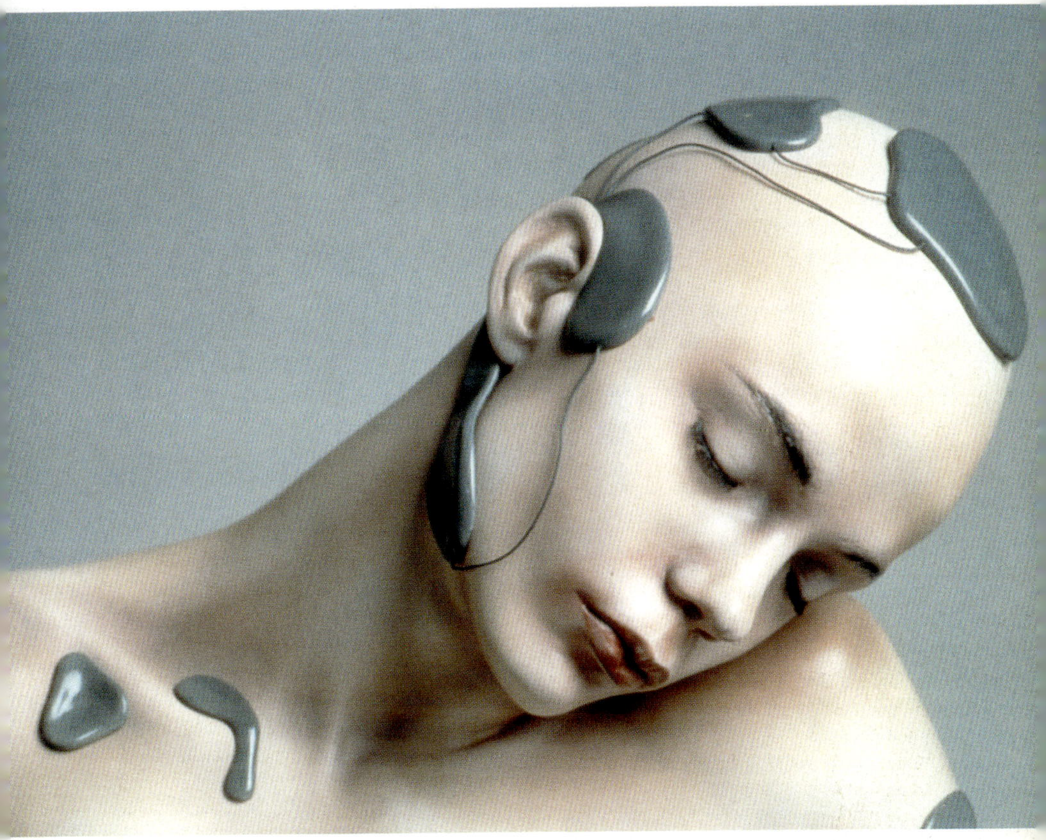

sculpture and painting and it never worked until the day I said to myself that this was stupid. Why not make a real person?... And so I made lots of casts and I also wounded plenty of models."

Q. To what degree are your characters "real"?

A. I want them to breathe.

Q. How important is painting to your sculptures?

A. I seek out the most indefinite colour possible. There are lots and lots of things that happen under the skin, and if you try to control them you can't obtain enough variation. With a first layer, I treat the extremities, especially the legs, as something that contains blood. I apply this blood red a little bit as if it were an abstract painting, then I wash, mix and densify it until the legs are purplish. When I paint the skin, I begin to work from the bottom, using a lot of red and violet.... I have studied the colours of skin and the differences in its various hues, and I try to paint these differences.... I don't use the same palette, but I invent a new one every time that I make a new character. In two or three years I will add new colours.

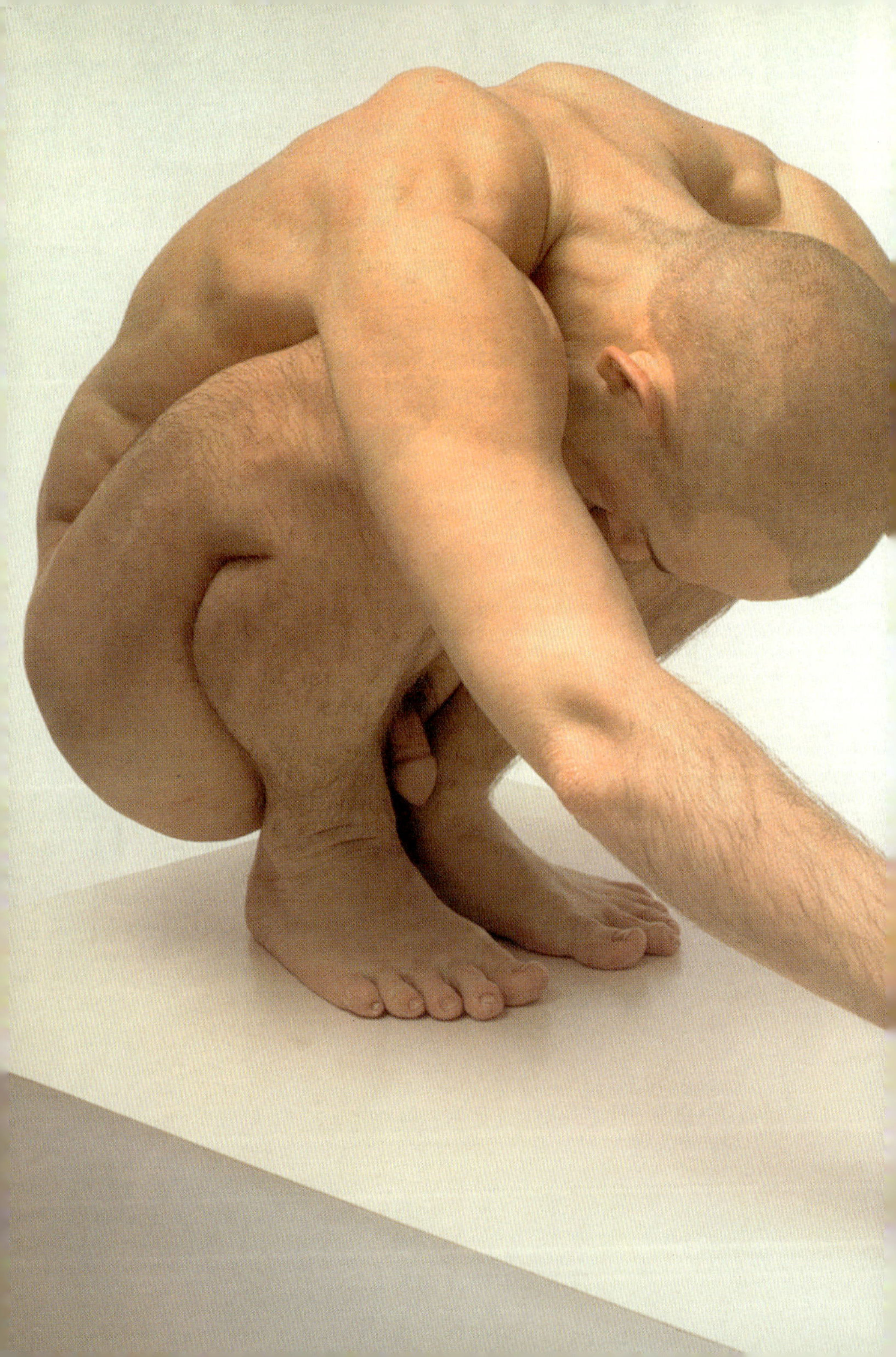

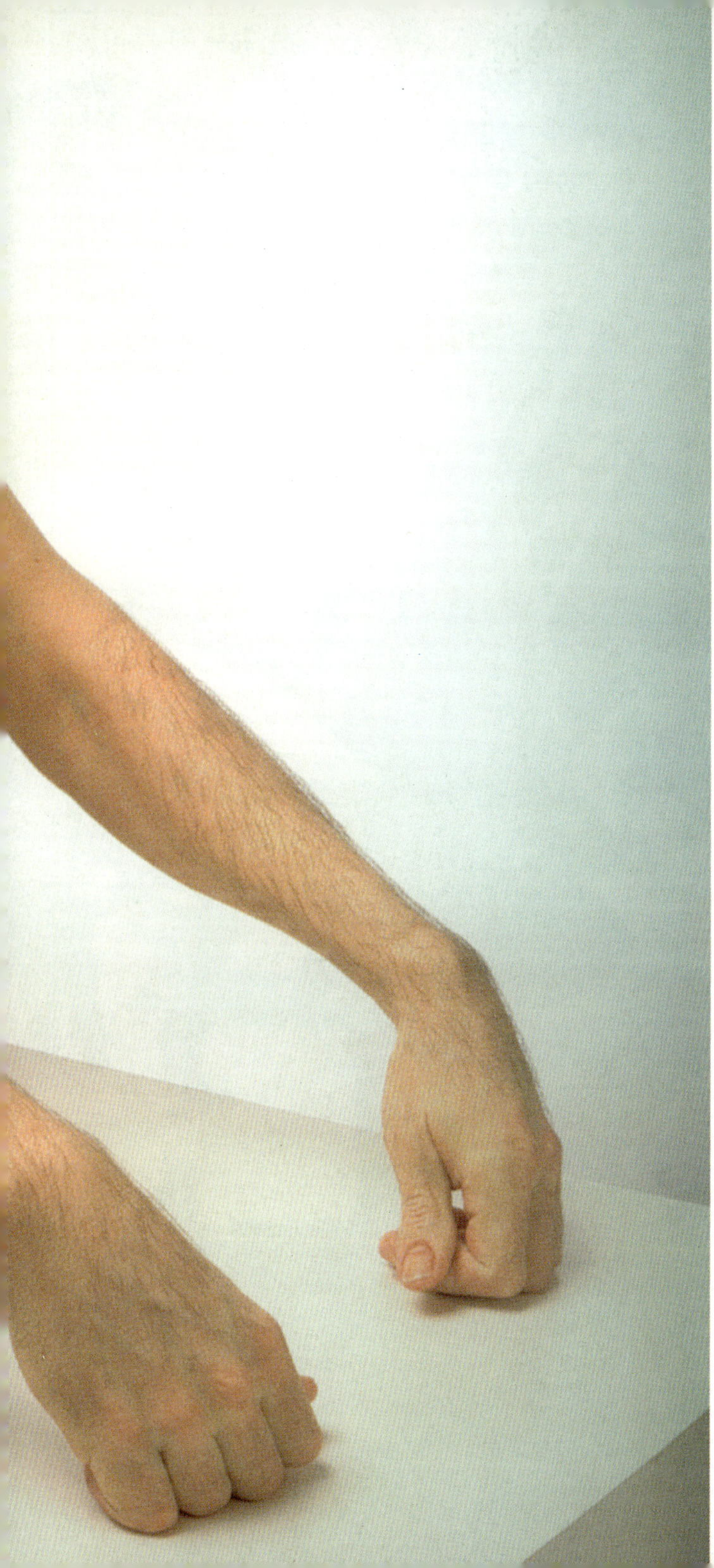

Ron Mueck,
Untitled (Shaved Head),
1998

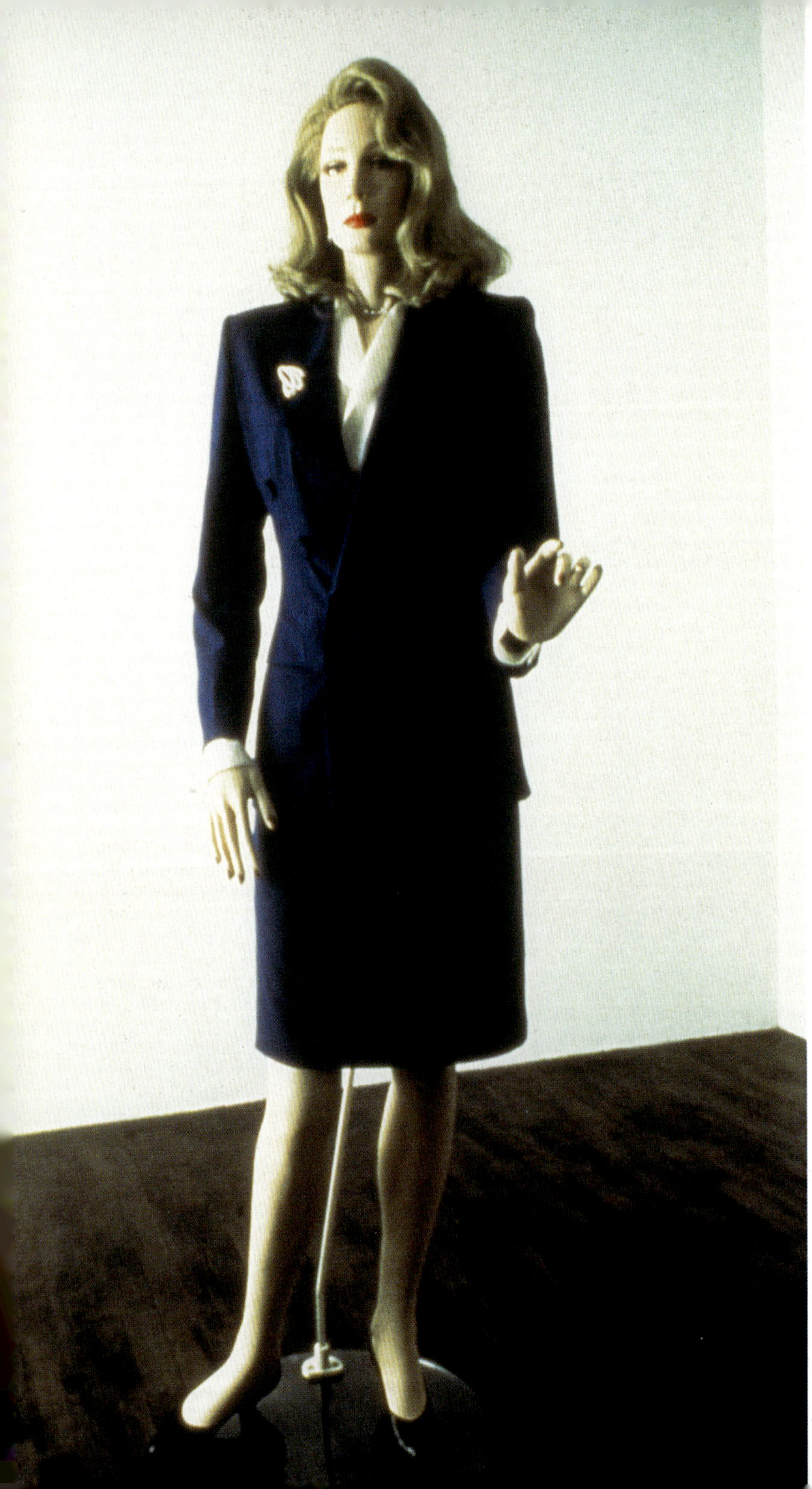

Charles Ray,
Mannequin
Fall '91,
1992

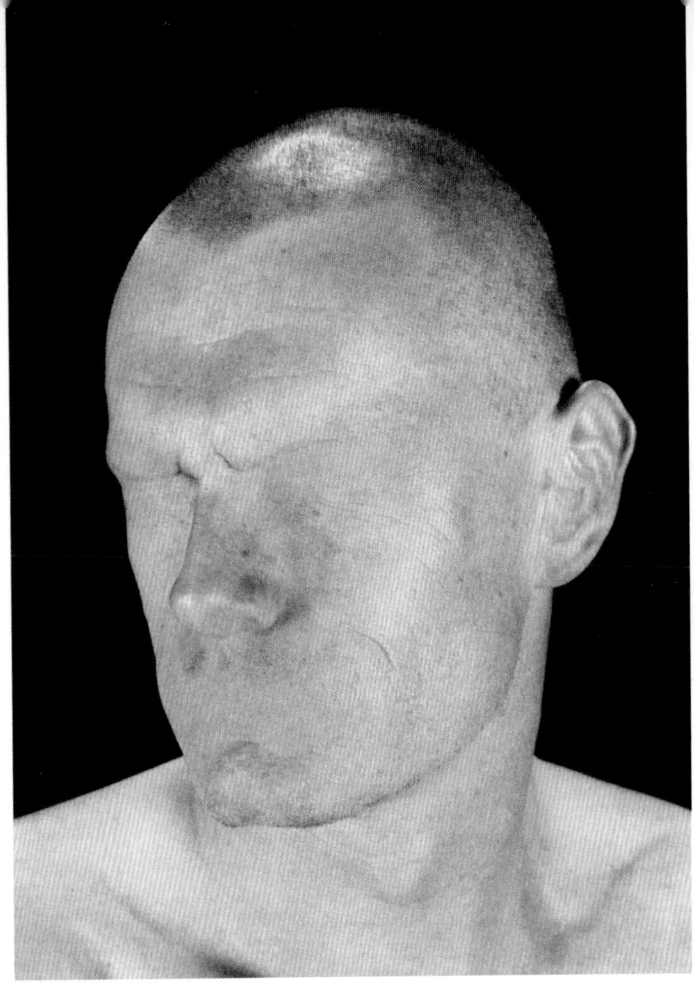

Aziz + Cucher,
Ken (from the
Dystopia series),
1995

Charles Close

I decided to work from photographs, not because I wanted my art to translate them but because, as interesting as the form might be, if it wasn't in a photograph I couldn't use it.... It seems to me that at times people think that when you use a photograph all that can emerge from it is one type of painting. From a photograph many different kinds of painting can emerge, as many as you can derive from reality.... I do canvases from photographs and that is not how the human eye sees. If I stare at something, I see it very clearly, if I look closely at something else, it is in focus too. The eye is very adaptable, but the camera sees the world with a single eye and I think that we know what blurring is only thanks to photography. Photography has definitively established what being out of focus is. It is this unquantifiable thing, the camera gives information that otherwise would have been too difficult to grasp.... I liked the fact of not thinking of a cheek in terms of the ear, trying to decide which was closer and which further away.... At this level, certain things are no longer in perfect shape, other zones at the same level fail to attain the same clarity. This allows me to treat different constants.

Mariko Mori, *Miko no Inori*, 1996

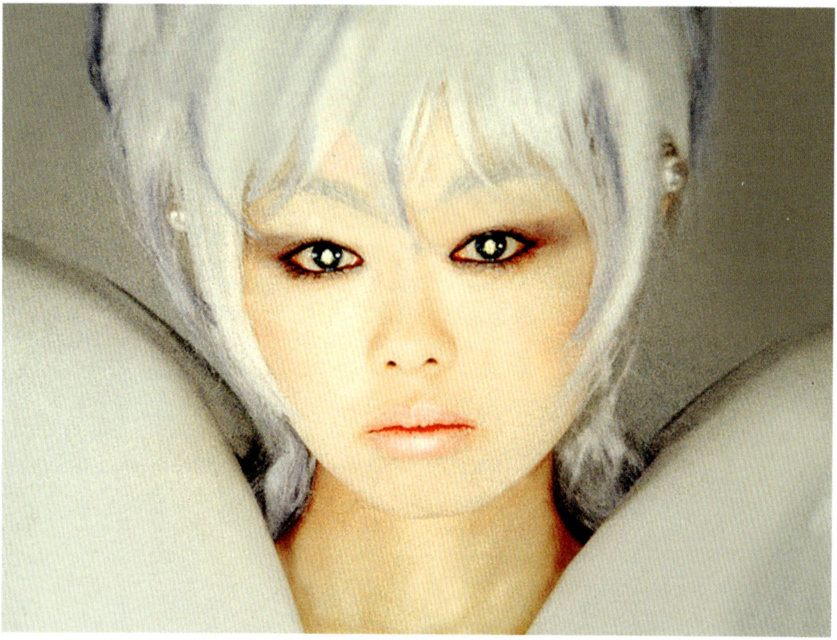

Richard Estes

Q. Do you try to reproduce photographs on canvas?

A. I don't try to reproduce photographs on canvas. I use it to make a painting.

Q. Could you make the same paintings without photography?

A. Certainly not. It is not possible. The advantage of photography is that you can block things; it consists of an instant.... The first step is to take a photograph, but I am not satisfied with enlarging a photograph.... There are some things that need to remain confused because they are that way by their nature. The eye sees this way when you look at things, some things are just out of focus. But I don't like to have some things in focus and some things blurry at the same time, because I am trying to keep the gaze from necessarily being attracted to certain parts. I want you to look at everything, and therefore for the focus to be more general.

We see the world through photography, and we accept it as reality. But if we show a photograph to someone from a primitive society, who has never seen one before, it may be that they will not know what it portrays.

Duane Hanson

In my sculpture I try to get free of the subject. My first artworks were fairly expressionistic, they took positions against war, crime, car crashes and violence in general; now my most successful pieces no longer set out from a theme or an idea, they are naturalistic and illusionistic, which entails, consequently, the shock, surprise and psychological impact of the spectator. The subject that I prefer to treat is the everyday life of the less well-to-do Americans or the middle class. The

Jeff Koons, *Bourgeois Bust - Jeff and Ilona*, 1991

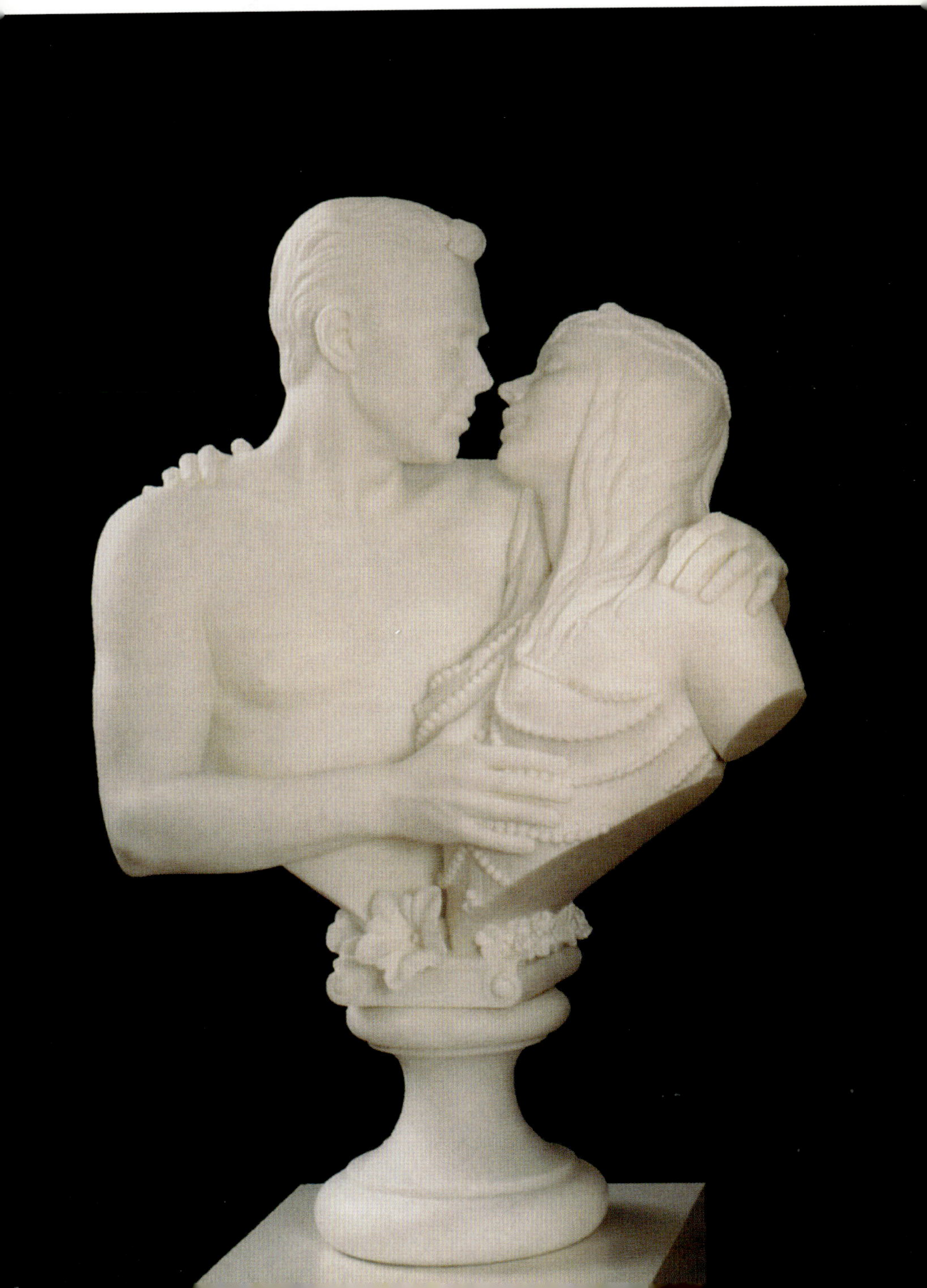

Inez Van Lamsweerde, *The Forest - Rob*, 1995

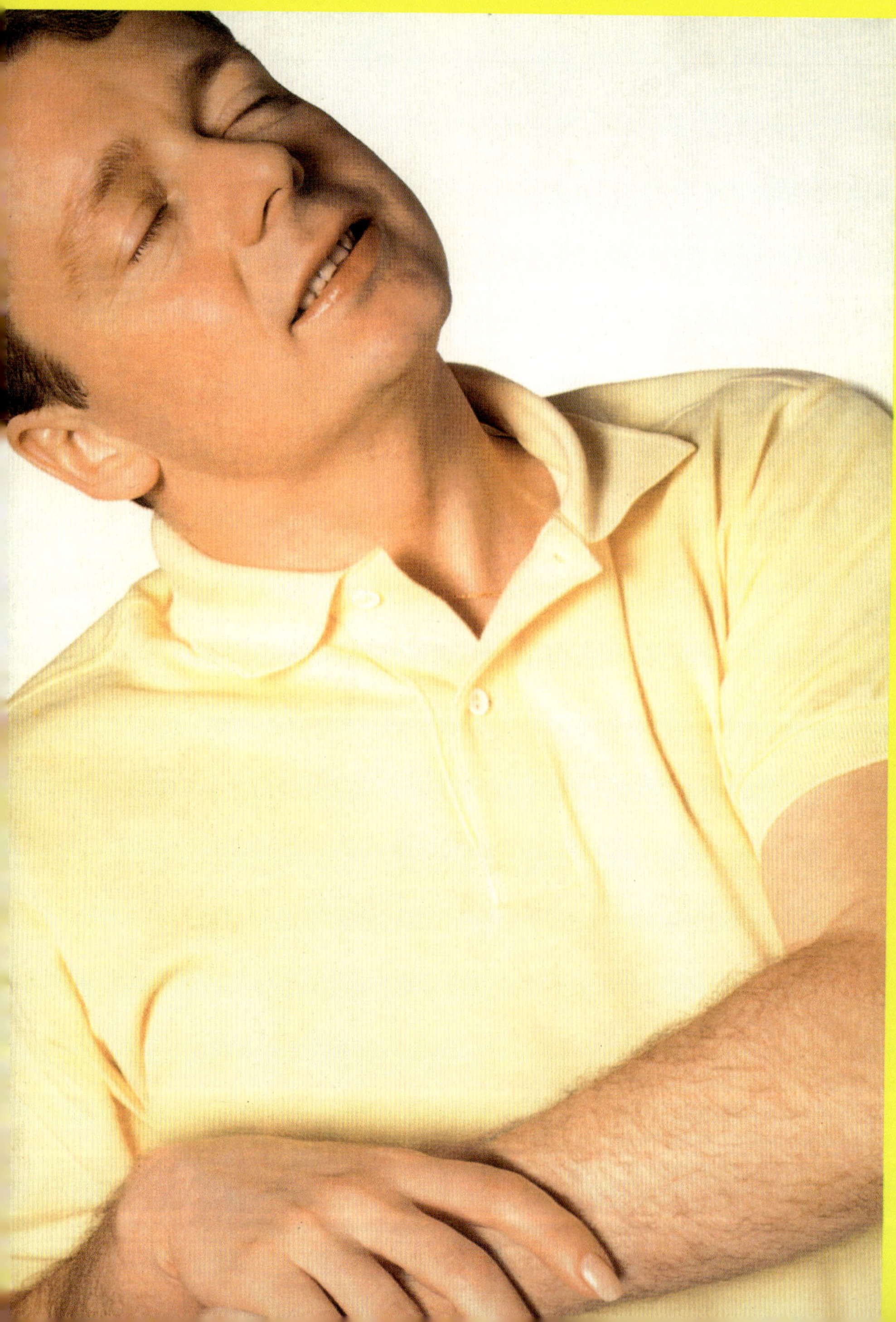

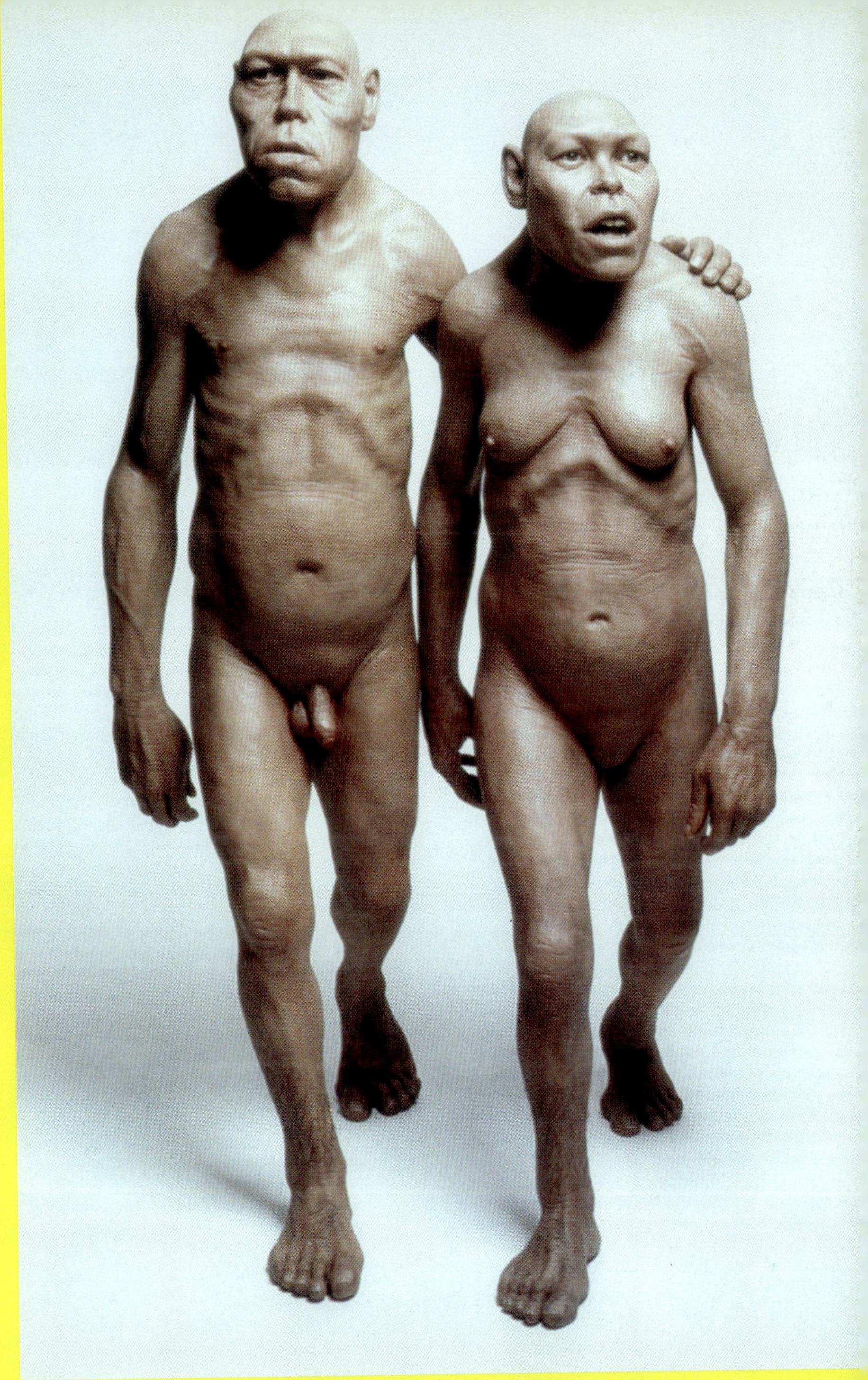

Tim Noble & Sue Webster, *The New Barbarians*, 1997–99

Cesare Fullone, *Tessy*, 2000

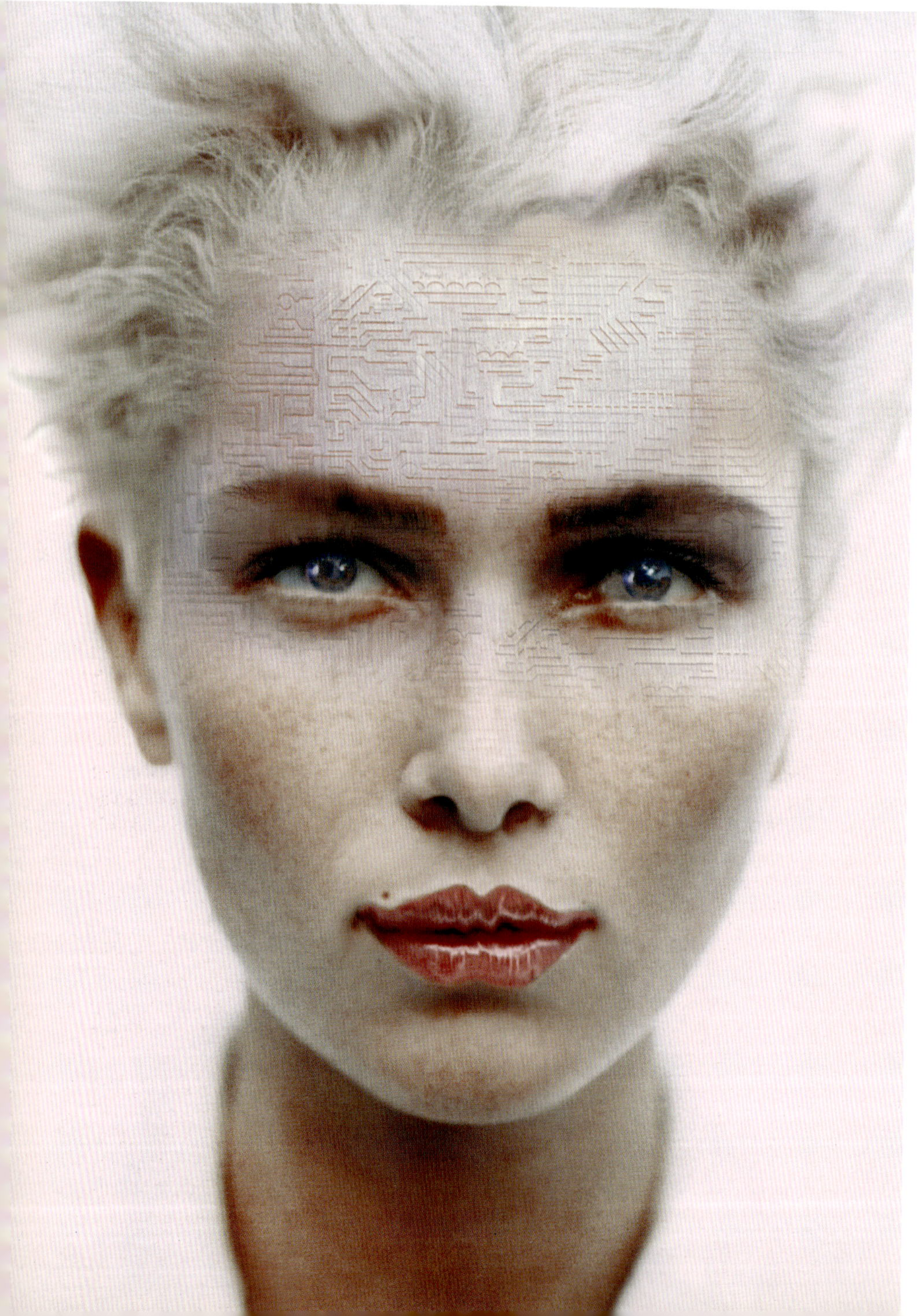

true reality of their lives is captured in this resignation, this emptiness, this solitude. Consequently, although it is realistic, the human form does not interest me... but rather the face or the body that has suffered as a territory from which emerges the erosion of time.... I try to obtain a harshness in the realism that speaks of the fascinating idiosyncrasy of our time. In my work I do not use photographs, because they are two-dimensional and I do not want to be restricted to a fixed and rigid visual concept.

"*Crash* is our world, nothing in it is 'invented': here everything is hyper-functional, the traffic and the accident, the technology and the death, the sex and the photographic lens; everything is like a huge simulated, synchronous machine.... In *Crash* there is no fiction nor is there any reality: the hyper-reality abolishes them both" (Jean Baudrillard). Ballard, in fact, in the so-called series of "natural catastrophes" and in the series of "urban catastrophes", unfailingly introduces the reader into something entirely and absolutely real, something absolutely familiar, verging on the banal; but it is precisely these elements that reveal the hallucinatory consistency of hyper-reality, in that dimension known to modern psychology as the "Ames room." The psychologist Adalbert Ames designed a series of rooms that appear absolutely normal to anyone who looks into them through a peephole; the supposed normality of the vision is in reality the product of a series of optical fictions, which reveal the mechanism whereby individuals see only what they expect to see. Ballard unhinges the mechanisms of a limited vision that separates "inner space" and "external space", distinguished only by the modes of a normalised and accommodating perception; he introduces the parameters of a "condensed novel" in which experimentation upon language intersects with the technologies and the neuroses of the metropolitan universe. The space of the real seems to plunge to an increasing degree into the forms and contents of a collective hallucination. "The Gulf War Won't Happen": that was the headline on an article by Jean Baudrillard that appeared in 1991 in *Libération*, a few days before the war actually did break out. During the conflict, Baudrillard wrote a second article entitled: "Is The Gulf War Actually Happening?", which he followed up with a third and final article, which appeared after the cessation of hostilities: "The Gulf War Never Happened". On 20 January 1991, the *Observer* headlined an article: "The Television Networks Are the True Directors of Saddam's Soap Opera", and on the same page Sue Masterman wrote: "This is the war; a war that is served up live in your living room. The biggest video game of all time is being played right before your eyes". And again, on 20 January 1991, the *Independent on Sunday*: "The exact moment in which a 2,000-pound bomb dropped down the ventilation shaft of the Ministry of Aeronautics in Baghdad was caught perfectly by the video camera located on the nose of an F-117A fighter-bomber, and a minute later the images were available for television broadcast. For 27 hours, that is, until the moment when the first Scud missiles began to fall on Israel, this war was played like an electronic game".

With the conflict in the Persian Gulf, the collaboration between information technology and war produced a new way of waging war and a new way of creating communications: the first electronic war, the first test of equipment that allowed a complete monitoring of all military operations. During the Gulf War, information coming from satellites, airplanes, radar, reconnaissance units, electronic maps and sensors were used and rendered available on a continual basis. Everything was like in a simulation visible upon a screen. For Baudrillard the "war that never was" took place in reality on the television screens of the whole world: "Our strategic deployment takes place on the television screen: it is from that screen that we are bombarded on a daily basis. A post-modern war, where reality does not exist, where all that exists is the simulation of reality.... The simulacrum is never that which conceals the truth; but it is truth that conceals the fact that there is no truth. The simulacrum is true.... Today, abstraction is something that, through models, generates a real that has neither origins nor reality: a hyper-reality".

Clone: A population of genetically identical unicellular organisms or viruses arising from successive replications of a single ancestral unicellular organism or virus.
(from the Human Genome Project)

It is the Los Alamos National Laboratories in New Mexico, financed by the Department of Energy, that serve as the sites of projects and researches on cloning, one of the central aspects of the scientific debate and the literary speculation of the last few years, a fragment of a trajectory of more precise mutation which belongs to the Human Genome Project, for the mapping of human DNA, the operation of decoding our genetic heritage and identity. The emergence of new technologies leads cultural events and their consequences to a different configuration: new cognitive models are elaborated, as are adaptive strategies in which the "practices" of mutation are undertaken. There are numerous basic questions that accompany the most recent biotechnology, a scientific practice that overflows into adjoining and stratified fields, becoming a new social, ethical, religious and aesthetic subject.

Duplication, replication and the creation of the human double has given life over time to a series of literary, science-fiction and artistic works: from the myth of the creation of Frankenstein to the Golem, to the cross-breeding of the human form with the machine, or the evolution of robots into a simulacrum of humanity in the figure of the android, the human imagination has progressively "thought up" a world in which the human being can project and coexist with forms of organic/artificial life. In the scenario in which cybernetics, genetics and complex systems merge and intertwine in the perspective of a neo-biological future, new and unpredictable alliances are established between organisms and mechanisms.

In a reality in which the spectacle produces new identities and new domesticated subjects, art, once again, signals the shift toward the realisation of an artificial life that produces a signal of alarm. In a phase in which new forms of life are experimented, the theoretical context and its references violently shift: they are no longer limited to Body Art, the last feverish impulse of humanity, but now they converge on hyper-realism, that signals the future of mutations in a culture that to an ever-increasing degree, both in terms of science and in terms of the spectacle, prepares new forms of artificial life and designs new biotechnological hybrids, inserting them directly into the marketplace, but without the usual amplification of communications and without the diffusion of data. Day after day, "idorus", constructs, avatars, electronic and technological identities are populating the horizons of movies, music, advertising, communications, information, and day after day the presence of these alien beings, designed and built as part of the spectacle, is "normalised". Art, once again, keeps for itself the diffusion and amplification of what are really the visible signs of mutation, apparently the most disquieting signs, but in reality the most innocuous ones. Charles Ray, Reuven Cohen, Ron Mueck, Aziz + Cucher, Alba D'Urbano, Judy Fox, Miran Fukuda, Cesare Fullone, Nancy Graves, Emiko Kasahara, Jeff Koons, Mariko Mori, Yasumasa Morimura, Inez Van Lamsweerde… there are now many artists who have chosen the stimulating and anomalous horizons of a further hyper-realistic prospect, creating morphologies and images of creatures as updated bodies, the consciousness of a mutation that brings with it its own fears. Absolutely canonical are the indications of modification for the bodies of these artists: mutation, multi-sexual identities, the fear of alteration, fiction, human scales of measurement that have been entirely altered… The current level of anthropological mutation is rendered evident by the weakening of the emotional sites of a culture of merchandise that no longer singles out emotional fields; it is the opening to discussion of the systems that propose a single model upon which to base themselves, systems that self-replicate, and these artists build bodies, or images of bodies, that take into account the changes that are emerging in the social and cultural fabric of the contemporary, bodies buffed in gymnasiums and experienced in the social spheres of the simulacrum, bodies that can scarcely be distinguished one from another. Artists aware of being part of the change that they undergo, who reproduce an attitude that is slightly ironic and slightly concerned with the idea of indicating a reality replaced by the aspects of superficial flashes of images, the illusion of perfection, the changes that are "forcing" the individual, who is obliged to follow the current codes of fashion. Changes that have become an integral and essential part of everyday life, which could also be changed in the night and replaced with another one the next morning through the use of hyper-sophisticated and fascinating effects, without anyone being the wiser, new identities and new relations alongside their replacements in keeping with their morphological appearance. Artworks that bring into being bodies devoid of physicality, bodies that have become a means of communication, bodies and identities that are expressed through pure appearance, bodies of the post-modern era and of a contemporary culture in which one witnesses the conjunction and the contrast of different subcultures, symbols, signs and images where the human body is transformed into a sort of multiform metamorphosis, transmitting the prospects of new forms of representation that become projects of reality in which the body becomes a perfect image, the illusion of perfection.

But technology cannot convert everything into happiness: physical conditions are very distant from perfection, and tensions only increase in an urban society in which one is accepted only if one is able to comply with certain physical standards.

The works of these artists are static three-dimensional semblances, the denunciation of humanity's inability to adapt naturally to the velocity of technological change, the precarious condition of the human being in contrast with materials considered to be eternal and indestructible, reproductions of figures with human semblances made of various elements, legs, arms, hands, faces, not necessarily harmonious or coordinated in a conventional manner, a series of combinations that cause various mutations underscoring the detachment between stereotypes, preconceptions and the present-day situation.

Personalities created by changes of perspective and code. Even the most intimate anatomical parts are by now dense with significance, we speak ironically about the role of men, the recognition of sex as an emblem of appearance, we take extreme stands about the possibilities that society offers today to be able to purchase the three-dimensional reproduction of the penis of a star as famous as Jeff Striker, autographed by him, to use for "personal pleasure" or else to display, the possibility of duplicating anyone's penis, keep it at home and substitute it for the real one in order to satisfy any fantasy. A work at the boundary between delirious behaviour and collective depression, the need for extraordinary events, the spectacularisation of anatomy and physical perfection, the fear of the indistinguishable doppelganger, the strategy of the spectacle in the hyper-reality of fluctuating values.

The body is the site of an experimentation blending creation and selection, the birth of a generation produced through models, through the morphologies of simulation, the necessity of the achievement of perfection and the implacable sensation of inadequacy. And so, finally, the contemporary celebrates its most spectacular result: man and machine fused into a single organism, the definitive culmination of the political and social conflict that opposed, in a radical materialism, man to machine. Nothing has been saved of the human body, transformed into a replica; the increase in the capacity of machine to simulate and emulate human properties and performances has been combined with the changes underway in the standing of the body, so as to give way to an "inevitable" being that consents to its transformation. The presence of technology in everyday life, visible and invisible, its necessity, has created the conditions for a "familiarity" of transformation, for its inevitability. A transformation that has little or nothing to do with the possibilities of mutation, of self-production of the self, of one's own decision to take on multiple identities.

What emerges is only the necessity of taking part in the spectacle, acquiring its semblances, upon penalty of exclusion.

Anthology

CONVERSATION BETWEEN FRANKO B AND FAM

How long ago did you introduce objects into your performances?
There have always been objects in my performances, some made by me, while others are objects — such as the hot-water bag — that are used at home or in the hospital, and which I use as apparatus. In any case, I have always made objects, ever since I studied painting and sculpture at art college in London.

What difference is there between your objects and your performances?
None, both still form part of my approach, of my way of evolving.

Which artists move you most profoundly?
There are so many... it depends... The ones that come to mind right away are Gina Pane, Rothko, Pier Paolo Pasolini, Mimmo Paladino, Cesare Fullone, Ron Athey, Jana Sterbak, Bill Viola, Force Entertainment, Louise Bourgeois, Giacomo Leopardi, Giacometti, Francis Bacon, Cage, Cunningham, Richard Billingham, Annie Sprinkle, Le Corbusier, Carol Christian Poell, Walter Van Berendock, Everything But the Girl, Stina Noordenstam, Green Velvet, Board of Canada, Jeff Mills, Joseph Beuys, Hans Haacke, Anselm Kiefer and of course many more...

All Western art has depicted a martyred, executed, tortured body. A special body. How much pain is there in art?
As much pain as there is in everyday life, even though I think that a person is unable to realise how much pain there is in everyday life.

What is censorship and how does it act today on works like yours and by artists like you?
Censorship exists through the use of the system of ignorance, fear and fiction.

What has changed nowadays in the concept of power?
I don't believe that the patriarchal concept of power has ever changed, it has only altered its appearance: the church, the state, etc., have been replaced by the emergence of multinationals such as Coca-Cola, Microsoft, Monsanto, and so on... The church and the state have become part of the multinationals: they are the new church, they are the sponsor of ignorance, fear, terror.

What importance will the idea of live art have in the art of the future?
A great deal, because it is alive, it has to do with life, and because it touches life.

Your performances have emphasised the awareness that no one is the owner of their own body, perhaps this is their strongest tension: the awareness of having a body to which anybody can do anything they want in many situations. Over the last few years, you have done a number of more essential, unadorned performances, with less choreography and less staging, you do a performance that becomes a "tableaux", a tableaux vivant. Why have you taken out so much of the staging?
For linguistic reasons. I thought that there were too many "words" and there is no reason for so many words when you want to say something. For me, it is important to try to be as pure as possible. I think it would also be arrogant to impose a language, or tell someone "you didn't understand", that would be offensive, because it would mean that the artist places himself on a pedestal, thinking that he or she is one step up from the others, like the pope... I want to communicate feelings and tensions, not impose a vision, even if I think that in fact many artists are dictators...

What does it mean to be as pure as possible to you?
People are very afraid of being called "naïve", they are terribly afraid, perhaps because it is like saying that someone is not very smart; but I don't want to be all that smart, I would rather be simple. Unfortunately I am not all that simple because I was contaminated by the education I received. The same thing is true where being pure is concerned, it's like being ingenuous... I am not afraid of these words, I want to be clear, pure, even naïve...

When people talk about body and performance many think of the performances of the 1960s. Do you think that the problem is necessarily a question of definition? Or is it simply that we use old language for new experiences?
Many people always think of things in term of the past. They usually only try to frame you and minimise you by reminding you that this type of experiment, in their opinion, has already been done. You know, the kind of people who have already seen everything, done everything, understood everything...

We should remind these people that the social and political context modifies experiences and actions: in this moment the climate is much more conservative and reactionary than things were at the end of the 1960s. What I think has remained the same is only the human race and the regimentation of individuals: there are still masters and slaves, the management of technology remains the same, the invention of the wheel was technology to the ancient Greeks, it meant you could conquer the world and now we find the same mentality with respect to the computer...

One thing that is especially striking about your work is the capacity to enter into relation with the private life of the spectator, with that intimate sphere of his or her pain, with the "off limits" areas.
I think that the artist should feel that type of responsibility, a responsibility to give and to have those feelings, even if I know that I am nothing more than a pretext, an element, a piece of a puzzle, perhaps I am only a link, but not an excuse. People don't need me to enter into their own personal "off limits" zone. It is very difficult to explain, but for me this is a very serious, very important aspect: feeling the responsibility of other people's emotions requires one to manage a great weight; for

me it is not an experiment or a game that I am playing with someone, it is not some clever little thing, because it would be too easy to play with the feelings and emotions of people. I am living an emotion myself, often I have nothing at all to do with that person, but I establish a link through the situation that I have created, that is coming about, and many times it is a situation without control, it is outside of the directing. Those are things for which five years later, or a month later or a day later you think, "yes, perhaps it is this, it is for this reason"; but I am not trying to find a reason, if there is one, there is one… Even if naturally the relationship that is created is not a relationship of power. For me this type of power has to do with the power that we have over ourselves, the "power of being", feeling that you can say something important for yourself, while the institutions try to establish control over you; at times I feel that I have power, but only over myself.

What sort of relationship do you create with the audience, what sort of feeling do you have in front of so many people who all come to see you, who want to understand, who want to come into contact with you?
For me this is very important, it makes me happy, it brings me contentment, because maybe, not just me but others as well, Ron Athey especially, we are actually doing something. Something that has to do with being honest, and I think that people recognise authenticity, maybe they think you are naïve, but being honest in this society is a taboo, being honest with your self, with reason, with emotions, with your own motivations. I think at any rate that there is a relationship that grows with various people, though with some it is really complicated: either they are afraid of what you do, but that is only if you put yourself on a pedestal, then people are afraid of you and they respect you only for this thing, or else they keep their distance.

I do not want to be respected only out of fear, or because they think that I am special only because it is wrapped up with the taboo. I think that love helps a great deal, I think that without love there is nothing; I think that there are people who come to see you because they think you are extreme, but maybe one day they will understand, or perhaps not, but it doesn't matter. I think that what helps you to go on if you are an artist is love, and I am not talking about the love for a person…

On your hands is written the phrase "blinded by love"…
For me, it is the quality of a love, not the quantity, that matters.

I don't know why people come to see me, even though I am happy if they feel involved. I like it because it is important to be appreciated, for the right reasons, and not because you want to be part of some club: I don't want to be part of any club, and I don't want to fit in with people. I think that the same thing is true on the other side, I don't think that people want to fit in with me. Mutation has to do with encounters; if you don't encounter people, spaces, possibilities, then you can't change. In order to change, even from without, you cannot be alone. But there is always a powerful negation. There are people who reject, reject, reject help and isolate themselves. They think that they are what they are because they are sure to be very smart and intelligent, but it's absurd. In practical terms these people live in a fictitious world, that they have created for themselves, with their stories, and they think that they are special because momma and poppa were very intelligent, so that this gene that was present in the sperm made them intelligent. A pity. Because I think that these people in the end are very unhappy. For this reason, perhaps, they need power, perhaps for them it means being recognised; it is artificial, it has to do with society, with being seen, being recognised. In the end I think that everybody needs to feel themselves full of something, which is love and which can arrive from any direction…

What do you think of the definition "extreme artist"?
I don't know; I think that some people need to find labels to protect themselves. People are afraid; it is ignorance, and it is nothing new. The strange thing is that they come to tell you: "it was done in the 1960s", and you say, "yes", but these are things people say out of ignorance; they criticise and they copy out of ignorance. The same thing is true for the "extreme" label: if you want to call me that, it's all the same to me. For me, people need something surreal to tranquillise them, people need distractions, banalities, stories made up for no reason. People are afraid, for whatever reason people need to establish distances and differences: this is accepted and that is not accepted, this is good… this is sugar and that is salt. A salty artist and a sugary artist. It's only a definition. For me, it is only a bad use of the language, but those who do it know that they are doing it, in fact they do it on purpose, with intention.

Some time ago you declared that style is a dictatorship. What did you mean?
Style is a ghetto. It is still the ghetto of art, the ghetto of form, the ghetto of language. If you always work in a given manner, you will die with it. People talk and they need to be able to define you with a single label: I am the artist who works with blood, with the body… as if all the rest of my work were somehow marginal… I think that it is not so much the object or the form that identifies the work; for example, take the body: if I paint it, I am "expressionistic" but if I present it I am "conceptual"…

To my mind, that is absurd. This is the ghetto: to have to be necessarily identified with a single artwork. Picasso himself was defined as the acrobat, the clown, a "pastiche"… It is like saying that if you like milk you can't like whisky too!

To my mind, an artist is an artist: if you limit the artist, then he isn't one anymore.

The latest artworks that you have made are very rigorous, with metal structures and carved crosses; why did you choose the cross, for these objects as well?
The cross has always been with me, it symbolises the body, my body. Before, for me, it was red: body, blood. Then I conceived it in a different manner, with other colours; people focus on the form — an obsession with form, instead for me it is a different code, it is the colour that I am using. For me there is no dictatorship of style, and so if you work in a certain way, you need to remain on that. The world is full of people who have the same needs but are not worried about belonging to a club. For me the best artists are people who have no fear, who have nothing to lose, and who don't want to fit in: people who have no particular interest in being accepted by one group or another. All of the ingredients that you put together are in reality very simple, but they appear complicated because you always

tend to tart them up a bit. That is why people think that perhaps with technology it will be better, we will become more independent, but maybe this is not the most likely scenario… That is my fear: that one day I will not have the power to decide. If I should happen to have an accident, if I were to be immobilised, someone else would decide for me that it was time to eat, maybe oatmeal every day, or sleep, at eight in the evening. It is a very simple example but it clearly explains the fear of being powerless.

I believe that one of the most violent forms of exercise of power is that of "intervening" upon bodies, on the non-physical aspect, from limitation in prisons and insane asylums, all the way down to the dictatorship of a fashion that wants us all to be tall, slim, handsome and identical, to the verge of anorexia.

It is people that you think are so "acceptable"; someone like me shouldn't take off their clothes because they should be ashamed of the body they have, and at times you hear them say: "you're fat, who wants to have sex with you?" Don't you worry about me! If I want to have sex, I have sex, believe me!

Have you ever had the sensation that power was trying to shape your body? Modify it?

It's too late now. In practical terms, this is the trip that I took to become what I have become, in order to escape from what I had and give myself power as a person in this world in which everyone judges you and they tell you what you can or you cannot do, in which you have to be ashamed. I think that I have this power over myself, and no one can take it away from me. I hope one day to be able to prevent what I fear, that is, to be able to say, "this is what I want to do" and that someone should say to me, "no, you can't decide", or "you are dangerous to others". I am afraid of things reaching that point, and I would like to be able to decide to escape: "I am going to overdose, see you later, thanks for everything. I'll knock down the stage myself".

For me this is a very important point. I always think that if you aren't happy with your life you need to have an alternative; for me it is inconceivable that you don't have the possibility or that you just can't decide. "Now you can't do that anymore because I'm taking charge here, for your own good, because we love you: you can't put those shoes on because they are ridiculous", that might happen when you are seventy years old and your daughter makes that decision because she is ashamed of you. But a person thinks to themselves: "If I can't do that, then what am I doing here? Maybe it's better for me to leave". I don't want to become a vegetable.

And what is the Red Cross for you today? Why is it always on your body, always in your work?

For me it is a rescue, help, it is like a home, it is part of my family, when I see it I think of the Swiss Red Cross… it is a symbol that I have chosen, like somebody who has loved firemen since he was a little boy and anything he sees that has anything to do with firemen or fire takes him back to that; it is also like someone who likes to dress in black and dresses in black… a little bit you can see that it is like an obsession. In any case, it is my obsession. There are guys who, at the age of sixteen, are obsessed with cars and tits; I like men. But it is something that also has to do with power as well: as soon as you are born they bombard you with what is right and what is wrong, a criterion to which you have to adapt, otherwise you are crazy or a loser. I prefer to be crazy, a loser is something that I really don't want to be...

Society, people are obsessed with being articulate, always being able to express yourself; I don't think that I am being very articulate right now; no, it has nothing to do with being articulate, but with expressing yourself. Being articulate is not the same as expressing yourself, it is a way of justifying yourself, it is a way of showing that you are intelligent, that you know how to do something. I think that being articulate, in practical terms, is a way of getting out of things, a dishonest way of dealing with things. Why should you have to be articulate? How is it possible to articulate the sense of having lost something, whether it is love, people, your parents, or your innocence? How can you articulate someone who is dying? Your mother or your father... like saying "daddy died ten years ago, quit busting my chops, get over it", but what if you don't want to get over it, what if you lay claim to that pain, that loss as a part of your life, it is yours, you need this, why should you have to get over it? It's your whole life; it is like someone who says, "when I was little I had a sister and I lost her, and I am very sad about it, but I am better now, I got married, I have two children..."

The obligation to pretend to be serene...
Yes, everything is normal and everything is fine. But it's absurd! There is this obsession with recovery. I don't want to recover.

Your performances oblige the spectators to be aware of unhappiness: they meet you, for instance, in the performance *Who Will Lick My Wound*?, presented as a dog, with a dog collar, with a wound, rolling on the ground... It's not simple, you cause a crisis in that whole quantity of forced serenity, fictitious, false... you express the discomfort of a state.
It's the same thing as the family, it doesn't matter what social group you come from, what your background might be: if you have no power for yourself, if you had an unhappy childhood, you have no choice. I think that in order to live you should be ingenuous. Many years ago I saw a movie by a Norwegian director, the story of a little boy who, when he was upset, would bark like a dog and that is how he managed to express himself... There was a period when if there was something that I didn't like I would bark, whoof, whoof... obviously lots of people looked angrily at me, others wouldn't, but many of them must have thought I was crazy when I barked at them!

Is there a desire that you have in your work?
My desire in work is always to express something, always do things that are powerfully communicative... I would like to be economically more independent, which would mean for me to be able to do more things, be crazier... But it's not bad now!

CONVERSATION BETWEEN RON ATHEY AND FAM

What does it mean to be a performer in the contemporary artistic context?
For me it means putting myself at risk. My work entails living the concept, through the live implementation of the concept itself, which can change. I think that performances in galleries have a value, which always seems linked to the 1970s because usually they are minimalistic, if not monotonous. The most absorbing work that I do has a strong link with theatre, which works on a different level but which has similar expectations in terms of timing, the technical production, the narrative and the technique. The values of high-tech productions amplify the work, if the work is strong.

What type of relationship do you establish with an audience that prefers to watch live performances rather than normal exhibitions?
The involvement of people in live art is much more intense than what you can create with an object or with videos. There is a requirement that audience observe and reflect, and sometimes even a chemical reaction is produced by seeing a live body performance. We have learned how to detach ourselves from photographs, monitors and projections. In live art the performer is not only responsible for the validity of the content, but also for the way and the impact that it provokes on those who see it.

What is the importance of shock in your work?
I try not to think that most of the West has fallen victim to a sense of guilt concerning the body which derives from Christianity. Every spectator penetrates into my own space with his or her personal history, their understanding of art, their images and their psychology. The responses vary, from expressions of pain to moral disgust to visual appreciation. I am obliged to create images that go beyond my own limits, which take me from my level of well being, repeatedly, until they become normal for me. The spectators have not developed themselves, nor have they tested themselves nor have they exhibited themselves as I have done, and I am aware of this. But there must be an openness in their mind in which automatically every action is judged that they were unable or unwilling to perform. Mutilation is shocking, but it has various aspects. Pornographic taboos are equally complex for the myriad of different effects that they have upon an audience.

Which artists do you feel now and have you felt in the past most in tune with?
I believe that anger inspires other artists the way it inspires me. I admire artists of

the feminist period such as Valerie Export, Carolee Schneedman, a number of pieces by Marina Abramović, who was admittedly very aesthetic but who still transmitted a message of great clarity. Lydia Lunch has inspired me from both an artistic and a personal point of view. AIDS has endowed the works of artists such as David Wojnarowicz, Karen Finley and Diamanda Galas with a passion that speaks to, and of, the human condition, not only of HIV. Fetishists such as Pierre Molinier and later Bob Flanagan have developed a message out of the very obsession that had turned them into nobodies. Certainly the hook-suspensions of Stelarc and the blood-work of Hermann Nitsch have had a profound effect upon me. Today the artists that I feel have inspired me most are Osseus Labyrint, the blood brother Franko B and Marcel.li Antunez Roca.

How has the body been changed by political, ecclesiastic and juridical power, over the last few years?
I have an American point of view, seeing that I have been here all my life. There is a false modesty (shame), which reeks of Victorian colonialism, even though modesty exists only when the body is not perfect (a perfectly muscular body is not seen as being nude); certainly technology, surgery and pharmaceuticals have created new possibilities for the body. Human hormones, silicone implants, testosterone injections, laser hair removal have all created what would appear to be a new race. Even in the face of HIV, the collateral effects of protein inhibitors have created a type of vascular structure, a discolouration of the skin and protuberances that have never been seen before. Even though they are radical, there is a possibility of returning from these changes. I thought that a penis that had been injected with fat was like a jellyfish. When it is hard it becomes like a jellyfish with a spinal cord. Many different messages have been sent. Things are sexier or less sexy than ever. Living in Los Angeles you understand that the image of the body is linked to age and it is obsessed with fitness. Politically, repression is always prelude to rebellion, and I think that in the age of Bush there will be an extreme need for representatives of the outsiders. People will continue to get tattoos, even though the effect is diminished by the general proliferation. Through my work I have been able to notice that if in the 1980s blood was shocking, in the 1990s it causes panic because of the explosion of HIV.

What is censorship?
There is censorship established by the state, whereby institutions and artists can be punished for the content of their work. Usually this censorship operates by preventing them from finding places in which to exhibit controversial work. There is also a form of malign neglect of the arts, whereby artists are worn out by the lack of funds and the continual rejections from the galleries, which refuse to offer a chance by allowing them to exhibit. The contradiction can be clearly seen in musical videos and movies, where any image can be used by the director.

One of the strictest censorships of our contemporary world is the exclusion of death from reality. Now only a spectacular death is acceptable. What is death for you?
I think that the fear of death is at the origin of so many repressive religions, as the rejection of old age. For me, death is quite simply the end. I don't want death, but

you can't deny that it is one of the realities of life that will never change. I have to ask every day if I am sufficiently alive today to justify the fact that I might die tomorrow. Do I have an emotional life? Am I doing work that satisfies me? Is there love in my life? Are there friends and acquaintances who know that they are treasures for me? Am I doing things just to do them, without understanding their meaning? It is not so difficult after all to embrace life with all that it offers, good, bad and ugly. To be more honest, in the 1980s, I thought that I would die of HIV but it didn't happen. I learned that the shadow of death cannot run my life.

Disease, sex, death. Why have you chosen to explore some of the most profound taboos of humanity?
I had no choice, and there was no reason not to treat these topics. I was born a homosexual into a fundamentalist Christian family. They almost died in Texas during the Great Depression in the 1930s, and they lived with a constant fear. As far as I am concerned, I was a heroin addict for seven years, involved in destructive sexual practices: I contracted HIV and hepatitis C. If I think about the 1980s and the 1990s, the parties and the dinners, I realise that I am one of the very few survivors from my group. The world rejects the truth about this disease; it is obsessed with sex but relegates it to a series of low-grade images, and cannot seem to reach a compromise with death in an overpopulated world. I remain constantly disconcerted by these accepted realities. The struggle for how we see our life and the determination to set it forth in a different light are the two single most important things to me. I am not experiencing a voyage toward death, I am only moving through a reality made up of tortures, redemption and survival.

What is the taboo of the contemporary world?
Not being a capitalist when you are older than thirty. As far as the body is concerned, mutilating the face is worse than mutilating the genitals. Being self-destructive is more taboo than ever, whether you are talking about drug-addiction or indulging in unsafe sexual practices. I think that even many liberals are still frightened by the transexual community; here you find same-gender sex, genital mutilations, and if you open a door you see that in appearance at least the polarity between the two sexes is not insuperable. I know two transexuals who have a very deep relationship. The younger of the two was still menstruating when she got pregnant, and now they are two men with beards who are raising a child and living together as a family. This is even more taboo because they don't alienate you.

Do you think that art is still the most open language, that is, the language that more than others shows the spirit of the time?
Sure, certain art forms, just like certain love affairs. I think that capitalism and the machinery of the galleries inhibit the language of art, giving priority to marketing and strategy. And academia can be considered partially at fault, since they probe so deeply into art that it is forced to refer only to itself and becomes quite boring.

To what degree does the Western body need to make itself special in its depictions (torture, martyrdom...)?
This becomes Jungian. In my first artwork, *Martyrs & Saints*, a powerful woman

supports a man who has been beaten bloody (a *Pietà*). I think that there are many signals of self-preservation in our fascination with the morbid. But it is our emotional response to the history and the images of the archetypes that makes us see the way we do. The Spanish Inquisition, the Holocaust, Vietnam. I saw the movie *Deliverance* when I was too small, and my stomach still gets queasy when I hear a southern accent. My understanding of the struggle for civil rights in Mississippi and Alabama has increased my repulsion.

How much influence does religion have on life today?
Religion is still a dominant culture. And so either you follow it or else you rebel. Nowadays, you don't hear the word atheist very often, it has been softened so that it is no longer directly in opposition. Religion is my weak point.

What is your concept of art?
I want a message. Art can channel, invent, incite, convince and reflect. I do not believe in rules, I think there should be more liberty and help for those who want to evolve. Making art is a calling, not a strategy. Perhaps I treat it too much like a religion, but I am certainly very passionate about it.

The Intruder
by Jean-Luc Nancy

The intruder makes his way in by force, surprise, or cunning, in any case without any right to do so and without an invitation. There must be an element of the intruder in the stranger, otherwise he loses his strangeness. If he has the right to enter and to stay, if he is an expected visitor, then he's no longer an intruder and he is no longer even a stranger. And so it is logically neither acceptable nor conceivable from an ethical standpoint to rule out the idea of intrusion in the arrival of a stranger.

Once he is in, if he remains a stranger, and for all the time he remains, instead of "naturalising himself", his arrival does not cease: he continues to come and he never stops being an intrusion; he continues to be without right and familiarity and habits, but he remains a disturbance, a turbulence amidst the intimacy. Otherwise the extraneousness of the stranger is eliminated before he walks over the threshold. Welcoming a stranger also means sensing his intrusion. Often we don't want to admit it: the motivation of the intruder is itself an intrusion in our moral correctness (indeed, a notable example of the politically correct). And yet this motivation is inseparable from the truth of the stranger. This moral correctness implies the welcoming of the stranger, cancelling out his extraneousness right on the threshold.... The stranger however insists and intrudes. And it is this precisely that is difficult to accept and perhaps conceive...

I have (I, who? That's the right question. Who is this subject of the statement, always extraneous to the subject of its enunciation, of whom it is necessarily not the intruder. And yet it is precisely the motor or the heart). I received the heart of another person about ten years ago. I received a heart transplant. My own heart (here it is the question of "my own": no mystery, no question, only the simple evidence of a transplant, as the physicians prefer to call it). My own heart, then, was out of operation for a reason that is as yet unclear. The last word that I heard on this subject was that of a physician who said to me: "Your heart was programmed to last fifty years. And so for you to go on living you needed to receive a heart from someone else". But what other programme was intersecting with my physiological programme? Twenty years ago, there was no such thing as a transplant, and there was certainly no such thing as cyclosporin, which helps to prevent rejection. In twenty years there will be new types of transplant thanks to new technologies. A personal contingency intersects with a contingency in the history of technology. Before, I would be a dead man, later, I would be just another survivor. But "I" depend on a series of technical possibilities. And so we see that there is no meaning or point to the debate between the followers of metaphysical adventure and those of technical miracles: we are talking here about both things, one concealed within the other.

From the very moment in which I was told that I would have to have a transplant, all of the signs could vacillate, all of the points of reference could be overturned. Without reflecting, certainly, indeed without identifying any act or any permutation. Quite simply, the physical sensation of a void already opening in my chest, a sort of apnœa where nothing, strictly nothing, even today could untangle the organic from the symbolic or from the imaginary, nor could it untangle the continuous from the interrupted. It was as a single breath... By now I was pushed through a strange cavern, already imperceptibly open, and it was as if, in a single representation, I were falling into the sea while still remaining on the deck.

If my heart were to abandon me, I wonder to what degree it was "mine" and "my own organ"...

For the past few years now I have felt a rhythm, sort of evenly spaced cracklings, not much, really: not an organ, not a dark red muscular mass packed with tubes that I now have to imagine in place of "my heart", beating incessantly, up till now absent, as were the soles of my feet when I was out walking.

It was becoming a stranger to me, it was intruding by default: as if by rejection, if not by extrusion. This heart was always on my lips, like some ill-advised food. Like a sweet nausea. A sweet slipperiness was separating me from myself. A "proper" immersion in me of a myself that had never been identified as body, far less as heart, and that suddenly was looking at itself.

How do we become a representation of ourselves? Or a montage of functions? Where is the powerful and mute evidence that once held all this together? My heart was becoming a stranger: a stranger precisely inasmuch as it was inside me. The strangeness came from the exterior, but only because it arose from within. What was this sudden emptiness opening in my chest or in my soul — much the same thing, when I was told: "you will have to have a transplant." Here the mind bumps up against a null object: nothing to be known, nothing to be understood, nothing to be felt. The intrusion of a body extraneous to thought. This emptiness will remain as the very thought of itself as well, simultaneously, as its opposite.

I was already no longer inside myself. I come from elsewhere and I no longer come. Up to today, I was a stranger inasmuch as I was insensible, indeed, not present. By now, this heart fails me and this standing as a stranger brings me back to myself. "I" exist inasmuch as I am sick ("sick" is not the exact term, my heart is not infected, it is only rusted, rigid, blocked). What no longer works is my heart, by now it is necessary to extrude this intruder.

Certainly, this will take place upon the condition that I want it, along with someone else, in this case, my beloved family, the doctors and myself. I now discover that I am double, or more manifold than ever before. All of these people must now decide whether or not it is worth the trouble for me to go on living. It is the doctors who must decide on the type of transplant that they will have to propose but not impose. The doctors will also have to decide whether to put me on a waiting list, they have to make a choice. I have not asked who makes the decision, and how, upon who will receive an organ that is available and that could be used by more than one person. And so my own survival depends upon a complex process filled with strangers and strangeness.

What do we all need to agree on for the final decision? Upon a survival that cannot be considered as strictly necessary. What would oblige me to survive? This question is followed by many others. Why me? Why survive in general? What does it mean to survive? In what way is the duration of life a good thing? At the time I was fifty years old, young in age only by the standards of the population of a developed country at the end of the twentieth century. To die at that age was not scandalous in the slightest just a few centuries ago.

Then where are fairness and justice? Who controls them and who pronounces them? In this story, everything came from elsewhere and from outside. Everything, including my heart, my body, which came to me from elsewhere, are an elsewhere "inside" me.

I do not look down on quantity nor do I claim to count on the length of life independently from the quality of life itself: life pushes us toward life. But it also moves toward death: because it was limited in me to this diseased heart.

Isolating death from life, do not accept one as intimately intertwined with the other, each intruding into the heart of the other — that is what we should never do.

At least as far back as Descartes, humanity has ensured that the vow of survival and immortality is one of the elements of the general programme of control and possession of nature. It has therefore programmed a certain growing estrangement from "nature". It has rendered stronger the absolute estrangement of the double enigma of mortality and immortality.

It has elevated that which the religions represented to the power of a technology that rejects the end in all the meanings of the expression, prolonging its termination, exhibiting an absence of end: what life should we extend, and for what purpose? Postpone death but also exhibit it, emphasise it.

We should add only that humanity has never been ready to deal with this question, and that its impreparedness for death is itself nothing other than death: its blow and its injustice.

So, the multiple stranger that is intruding into my life is nothing other than death, indeed life/death: a suspension of the *continuum* of being, a scanning in which I do not have much to do. Revolt or acceptance are equally estranged from this situation. In any case, a transplant imposes the image of a passage from nothing, finding oneself in a space emptied of all intimacy or, to the contrary, the image of the intrusion into me of this space.

What is this "own" life that we try to save? It is true that this property does not in fact reside in my body.

Life which does not occupy any particular organ but which cannot exist without organs. A life that not only survives but which lives on its own behalf under a triple influence: that of the decision, that of the organ and those of the aftermath of the transplant.

First of all the transplant presented itself as a *restitutio ad integrum*: I woke up with a beating heart. In this connection, all of the dubious symbolism of the gift from another immediately crumbles; it seems moreover that this custom, still quite common when I was transplanted, is already vanishing from the awareness of transplantees: there is already a history of the representations of transplants. A great deal of emphasis has been placed on the solidarity, indeed the fraternity, between donors and recipients, in order to encourage organ donors. And no one questions that this form of donation has become an elementary obligation for humanity (in the two meanings of the term) and that is establishes among everybody, with no other limit than incompatibility of blood types, the possibility of a network in which life/death is shared, in which life is connected with death, in which the incommunicable is communicated!

Immediately the other inasmuch as a stranger can manifest himself: not woman, or black, or youth, or Basque, but the other immune, the other irreplaceable who has been replaced. It is called rejection: my immune system rejects the immune system of the other. Many think that rejection consists of literally spitting out the heart, or vomiting it. After all, the word itself suggests that image. That is not how it is, but it is a matter of that which is intolerable in the intrusion of the intruder, and it is fatal if it is not treated.

The possibility of rejection establishes a two-fold strangeness: on the one hand the strangeness of a transplanted heart that the organism identifies and attacks as a foreign body; on the other hand, the strangeness of medicine which has to protect the transplantee. It lowers his immunity in order to allow him to accept the foreign body. It renders him a stranger to himself, to that immunitary identity that is in a sense his physiological signature.

In me there is an intruder and I become a stranger to myself. If the rejection is very powerful, it will be necessary to treat me in order to make me resist ordinary human defences. But becoming a stranger to myself does not bring me closer to the intruder. Rather, it would seem that there emerges a general law of intrusion: there is not a single intrusion because it multiplies, identifying itself in its renewed internal differences.

And so I shall encounter repeatedly the zoster virus or the Cytomegalovirus, dozing strangers that have always resided within me that wake up suddenly and attack me because of the necessary immuno-depression.

Here is what happens: identity applies to immunity, one identifies in the other. One cannot reduce one without lowering the other. Strangeness becomes common and everyday, bringing forth a constant externalisation: I have to control myself, subject myself to continual tests. They recommend various things (avoid crowds, swimming-pools, sick people), but our real enemies are within us: the old viruses, long-time intruders, always dozing away in the shadow of immunity.

In this last case, there is no form of prevention available. Only treatments that render us even more estranged because they exhaust us, or else the piercing pain of the zoster virus. Through all this, what "ego" follows which trajectory?

What a strange self!

They opened me up to change my heart and this wound can no longer be healed or closed up. I am open and closed. There is an opening through which an incessant flow of strangeness passes: the medicines, including those that are meant to combat secondary effects (such as the decay of the kidneys), continual checks and tests. Existence imprinted on new registers, each of which presents numerous other possibilities of death.

And so I myself become my own intruder because of all these accumulated and opposed manners.

It is much stronger than a sensation: never has the estrangement of my own identity touched me so sharply. "Ego" has clearly become the formal identifier of a succession of facts that cannot be verified or touched. Deep down, between me and myself, there was already a space-time *continuum*, but now there is an open wound and a thwarted immunity.

And here comes the cancer: a lymphoma due to the cyclosporin, which lowers my immunity. Cancer as the hooked and devastating face of the intruder. Extraneous to my self and I myself estranging myself.

Here once again the treatment demands a violent intrusion: it incorporates a quantity of chemotherapeutic and radiotherapeutic estrangement. While the lymphoma scrapes away and exhausts the body, the treatments attack it and make it suffer in various ways. Suffering is the relationship between an intrusion and its rejection.

The most elaborate treatment consists of the self-transplant of cells.

The drop in the immune system becomes extreme, causing high fevers, mycosis and various other disorders before the production of lymphocytes recommences. You emerge from this little adventure absolutely exhausted. You are no longer recognisable. You float, you are like a suspension of estrangements between various badly identified states, amidst pain, impotence and a general *defaillance*. Relating to oneself becomes a problem, indeed a major difficulty: it happens through pain and fear. There is no longer anything immediate, and mediating is tiresome. The empty identity of an "ego" no longer stands upon the simplest adequacy (in its "ego = ego") and when you state "I suffer", you are implying two egos, one extraneous to the other, and yet they touch.

I wind up becoming a fragile thread, from pain to pain and from estrangement to estrangement. I become inextricable from a polymorphic dissociation.

The lives of the sick or the old has always been like this, but I am neither sick nor old. What makes me recover infects me; what makes live ages me prematurely.

With a single gesture, one's own ego moves off to an infinite distance (where does it go? In what elusive point where it can once again proffer that this is "my" body?) tumbling into an intimacy far more profound than any inner life.

Corpus Meum et interior intimo meo, the two concepts to say — in a complete configuration of the death of God — that the truth of the subject is its estrangement and its excessiveness: its infinite exposure. The intruder exposes me excessively — it extrudes me, it exports me, it expropriates me. I become like an android out of science fiction, one of the living dead.

We are, with all our increasingly numerous peers, at the dawn of a mutation. In fact, man begins once again to think infinitely of man ("the death of God" always meant this). He becomes that which he is: the terrifying and the most disconcerting of technicians, as he was described by Sophocles twenty-five centuries ago. He becomes the one who denatures and remakes nature, who recreates the creation, extracting it from nothingness and perhaps ultimately consigning it to nothingness. He is capable of originating and ending.

The intruder is myself and man himself. No one other than him, who continues to alter, at one time refined and exhausted, stripped naked and over-equipped, an intruder both in the world and in himself, a disturbing impulse of strangeness, an attempt at an excrescent infinity.

OUR DESTINY AND LITERATURE

by Paul Valéry

But humanity never has enough. I don't know, for that matter, whether humanity perceives its own modification. It still believes that man is always the same.... And yet there are several reasons for believing that people change. Image... what things an observer might note, a Mephistophelean spectator of the destiny of our species, who happened to consider our condition, our life as a whole, just as it passes, it transforms itself, it has consumed itself over the past century or so.... We are convinced that we are dominating energy and matter, while there is not even one of these ingenious attacks against nature that, either directly or indirectly, fail to render us, to the contrary, just a little bit more subject to nature, and make us just a little bit more slaves to our own power, creatures that are just that much more incomplete as much as they are better equipped, and whose desires, whose needs and whose very existence are just so many playthings of their own cleverness. "Do you not see then", this light-eyed devil would say, "don't you see that you are just so many simple objects of extravagant experiments, that thousands of unknown actions and substances are being tested upon you? They want to know how your organs will react to high speeds and low pressures; if your blood can adapt to strongly carburated air; if your retinas can withstand increasingly energetic light and radiation... And that is without mentioning the odours and noises that you tolerate, the vibrations and currents of every frequency, the synthetic foods and lots more!... And as for your intellects, my friends, as for your sensibilities — these are the things that interest me most! — your mind is subjected twenty-four hours out of every twenty-four to an incredible quantity of incoherent information; your senses are obliged to absorb, without a single day's pause, so much music, art, drugs, strange drinks, spectacles, movement, sudden changes in elevation and temperature, political and economic anxiety, as all the rest of humanity put together was once able to absorb over the course of three centuries. You are so many guinea pigs, my dear humans, and guinea pigs treated particularly badly, since the tests to which you are subjected are inflicted, varied and repeated constantly and solely at random chance. There is no scientist, there is not even a laboratory assistant who regulates, adjusts, monitors, or interprets certain experiments, certain artificial vicissitudes, of which no one can foresee the effects, of greater or lesser profundity, upon your precious persons. But fashion, industry, the combined forces of invention and advertising possess you, they exhibit you on the beaches, they send you up onto the snow, they tan your thighs, they burn your hair; while politics aligns our multitudes, persuades them to raise their hands or to raise their fists, makes them march in unison, vote, hate or love or die in cadence, indistinctly, statistically!"

(from *Conferencia*, 1937)

INDEX